Ceremonies of the Horsemen

The Ranch & Reata Essays

Tom Russell

This book couldn't exist if the West wasn't still out there and that for five glorious years, *Ranch & Reata* magazine encouraged and published my writing. TR

Copyright ©2016 by Thomas George Russell

Published in the United States by
Alamar Media, Inc.
PO Box 1782
Santa Ynez, CA 93460
www.wcreynolds.com

Art and paintings by Tom Russell www.tomrussellart.com
All Tom Russell songs: Frontera Music (ASCAP/BUG) www.fronteramusic.com
Cover design by William Reynolds www.wcreynolds.com
Cover photo: Nadine Russell

ISBN-10: 0-9890701-5-8
ISBN-13: 978-0-9890701-5-7
Manufactured in the United States of America

All rights reserved. With the exception of short excerpts used for promotional, review, or academic purposes, no portion of this work may reproduced or distributed in any print or electronic form without written permission from the publisher.

*To Nadine with love,
and the entire Russell horse tribe – California to Ireland.*

Table of Contents

Forward vii
Preface xi
Never Leave Home for Second: The Ballad of Casey Tibbs 1
Ceremonies of the Horsemen: Horses of the L.A. Basin 15
Bitter Tears and Mean as Hell: Johnny Cash in the Wild West 29
Old Hank's Journey: How the Guitar Won the West 43
The Michelangelo of the Western Saloon: Guy Welch 59
Blood on the Saddle: The Long Shadow of Tex Ritter 67
Dancing on the Rim of Lorca's Well 79
Four Portraits of Women in the West: Rosalie Sorrels, Katie Lee, ... 87
    Patricia McCormick, Claudia Russell
Out Where the Horses are Tied: Marty Robbins' El Paso 101
The Wild West in Europe: Buffalo Bill 113
Hemingway in the West 127
When the Wolves No Longer Sing: 141
    Ian Tyson & the Reinvention of Cowboy Song
Gallo del Cielo: The Journey of the One Eyed Rooster 155
Margaritas with Monte Hellman, The Modernist Western, and 177
    a Nod to Jack Nicholson, Warren Oates, and Harry Dean Stanton
Fritz and Georgia: Indian Not Indian 187
Through the Looking Glass with Ramblin' Jack Elliott 199
The Falconer: A Journey into the Western Outback 211
A White Horse Named Tequila 223
Dispatches from Patagonia: The World of J.P.S. Brown 237
Four Dreamers on a Western Landscape: 251
    Chuck Steiner & Markus, George Malloy Jr., & Johnny Bean
Muleteer on the Edge of the World: Ross Knox 265
True Grit and Hard Scrabble: Charles Portis & John Graves 277
The Strawberry Roan: Curley Fletcher 291
Rhymns of a Recluse: Dick Gibford 305
In The Shadows of the Joshua Tree: 319
    Gram Parsons & the Lost Angels of Americana
Tom Russell Biography 333
Quotes 334

Forward

Long live freedom, and damn the ideologies.

— Robinson Jeffers

    Publishing print magazines today is not for the faint of heart. Gone are the days of "print it and they will come" approaches as the magazine is no longer the hand-held content device of choice. That's not all bad, even though I am a paper and ink person as I am of the generation that remembers the feel of letterpress. Way back in the 1970s, working in the music industry, we still created 12 x 12 album covers and the budgets for each one were based on artist's cred and sales. Some were nothing more than a wrapper while some allowed us art director types to dabble in the world of hand-set, metal type proofs creating truly glorious title blocks, pulled on proofing presses, later to printed by the thousands – hundreds of thousands and millions in some cases in hopes of reaching record gold.

    Back when I was toiling in those music art department dungeons and design studios, Tom Russell was already out there amongst them, singing and writing. Always writing. His view of songs, the good ones, is that they endure. "They amuse or hurt, divert and stop time for a holy moment," he says. "They suck us in, slap us around, kick us in the belly and heart, and then push us back out into the world with a memory we'll never purge from our blood. Songs travel."

    Above all Tom is a storyteller – be it in a song or in one of his paintings – or in our case, in his essays. The essays in this volume have come from two endeavors in the western magazine world Tom Russell and I had worked on before it all went over the cliff - *The Cowboy Way* and later in *Ranch & Reata*. The premise for the essays was pretty simple - I had known him for many years and knew of his story telling prowess – I figured the best thing to do was for us to just agree on a storyline and then for me to get the hell out of the way. I never worried. Tom never disappointed. The diverse nature of his stories – from all over the map – were greeted by readers literally waiting at the mailbox for an issue with "a new Tom Russell story" to arrive. It was the closest thing to a sure-enough-sure-thing-home run I ever got to in publishing.

    One of the most popular was his history of the horse and its place in the Los Angeles Basin especially dealing with the film and television industry during the "middle of the last century" as his family was in the thick of it when Tom and his brother Pat were growing up. Stables and trails and bars with sawdust covered floors and personalities long gone, filter back into his tale and take the reader to an almost forgotten time in L.A.

There are so many great stories in the thirty-one issues we did of *Ranch & Reata* and the seventeen, quarterlies of *The Cowboy Way* that it was pretty tough to figure which twenty-five we would use. One for sure was one of the near last ones we published – his homage to the great singer-songwriter, Gram Parsons. Parsons died in 1973 at the age of twenty-six after years of alcoholism and drug abuse at a motel in the California desert. His ashes were scattered under a big, table-shaped rock in Joshua Tree. Tom's story flows through the music business of the late 1960s and 70s to that lonely, wind blown, desert rock – celebrating Parsons' life and artistry.

Putting long-form magazine's together has changed so much lately that one wonders – fearfully – where grand words like Tom's will be featured in the near future. Paper and ink have a "carry" greater than words on a screen any day and Tom Russell's words deserve an appropriate tableau. Through all of his stories I can't remember changing anything as his construction was always great but it was his voice that mattered. He could turn a phone book into a gothic read.

The twenty-five stories in this book will seem to go by quickly. Russell is a fast read because his presentation is always so compelling. But savor each individually and give them air – like a fine pinot. They will in turn, leave you enhanced and satisfied.

It was a grand journey. We had a time.

— **Bill Reynolds**
Santa Ynez, CA
2016

Preface

West is where you go when the land gives out and the old-field pines encroach...it is where you go when you hear that 'thar's gold in them-thar hills.' It is where you go to grow up with the country. It is where you go to spend your old age. Or it is just where you go.

— **Robert Penn Warren**

The esteemed publisher of *Ranch & Reata* magazine, Bill Reynolds, allowed, hell, even *encouraged* me, to wax forth in essays centered around our West. 5000 words. Bi-monthly. No rules, as long as my musings loosely dealt with the West, and anything that touched it. Bill and I being Southern California boys whose forebears had *gone West* and unhitched their wagons near the City of the Angels, thus banging up against into the great Pacific Ocean, the movies, the dude ranches, racetracks, the *mariachis*, country bars, cowboy songs, Bohlin saddles, and such...Ed Bohlin himself was a Swede who came West to be a cowboy.

The West was where you went to re-invent yourself — in the manner of Will James, Roy Rodgers, or Ramblin' Jack Elliott. Your persona thus reinvented, you wrote or sung up your singular cowboy vision. The plot usually centered around, or led back to — the horse. In that respect I call these essays *Ceremonies of the Horsemen*, a phrase stolen from a Bob Dylan song.

I hail from The Irish, with a feint touch of Norwegian. My father's father settled in Iowa. He was the sheriff of Chickasaw County and a horse trader on the side. Or vice versa. I have his card here on my desk: *Russell Brothers – New Hampton Iowa – Dealers in Live Stock – Horses and Colts a Specialty*. We're Irish, and our besotted roots trace back to pirates and gypsies — a tribe or rascals who would sell a lame horse to a blind priest.

It wasn't long before my father left Iowa — gone west to *grow up with the country*. He worked his way up, discovered Hollywood Park Racetrack, played poker with Hopalong Cassidy on the backside of the track, and sired four kids. My brother Pat jumped out of the crib and was soon hot-walking racehorses, then building a bucking barrel in our backyard. *Hang and Rattle, kid.* Soon he was riding real bulls at Crash Corrigan's film ranch.

Brother Pat's record collection was well formed early on: Tex Ritter, Johnny Cash, Marty Robbins, George Jones, Hank Williams...and several LP recordings of bullfight music. The stage was set. I absorbed the music and stole his Tijuana gut-string guitar, learned a bunch of old cowboy songs and poems, and became the songwriter. He carried on with the rodeo and the family trade in livestock. To this day he's horseback, behind some arena in Nevada or California. Bringing in the fresh cattle.

These essays are my own *Moveable Feast* (to borrow from Hemingway) of a time spent mostly in The West. Bill Reynolds never altered a word, that I can recall, and also allowed your reporter to stumble, headlong, down grammatically innocent back roads at my own peril and pleasure, with a snorting distaste for the semi-colon. As the legendary Anton Chekhov stated: "It's not so much *what* I have seen as *how* I have seen it." The job.

Or to quote Ray Bradbury: "I have three rules to live by as a writer: 1. Get your work done. 2. If that doesn't work, shut up and drink your gin. 3. When all else fails, run like hell."

I lifted the lid off the stewpot of anything that interested me. Herein we have ruminations on tequila, Spanish cuisine, guitars, Johnny Cash, Casey Tibbs, cowboy bars, Buffalo Bill's Europe tours, Hemingway in the West, Ian Tyson, Ramblin' Jack Elliott (both best men at our wedding in Elko), falconry, J.P.S. Brown and the song *The Strawberry Roan*. And more. What a hoot.

And now? My wife and I have recently moved from El Paso to the outskirts of Santa Fe, New Mexico. We migrated up the historic Spanish conquistor route, the *Camino Real*, or *Hornado del Muerto* (*Oven of Death*) which the Spaniards trekked-up with their troops, horses, cattle, priests, guitars, and the odd bottle of fine wine. We followed their deep tracks up the dry old Rio Grande (from which I used to irrigate my pecan trees), and now live in the land of the coyote, bobcat, bull snake and raven. The high desert, twenty miles from the historic Santa Fe plaza.

We built an addition on the adobe – a painting and writing studio with a *torreon* tequila bar in the form of an old *Pueblo* Indian tower. The bar is staggering distance from my work area. About six feet. The tower-shaped bar marks my affinity for Robinson Jeffers and Carl

Jung, who became isolates during the second half of their lives and built their own towers, retreating there to waltz with the muse. The mystic priest, Fr. Richard Rohr, says the second half of life is the time we're finally able to *fall upward*, and find our *true selves*. Finger's crossed. Guitar in hand. The story's the thing. The myth. The legends. Whatever I couldn't fit into a three minute song I fleshed out into an essay. Here they are.

    The breath of God blows me where it wills, mostly west, and His eyes shine through the coyote fence every evening at happy hour. There is no retiring from this. And in that we are blessed.

—TR
8/16/16

Never Leave Home For Second
The Ballad of Casey Tibbs

If you wanna say a prayer from my purple angels, you can do that. But I'm gonna make it. And for all you youngsters that's gonna be a world's champion, never leave home for second. Adios.

— **Casey Tibbs**, August 10, 1989
(Recorded by Ivan Daines, five months before Casey passed on.)

I was twelve years old when I met Casey Tibbs. It was one of those childhood encounters when you know you're rubbing up against something greater than blood and bone. You're colliding with history. Against a force which reshapes the way we think or feel about life. I never met Muhammad Ali, but he was one of those humans. People who dance to their own radical music and lure us into applauding it.

I've met Bob Dylan once, and the Beatles, sang with Johnny Cash, and shook hands with John F. Kennedy. How's that for name dropping? Bob Dylan asked me where the nearest liquor store was. I was fifteen years old. I told him I was too young to know. Bob told me to check back when I grew up. Encounters with history. Before all that there was Casey Tibbs.

The scene was Hollywood Park Racetrack. Late 1950s. My father was still on his high-end swing of buying cheap claiming horses and turning them into winners. My brother worked as a hot walker and rode bulls on the weekend. Our family explored the odd angles of the Los Angeles horse and rodeo scene. It was in our bones. We descend from Irish horse traders. As did Casey.

That afternoon my father brought Casey Tibbs up to our box to meet me. Casey looked as if he'd just stepped off the cover of *Life Magazine*. Which indeed he had. Seven years before. I'd cut out that *Life* cover and taped to my bedroom wall, next to Willie Shoemaker and Duke Snider. It was the October 22, 1951 *Life Magazine* issue. The cover declared the *Life* circulation at 5,200,000. The magazine cost 20 cents.

Five million people held that cover and viewed young Casey

Tibbs, his hands on his hips, looking out at the world, high above a rodeo arena. Cocksure and ready to ride. The greatest bronc rider of all time.

In the lower left hand corner of the *Life* cover was an inset box which declared the news in the rest of the world: *Fateful Meeting: Churchill, Roosevelt and Stalin.* And there stood young Casey Tibbs, above it all. It looked like he was on a high wire, and as the great wire walker Karl Wallenda said – *life is on the wire, the rest is just waiting.* Casey would have loved that quote.

A few weeks ago I flew over what was left of Hollywood Park racetrack in Inglewood, California. I looked down on heavy equipment bulldozing the dry lakebed, knocking down the grandstand. Bulldozing childhood dreams. I remembered that moment, almost sixty years ago, when I met Casey Tibbs.

A magic afternoon. Silky Sullivan was running that day in the late 1950s. I'd bet on it. The legendary come-from-behind racehorse. Silky would close from forty lengths off the pace to win. His stretch runs took your breath away. They called him *the heart attack horse*. On February 25, 1958, Silky Sullivan came from 41 lengths behind to win a short 6½ furlong allowance race by a half-length. Think of it.

And there before me was Casey Tibbs. He stuck out his hand. "How you doin' kid?"

He looked over my head at a blonde, two boxes away. Casey Tibbs – with a high crease in his grey hat, the silver dollar bolo tie, the purple shirt, the perfect Hollywood-stitched western suit, the white boots with purple wings on the toes. His purple Cadillac was probably out in the park lot guarded by valets.

He smiled, nodded a quick goodbye, and moved off into the backslapping crowd to make a bet, for he was a betting man. And a drinking man. And a woman's man. And a saddle bronc rider. And damn good bareback rider, and a hell'uva bull rider.

In 1949, at age 19, Casey Tibbs became the youngest man ever to win the national Saddle Bronc-Riding crown. Between 1949 and 1955, he won a total of six PRCA Saddle Bronc-Riding championships, plus two All-Around Cowboy championships, and one Bareback-Riding crown.

In 1958 Casey temporarily retired from rodeo and tried the movies. When an ignorant director told him to dress "more cowboy" for a commercial Casey was insulted and went back to the saddle broncs. He won the first nine rodeos he entered and won the world again in '59.

Charlie Daniels called Casey Tibbs *the greatest cowboy who ever lived.* I wouldn't argue with that, if *greatest cowboy* entails a unique western force, a human who has carved out a lasting and memorable presence, *horseback*. Casey mastered the art of riding saddle broncs artfully, all of it washed in a charisma which made rodeo attractive to the wider public. He was the Mickey Mantle and Muhammad Ali of his time.

He was the man who *floated bucking horses.*

Anecdotes on Casey Tibbs are legion. Below are a few of my favorite yarns about Casey, formed loosely as an oral history, or a ballad. Real folk talking American lingo. This is our heritage, spilled off the tongues of savvy old bronc riders. Goin' down the road with Casey Tibbs. Minced words be damned.

Let's dance.

I   Casey at the Bat – Beginnings

There was ease in Casey's manner as he stepped into
  his place;
There was pride in Casey's bearing and a smile on
  Casey's face.
And when, responding to the cheers, he lightly doffed his hat,
No stranger in the crowd could doubt 'twas Casey at
  the bat.

— **Ernest Thayer**, 1888
Casey at the Bat

Tom Russell: He grew up on the Cheyenne River in South Dakota, fifty miles from the nearest town. The youngest of ten kids raised in a log shanty. His father, John Tibbs, was a tough Irishman who knew horseflesh. Casey's father liked to recite Ernest Thayer's famous baseball poem, *Casey at the Bat*, so he named his youngest son Casey. Their log cabin bordered the Cheyenne Indian reservation and the Indian kids were horsemen and bronc riders.

Casey Tibbs: My old man wasn't very sociable and there was a gulch out there made a kind of natural corral where we could work horses. If you ever seen pictures of the old homestead it looked pretty rugged, but I never knew I was poor 'til I left home. I never went hungry 'til I rodeo'ed for a little while. I might of got hungry at home a few times when my horse bucked me off and I had a long ways to walk. My dad raised ten children and we weren't church goin' people, because churches weren't there, but he taught us the religion of The Golden Rule and I think he done pretty good.

Jim Hannum: I ate many a dinner and slept many a night in that old log house of John Tibbs. Hell, that was horse country. Old John was running horses one day and his horses was running wide open, and his horse broke it's leg, and he's hollering to one of his kids, "Rope something!" And one of the boys roped a horse, running wide open, and drew him over to the old man, and old John choked him down and rode him right off the ground, and away they went. Running their horses.

Casey was raised on the Cheyenne River and I was raised on the Bad River. My dad's brother was married to Casey's sister. Me and Casey grew up together. You know their whole family could ride broncs. Men and women. Casey ain't the only one. He's just the only one that left there. And the old man, John, was one hell'uva bronc rider.

There was another brother named *Short Log*. He was my favorite. Frank Tibbs was his name. *Short Log*. A little bow-legged son-of-a-bitch. His legs was all bent around and he walked around funny like that.

It's a different world now, see. I worked for Casey's brother, Johnny Tibbs, and we broke horses for the government. Johnny done it for 25 years. I worked for him in 1951 the last year the government broke horses. 20 dollars a day and room and board. I got on 25 to 30 head a day. They were bronc sons-of-bitches. All you had to do was tame 'em down so you could ride 'em up and trot up back down a stockyard alley. For the Army. Them horses were not very broke. (*laughter*)

Kids like Casey and Billy Meyers rode broncs to school. Five miles. Slapping 'em over the eyeballs when they wanted 'em to turn one-way or the other. It was a different time. We learned to ride on them old meat-hook horses.

There was an old French Canadian guy there on the Cheyenne River name of Bullet Pierman. Old Bullet, he weighed 300 pounds. He had them meat-hook horses. They was a bunch of bad rascals and me and Casey learned to ride on 'em. They'd pitch, and you bet your bottom dollar they'd part your hair. They was bad sons-of- bitches on the ground.

We rode them horses to school. Twenty-four kids in a one room school and twenty-three of 'em road horseback to school. The other kid lived across the road, so he walked. One gal rode eight miles to school, 16 miles a day, and some days was 20 below zero, and she'd come on an old white horse. Different times, eh? Another little gal's horse got spooked by a jack rabbit and he bucked her off, and she got hung up in the stirrup, and he drug her all the way back home. Broke her arms and all.

Casey Tibbs: I'd start off every morning with a wild horse, and since I never knew what direction they'd take off in, I'd have to start out two or three hours early. When times were good my old man ran 2000 head of horses.

Rusty Richards: It's interesting for several reasons why Casey became an expert in his field. Consider the tremendous amount of rank bucking stock he climbed aboard. One year Albert Lopez paid him for breaking sixty head of horses. Once, in trying out horses for Ken and E.C. Roberts, Casey rode an incredible thirty-three head of bucking horses in one day.

Jim Hannum: We learned starting them colts. Some of them government horses we broke, were four or five years old. They didn't start horses 'til then. Four to seven years old. Solid colored horses. They did it different. They run a horse into a round corral and just neck 'em down, and forefoot 'em, choke 'em down, roll 'em around 'til he got down, roll him in a saddle.

Yeah, all summer long you ride him and he might not even be halter broke. And when he was caught he knew to stop. Didn't want no more. So if you was gonna work on one of them outfits and you couldn't ride him, well they'd put you to pitchin' hay or fixing a fence.

You toughened up and got 'em rode. I went to work for Johnny Tibbs. First horse bucked me off 34 times that first mornin'. And John come a riding up and he said, "I got more to do then keep catchin' your damn horse all mornin.'" I toughened up.

Rusty Richards: It's almost unimaginable how many broncs Casey rode (early on). That he did so without much injury gives silent testimony to his great skill.

Jim Hannum: Horses have changed. They got horses bred today so athletic and smart. But they bred the grit out of 'em. Everything is a product of the environment. You take this horse that's been raised in a pen all his life, from the time he was a colt to the time you start him, he ain't never stepped on a rock. He ain't got no sole to his foot. He ain't been able to go but thirty feet and hit a fence, so he don't know how to travel.

A lot of things have changed. Back when they raised horses (in South Dakota) there was lots of country and there was lots of horses, and a mare would go off by herself to have her colt. And she'll stay with that colt maybe three days before she goes to water. Well, just think about that. A product of the environment. The first day that mare goes to water, that colt follows her to water. He went fifteen miles. Maybe further. He went further on his first day than the other horse (the modern horse in the pen) went in a year.

It's survival of the fittest. These modern horses don't have no sense of survival. He's thinkin' you're gonna take care of him all his life. Them older horses were smart enough not to drink too much water and colic themselves. These newer horses you're always callin' the vet, cause they got a bellyache.

Casey Tibbs: It was a godforsaken place so I took off from there. I left at age thirteen and broke horses for the Diamond A, a big New Mexican outfit, then a cook shot a foreman (for getting into the biscuits too early), which is a long story, and they wanted me to work on the fence crew, which I didn't want to do, so I drifted around some, and when I was fourteen or so I started hittin' the rodeo pretty fair, and after that I just sort of busted loose.

Ernest Thayer: *From 5,000 throats and more there rose*
    a lusty yell,
It rumbled through the valley, it rattled in the dell,
It knocked upon the mountain and recoiled upon the flat,
For Casey, mighty Casey, was advancing to the bat.

II Busting Loose: The Man Who Floated Bucking Horses

When I nod
and they throw the gate open to the same
gravity, the same 8 ticks
of the clock, number 244 and I
will blow for better or worse
from this chute – flesh and destiny
up for grabs, a bride's bouquet
pitched blind

    — **Paul Zarzyski,** *All This Way For the Short Ride*

Jim Hannum: (Jim is pointing towards a wall of bucking horse photos in his ranch house.) See that picture of Casey? He's ridin' blindfolded for a thousand dollar bet, and he's looking over his shoulder and telling the guy who bet him to get his money ready. Yeah! Look at that!

Childhood Friend: I grew up with Casey, you know. He started winning bronc ridings right out of the eighth grade and went on the road with Billy Meyers. Another great bronc rider. (Meyers died in a car wreck.) Nobody ever told Casey to save money, or behave himself or nothin'. He just ran off with the wild bunch and never looked back, as long as the money rolled in.

Rusty Richards: Casey devised ways to take what he'd labeled a *mediocre horse* and make him look better (extra slack in the bucking rein, loose cinch to make the horse think he was winning, and full stroke spur licks) all this combined gave Casey the reputation for what became known as "floating" his horses. He had to ride on almost pure balance and agility. Many people in the rodeo business today give Casey credit for being the first to full-stroke a saddle bronc.

Winston Bruce: Casey took it to the next level.

Jim Hannum: Those was a different kind of bucking horses back then in the 40s and 50s. Big rank horses. You can't ride rank horses the way some of these guys today ride these little blooper horses. They got their toes turned down like this and they're missing them all the way back, the stirrups are a hole too long and the rein is way up high. Yeah it's fine on them blooper horses, but when a big horse is giving you a thrashin' and jerking you and sashaying this way and that, you can't be liftin' and you got to let him pull you through it to have contact. You can't float them big rank horses.

Pat Russell: Casey was the best. A natural. There was also Gene Rambo, Enoch Walker, Winston Bruce, and Marty Wood. And great buckin' horses like *Scene Shifter* and *Wild Portugee*.

Jim Hannum (When asked: *how did Casey float those big, rank horses?)* You're talkin' about a different kind of individual. Casey rode them out of the ass of his pants. There aren't many of them guys come along who have that natural ability. It's just like Michael Jordan (*pro basketball*). He could jump up in the air and float on forever.

Well, Casey, I've seen horses jump plum out from under Casey and he'd just jump and stick them, and pull himself back to them. Like I said, he rode them out of the ass of his pants. There was only a few guys who could ride broncs like that, guys like Casey and Marty Wood.

Casey Tibbs: The name of the game is *try*.

III Wide Open and Roaring – The King of the Practical Joke – The Man with the Hair Trigger Heart

A man is seen in fragments,
A scar, a limp, tattoos, and broken teeth
Scratch the surface on most men out here
And you'll find three men hiding underneath....
   Cowboys we are, cowboys we shall always be.

— **Tom Russell**, *Hair Trigger Heart*

Jim Hannum: I travelled with Casey a few years. He never drove. He slept. He'd buy a pint of whiskey and pretend he was drinkin' it, so he'd tell us he was too drunk to drive. But he wasn't drinkin' much of it at all.

That son of a bitch, he wouldn't drive and he'd let you drive forever. You'd drive 'til you couldn't see no more, and finally if you made him take over, he'd pull out and buy another pint of whiskey and pretend to start suckin' on that whiskey, but he wouldn't really be drinking it, but he'd be swerving and swishing into the gravel, so we'd be worried and have to take back the wheel.

You travelled 60 to 80,000 miles a year in them little cars back then. Lincolns and Chevys and Studebakers. 80 miles an hour, just wide open and roaring.

Harry Tompkins: If there was nothing going on, Casey would throw a firecracker at your feet.

Tom Russell: Casey was addicted to practical jokes. There's no better word for it. *Addicted*. Like any addict he sometimes blurred the line between a good old practical joke on your buddies and something that was over-the-line dangerous. Caught up in the adrenalin rush of a scheme, the jokes could get out of hand.

Glen Orhlin: Casey was pretty much always involved with the business of bein' Casey.

Jim Aplan: We'd been out at the ranch playing with dynamite and then drinkin in the Hopscotch bar. Billy Meyers and Jim Hannum decide they're gonna blow up the bank. I was startin' to sober up real fast, cause I knew they do it, and anybody knows 'em knows they would do it. We had a lot of wild guys in Fort Pierre. You know they had Casey on the Tonight Show eating a glass?

Jim Hannum: How do you eat a glass? You just bite a chunk out and start chewin' that's how. With your teeth. I just used it as intimidation when they told me I was cut-off at a bar. There were nine bars on one street in Ft Pierre where we grew up. The Hopscotch, and the Indian bar was called the Snake Pit. The Indians got off the reservation and they'd come to town. The Sioux was some good bronc riders. There was one guy named Johnny Iron Lightning. That kid rode a bronc called Broken Bones that Casey could never get covered. Johnny got kicked in the face by a horse so he had a hair lip. Talked funny. Tough bronc riders. At the Snake Pit.

Tom Russell: My sister in law Claudia gave me a bunch of old magazines Casey was in. He was on the cover of the June 1956 issue of *Western Horseman*. I opened to the article and out falls an old newspaper clipping someone had stuck in there. It shows a photo of Casey in a hospital bed, recovering from *self-inflicted abdominal knife wounds.*

Casey had fired a blank gun into a phone booth where Jim Shoulders was talking to his wife, and Shoulders was so pissed off he pulled out a knife and jammed it into Casey's gut. Severe wounds. Casey took the rap and told the police they were *self-inflicted* wounds. He and Shoulders eventually became friends again.

Casey Tibbs: I had it coming. My morbid sense of humor had finally caught up with me

Childhood Friend: He never grew up. When the money dried up he was living off women and trick horses. He died penniless. He could have made money in Hollywood but he was always playin' practical jokes at the wrong time. He almost killed a lot of people with his practical jokes. Never grew up. Nobody ever really figured out how he could ride broncs so well – he just did it. He always landed on his feet like a cat. Until one day, you know, you don't land on your feet.

Tom Russell: The reverse side of it was Casey went out of his way to visit sick kids and do charity work and lend money to broke bronc riders. He was a big-hearted kid for sure.

IV Captain Midnight and his Trick Horse – actor, drinker, gambler, stunt man, and rodeo producer.

His boots were purple, the Cadillac was purple
The sky was 1950s Blue
Green was the color of the greenback dollar
And he rode those broncs with a hoop and a holler
    Casey you're a Rainbow rider...

— **Ian Tyson,** *Casey Tibbs*

Jim Hannum: Casey was trying to quit rodeo in 1957 and he became Captain Midnight, cause he had this trick horse named *Midnight*. And he finally decided that wasn't gonna work and he came back and won the world in '59. The last time.

Pat Russell: It was about 1959 or '60. Andy Jauregui gave Casey about 40 head of horses. So Casey put on about five rodeos at Devonshire Downs. He was the promoter. He used to take his introduction on a little saddle bronc named Johnny Cake. He was a longhaired little brown horse who just jumped and kicked and Casey would just spur and drag the fur off of him. He could float him forever.

    The announcer would say, "Here's your rodeo producer, Casey Tibbs." And he'd come out of the chute on that little bronc and jump off and land on his feet after a few bucks and tip his hat.

    One time Johnny Cake got crippled and I told Casey there's this black mare that bucks pretty good, so he uses the black mare for his intro. Now Casey was gettin' a belly on him, he was fat and out of shape, and this mare really bucked and got Casey standing up in his left stirrup. Casey took the bucking rein, threw it over the horse's nose, when she was in the air and he was gettin' bucked off. He pulled the rein over her neck and when she hit the ground he cradled her head in his arm, took the flank off, took the saddle off, let her up and tipped his hat.

I never seen anything like it. Slim Pickens was there – Slim said "I never in my life seen anything like that."

Harry Tompkins: In Fort Worth once they introduced Casey and he came out on that buckin' horse Johnny Cake. It was the classiest ride. When he jumped off he landed on his feet and he held the bronc rein. He worked the horse in a circle just like he was on a long line, then he threw the rein to Slim Pickens and took off his hat and bowed as he left the arena. The applause just rained down.

Tom Russell: The director Budd Boetticher lured Casey back into the film business. When Boetticher died I picked up a box of his memorabilia at an auction. Stacks of signed photos from Anthony Quinn, Gilbert Roland, Audie Murphy, and Casey. They were all running around together. Casey was doing films, commercials, and Levi's magazine ads. He was in every Western magazine you opened up.

Then there was Casey's documentary *Born to Buck* where he swims a herd of horses across a river in South Dakota and almost drowns. Around 1977 Casey helped invent *Team Rodeo* (which didn't fly) where towns had different rodeo teams. He got Steve Ford, President Ford's son, involved.

Steve Ford: Team rodeo was a concept they came up with to make rodeo a team sport like football. Casey was a coach. One night in Salt Lake City one of our bronc riders from Canada couldn't show, so we were short a man.

Casey was drinkin' quite a bit back then and I think he was drinkin' before the rodeo. And he said, "Aw, hell! I'll just ride him!" He was listed as a player/coach so they could substitute him in the bronc riding. Here he was, thirty pounds overweight, drinking, and he hadn't been on a bucking horse in probably ten years.

He borrowed some guy's saddle, and he got some spurs and another guy's chaps. He takes his hat off and spits in it, then pulls his hat back on and calls for the gate. The gate opens, and for the first couple of jumps no one knows who's gonna get the best of it. Everybody's holding their breath, but about the third jump out, Casey starts reaching and spurring that bronc like it was fifteen years earlier. I mean it was just beautiful! He spurred the hell out of that horse.

He made the buzzer and it was a good ride, but he was feeling so good that he waved the pickup men away, and started fanning his horse with his hat. Well he was gonna jump off like he used to in the old days, and he jerked the flank strap off. But when he went to bail off the horse ducked to the right on him.

It just stuck him in the ground like a post. I thought he'd really hurt himself. We rubbed liniment on him for about three days – but he rode the hair off that horse.

Rusty Richards: (concerning Casey's drinking) At this point (1983) the old champion spirit rose again in Casey and he began to sail with the A.A. program.

Casey Tibbs: I went into A.A. to save my ass, but I found out that my ass was connected to my soul.

V When the Legends Die – The Last Go Round

We drank the rivers, we rode the twisters
We tumbled down to the ground
But we'll rake and ride, we'll spin to Glory
On our last go round...

— **Rosalie Sorrels,** *My Last Go Round*

When the legends die, the dream ends.
When the dream ends, there is no greatness.

— **Hal Borland,** *When the Legends Die*

Tom Russell: Thirty years after meeting Casey at the racetrack I was living in a storefront in Brooklyn. Driving a taxi and playing honkytonk music. I heard Casey was hurting, fighting a terminal sickness in San Diego, where he was a "greeter," more or less, at a new ranch-housing development. I couldn't believe it. It was like hearing Joe Louis ended up as a greeter at a Casino in Las Vegas. I guess Casey was broke.

I wrote him a note about how much it meant to me to meet him when I was a kid. He sent me back a card and a signed photo of himself riding a bronc called *Easy Money,* high above a pole corral in South Dakota. Full circle. It's the greatest bronc photo of all time. "Luck to Tom Russell," he said. Damn. He had no self-pity in him. He was all heart right to the end.

Casey: I want to send a word out to all you who heard I was on the down side. I'm gettin' better every day, and if you want to say a prayer to my purple angels you can do that, but I'm gonna make it.

Jim Shoulders: Back then a lot of the media wouldn't have talked about rodeo if it wasn't for Casey. He did a lot for rodeo. He dressed the part. He lived up to whatever he said.

Tom Russell: Casey Tibbs died in front of a television while watching the Super Bowl in January, 1990. He probably had a bet on the game.

Inscribed on Casey's grave was a quote from his last speech at the Rodeo Hall of Fame: "Thanks for makin' me look good...Hell, I *was* good."

In Congress on Monday, February 5, 1990, Congressman Duncan Hunter stood up and read this into *The Congressional Record*: "Mr. Speaker, one of America's greatest champions, Casey Tibbs, died this week in California. He will be greatly missed by all of us who treasure America's heritage of the Wild West cowboy."

Casey Tibbs: I was just another cowboy who done the best he could. I was blessed. And for all you youngsters that's gonna be a world champion, never leave home for second. Adios.

****

Note: Rusty Richards' quotes, some Casey quotes, and the Steve Ford quote, taken from Rusty's fine book: *Casey Tibbs: Born to Ride*. Hard cover copies autographed by Rusty available at: rustyrichards.com

Jim Hannum quotes were taken from our afternoon conversation at his ranch. Jim Aplan quote from the book: *Badlands: An Oral History of Rodeo – Doug and Kathy Jory*. Several quotes taken from Ivan Daines' interview with Casey, 1989, at The Rodeo Hall of Fame.

Three Bronc Sundown

Ceremonies of the Horsemen
(Horses of the L.A. Basin)

*After God, we owe our victory
to the horses.*

— R.B. Cunninghame Graham
Horses of the Conquest

We grew up on a three hundred thousand acre ranch the Spanish called *El Pueblo de la Reyna de los Angeles*, The Pueblo of the Queen of the Angels, or simply – Los Angeles. My mom and dad and four kids. That's us smiling from that black and white Christmas card in the 1950s. That's me holding the horse. *Tex Anne.* We bought her at the L.A. Horse and Mule Auction. That's my older brother Pat, kneeling in front. Ready to mount-up and ride off into the gunpowder sunset, across the L.A. Basin.

Our horse stables were Fox Hills Riding Academy, near the airport, and the stables on the backside of the now defunct Hollywood Park Race track. At the track my father played gin rummy on foggy mornings with Hopalong Cassidy (William Boyd) as we watched the morning workouts.

My father came out of Iowa, where his father was sheriff of Cochise County. The sheriff co-owned the *Russell Brothers – Dealers in Livestock* barn and auction yard. We're descendants of Irish horse traders and pirate queens. My 80-year-old Aunt Mary still lives in Templemore, Ireland. She keeps cows and horses. Up until a few years ago her roof was thatched straw.

My father, Charlie Russell, came out West to sup of the American dream. He drank deep from the toxic elixirs which tempt Mid-Western farm boys. *Hollywood. Money. Fast horses.* He operated gas stations, furniture stores, clothing outlets, eventually becoming a building contractor. His passion was horses. Pleasure horses and running nags. He had a fancy saddle made at Bohlin's in Hollywood. Then the money dried up.

Even in the lean years – there were always the horses.

My brother Pat began riding the pony-horses at the track and hot walking thoroughbreds. At age fifteen he was packing mules into the high sierras under the guidance of an Arkansas muleteer named Rayburn Crane. Pat came out of the mountains *cowboy to the core*, with old cowboy poems and songs on his tongue. His days, from then on, were spent horseback.

In the mid-1950s my brother built a bucking barrel in our backyard in Inglewood. The barrel was an empty fifty-gallon oil drum suspended from four telephone poles. The barrel danced on stout ropes tied to garage door springs. Powerful, badass springs.

My brother proceeded to launch the neighborhood kids into outer space. Some of 'em I never saw again. Others landed in Fergie Ferguson's chicken yard and crawled back home to their piano lessons. *Weeping*. The ones who survived grudgingly agreed to follow my brother to the weekend rodeos at the movie ranches in the San Fernando Valley, where Pat started riding bulls at age sixteen.

My brother is still in the rodeo game. The others faded. They didn't like the taste of blood, dirt and manure. But they loved to sit on the barrel while polishing up their opening lines: "Open the Chute," "Let Her Buck," "Ride a Bull," "Let's Dance," etc. They'd watched too much television. Most of them would never get on a live bull. Fear clawed at their sleep patterns, and law school or undertaker careers loomed. The barrel taught tough lessons.

Brother Pat never looked back. From bull riding, to bareback broncs, bulldogging, and on to horseshoeing, Agricultural Science at Cal Poly, to ranching, trading Navajo Rugs, collecting rare horse bits...on to rodeo contractor and stock contractor. He's at it today. If there's a major cutting horse competition somewhere near the West Coast or in Nevada, it's likely Pat Russell is behind the scenes, well mounted, moving fresh cattle through the action. He never got away from the backside of the track. The cowboy side.

Myself? I figured falling off a horse interfered with my guitar playing and I became the songwriter. He's the cowboy. And a damn good one. But what about the cowboy and horse tradition in Los Angeles? Where did it come from, where did it go?

I   The Russell Brothers in Deep Palaver: Horses of the L.A. Basin

In ceremonies of the horsemen
Sometimes the pawn must hold a grudge...

— **Bob Dylan,** Love Minus Zero/No Limit

Fast forward 50 years. I'm sitting across the table from brother Pat in The Peppermill Casino, in Reno, Nevada. I have a concert that night. This is a family meeting to discuss a topic we, and editor Bill Reynolds, are much interested in: *Horses of the L.A. Basin*. Pat has 12 handwritten pages in a spiral notebook. Notes and facts and statistics. He rips them out and throws them on the table. Then he starts in.

"What I'm talking about," he says, slapping his notes, "is *the sheer volume* of horses." He stops to spit tobacco into his Styrofoam coffee cup. I move my cup out of the way.

He takes up where he left off: "The *sheer volume* of horses that've come through the L.A. basin. In the four hundred years or so. Millions of 'em."

I look down at his notes and try to keep up. He knows what he's talking about. He points at the first page. It's all lined out there in ballpoint ink, in his own hand. This was not concocted on a computer. This was not summoned forth from the shallow wells of *Google*. This came from his blood memory. *Cowboy* blood memory.

The list begins with the early Spanish haciendas and the Missions and includes the Spanish Land Grant ranches. Onward through the wild horses, the military horses, the workhorses, the Japanese farm horses, the slaughter plants, sales barns, movie horses, racetracks, amusement parks, rodeos, dude ranches and rent stables.

Then Pat is talking about *the evolution of Horses becoming pets, rather than tools of the conquest.* This was becoming a damn good history lesson in a casino in Reno: *The Biggest Little City in the World.*

My brother spits again into the cup, and goes to list the rodeo and movie horse contractors: Fats Jones, Jack Lilly and Andy Jauregui. Then the specialty horses and the trick horses. He has the rodeos in the LA Basin listed. Over fifty of them. From the L.A. Coliseum to small towns, like Norco, Castaic, Hemet, Indio and Big Bear. He's got the horse farms marked down: Connie Ring and Rex Ellsworth and others. Then he's onto the slaughter plants.

There's a quick aside about horses being shipped by rail back in the 50s, but stock trains could only roll for 36 hours maximum before the horses were let out for exercise. Then he mentions of horses on the Channel Islands and on Catalina Island. I'd never thought about that. He rolls onward.

He lists the rent stables, saddle clubs, and drill teams. The Anadarko Riders. The Camp Pendleton Marine Color Guard. The hundreds of horses in the annual Rose Parade. The Sheriff's Posse. The Search and Rescue Posse. Then the racetracks: Hollywood Park, Santa Anita, Del Mar, Los Alamitos, and Devonshire Downs. Then the Amusement park horses: Knott's Berry Farm, Disneyland, and the Griffith Park Pony Rides.

We're talking about *volume* of horses, but also the deep history of cowboy and horse culture in the L.A. Basin. The Los Angeles Basin, in a geographic sense, includes the central part of The City of Los Angeles, as well as its southern and southeastern suburbs. The Basin is approximately 50 miles long and 25 miles wide, bounded on the north by the Santa Monica and San Gabriel Mountains, on the east by the Santa Ana Mountains, and in the South by the Pacific Ocean and the Palos Verdes Hills. The confluence of the Los Angeles and Rio Hondo rivers is the center of the basin.

A million years back this basin was under water. Currently it's a snake-nest of freeways. Just 60 years ago there were hundreds of thousands of horses here. And what does it come down to, this great quantity of horses in the recent past, after the conquistadors rode away?

Auctions, sure. And slaughterhouses. And pleasure mounts. Race horses. Plow horses. But in the end it comes down to *Western films*. Hay burners and classics. Thousands of them.

II The Sheriff of Monterey Weighs in on Western Film History

Well Jackie and his buddies,
　were hangin' out at Gower Gulch...
Waitin' for a call from the studio
　for a part in a cowboy movie...
Jackie wants to be a drugstore cowboy...

— **Maria McKee**, *Drugstore Cowboy*

My friend Gary Brown, former Sheriff of Monterey, is one of our leading authorities on cowboy and Western films. I asked Gary how many cowboy movies were filmed on the West Coast during the Golden Era: 1930-1960. Gary surmised there were 2962 Western films produced between those years – the average of about 99 per year.

Sound films began in 1929. The '30s and '40s were the big years for cowboy films, and number began dropping off by the late 1950s – from over a hundred a year, down to 38 films in 1959. Numbers have been dropping since. Now there's maybe one or two Western films per year.

Between 1930 and 1960 there were over 20 operative Western Film ranches in the greater L.A. area, including Corriganville, Circle J, Disney Oak Ranch, Iverson's, Jack Ingram's, Melody Ranch, Pioneer Town and The Spahn Ranch. Each ranch kept a decent size herd of horses, ponies, and mules. Maybe you recall *Francis the Talking Mule*? He had his own T.V. series.

The most popular Southern California movie ranch was the Iverson Ranch, located in the San Fernando Valley. There were more major studio productions shot there, per square mile, than any other location in America. *Stagecoach* was filmed at Iverson's and hundreds of other Westerns, along with the T.V shows *The Lone Ranger* and *Bonanza*.

The rise of the Western film signaled cowboy work for wranglers, extras, and stunt people – male and female. And the deep need for good horses. *The sheer volume*, my brother kept emphasizing.

Gary Brown sent me a photo of cowboys hanging out at the corner of Sunset and Gower back in the '40s. They called it *Gower Gulch*. You waited on the corner, near a local Hollywood drugstore, for work in cowboy films. You wore your best cowboy gear. That's where the term *drugstore cowboy* came from.

Gary forwarded to me a copy of the bill of sale for *Trigger,* when Roy Rodgers purchased the famous palomino horse from the Hudkins Brothers Ranch. Trigger cost $2500. *Mucho dinero* back then. He was a special horse, trained for movie stunts.

I promised brother Pat we'd work on it. The *sheer volume of horses*, and the stories which surrounded the hay day of horse culture in the City of the Angels. I figured a good place to begin would be the bars. I was comfortable with that. The infamous River Bottom's bars – those cowboy bars on Riverside Drive bounding Griffith Park, near the horse stables. The bars were a haven for great bronc riders making side money as film extras. As the fictional West unfolded in film, the real West of drinking, fighting, singing, and spinning rowdy yarns, came alive in the bars.

I went home to El Paso and dug through old boxes and unearthed a series of notes from eight or ten years ago. A folder marked: *Stories from The River Bottoms Bars.*

III Walt LaRue & Pat Richardson: Tales From the River Bottoms

Will James, he'd stay in his room for days.
Drinking. He would take a piece of soap
and draw a bucking horse on the mirror,
drunk as hell...

— **Walt LaRue**

Walt LaRue was a bronc rider, stunt double, wrangler, cowboy singer, story-teller, artist, cartoonist, and occasional illustrator for *The Western Horseman* and other cowboy publications. I met Walt at *The Elko Cowboy Poetry Gathering* a few years before he passed away. I'd call him up at his place in Burbank and we chat about the old days and the River Bottom's bars along Griffith Park in L.A. Walt was not a man to mince words or prettify them. He spoke like the old songs spoke. Straightforward, hard edged, and colorful. *Hang and rattle, Tom,* was always his closing line.

Let's start in the middle (*en media res*) of Walt's chats and wind our way to both ends of the L.A cowboy deal. Here's Walt LaRue:

> *I worked on* Paint Your Wagon *with Clint Eastwood and Lee Marvin...Lee could drink a little, ya know. Gawd, yes. I'd work out at the Corrigan's and Iverson's movie ranches shootin' them quick pictures with Roy Rogers and Bob Wills. I tell you Bob Wills would play in a ballroom out on the end of the Santa Monica Pier and that damn pier would be a rockin', and you couldn't help but stomp your feet to the music.*
>
> *Stunt men and musicians stayed at the same hotel over there on Santa Monica Boulevard. Paramount Studios was near there. Near Teeny's Bar. Keystone Cops and midgets and cowboys all slippin' upstairs with gals. All of 'em drunk. Same street Valentino was buried on in that Hollywood graveyard over there.*
>
> *Red River Dave was around. Famous for "Amelia Earhart's Last Flight," and he had a song about a little blind kid that was*

gonna donate his seeing-eye dog to Uncle Sam for the war effort. Can you imagine?

I didn't know Will James. But I loved to hear Will James stories. You think he couldn't write? Go read the last goddamn paragraph of Smoky The Cow Horse *and that will jerk you around, kid. Read one of Will's stories and you'd want to quit school. He'd drink at The Green Spot in Victorville and get a room upstairs and stay in his room for days. Drinking. He'd take a piece of soap and draw a bucking horse on the mirror. Drunk as hell. They'd have to come up from Hollywood to get him. He went to hell drinkin'.*

He died in 1942 when I was in Montana breaking horses. He died from drinking too much. Died in the Presbyterian Hospital. Then I discovered Charles Russell and Joe D. Young and Ed Borein. Joe D. Young would draw cowboys to show the movie folks what cowboys looked like.

Casey Tibbs came through those L.A. bars. I first saw Casey up in Salinas in '47 or '48. Rodeo grounds. He was in the office when I come in. He had on a purple shirt with horseshoes on the pocket. I said, "who in the hell is that guy?" Wag Blessing says "That's Casey Tibbs." I may of thought he was some kinda' dude. But later on I watched him ride and he sure showed me who he was. Nobody ever done it as good. With such class. Casey was great, cause he floated them broncs...but for my money Gene Rambo was the greatest all-around bronc rider who ever lived. It was kind spooky how he died. They said his gun went off when he was crawlin' under a fence.

Casey Tibbs come out of the chute a spurrin' em. Hang and rattle, that's what you did. Casey worked on the Stony Burke *TV show, but was so phony it drove him nuts. But he took their money. Casey would drink and play around, but he never showed up drunk to a rodeo...now Bud Linderman could ride drunk.*

I started stunt doublin' for Gabby Hayes and Audie Murphy. I doubled for Warren Oates one time. Had to jump off a train onto a horse. I saw Warren Oates ride a pig through a train. Won a 800 dollar bet. Rode the pig with a loose rope...

Well, gotta sign off, Tom. Hang and rattle.

Pat Richardson is a cowboy poet, artist, and ex-bronc rider out of Merced California. Pat shared a few River Bottoms stories with me. Most of 'em I couldn't repeat even in the most *impolite of companies*. They're blue humdingers. Raw and funny. Here's a cleaner one about the infamous rodeo brothers – the Linderman's.

One of Pat Richardson's arms has been crippled since childhood, but it didn't hurt his bronc riding or fighting skills any. Pat was 18 and riding broncs around the L.A area. He was sitting in the Pickwick Bar when a cowboy came up and tapped him on the shoulder. Pat turned around and the cowboy threw a punch that glanced off Pat's jaw.

Pat, half-dazed, stood up and decked the cowboy with one punch from his good arm. Pat sat back down to mind his own business. A few days later the same thing happened at The Pickwick. Another cowboy came in and started swinging and Pat had to deck him. This time Pat noticed one of the Linderman brothers, behind the bar, laughing. So Pat, pissed off now, walks up and asked what was going on – what was so damn funny?

Linderman finally quit laughing and told him.

"Hell, Pat, I've been making money off you. These tough old cowboys come in here and I make a bet with 'em...I say 'you ain't so tough. I'll bet you five dollars you can't even go over and knock down that cripple kid.'"

The rest of Pat's stories will stay under the counter with the *Tijuana bibles*.

IV Blood Buckets and Bronc Riders: Glenn Orhlin Remembers

Casey Tibbs had a trick horse act, ya know. The horse sat and counted and all that. Casey, himself, didn't have to do much but tip his hat and smile. Casey was pretty much involved full time in being Casey.

— **Glenn Orhlin**

Another fine cowboy I met at Elko is Glenn Orhlin. Glenn's an ex-bronc rider, singer, storyteller, and cowboy folklorist and authored the timeless cowboy collection: *The Hell Bound Train*. Glenn has recorded several classic traditional cowboy records. He ranches in Arkansas. But in the late '40s and '50s he used to hang out in L.A.

According to Glenn:

> There were the two cowboy bars there in The River Bottoms: The Pickwick and The Hitching Post. Jerry Ambler owned the Pickwick and Wag Blessing was involved. The Linderman's were around. All these guys were great rodeo cowboys. Cowboy actors and stuntmen would sit in there and wait for the phone to ring for a movie job. Sometimes they'd wait for months. That wasn't so appealing to me, so I went out and rodeo'd some. Came back now and then.
>
> Ya' know you'd see these guys who were once big...Ken Maynard, he ended up doin' trick shootin' in a fancy suit. He could barely fit into it. It was kinda' sad.
>
> Jerry Ambler was Saddle Bronc Champion of the world in 1946, predated Casey Tibbs a little, and he took up part ownership in The Pickwick Bar. Jerry would hold forth on the art of bronc riding and say that it was all balance, timing, and science...he could make a mediocre horse look better by his own motion and artistry. But Jerry claimed the best of 'em all was Pete Knight, who died after being bucked off and stepped-on at the Hayward rodeo grounds in 1937.
>
> The River Bottom's bars were a home place for cowboys of all kinds. They weren't necessarily all rodeo or movie people. It was a gathering place for 'em...a block away, up the street it wouldn't be. Cowboys are like anyone else, they like to be with their own kind.
>
> There were probably more that 100,000 horses in the city limits back then and a maybe a million in Southern California. The Hudkins family had a thousand acre ranch just over the L.A River...they had lots of movie horses. Over 500 head at a time, at least.
>
> Jerry Ambler and Wag Blessing were always around. Ambler was one of the best saddle bronc riders ever, and Wag Blessing was world champion bull rider in 1947. Bud and Bill Linderman also hung out there. Bartending. Bill Linderman was the first rodeo cowboy I know to win over 40,000 dollars back then. They were from Red Lodge, Montana.
>
> The Pickwick Stables were behind the Pickwick Bar. The Hitching Post, at one time, was owned by the Olmstead brothers, and their boarding stables were behind the bar. Their place was called The Stock Farm.

Tommy Coates was a bartender at the Pickwick. He was a stunt man. He could sing with a real New York, wise-guy accent...so he'd jump up on the bar and sing "Ace in the Hole." I'll leave you with that one:

There's con men and there's boosters
Card sharks and crapshooters
They congregate around The Metropole....
They wear flashy ties and collars
But where'd they get their dollars?
If they'd lose that old ace in the hole?

V The L.A. Horse and Mule Auction, Slaughterhouse Afternoons, and Crap Games on Bandini Road: The Lost Pat Russell Transcriptions

We'd get these killer horses in the alley,
and we'd rope one, put a bareback riggin'
on 'em, and that's where we'd practice...

— **Pat Russell**

Inside the box of notes on the River Bottom's bars I found an old postcard from my parents. The message on the back stated my older brother Pat was conceived right here in El Paso, at the *The Paso del Norte*, an old cattleman's hotel downtown. It figured brother Pat was conceived on the edge of the last frontier. The card was clipped to the transcription of an old interview I did with my brother, maybe eight or ten years ago. The missing link in this story.

Picture the dialogue below punctuated with chewing tobacco, spit out between the wild pig's teeth my brother planted into his lower jaw with crazy glue. So goes the legend. The sound of his voice and way of speakin'? Think Ben Johnson crossed with Slim Pickens, in a documentary filmed by Sam Peckinpah.

Brother Pat Remembers:

Well, you know one of the best cowboy poets ever, Bruce Kiskaddon was cowboy-ing on some Southern California ranches with Bill Gibford (father of cowboy poet Dickie Gibford), and he give it up and went to be a bellhop at the

Mayfair Hotel in downtown L.A. They used his poems on the cover of the program they used at the Livestock auctions in L.A. "The Little Blue Roan" and stuff like that.

I started ridin' bulls in the early 1950s. I was sixteen. Out on all the movie ranches. There was Dee Cooper's, Devonshire Downs, and Corriganville – which was Crash Corrigan's ranch. A lot of rodeo champions where living in Burbank, working in the movies. Lots of 'em. Wallace Brooks, Louis Brooks, Montie Montana – they were all working for Fats Jones.

Fats Jones was supplying movie horses. He had hundreds of 'em. And these cowboys lived around what they called The River Bottoms, all along Riverside Drive, working for those different stables. Startin' colts or workin' in the movies.

Andy Jauregui was one of the big stock contractors. He did all the local rodeos within 150 miles of L.A., to about as far as Prescott, Arizona. He had some great animals. One of his best bareback horses was "Cheyenne." He had a little Buckskin horse called "Whiz Bang," who went on to become a National Finals horse. Jauregui sold out to Cotton Rosser in the 1960s. And Dee Cooper, who was a stuntman in the movies, had his own string of horses that did the California rodeos and the weekend rodeo at his movie ranch.

I got a job at the track (Hollywood Park) walkin' hots in the morning. (Walking racehorses to cool them down after a workout.) You got to work at four thirty in the morning and work 'til about ten thirty or eleven walkin' the hots, then hand them over to the groom.

One day a week you'd come back and walk the horses that were up in the races that day. Our dad would play gin rummy in the morning with Bill Boyd who played Hopalong Cassidy. (Our father had worked for The Academy of Motion Pictures in the mid 1940s – handing the Oscars onstage to the presenter – Bob Hope.)

In L.A., there was a horse auction twice a week. They had a trader sale on Wednesday afternoon. Bob Scott, who was half Indian and half black, rode the horses through the ring, and he could make any horse lay down if he wanted. They'd come in by the hundreds and he'd never seen 'em before.

He worked with a lot of the movie horses. He could make 'em do anything. He could make a horse lay down and roll over.

With a halter rope. He had the knack. And a guy named Red Foster was trying to start the American Model Quarter Horse Association, and he'd ship horses from New Mexico and Arizona.

The trader's sale was just for horse traders on Wednesday afternoon. There'd be three or four hundred horses in there and they wrote out the horses' names and held them up. They'd shave their tails down each side so their butts would look bigger and their neck would look stouter.

And a lot of those horses had their manes rubbed out, and they'd sell the mane and tail hair. They'd keep the horsehair separate. Load after load of it. The horses would come off the trains and trucks, and also carloads of hair. Bob Scott would ride those horses through, and what didn't sell they'd put on feed and sell them at the public sale on Friday. The hair was sold to guys who would use junk hair in furniture. Ottomans and cushions. And the rest would go to making hair ropes.

Behind the L.A Horse and Mule Auction, on Bandini Road, was Snowdon Brothers. A horse killin' plant. They'd kill like 80 to 500 horses a day. For dog food. And Alvin Deal and I would go over to the horse killin' plant when the sale was going on back at the auction. We'd get these killer horses in the alley, and we'd rope one, put a bareback riggin' on 'em, and that's where we'd practice. And we'd have to catch him to get our riggin' off.

Over in the hay barns, behind the auction, there was always a crap game going on. One Friday night they shot a guy.

Gotta go. Adios, kid.

Brother Pat rides off towards the Cuyama Mountains. *Lonely Are the Brave.*

VI Coda: The Sheer Volume Thins Out — Roll the Credits.

Oh, Midnight was the champion
He is the only bronc I couldn't ride
But now I hear old Midnight's blind
And rides little children for a dime...

— **Paul Davis,** *Ride 'Em Cowboy*

> *I sat on a horse and watched the aftermath*
> *of the Pickwick Stables fire, and remember*
> *all the dead horses in the sun, bloating. So sad.*
> *I left the River Bottoms in '53.*
>
> — **Sylvia Durando**, Horse Trainer/Stunt Woman

The Western film era began to decline in the mid-1960s. The bars closed down. The bronc riders moved on. *The L.A. Horse and Mule Auction* moved out to the City of Industry, in the L.A. suburbs. Dave Winn operated the auction for at least 25 years, into the late 1970s. Winn stood in the sales ring with a long stock whip and moved the horses and mules around the ring, after he'd eyeballed the animal and shouted the starting bid to the auctioneer.

Brother Pat Russell still handles livestock behind the scenes at cutting horse competitions. His bucking barrel should be in The Cowboy Hall of Fame, along with those pig's teeth he glued into his lower jaw. And that spiral notebook with the horse volume facts.

Pat weighed-in as I wrapped up this essay. He'd read the rough draft. He called up and said he wished there were more statistics on the number of horses. He emphasized what a huge boon to the L.A. economy the horse business was during those golden years. He didn't much take to the personal hogwash about our family and himself. It didn't interest him. He's a humble individual. I told him *personal hogwash* was my stock and trade. I'm a storyteller and a songwriter. I flunked statistics in college.

He spit into a cup, said *adios*, and hung up the phone.

We're back where we began — thinking of those *horses of the conquest*, and the sheer volume of hoof prints across the Los Angeles Basin. The research goes onward.

I'll leave you with a quote:

> *I who have ridden thousands of horses descended from the horses of the conquerors, have written that which I have written out of gratitude to all of them — bays, browns, blacks, chestnuts, piebalds, roans, grays, whites, cream-colored with black points, duns, skewbalds, claybanks, calicos, pintos, pangares, lobunios, grullos, zebrunos, malacaras, pampas, picazos, gateados, zainos, tordillos, melados, doradillos, overos,*

moros, barrosos, ruanos, rosillos, bayos, and all the rest of the infinity of colors that the Americas bring forth....for after God, we owe our victory to the horses.

— **R.B. Cunninghame Graham,** 1930
The Horses of the Conquest

Bitter Tears & Mean as Hell
Johnny Cash in the Wild West

I   Visions from an Indian Burial Ground

*I seemed to be surrounded by a mystery
so heavy and oppressive I could scarcely breath...
For weeks I wandered aimlessly, seeking answers.
How I arranged to escape from the valley,
I don't know...but I must tell you what I learned
out on the desert...and the secrets of the shifting,
whispering sands.*

— **Johnny Cash**
"The Shifting Whispering Sands" (Part 1)
Ballads of the True West

Maricopa, California, lies in the San Joaquin Valley, just over the Grapevine Hill from Los Angles County. It's due west of Highway 5 and a few miles east of the Carrizo Plain. Steinbeck territory. *Almost.* A little crossroads town circled by blown- out oil wells, cattle ranches, and citrus groves. Thirty years ago I recall a one-armed guy named *Shorty* running the gas station at the stop sign. A character right out of *The Grapes of Wrath*. Bakersfield is further down the road, forty miles deeper into the Valley. Tulare dust and neon lights.

In the early 1960s Johnny Cash used to roam around out here, kicking at cow skulls and digging up old bottles and bones – communing with the desert spirits. *Talking to himself.* Something was gnawing at him. What happened to the old-time cowboys and prospectors? Where had the Old West gone? The Indians who'd painted on these cave walls? What was their story? Johnny was *acrawl with nerves* back then. Fidgety. Restless. He'd trek deep into the Western outback. Disappearing for days. Hearing voices. Talking to the ghosts inside his skull.

He wrote:
> *I often go to an old abandoned ranch near Maricopa in my 1946 Jeep. No electricity. No running water no phone. There are rabbits, deer, badgers, coyotes, squirrels and, once and awhile, a bear. I know the 480 acres like the back of my hand. I sleep in a little cabin heated by a wood burning stove and use candles for light...I sat under a Manzanita bush one hot day, with pen and paper, all set for song inspiration...I was in an Indian burial ground...to my knowledge no one else knows of this Indian graveyard and I won't show you where it is.*

Cash was mining for material for what would later become a two record set of cowboy songs, eventually titled: *Ballads of the True West*, and re-issued in short form as *Mean as Hell*. The initial record was released in 1965, following on the heels of his Native American collection: *Bitter Tears*. A pair of folkloric masterworks. There is a great dose of rage in these records, for these were troubled years for Johnny. He'd been indited for starting a forest fire – with the spark coming out of the exhaust of his old pickup truck. 400 acres burned. He was also developing a craving for speed pills, an addiction that would land him in an El Paso jail. He was caught crossing back from Juarez with a thousand pills inside his guitar case. He was also going through a divorce, and performing over 300 road dates per year.

To top off the mayhem, Johnny was kicked off the Grand Ole Opry for smashing out the footlights with a microphone stand. *Who gave a damn, heh?* The Opry had kicked off Hank Williams, didn't they? Johnny's plate was overflowing with turmoil and wrath. Hunter S. Thompson once wrote: *a man doesn't know where the edge is until he jumps over it.* Johnny was performing backflips off the rim of a *grand* canyon. Yet he'd recorded at least ten great records in the previous decade. All of them included a hit song or two. Records which re-invented country music.

All this pain, chaos, and road-weariness played out in his voice. You could hear the rattle dance of a man fighting hard with his soul. The perfect voice for an old cowboy song, like "The Streets of Laredo" or "Sam Hall." No one, save Tex Ritter, had given such a rugged and authentic reading to the lyric of a man dying outside a whorehouse, or the whine and wail of a gunfighter about to be hung.

The golden years of Western music, the last major wave, had all but played out by the time Cash got around to recording this record in 1965. The 1930s through the mid '60s were fruitful years. The B-

Westerns, the Singing Cowboys, the Western T.V. serials, and the Broadway Frontier Musicals (*Oklahoma!*, *Annie Get Your Gun*, *Calamity Jane*, *Seven Brides for Seven Brothers*, and others) were simmering down in appeal as "pop country," modern folk, and rock and roll hit town for good. Even a few Jazz greats had been on board the Western train. Saxophonist Sonny Rollins recorded a Western jazz record titled *Way Out West* in 1957. Sonny lets loose on a bop version of Johnny Mercer's *I'm An Old Cowhand (From the Rio Grande)*.

It would take Nashville another dozen years or so to bleach the word *Western* out of *Country & Western*. A*dios* to the image of a cowboy with a guitar, sitting on a horse. Say goodbye to the gunfighter ballad. Welcome the *new country* sounds aimed at strip mall suburbia with singers with fake twangs and stove-in, cheap straw hats. Goodbye to classic songwriting. Of these changeling music-cultural trends – I feel *sorta* like Winston Churchill, when he remarked: *The substitution of the internal combustion engine for the horse marked a very gloomy milestone for mankind.*

Johnny Cash wasn't concerned with fading fashions. He'd been toying with cowboy songs for a long while. He'd crawled across those old ranches and Indian burial grounds. He'd already written and recorded: "Don't Take Your Guns to Town," which proved a minor hit, and he didn't give a damn how the winds had shifted in Nashville. He had a vision of The West.

Marty Robbins re-invented the western wheel with his song "El Paso," and that song, and Marty's eight Cowboy-based records, were a hard act to follow. But Marty was almost a *crooner* with a polished voice and a deep respect for Gene Autry and the singing cowboys. Cash sang from the other end of the spectrum. *Mean as Hell.* Cash's sound and snarl gave off the feeling of walking the wrong way around a outcropping of prickly pear and stepping on a gila monster. Tension hung in the air above each song. There was no over-romanticizing to his approach. Some of the vocals on the Native American and Cowboy records are almost hysterical with venom. No matter. Johnny Cash had lived it. And he had done his homework.

> *I went through a period in my career when I collected Cowboy songs. Westerns. And I went to the source, John Lomax's Cowboy songs which was published in 1910...I listened to cowboy singers...just to weed them out and choose for myself the right songs...I had a total collection of cowboy songs and I've lived with them and I've loved them and then I recorded some.*

He also read books by J. Frank Dobie and perused the Carl Sandburg song collections, but became confused with the possibilities of a direction. He called on Tex Ritter for advice. *Birds of a feather.* Tex was not only a great cowboy singer, in that raw and real vein, but a folklorist with a wide knowledge of traditional Cowboy songs. Both men possessed rugged voices and appreciated hard, truthful cowboy poetry.

Tex had appeared on Broadway in the 1930 play *Green Grow the Lilacs*, which later became the basis for Rodgers and Hammerstein's successful Broadway hit *Oklahoma!* Here's a bit of cowboy-trivia for you: "Green Grow the Lilacs" is an old Scots-Irish song. When American soldiers sang it during the Mexican-American War of the 1840s (with its first line: *Green grow the lilacs, and so does the dew...*) The Mexicans thought the US soldiers were always singing the word *gringo* instead of *green grow*. Thus came the Mexican slang word for white men – *gringo*. That's one version of the etymology.

Tex and Johnny sat down and narrowed in on the material. Cash later acknowledged the influence of Peter LaFarge (composer of "The Ballad of Ira Hayes"), and Ramblin Jack Elliott, who knew a hell of a lot of old cowboy songs. Jack gave Cash a version of "Mister Garfield," about President Garfield being assassinated.

Don Law, Cash's producer at Columbia records, wanted the cowboy album *pronto* – but Johnny kept disappearing out in Maricopa, or deep into the Mojave Desert, allowing the material to distil inside his gut.

> *I slept under mesquite trees. I ate mesquite beans and squeezed the water from a barrel cactus. I was saved once by a forest ranger, lying flat on my face, starving. I learned to throw a Bowie Knife and kill a jackrabbit at forty yards, not for sport, but because I was hungry...I learned the way of the True West the hard way.*

The record was an odd watermark for Western music. 180 degrees away from Marty Robbins territory. (And I love both slants) The album artwork tells the story. On his record *More Gunfighter Ballads and Trail Songs*, Marty is crouched under a cottonwood tree with a pistol raised. His clothes looked laundered, his face seems to indicate he is well fed. His flat-brimmed hat is perfectly creased. Marty was a gentleman. He's dressed in black, but doesn't look like a rake that frequents whorehouses, card rooms, or saloons.

Cash, on the front of *The Balluds of the True West*, is also lying beneath a tree. A thorny Mesquite. He looks like a bushwhacker who woke up on the wrong side of his bedroll – after sleeping off a three-day bender. He's unshaven. His hat is caved-in and there's a cigarette pack stashed down into the band, or is that envelope of hop-opium? His pistol is cocked and a snarl is locked into his face. A man about to be run down by a posse. And *hung*.

The music follows the cover art. *Mean as Hell*. Whatever Johnny went searching for in the desert, he seems to have found. And he's fixing to tell us about it in a voice that wavers between death and frenzy – an hombre who's seen a ghost in a cracked mirror that turned out to be himself. If the overall feel of the music resembles anything – it's Tex Ritter's *Blood on the Saddle* album. The stories crawl up your spine.

There are twenty reflections on the West, some of them straight ahead and stark. Others are backed with string arrangements and added vocals from the Carter Family. All of it is grounded by the bottom line of Cash's voice. An honest *American Voice*. In capital letters. A man who's been to places you don't want to pass through.

There's a mixed bag of traditional standards like "Old Paint," "Streets of Laredo," and "Bury Me Not on the Lone Prairie," along with originals songs by Shel Silverstein Ramblin Jack Elliott, Peter LaFarge, and Harlan Howard. Cash has added a few of his own songs, and three spoken-word ruminations on the West.

Here are the highlights.

II "Hardin Wouldn't Run" and other Tales

I never killed a man who didn't need killin'

— **John Wesley Hardin**

Ten miles east of our hacienda, in El Paso, sits one of the best Mexican restaurants in the West: *The L and J*. It's been there forever, and was originally called *Tony's Place*. Soldiers from Fort Bliss, fifty years ago, used to send a trained mule down to pick up a bucket of beer and bring it back to the base. It's also called *that restaurant next to the graveyard*. The graveyard in question is *The Concordia*, which embraces the remains of John Wesley Hardin, as well as dozens of Chinese railroad workers, various Buffalo Soldiers, and the odd Texas Ranger. Hardin is the star of the show.

There's no telling how many men Wes Hardin killed. Like most gunfighter legends he fine-tuned his own myth, embellished the details, and published a hero-rigged autobiography. The El Paso locals gave Hardin a wide berth. He was a card cheat, a bully, and a mean drunk. Sherriff John Selman finally shot him in the back of the head, and then drug John Wesley out into the El Paso street, so the citizens could gawk at another dead gunfighter with a big mouth.

Hardin was also a half-assed lawyer. He'd earned his law degree during the fifteen years he spent in Huntsville prison. Clients in El Paso were scarce, so Hardin resorted to extortion and cheating at craps and poker. Until Selman intervened. You notice how many of our outlaw legends were shot in the back? Jesse James, Wes Hardin and others? You didn't approach a rattlesnake from the front.

Johnny Cash read Hardin's book, and other history tomes, and wrote the song "Hardin Wouldn't Run." He takes us into the barroom where John Selman *came with a swinging gun*. Hardin doesn't have a chance to raise his *plow handle hand* and lift his pistol. No eyeballs in the back of his head. Cash's liner notes illuminate the details of the action, western jargon, and history of the Colt firearm:

> *Plow handle hand is the (gun) drawing hand...plow handle is a nickname for the shape of the Colt single-action army Revolver. Colonel Sam Colt invented the revolver...his firstone was a five-shooter, not six. He said he got the idea from watching the paddle wheel of a ship he was going on to India in 1835.*

Sherriff John Selman evidently shot Hardin because Hardin's Mexican girlfriend had "pistol whipped" Selman's son. I'm sure you can dig out the rest of the story. A fine El Paso historian, Leon Metz, has written plenty about Hardin. Cash wrote the song.

Cash found *The Streets of Laredo* in John Lomax's 1910 edition of *Cowboy Songs*. The song dates back to various Scots-Irish sources such as "The Unfortunate Rake," which also spawned a later version know as "St. James Hospital" or "St. James Infirmary." The early variant concerns a young man dying of syphilis in a London infirmary due to an unwise encounter with a *soiled dove*. The cowboy version replaces London with Laredo.

Cash does the best version of "Sam Hall" this side of Tex Ritter. Sam is singing to us from the gallows – a rope around his neck, as he curses the crowd, his girlfriend, the Sherriff and all of mankind. He stops short of messing with God. Seems he hasn't been rehabilitated in the clink. This song is a variant of an old English ballad: "The Climbing Boy," about a rotten-hearted chimney sweep in England.

Cash's screedy rant, as he portrays the doomed Sam Hall, reminds me of Warren Oates in *Bring Me The Head of Alfred Garcia*, or Harry Dean Stanton in *Paris, Texas*. Or maybe the character *Festus* on the old *Gunsmoke* TV show. Creepy and sly and Western as all hell. Ben Johnson and Slim Pickens territory.

Then there's "Mean as Hell," a traditional poem Cash has adapted to suit the rough texture of the record. We reside in the border-badlands of West Texas, so I take this one to heart. It seems the Devil is seeking a place to make a decent hell, and God talks him into utilizing sorry ground down near the Rio Grande (El Paso-Juarez will do just fine.) God set the landscape tones:

He began to put thorns on all the trees,
And he mixed the sand with millions of fleas,
He scattered tarantulas along all the roads,
Put thorns on the cactus and horns on the toads...

The heat in the summer is a hundred and ten,
Too hot for the devil and too hot for men.
The wild boar roams through the black chaparral,
It's a hell of a place he has for a hell...

There's a dozen verses, and much more to the rest of this record, but you get the picture. *Raw*. Concocted 'neath a mesquite tree in Maricopa, by an artist seemingly reaching the end of his tether. Johnny barely made it out alive. Balance this one with *Bitter Tears* and you have Cash's rugged, historical vision of the True West.

III *Bitter Tears* & Peter Bucking Horse

Of the new songwriters I'm the oldest and most
evil with my past. I have no lies to tell about
my past and sometimes it strangles me like a black dog
putting his foot down my throat...someone once
said to me: "I envy you your heart, but I couldn't stand
your hangovers."

— **Peter LaFarge**

I once owned an original 8 by 10 black and white photo of the songwriter Peter LaFarge. Peter was riding a bronc named *War Paint* in a Denver rodeo. Must have been the late 1950s. At the bottom of the photo Peter signed it: *To Woody, from Peter,* in ballpoint ink. I assume that was aimed at Woody Guthrie, who died before Peter would give it to him. I copied the photo and gave the original to Peter's sister, Povy, who lives down the road from us in El Paso. The horse in the photo doesn't appear to be the famous *War Paint,* who was PRCA Bucking Horse of the year (1956-57). That *War Paint* was the son of a registered quarter horse stud and a wild pinto mare, and came off the Klamath Indian Reservation in Oregon.

That half-breed, Indian blood deal fits our story. Johnny Cash had Cherokee blood, and Peter LaFarge, who wrote songs about Indian issues, is the key to *Bitter Tears* – Cash's Native American record. LaFarge wrote the classic protest song: "The Ballad of Ira Hayes." Peter's father was Oliver LaFarge, a fighter for Indians rights who won the Pulitzer Prize for the novel *Laughing Boy*. Peter's mother, Wanda Kane, was the organizer and first secretary of *The Rodeo Cowboys Association,* known originally as *The Turtle Association.*

What to say of Peter LaFarge? There's plenty of color. Too much. In 1959 LaFarge rode a saddle bronc in Madison Square Garden – rode with one broken foot in a cast – a spur set into the plaster. That same week he was appearing in a New York production of *King Lear.*

Peter was not a full blooded-Indian, though he was "adopted" into the Hopi tribe at an early age. He *thought of himself* as Indian. He had a cowboy radio show in Colorado when he was fourteen and worked on the ranch of his stepfather, rodeo producer Andy Kane. Later Peter joined the Navy and fought in the Korean War, boxed professionally, rode broncs, acted, wrote plays, poems, and songs, and stumbled in and out of mental health programs. He passed away under cloudy circumstances in a New York hotel room in 1965. La Farge's short, tragic life mirrored that of *Ira Hayes.*

"The Ballad of Ira Hayes" is the true story of a Pima Indian from Arizona who was one of the marines who raised the flag on Iwo Jima. You've seen that photo. It's iconic. Ira Hayes came back home to die a forgotten drunk. The lyrics seethe with dark irony:

Then Ira started drinking hard...
Jail was often his home
They let him raise the flag and lower it there
Like you'd throw a dog a bone.

He died drunk one Sunday morning
Alone in the land he'd fought to save
Two inches of water in a lonely ditch
Was a grave for Ira Hayes.

The poetic irony is based in the fact that Ira's people, the Pima, had lost their water rights in Arizona – or the rights *were stolen* from them. Ira dies drunk, in a ditch filled with *two inches of water*. Ira raised the flag on Iwo Jima and was later allowed to raise the flag every day in jail, where he was doing time for drunkenness and vagrancy. The paradoxes of Ira's sad life are embedded deep in the lyric, and LaFarge admitted crafting the song over a long period of time, with help from Cisco Houston.

Johnny Cash's Cherokee blood was stirred. His voice bit into the heart of the story. The song hit the charts, but there was backlash from radio folk. Cash was so perturbed at the response of programmers and D.J.s, many whom refused to play "Ira Hayes," he took out a full-page ad out in *Billboard* magazine:

As an American who is almost half breed
Cherokee-Mohawk (and who knows what else)
I had to fight back...D.Js, stations managers,
*owners, etc...where are your **guts**? I'm not*
afraid to sing the hard, bitter lines that the
son of Oliver LaFarge wrote. "Ballad of Ira
Hayes" is strong medicine..

Bitter Tears and "Ira Hayes" proved that Johnny was turning his attention toward the *new-folk* crowd in Greenwich Village – writers like Peter LaFarge, Bob Dylan, Phil Ochs, Tim Hardin, and others, who were hammering out strong lyrics which would change the face of folk music and create the new image of the *singer-songwriter*. These artists wrote and performed their own material, rather than relying on Tin-Pan Alley or the Nashville songwriting mill. Johnny Cash had a deep respect for singer-songwriters. I know this first hand.

Peter LaFarge didn't have much time to enjoy the recognition that Cash's *Bitter Tears* brought him. Peter died of a stroke (or pill overdose, or suicide...there's many theories) in 1965. Peter had lived a hundred years of hell in his thirty-four years on earth. He rode the *big bronc* to a standstill and said goodbye.

*There's many a fall, and I've had them all
In life's great rodeo...*

> — **Peter LaFarge,** "Don't Tell Me How I Looked Falling"

How about these words scribbled on three cocktail napkins:

*I always love like a high jackrabbit going through
a bramble. Or a hawk up there twining the world
around him, just before he falls to get the jack.
Like an eight-wheeler going through a Kansas town
at midnight, with only a little boy watching from
his bedroom window, riding every non-stop car out.
I love like an act of nature...hear me, people, hear Peter
Bucking-Horse cry in the New York's dark dawn...
hear me Indian-strange...*

His fellow bronc riders called him *Peter Bucking-Horse.* The Indian-Cowboy singer. Peter had been the first of the village songwriters to be signed to Columbia Records (by John Hammond) in 1962. Columbia dropped him after one record. (*I thought the best way to make a record was with a bottle of brandy,* Peter said. *I was wrong.*) He then recorded five albums for *Folkways* records – Cowboy Songs, Native American ballads, protest songs, blues, and poetry.

It's hard to focus in on such a brief, fractured career. A life which left its mark on Johnny Cash. Peter La Farge was what the Navajo called *a seldom man.* This is what Peter called his own father. A *seldom man.* A man *the likes of which* we will *seldom* see again. He was also a bad drunk, suffered from stage fright, and never recovered from his war experiences as a spy aboard an aircraft carrier.

There are eight songs on *Bitter Tears* – two written by Johnny Cash and one by Johnny Horton. Cash wrote the songs "Apache Tears" and "The Talking Leaves," which celebrates *Sequoia* creating the Cherokee alphabet. Peter wrote the remaining five songs. "Ira Hayes" stands out among these – the *war cry.*

La Farge, along with Woody Guthrie, Ramblin Jack Elliott, Harry Jackson, and Ian Tyson, brought cowboy music to 1960s Greenwich Village folk scene. LaFarge loved the old traditional cowboy songs and once noted: *all cowboy songs are done to one gait or another of the horse, as you can feel the ship and sea in sailor ballads, here you can feel the horse.*

As Peter Lafarge dissolved in self-destruction, Johnny Cash endured and seemed to turn his life around, conquering his demons – but not before registering his passionate, well researched thoughts on the Cowboy West and Native Americans. Cash moved on to record his two groundbreaking prison records, live at Folsom and San Quentin. A tremendous legacy in music.

The town of Maricopa, Johnny Cash, Peter LaFarge, and "Ira Hayes" – we've come almost full circle in this tale. I have a sister-in-law, Claudia, with a ranch near Maricopa. And Johnny Cash, Peter LaFarge and "Ira Hayes" left their mark on several of my early songs, particularly "Veterans Day" and "Blue Wing." "Veteran's Day" tells of a solider missing in action in Viet Nam, and "Blue Wing," concerns an Alaskan Indian dying on Skid Row in Los Angeles – and one day these two songs came to the attention of Johnny Cash.

IV Encounters with The Man in Black

> *I got sidetracked in El Paso*
> *Stopped to get myself a map*
> *Went the wrong way into Juarez*
> *With Juanita on my lap....*
> Johnny Cash & Bob Dylan,
>
> — "Wanted Man"

It was 1989, or *there-abouts*. My bedside phone rang in a hotel in Switzerland. One of my band members:

> *Tom, you gotta come down here. We're having breakfast with Johnny Cash and his family. He's talking about cowboys, and your songs. We're afraid to talk. It's awkward. You gotta come down and meet him...*

I took the elevator down. Cash was at the table, fiddling with the bowl of sugar packets. He'd grab a little sack of sugar, bite the end off the top, and pour the whole deal directly down his throat. A man who had kicked pills, long time back, might need whatever civilized *pick-me-up* he could get. Besides, *he was Johnny Cash.* He could not make a false move. Not in my eyes.

He stood up: *Glad to meet you in the flesh, Tom. Join us.*

Cash sat down and focused his eyes on me. He told me how much he liked my songs "Blue Wing" and "Veteran's Day," and he was fixing to record both of them. I was trying to hold onto my chair, so I wouldn't float up and hit my head on the ornate Swiss ceiling.

We talked for a while, then a horde of Swiss photographers swarmed around Johnny. He tapped me on the shoulder and said: *Let's go up to my room, Tom.* We walked toward the elevators. The *Man in Black*, myself, and 20 Swiss paparazzi walked behind us. The elevator door opened and Johnny and I got in. He turned to face the paparazzi. He held his hand up.

"*Stop!*" he ordered.

They stopped. Trust me.

"I'll be right back," Johnny said.

Then the elevator doors shut on them. Cash turned to me.

"Yeah...in about a million years."

That night Johnny called me out of the audience in front of ten thousand people. He wanted me to join him for the encore. "Peace in the Valley." There I stood next to a hero of mine. I thought I'd try to sing along in the background. The last verse came around and Johnny said: *Take it, Tom.*

I had to mumble to him that I didn't know it – so Johnny said: *I'll tell it to you*, and he sang the last verse into my ear. Something about *lions lying down with the sheep*. It was a biblical moment. Old testament style. I sang the verse and it came out sounding like I was Johnny Cash's ventriloquist dummy. You should have been there.

I watched him the next afternoon, backstage, as he was about to go on for an added, sold-out matinee. He was *hurting*. Bent over in some kind of internal pain. Or a bad back, or muscle memory from the wild years. Then the MC announced him. Cash pulled himself upright, like Lazarus, and planted a smile on his face, and then walked out and declared: *Hello, I'm Johnny Cash.* The crowd, of course, went wild. A chill ran down my backside. He had resurrected himself for the people. I'll never forget that moment of bravery. Of a big soul *sucking it up* and delivering.

After the show Johnny ran for the cover of his limousine. Reporters were descending. He stopped, and turned around and looked for me, eye to eye across forty yards of Swiss parking lot. He raised his hand in a Cherokee salute and yelled: *Keep writing them, Tom. Keep on writing them*...then his head disappeared down into the long black car.

I never saw him again.

I'll hold on to these visions. The *man* resurrected backstage, and then the Cherokee salute. I think of him when I pass through Maricopa on my way to Cuyama. I scan the hills for that scraggy Mesquite tree he might have sat under as he envisioned his epic *Ballads of the True West*, almost fifty years ago. After *Bitter Tears* and "Ira Hayes" and all of it.

Now the Post Office has issued the *Johnny Cash Forever* stamp. On top of the stamp sheet it states: *Johnny Cash sang of love, loss, hardship, and faith, telling the story of the nation one person at a time.* And he sang of the Cowboy and the Native American, and sang it true. One person at a time. He was a *seldom man*, was Johnny Cash. A *seldom man*. He went searching for The West and crawled through the desert, and dug deep into his gut and heart until he found his own vision. Then he sang it true, in that soul-wrenching voice.
For The Ages.

Django Reinhardt in New York, 1946

Old Hank's Journey
How the Guitar Won the West

The minstrel boy to the war is gone,
In the ranks of death you'll find him,
His father's sword he has girded on,
And his wild harp slung behind him

— **Thomas Moore** (1779–1852)
The Minstrel Boy

I   Old Hank's Nine Lives

I bought my first serious guitar in a used instrument store in San Luis Obispo, California, in 1967. It's sitting here behind me now. I call him, or her, *Old Hank*. Old Hank is a 1946 Martin D-18. I paid $150 for it, back in the days when such miracles were possible. The sundown days of hockshops and pawnbrokers. Walls of guitars that were cleaned out of attics, cellars, and closets, smelling of grandma's cedar chest with a lingering twist of had-rolled cigarette smoke. Tortoise shell pick guards. Abalone inlays. Sitka Spruce, mahogany, Brazilian rosewood, and ebony.

This old Martin was, and is, beat all to hell. Wounded, scarred and *proud of it*. I know nothing of the previous owner – an obsessed flat picker who tore into Old Hank. Deep grooves are worn into the top, extending beyond the pick guard and bordering the sound hole. Running off in wild directions. Civilization be damned.

Like *The Minstrel Boy* in Thomas Moore's song of old, I consider old Hank my *wild harp*, slung over the shoulder and carried to the song wars. I put a few of those grooves and dents in there myself. Fifty years of picking. And I have fallen off stages. And slobbered beer and cheap white wine down onto old song lists rigged with tape on the side. Then there's the bullet hole, but I'll get to that.

I'd like to talk about the journey of this old guitar, alongside a glimpse of guitar and troubadour history, and surmise how the guitar won the West. In our romantic mind the guitar is the cowboy's best friend, next to his horse, his dog, his gal, his sidekick, and the occasional shot of hooch – according to his or her order of ranked preferences. Good guitars never lie to you.

Dream up an image of Gene Autry and you'll likely conjure up Gene, with guitar, sitting on *Champion the Wonder Horse*. Gene would be cradling his Martin D-45, the first one ever produced. It was custom-made for him in 1933 by Martin, and his name was inlaid in pearl script along the fingerboard. And how about Roy Rodgers singing *Happy Trails to You*, strumming his 1930 OM-45 Martin Deluxe – one of only 14 made. It now rests in a glass display case in Branson, Missouri.

Any fool can learn three chords, and then the doors are open to the old songs and the magic of rhymed yarns filled with ghost riders, lone prairies, dark *senoritas*, paint horses, strawberry roans, and dogs named Blue.

Blue chased a possum, way out on a limb,
Then Blue sat down and talked to him.

No one ages during the course of a great song. Time stops. *Old Blue* corners a possum. *The Strawberry Roan* twists and rolls high in the air. God holds his breath. The angels applaud. The D-45 keeps ringing.

I believe a guitar absorbs the spirit of every room and circumstance it passes through. It inhales the silence, spit, and spilled whiskey in the sing-along world of campfires, parlors, back porches, honkytonks, and dressing rooms. The situations are ingrained in the living wood, as the guitar changes its *voice* for the better. The journey informs the sound. First it must grow out of adolescence.

There comes a moment in a guitar's young life when it leaps beyond puberty and develops a sonic personality. Most well made guitars (and people and violins) get better with age. The spruce or rosewood or mahogany tempers, much like *anejo* tequila aged in whiskey barrels. The sound becomes subtly louder, more *wooden* and rounder, a voice that speaks with more assurance and authority. It will tell any tale you have the guts to coax out of it.

II Old Hank's Journey: A Wild Harp in The Biafra War

Mother Africa, you lay heavy on my breath
You old cradle of civilization
Heart of Darkness, blood and death...
But we had to flee you, running scared
When the crocodile ate the sun
East of Woodstock, West of Viet Nam

— **Tom Russell,** East of Woodstock, West of Viet Nam

Old Hank's first major excursion was to Nigeria, West Africa, in 1969. I had a year-long job as a student teacher in Criminology. The Biafra War was on, and the frontlines were 300 miles away from our ancient stone dwelling. We lived in the native quarter, in the middle of a palm grove, outside Ibadan. Up in those trees palm wine was naturally fermented. I learned to stay away from it. It coaxed weird rhythms out of Old Hank.

I was arrested coming into the country for taking photos in a war zone, and I was arrested going out a year later. By then I'd learned the art of the bribe. I had bribed armed policemen with English pounds, American dollars, chocolate, cigarettes, and a grapefruit, once, at a back road security stop.

That night I was in deeply over my head, lost on an off-limits road. The armed road guard was drunk on palm wine. He was swaying and sweating and his machine gun kept waving in my face as he was eyeing Old Hank in the back seat. Lord knows where Old Hank might have ended up.

Then the soldier's eyes widened when he saw the grapefruit on the dashboard, as if he'd never seen one. I offered it to him and sped away. I kept my head down low, beneath the wheel. He did not fire his weapon.

I didn't teach much Criminology because of the war and riots and such. I read Graham Greene novels, played Old Hank, and sat in with African *high life* bands in local bars. I dreamed of being a songwriter as I grew bored with the academic life. All the professors were sleeping with each other's wives, or hiding in their University compounds with three servants, a night guard, and a pet monkey. I stayed outside the compound. I learned to carve wood in the marketplace and from that vantage point witnessed a few miraculous cowboy moments.

Ibadan is one of the most populated cities in Africa. One morning, in the middle of the teeming, chaotic downtown traffic, I watched one lone Fulani tribesman move three-dozen head of long horn cattle through the jammed-up chaos. He swung a long stick and sang a herding chant. He moved them around cars, market stalls, and sharp corners. I told myself I'd just seen God's own cowhand and heard the oldest herding song in history. The ancestor to *The Night Herding Song*.

On another evening I watched a drumming exhibition – a dozen *talking* drummers creating a loud, jazz-like percussive piece. Talking drums have strings on the sides, which are attached to the drum heads – when the strings are pulled the drum changes pitch and *talks*.

The woman conducting this troupe looked like Betty Davis. A middle-aged white woman in an African print dress and a floppy straw hat. She was a white priestess of the Yoruba Cult – an Austrian named Suzanne Wenger who ran off with a Nigerian drummer and created her own art colony. She lived to be almost 100 and died a few years back. She possessed powerful *musical juju*, and I'll never forget her.

What do African cults and cowhands have to do with guitars, the West, and old Hank's trip? Try this one.

Consider *The Father of Country Music*, Jimmie Rodgers. *The Singing Brakeman*. Then cogitate on the *Chemirocha* cult and the Kipsigis tribe of Kenya. This is a tribe of traditional herders. Cowboys. At some moment in time, during the 1940s or '50s, a stack of Jimmie Rodgers 78s turned up in Kenya, either shipped there by mistake, or smuggled in by missionaries.

The Kipsigis became fixated on *The Singing Brakeman's* music – his singing, yodeling, and guitar strumming. It sounded otherworldly and lured them into a trance state. They called him *Chemirocha,* their pronunciation of *Jimmie Rodgers.* The tribe thought *Chemirocha* must have been half-man and half-antelope in order to make those melodic noises.

Now consider that the ancestral links of the guitar lead back to Africa and we see guitar history swirling back and forth in cross-pollinating anthropological weirdness.

The Kipsigis singers played a 6-string bowl-lyre known as the *chepkongo*, and the lyre is great grandfather of the guitar. Jimmie Rodgers played a custom-ordered 1927 Martin 000-45, with his name in pearl inlay on the neck, and the word *Thanks* inlaid upside down on the back. After Jimmie's death his wife loaned the 000-45 to

Ernest Tubb, who played it for forty years.

I opened a show once for Ernest Tubb on the West Coast, in the 1970s. After every song he'd flip the guitar over and show the *Thanks* to the crowd. I didn't know at the time that this was Jimmy Rodger's guitar. But I knew of the *Chemirocha* cult.

Charmed moments in my life have centered around the guitar, and encounters with guitar and troubadour history.

III *La Breve Historia de la Guitarra* – Lutes, Minstrels, Troubadours, and Buskers

Modern storytellers are the descendants of an immense and ancient community of holy people, troubadours, bards, griots, cantadores, travelling poets, bums, hags, and crazy people.

— **Clarissa Pinkola Estes**

The troubadours invented love.

— **Graham Greene**

It's those bloody Moors again. They not only brought us paper, sugar cane, cuisine, horsemanship, bullfighting and such – they carried the fretless *oud* into Spain when they invaded in 711. From the *oud* came the fretted lute, then cometh the troubadours, who invented the love song. After the lute came the guitar.

The evolution of the classical guitar began with the influences of the *vihuela* and Moorish *gittern* in the sixteenth century. The guitar evolved into the modern classical shape by the mid nineteenth century. Here's a poem, called "The Book of Good Love," from the year 1330:

Then came out, with a strident sound,
the two-stringed Moor's gittern,
high-pitched as to its range,
as to its tone both harsh and bold.

Big-bellied lute which marks the time
for merry, rustic dance,
And Spanish guitar which with the rest
was herded in the fold...

The guitar and the old songs came to Western America with horses and cattle herds travelling on ships with Cortez and the boys. When Don Juan Onate crossed the Rio Grande in 1598, near what is now El Paso, he travelled with his troops, horses, cattle, wine bags, and a priest who played a Spanish guitar and sang olden songs. The first folksinger to enter the West.

Around the year 1900, the steel string guitar appeared in America, as the quieter Spanish gut string couldn't compete with banjos, fiddles, and mandolins, volume-wise. Steel strings were louder, but the interior of the guitar needed more bracing. Then cometh the hillbilly flat pickers, bluegrass boys, country, and folk singers – the progeny of the troubadours and minstrels. I count myself amongst this crew.

Around 1931, the electric guitar was invented as an even louder necessity for jazz, big band, and blues guitar players like Charlie Christian, Les Paul, and T-Bone Walker. Next stop, Rock and Roll and *Johnny B. Goode*, who *carried his guitar in a gunnysack*. Then cometh Keith Richards and The Rolling Stones. Still on the road.

But what of those minstrels and troubadours, the forerunners of the guitar-toting folksingers and songwriters? Minstrels were prominent in medieval times, usually employed by King and Royal Court, performing songs and stories of foreign places and historic events. They created their own tales or stole a story from another minstrel and embellished it. It's now called *the folk process.*

The troubadours were educated amateur poets of higher social rank than minstrels. They flourished in the period 1100–1350, composing ornate lyrics of courtly love, which had a broad influence on Western poetry and culture.

Buskers were street singers, thriving in the mid-1800s in Great Britain. The verb *to busk*, from the noun *busker*, comes from the Spanish root word *buscar*, meaning *to seek*. The guitar is the preferred instrument of the modern busker.

Old Hank and I *busked* for a few days, a long time back, on the streets of Oslo, Norway. If needs be, I'd do it again. It's the bottom line. There's nothing like buying bread, cheese, and a bottle of wine with money you've made as a *busker.*

IV Old Hank on Skid Row and The Carnival on The Road to Bayamon

In a parking lot down in old San Juan
Out on the road to Bayamon
We set up tents and the alibi joints
And the freak show from Leon

— **Tom Russell,** The Road to Bayamon

After Africa I wound up in Vancouver, B.C., and began my show biz career in the dives along Hastings Street, Vancouver's Skid Row. Eight sets a night, six nights a week, backing up topless dancers, sword swallowers and female impersonators. We were *Skid Row's finest band, The Mule Train Review,* and these were the same bars Ian Tyson came out of a decade before. Knife and gun clubs. Old Hank felt right at home. Nothing Old Hank loved better than to accompany a Hank Williams or Lefty Frizzell song.

Fast-forward ten years through fifty sets of strings and a thousand bad gigs. Vancouver, Prince Rupert, Prince George, down to Austin Texas, back to San Francisco, then across the New York – playing the mechanical bull bars during the *Urban Cowboy* scare. Endless nights of *Cotton Eyed Joe.* Old Hank and I thought we'd seen it all – until we hit that Puerto Rican carnival.

Now, as I've stated, this Martin D-18 also has a bullet hole in the back – an odd angled hole caused by a .22 caliber bullet passing through the sound hole and out the back. The shootout took place in a dressing room in a carnival tent in Puerto Rico. Back in the days (to paraphrase Warren Zevon) when my career had all the potential of a civil war leg wound.

No, I wasn't holding the guitar at the time. I was passed out about five miles away. I was the featured Urban Cowboy Singer on a two month gig on the largest carnival midway ever assembled. The gigantic Midway was in San Juan, Puerto Rico, near the Roberto Clemente Stadium, out on the road to Bayamon. Mid 1980s. A French Canadian disco band backed me up and I sang all the Johnny Cash songs I could muster up, as well as my freshly written chicken-fighting saga, *Gallo del Cielo.*

My biggest fan and bodyguard was a 250-pound *ride jockey* and biker woman named *Gypsy* who ran the Astro Ride. Gypsy schooled me in carny jargon – for instance *possum belly queens* were hookers who enacted their trade in the possum belly (tool boxes) of semi trucks. And so on.

Gypsy had my back, except for the night when we went out drinking and I carelessly left the guitar in the dressing room of the performance tent. Somebody broke in and shot the joint up. Old Hank took a round in the gut.

Gypsy surmised the shooter was the night guard who didn't dig my Johnny Cash imitations. Gypsy, and her carny henchmen, took care of the gentleman with the gun. He ended up a *Bozo* in the *Dunk the Clown* game – the last carnival stop on the road to being a geek and biting the heads off of live chickens. Gypsy's last words to me when I left Puerto Rico: *Don't let anybody mess with Old Hank.* I took that to the heart.

Time for a brief *intermezzo* of guitar anecdotes to freshen the *palette*.

V How the Guitar Won the West: Worthy Guitar Anecdotes

The guitar is a small orchestra. It is polyphonic. Every string is a different color, a different voice.

— **Andre Segovia**

My brother was running a filling station, and he took in a guitar and gave a guy a couple of dollars worth of gas when I was about 10. He brought it over to the house and set it there in the closet, and it stayed there for a while.

My mother got it out and showed me a couple of chords my dad had showed her...

— **Merle Haggard**

I always thought that one man, the lone balladeer with the guitar could blow a whole army off the stage if he knew what he was doing. I've seen it happen.

— **Bob Dylan**

*One man with an acoustic guitar. It goes back to the 11th
century one troubadour with a lute. Troubadours to the Bards
of Senegal to the traveling bluesman the solo songsters. In
any case, one man and his guitar make a powerful statement.*

— **Don Edwards**

*Black Diamond Strings on a catalog guitar
That's pretty high cotton whoever you are
You break one you change one, that's as good as it gets
You can play all year long on two or three sets*

— **Guy Clark**, Black Diamond Strings

*I saw a drunken, angry, Hoyt Axton pour a glass of white wine
into the sound hole of his Martin guitar, in front of five
thousand people at a Berkeley folk festival...he poured the
glass into the hole and a thousand folkies gasped in shock.
"What the hell," declared Hoyt, " if it can't take it – it
shouldn't be on the road!"*

— **Tom Russell**

*Remember that guitar in a museum in Tennessee?
The nameplate on the glass brought back twenty memories
And the scratches on the face told of all the times he'd fell
Singin' and the stories he could tell*

— **John Sebastian**, Stories We Could Tell

*The guitar almost played itself
There was nothing I could do
It was getting hard to tell
Just who was playing who...*

— **Guy Clark**, The Guitar

*My first guitar was an F hole sunburst Silvertone my parents
gave me for Christmas around 1949 or 50...my favorite guitar
would be a 1921 Martin OO-45, one of only six made that
year braced for steel strings...Gene Autry's D-45 Custom is*

the "Holy Grail" of acoustic guitars...Said to be worth a million dollars.

— **Don Edwards**

My first guitar was some cheap German one that I can't remember the name of...the guitar I wrote "Four Strong Winds" and "Someday Soon" on is an old Martin D-28...I gave it to my son, Clay.

— **Ian Tyson**

There's a great photo of the song list taped to the top of Gordon Lightfoot's guitar in the early '60s. It speaks of Lightfoot's journey...It lists early Lightfoot classics as well as traditional cowboy songs...

I got to play that old Martin Guitar of his at a tribute to Gordon Lightfoot concert...Lightfoot magically appeared out of the hospital...he was in the dressing room, and he called me over and handed me his guitar and said "play me the song of mine you're gonna sing out there..."

So I auditioned his song "For Lovin' Me" on his old guitar...and he smiled and said "one of the best versions I've ever heard..." What a great heart he has. You could see the old song-list tape marks on the top from thirty years back... And I could feel the ghosts of all those great old songs in that guitar.

— **Tom Russell**

Will C. Barnes observed the traveling musicians who followed the cow-trails from ranch to camp to saloons and medicine shows. Will observed first hand these were professional musicians and the best of them were "colored men from Texas." Was he hearing music that would later be known as "The Blues?" More than likely it was.

— **Don Edwards**

*Sam tenderly and carefully tied his guitar across his saddle
on top of his slicker and coat. The guitar was in a green duck
bag...Sam Galloway was The Last of the Troubadours...The
encyclopedia says they flourished between the eleventh and
the thirteenth centuries...*

> — **Oh Henry**, *The Last of the Troubadours*
> (Thanks, Don Edwards)

*There never will be an end to the troubadours, and now and
then it does seem that the jingle of their guitars will drown
the sound of the muffled blows of the pickaxes and trip-
hammers of all the Workers in the world.*

> — **Oh Henry**

*I inhaled the fragrance of cedar as fresh as
the first day that I acquired the guitar. And a voice
seemed to say to me, "You are an old man
and you have not said 'thank you.' You have not
brought your gratitude back to the soil from which
this fragrance arose.*

> — **Leonard Cohen**

VI Wood Never Dies: Leonard Cohen's Guitar and The King of Spain

*If I knew where the good songs came from
I'd go there more often.*

> — **Leonard Cohen**

Leonard Cohen is standing at a podium, in front of an audience in Spain, in receipt of The Prince of Asturias Award on October 21, 2011. He is addressing the audience, The King of Spain, and attendant royalty. Hear his words. I have yet to encounter a more articulate statement on the profound meaning of a guitar in a musician's life.

Here's a capsule of Leonard's speech:

> *Your Majesty, Your Royal Highnesses, Excellency's, Members of the Jury, Distinguished Laureates, Ladies and Gentlemen:*
>
> *It is a great honor to stand here before you tonight...*
> *I stayed up all night last night, wondering what I might say to this august assembly. And after I had eaten all the chocolate bars and peanuts in the mini-bar, I scribbled a few words.*
> *When I was packing in Los Angeles to come here, I had a sense of unease because I've always felt some ambiguity about an award for poetry. Poetry comes from a place that no one commands and no one conquers. So I feel somewhat like a charlatan to accept an award for an activity which I do not command. In other words, if I knew where the good songs came from I'd go there more often.*
> *I was compelled in the midst of that ordeal of packing to go and open my guitar. I have a Conde guitar, which was made in Spain in the great workshop at Number 7 Gravina Street – a beautiful instrument that I acquired over 40 years ago. I took it out of the case and I lifted it. It seemed to be filled with helium – it was so light. And I brought it to my face. I put my face close to the beautifully designed rosette, and I inhaled the fragrance of the living wood. You know that wood never dies.*
> *I inhaled the fragrance of cedar as fresh as the first day that I acquired the guitar. And a voice seemed to say to me, "You are an old man and you have not said thank you – you have not brought your gratitude back to the soil from which this fragrance arose." And so I come here tonight to thank the soil and the soul of this people that has given me so much...*

Leonard then talks about the great Spanish poet Federico Garcia Lorca. Cohen had studied the great English poets, but when he discovered the works of Lorca, Cohen realized that he could find a voice like Lorca's – *a voice that struggles for it's own existence.*

He goes on:

> *And as I grew older I understood that instructions came with this voice. What were these instructions? The instructions were never to lament casually. And if one is to express the great*

inevitable defeat that awaits us all, it must be done within the strict confines of dignity and beauty. And so I had a voice, but I did not have an instrument. I did not have a song.

And now I'm going to tell you very briefly a story of how I got my song. Because – I was an indifferent guitar player. I banged the chords. I only knew a few of them...

In the early 1960s Leonard was visiting his mother's house in Montreal. Near the house was a park, and Leonard walked over and heard a young man playing a Spanish *flamenco* guitar and there were several pretty girls listening. The sound and the way the young man played *captured* the young poet, Cohen. I would assume Leonard also noticed the effect the guitar playing had on the ladies.

As the speech (and story) go forward, Leonard approached the guitarist and asked for guitar lessons. They made a deal, and the young man came to Leonard's mother's house each morning. At first Leonard couldn't make the chords correctly. He was frustrated. The Spaniard urged Leonard on, assured him, and gradually Cohen learned six chords in a progression that many flamenco songs are based on. Cohen began to improve. On the third day the Spaniard did not appear.

Back to Leonard:

The next day, he didn't come...I had the number of his boarding house in Montreal. I phoned to find out why he had missed the appointment, and they told me that he'd taken his life – that he'd committed suicide. I knew nothing about the man...I did not know what part of Spain he came from. I did not know why he came to Montreal... I did not know why he took his life. I was deeply saddened, of course.

But now I disclose something that I've never spoken in public. It was those six chords – it was that guitar pattern that has been the basis of all my songs and all my music. So now you will begin to understand the dimensions of the gratitude I have for this country (Spain).

Everything that you have found favorable in my work comes from this place. Everything that you have found favorable in my songs and my poetry are inspired by this soil.

So I thank you so much for the warm hospitality that you have shown my work, because it is really yours, and you have allowed me to affix my signature to the bottom of the page. Thank you so much, ladies and gentlemen.

VII Summation: Will the Wolf Survive?

*Sounds across the nation
Coming from your hearts and minds
Battered drums and old guitars
Singing songs of passion
It's the truth that they all look for
The one thing they must keep alive
Will the wolf survive?
Will the wolf survive?*

— **David Hidalgo, Louie Perez
Los Lobos**

*The Minstrel Boy will return we pray
When we hear the news we all will cheer it,
The minstrel boy will return one day,
Torn perhaps in body, not in spirit.*

— The Minstrel Boy

So I come here, in the manner of Leonard Cohen, to give thanks to Old Hank. The Minstrel Boy to the war has gone, and will go again. Wild harp slung behind me. But Old Hank is semi-retired from the fray now. He's sitting behind me a few feet away, staring out at the cows and workhorses. I still pick him up and sing a few songs every day, to keep our chops up.

Since that Puerto Rican carnival we've rounded the world: hundreds of nights in Oslo, Norway, in the '80s and '90s, where one time we were thrown in the Oslo drunk tank, and Old Hank and I entertained our fellow besotted pilgrims all night. In Finland we've jammed with a band named *Engels, Marx, Freud, and Jung*, who recorded my songs in Finnish.

Hank and I played the Irish bars of New York, the back street theaters in Lyon, France, summer street fairs in Italy, a *Western Saloon* in the mountains of Switzerland, where I met my wife, every honkytonk in Canada, a church in the Yukon with a dome made out of hockey sticks, the bars and concert halls of Alaska, joints in New

Zealand and Australia, music trains across Canada, trains down into the Copper Canyon of Mexico, and on and on.

As I write this, the next gig is a sold out show in a pub in Belfast, Ireland. And then on to Dublin and London. Old Hank won't make this tour, but he wishes me luck. He's seen it all. He's still a bit disgruntled at the wind whistling out of the bullet hole in his back. I've never had it repaired. I've let it remain as a souvenir of the wars we've fought together.

I take an old Gibson LG-1 on the road now, and have another 1948 Gibson J-45 I bought from a sailor in San Francisco. There's a decal on the back of a naked lady with a snake wrapped around her middle. That's a whole other story. I also have a few hand-made Collings guitars, but I'm downsizing. I don't believe in hoarding guitars that don't get played, or mummifying guitars inside glass display cases. They yearn to ring.

Yes, the guitar won the West, and Old Hank has enabled me to make sense of a world in which I've always felt an outsider – never good at playing the academic game, the music business game, nor gifted in the art of socializing with chat or small talk. Never much interested in Nashville or the long lines you have to stand in to sell your soul. I sing and write and paint.

I wake up every morning as confused as any other person, but my world becomes centered and joyful after the first two cups of coffee, when I reach for my guitar.

"Land of Song!" said the warrior bard,
"Though all the world betrays thee,
One sword, at least, thy rights shall guard,
One faithful harp shall praise thee!"

Pancho Villa's Horse

The Michelangelo of the Western Saloon

"I was once a painter, boys,
 Not one who daubed on bricks and wood,
But an artist! And for my age was rated pretty good...
 And then I met a woman...now comes the funny part.
Come, boys, who'll buy me a drink?
 And I'll draw here a picture of the face that drove me mad...."

— **Hugh Antoine D'Arcy**, 1887
The Face on the Barroom Floor

There's a rusted-out pickup truck filled with art supplies and cowboy gear, parked in a back alley in Calexico in 1932. A man is passed out across the front seat, grabbing a few hours of shut-eye. Dawn is coming on. The heat rises. The truck's cab is filled with empty beer bottles, rags, and paint brushes. Our man is a cowboy artist, and he stirs and snores and dreams in full color. His hands are stained with tobacco, charcoal, chalk, and red and yellow paint. A wasp is chasing a fly around the rear view mirror. The border cantina, a few yards away, is opening up for the day. "*Volver, Volver*" is whistled and sung and howled by an old Mexican cook in the kitchen.

The sun rises higher and shines through the back window of the barroom, illuminating a half-finished cowboy mural on the white-washed adobe wall. The painting depicts cowboys spurring bony broncs and Mexican vaqueros throwing loops over skeletal wild cows, against a landscape of saguaros and prickly-pear cactus. On an opposite wall there's a panorama of covered wagons attacked by Sioux Indians. *The West of the imagination.* Our cowboy painter jerks awake as the wasp lands on his cheek. The movie begins. *Fade on scene one.*

Here's the back story: Our cowboy Michelangelo, waking up in his truck, plies his trade in the border saloons, cantinas, cowboy bars, and whore houses – from the Mexican border up to the Canadian medicine line. He's a wandering cowboy muralist. One of the last of a breed of travelling folk artists, cowboy sign painters, carnival Botticelli's, and vagabond portrait sketchers. When his chips are low, and the cash runs out, he trades drawings for drinks, or offers to paint a sign or a mural in exchange for a meal and a place to park his truck.

Back to the movie. In the next scene, *let's say,* he rolls out of the truck, squeezes his eyes open, and yanks on a sweat stained cowboy hat. He staggers inside for a cup of coffee and a little hair of the dog. Maybe he's feeling healthy enough to tackle the *huevos rancheros.* Red salsa and *Asadero* cheese running over the top of egg yolks and corn tortillas. Once the artist is feeling human he goes to work, mixing up a concoction of shoe polish, coffee, chalk, Epsom salts and fish glue. It becomes a thick black tint.

He squints up at one of the bare spots on the wall, grabs a charcoal stick and begins to sketch the famous *Strawberry Roan* horse of song and folklore. The ballad about the bronc who *could never be rode* encountering the cowboy who *could never be throw'd.* The renegade *cayuse* with spavined legs, pigeon toes, little pin ears, and a big roman nose. The u-necked, rank old sun fishin' son-of-a-gun who *only lacks wings for the be on the fly.* Yes, that very horse. The Strawberry Roan is probably the most descriptive bronc song ever written. The *Roan* deserves to be painted.

The cowboy muralist likes the look of the horse's anatomy lines and traces them again with the shoe polish concoction. Then he begins to fill the Roan in with a red tint made from crayon wax, pink ink and pigeon blood. The Mexican bar owner walks over and admires the bronc. *Es un caballo muy bravo!* The old man goes back to the bar and brings the artist a bottle of cold Mexican beer. The work day has begun in earnest. The cook in the kitchen is now singing *Siete Leguas,* the song about Pancho Villa's horse. The beers arrive in regular half hour intervals as the *Strawberry Roan* comes to life on the old adobe wall. The cantina fills up with charros and vaqueros and gringo tourists, as the morning fades into afternoon border light. Our artist begins to sway back and forth from the beer and the loud mariachichi *corridos* on the radio. *Fade on scene two.*

Roll the film title across the screen: *The Michelangelo of the Western Saloon.*

Consider the history of art and drink. Pablo Picasso was known to doodle on bar napkins and sign them. Then he'd tear them up and laugh. *There goes a million dollars, boys.* Van Gogh must have tried the bar-sketching ruse to handle his wine and absinthe tab in Arles. The poverty stricken impressionists, expressionists, and cubists were known to coin their drink money with pencil and pen on the boulevards and in the bistros of Paris. Ragged and thirsty bohemians, drawing for drinks. It's a tradition which goes back to the cave men, who painted bulls and horses on ancient walls. They needed their grog. An artist has to eat and drink. Exchanging art for booze and grub eliminates needless middlemen and agents.

Trading art for drinks is also a notable tradition the American West. The young maestro, Charles M. Russell, swapped early drawings for drink and grub. Ed Borein, Will James, Maynard Dixon, and the best of 'em, were not beneath doodling on napkins in local watering holes. I'm assuming this, of course. I imagine Will James left hundreds of bronc scribbles on Hollywood cocktail napkins. Will was known to imbibe on occasion.

Then there was Pete Martinez, an itinerant bronc rider and cowhand who hung out at the *Tap Room Bar* in the Congress Hotel in Tucson, circa 1939. Pete drew bucking horses, wild cows, vaqueros, and desert scenes. He traded drawings for drinks. Pete's paintings and western drawings are still there, in the coffee shop and *Tap Room Bar* of the old Congress Hotel, long after Pete has drawn and drunk himself into the big railroad hotel up yonder. I'd recommend a stop at the Congress and a drink in the Tap Room. Beer, whiskey, tequila, coffee: *your call, amigo.* My favorite is the fresh lime juice Margaritas with 100% agave tequila. Pete's drawings look better with every round. They come alive, as bronc dust rolls off the pictures.

The Congress sits across from the train station in Tucson. It's one of the fine historic hotels of the Southwest, and the Tap Room is *vintage outlaw.* John Dillinger was caught outside the Congress during a hotel fire in the '30s. He'd bribed a fireman to go back up to his room and retrieve a suitcase. The fireman fetched the bag, which broke open, and Tommy Guns and revolvers fell out and rattled down the fire escape. Dillinger was busted. He was reported to have muttered: "*Well, I'll be damned.*" They say he broke out of jail with a gun carved out of soap. Another folk artist gone wrong. I used to sit in the Tap Room and ruminate over all of this history, right beneath the bucking horse art of Pete Martinez. *The cowboy who drew for drinks.*

That leads us back to the story of our cowboy artist in Calexico; Guy Welch. It's a *western* movie, sure enough. Guy Welch damn sure drew and painted for food and drinks. *The Michelangelo of the western saloon,* that's how Guy's daughter described her father's life. I'll tell you how I stumbled upon Guy's work. Seven years ago I was driving through the outback of Alberta, forty miles away from Ian Tyson's ranch. I'd been co-writing songs with Ian and needed a break. Those long cowboy ballads like *Claude Dallas* take a lot of energy to compose, face to face, *mano a mano*, with the legendary Tyson. He's a master writer. I needed to clear my head and think about a few verses. Near the town of Nanton I saw a worn sign that heralded a "Ranch Antique Store," five miles outside of town. Figuring I might unearth something like an old Navajo rug, I drove down the gravel road.

The store stood on high ground near the main house of an old horse and cow operation. Two women ran the place, and they were quite knowledgeable about the West of yesteryear. We chatted and I perused the stock. Lots of first editions of Will James books. I thought of Will, or whatever his real name was, drinking himself to death in a Hollywood hotel bar. A French Canadian who had re-invented his destiny in the West, as did many more western artists, novelists, and ranch hands. One of the appeals of the far west was that a man could walk away from his past, concoct a new name, and cowboy, *paint*, or write himself into history. Will James could sure enough write yarns and draw bucking horses, and his illustrations inspired Ian Tyson to write the great cowboy song "*Will James.*"

I was thinking of Will's story and those old Hollywood hotels, when I spied and odd piece of art hanging from the back wall of the store. It was a crayon drawing on newspaper. Black crayon, with reds and blues. Wild scrawls set against newsprint and yellowing paper. A cowboy on a saddle bronc. The bronc rider was a rather toothy, cartoonish looking buckaroo with pop-eyes and a red bandana. He was waving his hat and fanning the bronc, like the *top hands* used to do on old postcards, when their horses were *going some.*

The bronc is coming directly toward the viewer, jumping off that yellow want-ad page of long ago. The horse's tongue is hanging out and, with hundreds of wild crayon lines, the artist has done a fine job of creating action. It's almost as good as a Borein or a Charles Russell sketch. Welch's work was not as controlled as these masters, but the picture's essence shimmers with that gut knowledge of western life. The drawing is signed "*Guy Welch '49.*" Beneath the bronc the artist wrote: "*They sure go in for horseback ridin' down this way!*"

I loved it. The ladies hauled it down from the wall. I took a closer look. The newspaper which served as a "canvas," was a June 5, 1949 page from the want ads of the *Los Angeles Times*. A nice co-incidence, since I was born in Los Angeles around that year. As I looked closer, the real estate ads declared that houses near Wilshire Boulevard, in West L.A., were going for twelve thousand dollars in 1949. *Helluva deal.*

There was a letter written in crayon on the backside of the drawing, from Guy Welch to a friend named "Bill."

Dear Bill: this is a sample of what I can sell for $1.00. Will
send postpaid to anyone six of this size. All of different
scenes of the old west.
Cowboys, Indians, covered wagons, Buffalo, Long Horn
steers and etc.
So long for now,
Guy

The other newsprint drawing was dated *April 6, 1949, North Hollywood*. On the front it said: *"Dear Friend Bill: How's every little thing up in the old cow country? Okay I hope."* Below is a drawing of mounted cowboy leading his packhorse away from a saloon. On the backside was another letter and a crayon drawing of two cowboys herding longhorns. Crayons are limited as to possibilities for shading line and color, but Welch was a *crayola maestro*. He pushed kids' coloring sticks to their limits. The letter read:

"Well, Bill, looks like spring is just around the corner and
it's time to get the old chuck wagon loaded and start feedin'
the work stock some oats about twice a day with their hay.
If there is any hay. I'll bet you're glad to see the snow go. I
hope someday I'll be able to take a trip up that way again. I
sure do. So long for now. Guy."

Once again this letter was drawn on the *Los Angeles Times* real estate section. April 3, 1949. I peered closer at the ads, and saw a 20 acre horse ranch listed, with barns, ranch house, and a half-mile racetrack, going for $135,000. The house had four fireplaces. The ranch was *30 minutes from downtown Hollywood.* Looked like a race horse operation gone belly-up. I wondered if my father might have been involved. Listed beneath this was a two acre chicken ranch with houses and barn for $17,000. The price included *"500 laying hens."* The headline of another ad read: *"Famous Singer Making European Tour Forced to Sell His Home:"* featuring three bedrooms, three bathes, a patio, badminton court, and gorgeous swimming pool. *Frank Sinatra? Nat King Cole? Gene Autry?* Who knew? I couldn't read the price, because Guy Welch had drawn a longhorn steer over that portion of the ad.

I kept perusing his curious form of art and I imagined old Guy Welch holed up in a North Hollywood apartment with a pile of newspapers stacked beside his easy chair. I imagined him smoking a hand-rolled cigarette and tossing back beers, as he sketched his letter-art, destined for his old cowboy drinking buddies back down the painterly trail.

I bought two of the newspaper drawings and eventually framed them. Then I began digging around for any further information about Guy Welch. He'd evidently been living in that L.A./Hollywood era of stockyards, horse and mule auctions, rodeos at Crash Corrigan's ranch, movie-horse stables near Griffith Park, and cowboy bars near the "river bottoms" in Glendale. These were cowboy watering holes where Casey Tibbs hung out, and cowboy stunt men drank and used the public phones as their business contact numbers with the film studios. The territory my father came from. The old cowboy edge of Hollywood. Welch always returned to this area.

I kept digging for more facts on Guy Welch. The Glenbow Museum in Calgary had a file on Guy because he'd painted murals in Calgary back in the 1940s. There were a few biographical facts and letters. Fragments of a roving artist's life. Welch was born in Valentine, Nebraska in 1886 and died in Vallejo, California in 1958. He grew up near the Rosebud Indian reservation and eventually married and fathered five children. He learned to sketch. He gathered up art supplies and hit the trail. The *lean years*. A man had to feed his family.

Welch took off during the depression and made a hand-to-mouth living as painter of barroom walls. His range extended from the Mexican desert and the border towns, up to the Rockies. He established his own migratory trail. He made a few bucks here and there, or traded art murals for food, drink, and tobacco. He sent the extra money home. I don't wish to create the picture of a dissolute old cowboy bum drawing and drinking up his life. It seems Guy tried to take care of his family in the best way he knew how.

There are rumors of Guy Welch murals in Arizona, Mexicali, and the Morongo Valley of California, but I've never seen one. Time erodes mural art. I'd bet if you scraped off the walls of a dozen old cowboy bars in Salinas or Bisbee or Calexico, you might unearth interesting bucking horse frescoes by Welch. Or at least a covered wagon or a longhorn steer, or maybe faded chips of black coffee paint and a bronc head. I keep my eyes open in the old bars. I sometimes think that an extra strong Margarita might make one of those Guy Welch bucking horse scenes magically appear, like the image of our Lady of Guadalupe on the cape of Juan Diego.

The western saloon mural faced a curious shelf life. The art wasn't made to last forever. It was designed as a colorful backdrop for beer drinking and boozy contemplation over ranch palaver and a beer and a brisket sandwich, or a trio of *carne asada* tacos. Guy Welch, living dollar to dollar, beer to beer, and sleeping in his truck, was inventing his own art materials as he conjured up his personal vision of the west. He painted on burlap, newspaper print, cardboard and whitewashed adobe saloon walls. His paint was an odd concoction of chalk and fish glue; Epsom salts, beer, and ground-up crayon chunks. He alchemized his colors and filled in the pencil and charcoal lines with homemade hues.

The fish-glue tints would fade with time, dust, cigar smoke, and afternoon sunlight. The murals went the way of the saloon and cantina west, and Guy Welch's painterly road slowed to a stall somewhere near North Hollywood, and finally Vallejo. He sent off his newspaper letters and occasionally sold his crayon bucking horses and western scenes. A dollar bought you six. They were probably mailed off in manila legal size envelopes which had drawings on front and back. That was in an era when people actually *wrote* letters and drew on them. These days not many of us can't hand-write a page without having our hand seize up.

I came across more pieces of Guy's art in a Bakersfield antique store. I bought two more paintings. They were fashioned with crayon, watercolor and ink on cardboard. The frames were handmade out of old fence slats tacked together with nails and wood glue. The corners were whittled down with a pocket knife. *True folk art.* These were scenes of cowboys and cattle drives. On the backside of one of the paintings were more little studies of horses and cattle. Wonderful little unfinished renderings in the tradition of Russell and Borein.

The Glenbow Museum unearthed even more fragments of Welch's life and sent me files. There was an odd newspaper column from Alberta about the discovery of a large Guy Welch painting on a canvas tarp that had been thrown over a Farmer's haystack. Guy might have enjoyed that particular ending. There were also pictures of a few bars in which Guy painted murals. One was the *Rodeo Card Room* in Salinas. Another was the *Morongo Valley Inn* in California. Finally, there were tell-tale letters and anecdotes from Welch's daughter about her father's creative process:

> *My father was sort of a Michelangelo of the Western Saloon...when he painted, he forgot to eat. He drank beer all day, because it was offered to him by the bar owners... during the great depression he slept in his car in the alley behind saloons...when he ran out of paint he painted with a concoction of shoe polish, beer and Epsom salts...*

I have an affinity for Guy Welch' story. I've dabbled with the brush myself. And I've drawn for drinks. A few years ago I painted a six foot painting of two Mexican vaqueros with jars of *pulque* in their hands. Pulque is the fermented sap of the *maguey* plant and a traditional native beverage in Mexico. It was my first large, rudimentary oil. I called it *"The Pulque Drinkers,"* and hung it in our laundry room out here in El Paso. I'd always imagined it would look good in the right Mexican bar. Eventually my wife hauled it over to a famous cantina in Austin, Texas, and traded it for a voucher for 500 bucks in dinners and drinks. *Homage to Guy Welch*. Those Margaritas and taco plates, enjoyed over span of a year or two, have tasted great, since they were bartered for with art. As I drank up the voucher I sometimes lifted a glass to Will James, Pete Martinez and Guy Welch. The Western brotherhood of all those who've drawn and painted for drinks.

Guy Welch's life is worthy of a movie, or at least a cowboy ballad. He stepped right out of the classic cowboy verse: *"The Face on the Barroom Floor."* I first heard that poem recited by my tobacco-chewing cowboy brother Pat, who'd packed mules into the Sierra Nevada's in the 1950s. I think Pat might have learned the poem from an old muleteer named Rayburn Crane. I heard the poem again, in different variation, on an old Tex Ritter 78 record. Whenever I hear it now I close my eyes and see a beat up truck parked in an alley down in a Mexican border town. This old cowboy painter is sleeping on the front seat, you see. He wakes up and staggers into the cantina, and right into our poem and movie:

> "And as the songs and witty stories came through the open door
> A vagabond crept slowly in and posed upon the floor...
> "Say, boys, if you give me another whiskey I'll be glad
> To draw right here a picture of the face that drove me mad..."

He draws a woman's face. Then maybe a bucking horse. A long horn steer. A blood-red sunset over giant saguaros. The true west of the spirit, rendered in tints of shoe polish, beer, fish glue and Epsom salts. Art conjured up by a wayfaring cowboy artist living hand to mouth. Beer to beer. Guy Welch. The Michelangelo of the western saloon.

Roll the credits, boys.

Blood on the Saddle
The Long Shadow of Tex Ritter

Black horses and sinister people
Travel the deep roads of the guitar

— **Federico Garcia Lorca,**
Malaguena

High Noon struck me as a strange film. Dark. *Ponderous*. It wasn't your typical western. Back *then*. There were grey variations on the *bad guy* verses *good guy* routine. Many characters wore the gray hat. It was made in 1952, featuring the lovely Grace Kelley and the fine, understated acting of Gary Cooper who played the town marshal. The town folk were portrayed as cowards who wouldn't back up the Marshal when the chips were down. Still, the film won four academy awards, one of them for best song, and it was that song and the singer that stick deepest in my memory.

The movie opens with cowboy loping his horse across a stony ridge while the theme "High Noon" is sung by Tex Ritter. Tex sets a dark, foreboding tone. Something *bad* is gonna happen. An outlaw gang is up in the hills. The marshal's freshly married. He's turning in his badge in order to farm. A man he sent to prison was just released, and he's on his way to seek revenge. The bad guy is coming in on the noon train. His gunsel-outlaw buddies are waiting to join him. The marshal's wife, a pacifist Quaker (Grace Kelly), is pleading with the marshal to leave town. Gary Cooper, our hero, is torn between "love and duty." He won't run. *Roll the film*. The chickens are all hiding 'neath the coop, as a train whistle blows in the distance. *Noir* western.

Tex sings: *"I'm not afraid of death, but oh...what will I do if you leave me? Do not forsake me, oh my darlin'...on this our wedding day..."*

I could never wrench that *voice* out of my mind. I remember its first effect, even today, long after the plot of the movie has faded away in memory. It was that haunting voice of Tex Ritter which first attracted me to cowboy music. His voice stands out in my mind like the western movie voices of Ben Johnson and Slim Pickens. *Wise. Down in the dirt. Rawhiders and bronc-twisters.* Not so much *heroic* voices with beautiful tone, but gritty, western instruments. Watch their faces when they sing or act or speak. These folks *squinted* a lot, and in their squinting they saw *through* people.

Tex Ritter was my idea of a singing cowboy. Never pretty. *That voice.* It could be a *sinister* thing that held warning, like the hissing of a pit viper crawling near your leg. That voice was a sign on the door of a cheap hotel that said, *Go Away.* At times Tex sounded downright *creepy*, even when he was singing love songs or children's ballads. He sang "Froggy Went a Courtin'" with a cocked-sneer that would scare the hell out of any four year old kid. He meant every word. I never trusted frogs after I heard that one. At least frogs that *talk* and carried *swords and pistols* by their side.

"Rye Whiskey" was one of Tex's definitive performances. He slurred out the song as if he were God's Own Drunk. Like an alcoholic duck he was fixin' to dive to the bottom of a whiskey ocean and *never come up.* Tex Ritter's singing voice had the capability of scraping the frosting off of the American folk song, and cutting down to the bone of the lyric. It was not pretty, folks, but it was real. He *understood.* He'd studied folklore in college, didn't he?

Tex's scariest reading might be embodied in "Blood on the Saddle," the goriest cowboy song of all time.

> *There was blood on the saddle,*
> *And blood all around*
> *And a great big puddle*
> *Of blood on the ground.*
>
> *A cowboy lay in it,*
> *All bloody and red*
> *Cause a bronco fell on him*
> *And mashed in his head.*

Yes, *mashed.* One helluva' verb. You don't hear that word employed at your cowboy poetry get-togethers. Folklorists trace the origins of this ballad back to a description of hell written during the middle ages by a monk named Mathew Paris. That verse inspired the Scottish Ballad, *Halbert the Grim,* about the bloody death, in the saddle, of a medieval tyrant.

Later versions of the song made their way to America in the form of a long cowboy ballad simply titled "Blood." Reference books state the song was: *"taken from the singing of a fifteen-year-old Negro boy in a detention home in Detroit, Michigan in the early 1930s."* Songs travel their own gothic, winding trails. They make their mark and are passed along, altered by the *folk* who interpret and sing them. Tex nailed his version to the wall. *Horsemen pass by, there's blood in the street.*

I found a 78 rpm version of *Blood on the Saddle* and set the needle down on the scratched grooves. A low-tuned baritone guitar opens, like a coffin, and out steps Tex, who slurs *"blood"* into a three syllable word. *"There was buu-la-ud on the say-dull."* Frightening. Then I dug up the original LP album version of the full record, *Blood on the Saddle*. Turns out I have three copies. It was released in 1960. There're twelve songs on the album, all about: death, hangings, bronc-stompings, heartbreak, funerals, stampedes, boll weevil plagues, outlaws, and drink.

Eleven people die by the end of side one, and dozens are slaughtered and lying in the street on side two. This record left its mark on my young mind back in 1960.

Twenty years ago Ian Tyson declared me the *master* of the *whore and knife* ballad, because I'd written dark cowboy songs such as: "Gallo del Cielo," "The Sky Above and the Mud Below," "Tonight We Ride," and also co-wrote, with Ian, "Claude Dallas" and "The Banks of The Musselshell," as well as the hit, "Navajo Rug." I blame my folk-western roots for any dark leanings. *And Tex Ritter.* You take a kid and raise him on *Grimm's Fairytales*, *The Lives of the Saints and Martyrs*, Catholic fear, *Pinocchio,* and *Blood on the Saddle,* and that kid might end up writing *whore and knife ballads.* For a spell. I've mellowed a touch.

I credit my older brother Pat with informing me about Tex Ritter. Pat ran off to the high Sierra at age sixteen to become a mule packer. I stole his Tijuana gut-string guitar and learned a few chords and folk songs. When my brother came down from the mountains, three months later, he was *different*. His teeth were brown from chewing *Red Man Tobacco* and he could recite every song on *Blood on the Saddle*, including the long and classic narration of *The Face on the Barroom Floor*. He imitated Tex Ritter and scared the hell out of all the kids in the neighborhood. The old packers in the high mountains had sung and recited these ditties as they led their mules and the tourists over the trail and up through the giant redwoods.

Let's take a closer look at the list of songs collected on the album *Blood on the Saddle*. There are twelve: "Blood on the Saddle," "Barbra Allen" (a take on the ancient folk song – *western style*), "Samuel Hall," "Bury Me Not on the Lone Prairie," "Little Joe the Wrangler," "When the Works all Done this Fall," "The Face on the Barroom Floor," "Boll Weevil," "Billy the Kid," "Streets of Laredo," "Sam Bass," and "Rye Whiskey." A classic collection.

Many of these are sung from the lyrical perspective of a cowboy about to die from hanging, heartache, or gunshot wounds. Once he's bound for boot hill, our dying cowboy is unusually worried about the details of his burial, and where to send his belongings and love letters. Either that or he doesn't give a damn, like Sam Hall: *"I hate you one and all, blast your eyes!"*

These types of songs were Tex's forte. Whiskey and blood. Gunplay and alcohol. Roses growing out of dead bodies, and mashed-in heads. Why not? This was cowboy-folk music and Tex Ritter *sounded* like the marshal of Tombstone. Or the undertaker. Tex's style was the opposite end of the sonic/operatic spectrum from Marty Robbins. Marty was a crooner compared to Tex. Tex was a growler. He had the gun in your back and he was whispering in your ear. Stick 'em up. *Manos arriba.* Your money or your life.

I believed every word he sang. Still do.

I   The Kid from Panola County

Tex Ritter is no drugstore cowboy. The pride of Panola County Texas grew up on a ranch, helped his parents raise cattle and hogs, attended university and arrived in Hollywood...indeed one of the most popular stars in the history of motion pictures.

— Liner Notes: 78 RPM Album
of Tex Ritter's Children Songs

My interest in Tex Ritter lies embedded in his voice and those early cowboy songs, particularly the record *Blood on the Saddle*. I consider *Blood on the Saddle*, along with Marty Robbins' *Gunfighter Ballads and Trail Songs,* and Ian Tyson's *Cowboyography,* to be the cornerstones of western music. I want to share with you a few personal tales linking Tex with his great impact on a wider, stranger world; showing the grand influence of western music as it sweeps through our history. First let's scan over a few biographical facts. *For the record.* There's too much of Tex's historic and full life to include here, but I'll shout out a few highlights.

Woodward Maurice Ritter was born in 1905 Murvaul, Texas, and grew up on a farm in Panola county. He died in 1972 in Nashville. In between he made his mark as a lecturer, actor, cowboy singer and champion of western folklore. He even took a Wild West show to Europe. As a teenager Tex yearned to be a lawyer, and he eventually entered the University of Texas. The law path didn't work out and Tex became focused on cowboy and western lore. J. Frank Dobie and John Lomax encouraged Tex to pursue a career in singing cowboy songs.

Tex began in radio and then moved to New York City in 1928, where he appeared in Broadway in musicals like *Green Grow the Lilacs*. That musical would later become the basis of Roger's and Hammerstein's *Oklahoma*.

This was a time when western music, cowboy songs and western sing music were entering their prime in the popular market place. In the early part of the last century the cowboy became an icon which permeated the culture, from Broadway to Hollywood. Tin Pan Alley writers were re-writing old cowboy songs and inventing new twists. Cole Porter wrote *Don't Fence Me In*, and Johnny Mercer chimed in with *I'm an Old Cowhand from the Rio Grande*. Bing Crosby released several full collections of cowboy songs on 78 rpm. Bing wore a white hat, of course.

I'm sitting here leafing through my collection of old cowboy song folios from the 1920s through the 1950s, the hay-day of cowboy publishing. There's the *Ballads of the Badlands* by Curley Fletcher, Gene Autry's *Cowboy Songs and Mountain Ballads, The World Greatest Collection of Hill Billy and Western Songs, The Arkansas Woodchopper's Cowboy Songs with Yodel Arrangements*, and *Powder River Jack Lee's Cowboy Wails and Cattle Trails of the Wild West*. Also a beautiful folio of *Tex Ritter's Mountain Ballads and Cowboy Songs*.

Many of these books came with the music and chords for guitar, banjo, ukulele, piano and Hawaiian guitar. Some of the folios were filled with bad re-writes of cowboy folk songs. The writers changed the odd lyric, altered the melody a twist, and claimed the copyright. Many of the key themes and melodies had, in fact, first evolved from Scots-Irish folk ballads. Tex Ritter knew the history.

In 1936 Tex moved to Hollywood, and for the next twenty years stared in dozens of grade B hay-burner westerns as a singing cowboy. In 1942 he was signed to Capitol records, after a stint with two minor labels. He was the Capitol's first western singer. He registered seven consecutive hits including: "There's a New Moon Over My Shoulder," "Jingle Jangle Jingle," "Rye Whiskey" and "The Deck of Cards."

In 1952 he recorded "High Noon," for the movie of the same name, and sang it on the academy awards when it won best song. Tex

Ritter had arrived. As had the *western* part of country-western. Tex was the first cowboy singer to be inducted into the Country Music Hall of Fame, and was a longtime member of the Grand Old Opry.

On the 2nd day of January, 1974, Tex was on his way to the Nashville jail to bail out one of his band members. Tex suffered a massive heart attack at the jail, and died on the way to the hospital. He had just recorded his last hit, the recitation titled "The Americans." Tex's bronze star now sits embedded in the Hollywood Walk of Fame. He is one of the heroes of western music and cowboy culture.

Stuffed inside an old Tex Ritter collection of LPs, I found a copy of the form Tex completed for the publicity department at Capitol records in 1942. Tex filled in the blanks with personal information: his first job was on a "bull gang" of a construction crew; *homemade vegetable soup* was his favorite food; "The Last Roundup" was his favorite song; his pet hate was *song sharks*; his horse was named *White Flash;* and his dog was named *Dittybo*. His favorite books were *The Bible, the Dictionary and the Encyclopedia.* In case you were wondering.

Let's leave behind the facts and the high water marks of his tremendously rich life and follow the long shadow into far reaching cultural terrain.

II Cowboy Melts into Rock and Roll

Well a bless a my soul, what's a wrong with me?
I'm itchin' like a man on a fuzzy tree!
My friends say I'm actin' wild as a pup,
I'm in love, yeah, I'm all shook up!

— **Otis Blackwell,** *All Shook Up*

In 1985 the rock and roll songwriter, Otis Blackwell, shared wonderful songwriting anecdotes with me about the 1950s in the Brill building in New York. Otis had pumped out songs from nine to five, six days a week. One day a producer walked in and shook up a *coca cola* bottle near Otis's face and challenged him to write a song about it in one hour. Otis wrote *All Shook Up* in ten minutes. They sent it to Elvis Presley's manager, and the rest is Rock 'n Roll history.

After hearing Otis's self-made demos and records I had no doubt where Presley's vocal style came from. Otis invented sort of a percussive, hic-up, rocking-swing style on medium-tempo songs. Elvis copied that style on early hits, imitating Otis' approach. Otis affirmed this fact, but said it didn't bother him. Otis was also informed, by Elvis' manager, that Otis would be sharing the publishing credits with Elvis, even though Elvis didn't write any of the songs. That's the way deals went down back then. *Take it or leave it.*

Otis went on to write more of Presley's early songs, including "Don't Be Cruel," and "Return to Sender." He also wrote Jerry Lee Lewis hits like "Great Balls of Fire," and penned Peggy Lee's "Fever," with Little Willie John. What's this got to do with cowboy music and Tex Ritter? Hang with me, partners.

Otis was a half-blind African American gentleman from Bed-Stuy Brooklyn. Bedford Stuyvesant is an area you wouldn't wish to loiter in, even at high noon. In '85 I was working on a rock and roll essay about the roots of the genre and I went in search of Otis Blackwell. I found Malcolm X Boulevard and five thousand boarded-over storefronts, and the odd Chinese takeout joint. All of it near Otis' home. It was tough country. A battle ground. Otis and I eventually connected and several afternoons I entertained him in my little *bunker* writing studio in Park Slope, Brooklyn. This was the same little garret where Ian Tyson and I began the song "Navajo Rug" in 1986, before I moved back out to the Southwest.

Otis told me of his early days growing up in the Brooklyn ghetto, learning the dry cleaning trade. Years of being around cleaning solution had cost him most of his eyesight. Here's the heart of the matter. As a kid, Otis said he used to go to Saturday matinee movies in Brooklyn and loved the singing cowboy movies. He was always the first in line and he told me they gave a souvenir cowboy plate and drinking cup to the first twenty kids in line. Otis had the full collection. His favorite cowboy?

> *Tex Ritter was always my favorite singer. I loved that voice of his! Man, it was authentic. He didn't try to pretty things up. He told it like it was. Man I loved that. It was a deep influence on me and my music writing. Oh yeah, Tex Ritter!*

Otis told me he built his rock and roll hits out of little things he'd learned from Tex Ritter songs, and also cartoons and cowboy comic books. He would take a phrase or an idea or a story from here and there, turn it upside down, and add a melody. He would imitate Tex's attitude. That *cowboy thing* that appealed to this black kid from Brooklyn. *Bang Bang.* Rock was born. Tex, Otis, and Elvis.

Otis Blackwell is considered one of the greatest American

songwriters of our time, and a man who left his mark on popular music. A black dry cleaner from Brooklyn and a singing cowboy from Murvaul, Texas. The long shadow of Tex Ritter.

III Whatever Happened to Country-Western?

The cowboy is not to be lamented as a character now lost to American life. Cowboy songs tell us the cowboy is still with us... a colorful, hard riding, hard living denizen of the still existent Wild West.

— *Singing in the Saddle Songbook*, 1944

Let's pause a moment before I lead you to a final Tex Ritter expedition into the high Alps of Switzerland. Do you remember when country music was actually called *Country and Western*? I still have older folks come up to me and ask if I'm a *Country-Western* singer. That category was shelved thirty years ago. Whatever happened to the *western* part?

Western was dropped from the chart designation in a very conscious move by Nashville in the 1980s. FM radio expanded its docket and added FM stations in rural and suburban areas, and the business folks wished to hip up and expand the image of country. Prior to this move country music was usually heard on AM radio. The wider availability of country music led Nashville to aim their product at a more "sophisticated" urban and suburban audience. Enter the *pop, fast food* era of country.

Voices such as Johnny Cash, George Jones, Buck Owens and Merle Haggard were politely *honored*, but deemed a little *too real* and *rural* for major airplay in the growing new market. The old boys were closeted as *classic country*. They were pioneers, but their image no longer fit.

The audience wasn't blue collar any more, it was everybody who liked their disposable pop music served up with a homogenized, country feel, and a touch of artificial twang. Country music became a musical soap opera, and the song writing suffered for it. I was fortunate enough to have worked a few times with Johnny Cash and later Merle Haggard, as they stuck to their guns in spite of the turning of the screw. Their work will last forever. Haggard is still out there, *firing away*.

And the cowboy singers on radio? The *western* part of the deal?

The cowboy connection seemed far too *hillbilly* or deep-rural for Music Row and the new image of the pop-country charts. Bye-bye *country western*. The cowboy-song movement eventually re-surfaced at western festivals and folk-life gatherings across the country. The cowboy song didn't die, it was pushed into the margins. It survives.

But there was a time, folks. And 1959 and '60 were the prime years. Tex Ritter's *Blood on the Saddle,* The Sons of the Pioneers' *Cool Water,* and Marty Robbins' *Gunfighter Ballads and Trail Songs* were high water marks. Marty's album included the song "El Paso" an epic seven minute gunfighter ballad which topped both the country and pop charts for over a year. If you haven't heard "El Paso" for awhile I challenge you to dust it off. It sounds as fresh, dynamic and wonderful as it ever did. A masterpiece of writing and singing. I may be prejudiced, because I live down the road from Rosas' Cantina. Listening to "El Paso" is like hearing Pavarotti sing "O Sole Mio."

Let's get back to Tex. Put on your hiking boots.

IV Long Trail into the High Alps

> *...the brave cowboy, his six-gun always at his side,*
> *often brought into tragic conflict with a spirit as*
> *heedless and daring as his own – he died as he*
> *had lived, quickly and violently.*
>
> — Liner Notes: *Blood on the Saddle*

I'm a Sunday painter and have a collection of art books. I like to read about painters, and view pictures of their studios. Picasso. Matisse. Francis Bacon. Giacometti. Charlie Russell. Maynard Dixon. Ed Borein. Fritz Scholder. I like to see where they lived and worked and where they spilled their paint. There was a painter named Balthus *(Count Balthus, he called himself)* who was a contemporary of Picasso. In fact he outlived Picasso and Matisse, and died a few decades ago in a weird old chalet in the high Alps of Switzerland.

I was leafing through a large book on his life one day and I kept staring at that Chalet; all that ancient dark wood and high eaves and plunging rooftops. The book said it was the largest private chalet in Switzerland. And the *oldest.* It looked Medieval. *Draculian.* In the book there was a photo of Balthus with his beautiful Japanese wife, *Countess Setsuko,* and their daughter. Quite a family. Quite a dwelling.

I showed the photos to my wife, who's Swiss. I told her I'd like to see this place sometime. The chalet held this bizarre magnetism for me. An old art palace. My wife looked over the pictures and said: "That's in *Rossiniere*, just up the valley from where my parents have an apartment. It's a fifteen minute train ride."

And, so, that Christmas, in the middle of a gentle snowstorm, we climbed aboard a local Swiss train and chugged up the valley towards Rossiniere. I had made inquiries, via mail, to Countess Setsuko, Balthus' widow. I didn't expect a response, but one afternoon she'd left a message on my phone machine in Texas.

"You are invited to tea at Christmas time. This is Setsuko."

Then she hung up. There you have it. There we were on the toy train chugging up the dark valley. Are we far enough away from Texas and the West for you yet? Is Tex scratching his chin in *Hillbilly Heaven*?

We arrived at a little deserted station. The snow was coming down in shimmering flat leaves, and there was no coach-and-four to meet us. There was only that huge, dark chalet half way up the mountain, with one light on the top floor. *Ominous*. I was thinking *Frankenstein* or *Dracula*. Or *both*.

We began our trek up through the snow and finally arrived at the front entrance; there was a ten foot oak door and a medieval iron bell hanging from a chain. I pulled the chain and the bell rang out across the valley, and we stood there shaking from the cold; half-assuming the door would be opened by a hunch-backed dwarf who assisted the Countess.

Well, *almost*. A little Mongolian-looking man peeked out and asked us what we wanted. In *French* I believe. He looked like Genghis Kahn with a migraine. I told him Setsuko had invited us to tea. He wasn't buying that one, but he let us into the waiting room and hobbled off to find the Countess. I began to think we'd made a terrible mistake. We'd end up chained in the cellar. Or thrown to the wolves. Then I noticed the paintings on the candle-lit wall. There were six or seven original *Balthus* paintings and one Picasso. A *real Picasso*. We'd stumbled into a castle of lost treasures, and stood there for a good ten minutes, until we heard the clicking of wooden shoes coming down the hallway.

And there she was, *Countess Setsuko*, resplendent in a full ceremonial kimono, with her hair stacked upon her head, and her hands folded in front. She wore Chinese wooden shoes. She bowed slightly and introduced herself, *in English*, and held out a small, porcelain hand. She led us into the tea room and clapped her hands for the tea-boy (the Mongolian again *in a different jacket*). She instructed us to sit in certain places, to her right and left, and then, very stiffly began to interrogate us about what we were *pursuing* in life. We were a long way from El Paso.

The Mongolian brought the tea tray with Italian biscuits. He bowed and left. Setsuko told us about her work with charities and all the celebrities that showed up at the chalet, and her menagerie of birds that she kept on one of the upper floors. An entire floor filled with free-flying canaries. You could hear them twittering and singing up there. *Odd.*

My wife and I were feeling uncomfortable with the strange formality of it all, and the whiny noise from the *Hitchcock* birds above us. I'd forgotten why we'd wanted to come up here, and I didn't like the way the little Mongolian stared at us. I've already established here that I have a dark sensibility and I was playing out all the possible scenarios in my head. *King of the whore and knife ballads attacked by Dracula in the high Alps. Sordid end of the trail for cowboy songwriter.* They'd be talking about it around the campfire back in El Paso or Elko. *Russell lost his mind up there. He was never the same. Why in hell was he up there?*

Finally the Countess turned toward me. She was getting tired, and perhaps irritated with our intrusion. I think she'd forgotten about her invitation. The chips were down. The birds were screaming.

"And what sort of *music* do you *do*?" she asked.

I ran down the usual *folk* and *sorta country* hob gob that I spit out when someone asks; when I'm trying and to decide what sort of music I write. People want quick categorization. I had to be gentle with her, and the conversation was a might rigid. I thought maybe I should say *classical.* Or *modern jazz.* Or French *bal musette.* Maybe that would save us. Then she opened a bizarre door on our chat.

"Do you ever sing *cowboy songs?*"

Her eyebrows were raised. It was like she was asking if I had any opium hidden on me. Maybe a *trick question.* The Mongolian dwarf was standing in the corner. *At the ready.*

"Well, *yes*," I said.

"What do you *mean*?" she asked.

"Well, uh, I've written cowboy songs." I was guarded.

"Ah!" she exclaimed. Her eyebrows arched and she clapped her tiny white hands together. "I like the *dark* cowboy songs!"

"You mean," I said hesitantly, "You mean, uh, like *Tex Ritter*?"

"Yes!" Her eyebrows arched even higher, and a high giggle emerged from her fragile mouth. "Yes! Yes! Tex Ritter! Yes! I love Tex

Ritter! Tex Ritter! Tex Ritter! Tex Ritter!"

She was pounding the table with her fragile hands. The birds were whistling *High Noon* and the Mongolian was smiling.

With those magical two words, *Tex Ritter*, we were spared the dungeons of Rossiniere. The conversation and tea and biscuits took a savage, and wonderful turn for the better. Out came the cognac. Glasses were raised all around. We ran down a list of the great Tex Ritter songs. The darker the better.

An hour later I said a prayer to Woodrow Maurice Ritter as we staggered out of there into the snow storm, and back down the valley in that little train. I looked back at the old chalet, up in the high floors where I thought I could see the little yellow birds flying around, and I started singing "Blood on the Saddle," and I imagined the canaries were harmonizing with me.

V Epilogue

A few days ago I was relating some of these Tex Ritter stories to a doctor friend of ours, a renowned physiatrist from Texas, Dr. Eric Spier. Eric is an expert on physical rehabilitation, fine wines, and French techno music. I don't think he owns a cowboy record. We were drinking a decent Spanish Rioja, and I was going on and on about Tex, but Dr. Spier didn't seem to take much interest. Then I mentioned the song "Blood on the Saddle." It happened again. The shadow started hovering over us. A spark came into the doctor's eye.

"You're *kidding* me," said the good doctor. "'*Blood on the Saddle?*' My brother gave me a mix tape once when I was nineteen. It was a weird mix of techno and punk. But for some reason "Blood on the Saddle" was on it. I didn't know who the singer was, but it resonated in a way in which you could not ignore the words. *Scary*. The kind of song that follows you into your dreams."

And there you have it. The long shadow of Tex Ritter. *And "Blood on the Saddle."* Twisting across cultures and wiping away musical prejudices and boundaries. True cowboy music.

Black horses and dark voices travel the deep roads of the guitar.

Dancing on the Rim
of Lorca's Well

*With idea, sound, or gesture, the Duende
enjoys fighting the creator on the very
rim of the well. Angel and muse escape
with violin, meter, and compass; the Duende
wounds. In the healing wound, which never closes,
lie the strange invented qualities of a man's work.*

— **Federico Garcia Lorca**

In the winter of 1998 a fifteen year old Spanish kid named Julian Lopez walked out into the center of the biggest bullring in the world and called out to a brave little grey bull named "*Feligres.*" The bull came on a run, from a long way off and at full speed, with intent to kill. The kid, nicknamed "*El Juli,*" stood in profile to the charging bull and held the *muleta* in front of himself. At the last moment he swung the cloth back behind his own body, forcing the bull to swerve, change direction and now pass behind his *(Juli's)* back, missing his legs (and femoral arteries) by inches. The pass is called the "*pendulo*" or pendulum, and the business is risky. To be able to execute a pass on a fresh bull coming from a distance – the very first *muleta* pass of the *faena* – indicated extreme braveness in the character of both the torero and the little bull. Something had transpired. Something was coming. There, in Mexico City, the Rome of Western Civilization, this teenaged kid, who looked like a rosy cheeked graduate of a Jesuit secondary school, danced on the rim of the very ancient well of *duende*, and he invited a bedraggled ring of spectators to dance with him.

A few thousand desultory and half-drunk Mexican and *gringo aficionados*, watching a late evening *novillera*, saw the pass, or *thought* they saw it, and felt their incurious hearts jump up into their throats. The bile was rising up from a thousand year old pool of dark blood traced back to coming of the Moors. The shout of "*Ole*" came up like a besotted, passionate *Andalusian* chorus of approval, and it was followed by more "*Oles*" as the kid proceeded to lead the brave little bull through one of the most phenomenal, artful, and scary *faenas* in recent t*aurine* history. The crowd was on its feet. For a moment mortal working men, and even the candy hawking girls, became angels as their boots and sandals were no longer shackled to the concrete earth of beer-drenched aisles littered with cigar butts and pistachio shells.

And *I* was lifted, and pulled back inside the world of the bulls.

I was on my feet in front of an old black and white television screen in a backstreet bar on the border, in *Juarez*, Mexico. The room was filled with *panatela* smoke and the aroma of peppers cooking. It was a weekly meeting place for old men whose club was called "*Aficionados de Juarez.*" In this holy sanctum I was admitted as a gringo observer. I was sitting at a little beer table, with my barber, the former *banderillero*- "*El Pipo*," watching the *corrida* in Mexico City. We were with that kid who was dancing on the rim of the well in the center of our western world. God was afoot. It was a gathering of muses and angels; barbers, bullfighters, and bums, and *Duende* was squeezing the juice out of the lemons of death. *Comprende*?

Forgive the ecstatic poetry. I'm misquoting Federico Garcia Lorca. It's addictive. But it captures some of the inexpressible feeling of that moment.

The *muleta* passes went on and on. The kid knew every elegant pass in the book and his *Duende* – his ability to pull emotion out of himself and the bull and send it like sparks through the crowd, was pulsating at full bore. *He was in the zone.* He passed the bull from the right and left; *naturales* and *manoletina*s. He curved the bull around and around his own body until the black and white television, in this border bar, lit up with the colors of Picasso and Soutine. He was in the *terrain*, down inside the well now, and swirling in the inner ground of spiritual experience that was causing the wind of the spirit to blow gales across the ring and up into the cheap seats and through the airwaves, arcing a thousand miles up to Juarez.

He passed the bull closer and closer until his suit of lights was drenched in blood. After the prescribed time was up, and the *aviso* horns blew, the crowd was shrieking for more and waving handkerchiefs to pardon the brave little grey bull, and the sombreros and ball caps and seat cushions were raining down into the ring.

The kid danced around the sombreros and kept passing the bull until the world of Mexico City and the smoky little bar I was standing in appeared to melt into one shrieking and forceful "Ole!" – which may be traced back to the Moorish "*Allah*! An ecstatic cry to God. The judge granted the *indulto*, or pardon for the bull, and the brave kid led the brave little bull back to the gate which led into the corrals.

But wait.

The bull trotted through the gate, which swung closed. The kid turned around, tears streaming down his face, and the crowd surged into the ring and seized him and carried him *en hombros*, on shoulders, around the ring and eventually out the main doors, into the streets of Mexico City. Into history. The kid was crying hysterically with a joy and emotion which had boiled over the top of a very deep kettle. It was something to see. And *feel*.

A thousand miles away, the drunks in that smoky little club in Juarez kept slapping me on the back. As if to tell me: "*See! See Gringo! You didn't believe! Now you have seen! You must be patient with la Fiesta Brava, but now you have seen!*" In fact I didn't know exactly what I *had* seen, or why I'd felt so moved. But I was hooked again. Hooked by this "thing" – mesmerized by this shape changing shadow dance which can force the smoldering boredom of daily life up and out of your soul. A momentary glimpse when the door opens a fraction and you experience the possibilities of *Duende* and art. When a man (*in this case a boy*) and a wild animal redefine the boundary between magic and art, and ritual and dance, and *aficion. Ole! Indeed.* I was charged. And the bull lived.

That night the sidewalks didn't appear as filthy as I crossed the border bridge into El Paso, on my long walk home. The world had been spray-painted a miraculous white, and new colors were appearing on the canvas. This was many years before Juarez had turned into a drug battle ground called: "*the most dangerous city in the world*," and before they tore down the Plaza Monumental bull ring to build a *Walmart* store. Before the *end of the world*. That night in a Juarez bar I had rediscovered the lure of *duende* attached to the ancient rituals.

I had seen *corridas* in Spain in 1970 and now I was hooked again, and the only way to understand it, or dis-understand it, and rake all of the civilized false truths out of the marrow; the only way to comprehend the depth of feeling was perhaps by reading Lorca's lectures on *Duende*. And in reading these thoughts one might come to an understanding of why we are moved by art and music and love, and *La Fiesta Brava*. Why we will suffer dozens and dozens of bad afternoons until magic appears.

All that was twelve years ago; *as I write this*. The kid, *El Juli*, grew up and named his own bull ranch "*Feligres*" in honor of the brave little bull who led him across the abyss into a temporary eternity. I believe the little bull now lives on Juli's ranch. They will share a memory together, forever. Julian Lopez, no longer the kid genius, is not brilliant now on every afternoon. Bullfight fans, at times, turn against him, as they always will. He has tasted that sour taste of mortality on days when the luck wasn't with him and the bulls were mediocre, and there was no zone or well to fall inside.

But *Duende* is the killer of snakes in the garden of boredom, mortality, and artistic ignorance. I'd been re-introduced to the *corrida* by this kid, and I wanted to see, and feel, more.

Take Two

> *"When you see a torero whose performance causes*
> *you pain; makes you want to leave your wife and children*
> *abandon cigarettes, drink or God, and reminds you of your*
> *own death, then you are seeing a maestro. You may go to*
> > *corridas*
> *all your life and never see this, but if you are lucky enough*
> *to see it just once, to know what torero is all about – why men*
> *become toreros and why even if they have no talent they*
> > *come back again and again."*

> — **John McCormick**

I decided to go to bullfight school. *Amateur* bullfight school. Bloodless. Let's get that straight, *por favor*. I wanted to see if I could step inside, or at least *near* that deep well, and spin around a bit with the *Duende*. At the very least I might extend my understanding, or a horn might carve out a piece of my thigh and extinguish my desire to get involved. What I didn't want was to run after a small piece of what I call "airplane journalism," where a half-assed travel reporter learns to drive a race car, climbs up to a Mt. Everest base camp, or chase turtles in Patagonia, then wrap it up in a pithy, arch-humorous piece for a flight magazine. "*Around the world in eighty days.*" *Travel lit*. These journalists usually leave themselves a very wide back door out of danger, and away from committed art. They end up writing second rate novels where, in fawning introductions, they thank their tortured wives for putting up with the years of living with a whiny hack in the attic. But I *digress*.

I wanted to approach the ring as who I was; a gringo aged 50, or thereabouts, who wrote songs and painted, and had a yen for understanding the depth of passion. Passion as seen and experienced in flamenco, painting, song and the bull ring. This *"thing"* I saw El Juli spin in Mexico City. I wanted to try and follow the poetic footprints of Lorca, and go beyond that by actually facing a bull, albeit a small one. It was better than reading Hemingway on the back porch, pretending you were there in the 1920s drinking your young life away in Pamplona.

And so, as they say, I found myself in Salamanca, Spain, where the central plaza is filled with beautiful women from around the world, and the ancient brick towers are high and likely to be occupied by the nest of giant storks. The cafes were full at sundown, and the little tapas plates danced around the half-filled wine glasses. My ignorance on wine could fill up a book, but I liked the *Rioja*, both *red and white*, or even the touristic *sangria* with its apples and peaches doused in the blood of the gods. What the hell. The Spanish café chat was usually serious talk: romance, politics, literature, bulls. There was no need to read a newspaper, or watch the television news, if you hung out in the Salamanca cafes and spoke a little Spanish.

I had prepared myself in Mexico in a few sessions with a California based bullfighting academy. I don't recall much of the early training, except for long breakfasts in wonderful backstreet cafes and my getting tossed and eating a lot of sand in the practice ring. I was in the air quite a few times, looking back down at the little horns of a brave animal. I learned never to take a backward step. *Always move forward*. The tenets of torero were simple, and yet almost impossible to implement with *finesse*: Parar; *hold your ground*. Templar: *swing the cloth with slow artfulness*. Mandar: *mandate the action and direct the animal* and the flow of passes towards an artistic *denouement*. Looking at old films of my work I've decided I never *ever* mandated an animal. I was usually at *their* mercy, and they could smell it and take advantage of my hesitation. Which they proceeded to do.

My first clear memory is of a football field in the center of Salamanca. We were learning to swing the *muleta* with the instructor. The old Spanish men in their black berets, who sit all day like ravens on Spanish park benches, were quite amused with the gringo students playing bullfighter. It gave the old men much to chatter and laugh about through their tobacco and wine stained choppers.

One hot morning we were swinging away. One student would play bull, the other *torero*, and back and forth the bull would run, a mythical human-beast with a set of practice horns. One of the old black-capped Spaniards kept whistling at us and shouting, "*No, No derecho! Derecho! Con temple! Yi Yi Yi!*" He couldn't stand being a spectator to this offense against the dignity of the art.

His cronies urged him up off the bench and he limped forward in his black slippers. His eyes were gleaming below that black beret. He was an old bullfighter. At least that's what he told us. There are a lot of old bullfighters in the bars and on the park benches of Spain. Many who have never been in a ring. He asked permission to swing the *muleta* a few times and show his stuff. He could have been sixty years old or ninety. Hard to say. He wore the air about him of olive groves and basket-covered gallons of red wine and cigars and hard cheese carved with a handmade knife. And a half century of hard work. He was seriously *of* the country.

He took the *muleta* in his hands. Hands that looked like little broken roots or *raices* of a dry, overturned grapevine. He planted his small feet and focused his eyes far off on the towers of Salamanca, where storks were sitting on high nests. There was an imaginary bull out there and he called to it. "*Huh, toro. Huh!*" The sound came from a cavernous place in his throat that had been coated by a half century of cheap tobacco and second rate brandy. "*Huh, huh. Toro!*"

And then the bull came, and the storks took flight from the high tower and the little man in the beret swung the *muleta* as the imagined bull charged past. Then the man turned and called the bull again and swung around, once again finishing with a high *pase de pecho,* as he dismissed the bull and walked away. He turned his eyes proudly toward us. He thrust his chin up and shuffle stepped.

The *"Oles"* rose up from our throats. The old men on the benches whistled and clapped. The storks circled high above their nests.

He was not finished. He turned and passed his bull from the left side this time, showing us his very good form in the *naturales;* passes where the bull is lured dangerously close on the left side of the man. He linked a set of four passes and finished with a high pass. *Ole!* If I were Norman Mailer, I might say that butterflies flew out of the red cloth, as this little old man *conjured the magic*. He was waving a divining rod over Lorca's deep well. A cry issued from the empty arches and towers of this ancient city and was floating on the wind, and the wind was "*blowing relentlessly over the heads of the dead...the wind that smells of baby spittle, crushed grass and jellyfish veil.*" Forgive me, again. More of Garcia Lorca's poetic notion of *Duende*.

Those were the afternoons in Salamanca I'll never forget. In that little man's movements I saw a glimpse of what I'd come to Spain to understand. I went on to face a few small *vacas* in the *tienta* ring, and there were brief seconds of slight mastery when the black animal brushed past me and came again and again. But mostly it was awkwardness and fear. Fear of looking stupid. Fear of death and all the other rag tag components of humanness and vulnerability. But for a moment, once or twice, I stood feet firm on the Spanish sand and saw *the glimpse.*

Ah, *yes*, in Mexico and Spain I'd made an attempt to understand the *duende* which, in Lorca's eyes, was more important than the *muse* and the *angel*. The angel might bring us light, and the muse may help us create artistic form, but the *Duende* arises from the *remotest mansions of the blood*. It foments passion and lights up the dark soul of the *cante hondo* singer. On the rare afternoon or evening it might spark a *torero*, a painter or a troubadour. I *needed* that lesson. I write songs. I sing them.

In that Mexico City *corrida* with the kid "*El Juli*," and in the expressive, broken hands of an old Salamanca man swinging a red cloth on a football field, I found the echoes of Lorca's poetical and passionate definition of art. This earthy knowledge resonated in the mansions of my own blood. I would dream on these experiences and try to contemplate *who we are*, as artists and humans, and why we're here, and how we might direct our talents with spark and passion. These moments which create the *"healing wound which never closes, and lies in the invented qualities of a man's work."*

That miraculous piece of time, *out of time*, when we dance on the rim of the deep well of eternity.

Author's Note: Traditional bullfighting is illegal in the United States, but bloodless bullfighting has made a comeback. One of the first bloodless events took place in 1880 in New York City. Angel Fernandez received permission to stage a bullfight at the corner of 168TH and Broadway. The "judge" was Henry Bergh, who was the founder of the American Society for the Prevention of Cruelty to Animals. Henry made sure the event was devoid of cruelty. Bloodless events still take place on Portuguese Feast Days, on ranches in the San Joaquin Valley of California, and an organization called "Don Bull Productions" has planned six bloodless events this April – including stops in San Diego, Las Vegas, Chicago and New York. The star of the show is Pablo Hermoso de Mendoza, the great figure who fights via horseback, in the Portuguese style. His magnificent Spanish stallions are worth seeing in action.

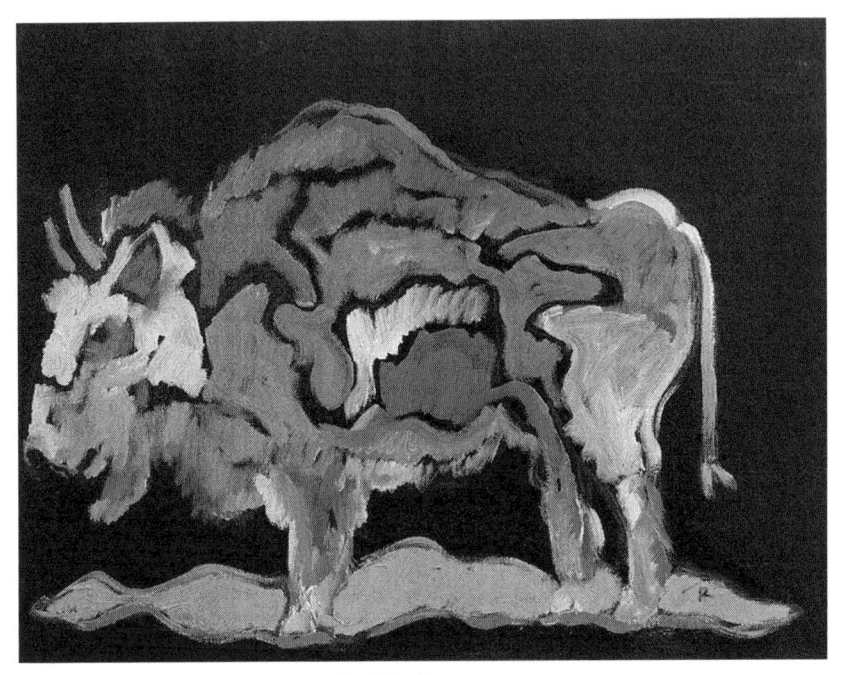

Old Shakespeare

Four Portraits of Women in the West

I've gained a deeper insight into our West through knowing these four women – each a pioneer in her own way. —T.R.

I   **A Hard Life a Long Way From Town: Claudia Russell**

I feel that it's real easy for that guy to sit there in town and tell me how to live out here (on the ranch). I abide the law to a point, but I'm gonna survive. If it means breaking the law to survive, I guess that's what I'll do.

— **Claudia Russell**, 2003

At her ranch, Claudia is surrounded by her heritage, a rare instance of the history of the place being commensurate with the history of the individual.

— ***The Los Angeles Times***, 12/5/82

It was past midnight. The bear was climbing up the second-story wall of the ranch house. Towards Claudia's bedroom window. She grabbed a rifle, opened the window, and fired a warning shot over the bear's head. The bear kept coming. *"That was his mistake,"* she said later. She fired again and wounded him in the neck. The bear dropped down to the porch and took off across the yard, leaving a blood spoor which led toward the Cuyama River. Claudia, alone on her family's three thousand acre ranch, knew her responsibility. *Finish the job.*

She dressed, grabbed gun and flashlight, called her dogs, and started the pickup truck. The dogs tracked the bear down into the river breaks. The wounded bear had come to ground in the high reeds. Still alive. This sounds like Hemingway's short tale: *The Short Happy Life of Francis McComber*. If I were Hemingway I'd suddenly switch to the perspective of the wounded bear, waiting in the cane breaks. Smelling the human. Gathering strength for a last charge. But I'm not

Hemingway. Nobody is. This was real. The woman is my sister-in-law, Claudia Russell. This was the second bear she'd shot trying to break into her house.

She was able to track the blood spoor and get the truck close enough to the bear to reach out the window with the rifle. She dispatched the bear. I am assuming the bear was eventually cut up into steaks or dog food and what not. She told me once: "*Wild pig makes good sausage. Bear lard makes the best pie crust.*" She's told me a lot of things. Words that stayed with me, stuck in my mind, and resonated around in my gut. The grist for a hundred songs echoing with a woman's hard-earned personal history. True grit from the historic Cuyama Valley of California.

The country out there looks nearly the same as when the Spanish first rode through: oak trees, rolling hills, *Chamisa*, and Chumash Indian caves. Wild pig, turkey, bear, lion, antelope, elk, deer...The Spanish *vaqueros* established the old land grant ranchos and roped grizzly bears on the beach. The grizzly bear is gone from California. The ranchos have been cut up. There's a new age of *vaqueros* now – ranching survives.

"My family in this country goes back to the early 1800s," Claudia says. "They went to town once a year. They grew their own food. It was a hard life, a long way from town."

A hard life. Ongoing. I've walked across the ranch with Claudia through ancient Spanish Oak Trees – as she spoke of her history and picked up fossils and Chumash mortar bowls in dry creek beds. She once pointed up to the skeleton of a baby black bear that had been stranded in the high limbs of an oak tree. I've also stood with her on a hill next to her great grandmother's grave – a hill overlooking the Carissa Plains – the only grave for fifty miles. Her great grandmother walked all the way from Texas to homestead in California. She died out there on The Plains. *Working*.

Claudia, and her twin sister Kate, grew up on the historic *Chimeneas* ranch. Her father, Claude, hand-dug seven water wells. He ran a dual ranching and farming operation, back when a man could pull that off. He sent his cattle to the Los Angeles stockyards in freight cars, which ran out of Maricopa. He taught his daughters the way of the West. The world has changed. The basics of ranch life have not changed. "Cows are cows," Claudia says. "Grass is grass. We still pray for rain."

There is a deep Western story here, and I've struggled for twenty years to get it in song and film. I'll keep working. Writing it and rhyming it is easier than living it day to day. I've known Claudia for over three-quarters of my life. She's *family*. We've been friends long after my brother went down the road, moved on to another ranch and another relationship. My talks with Claudia have revealed poetic masterpieces of ranch wisdom – poetry carved from a life of family tradition, hard work, principle, frontier character, survival, and a love of the land.

I jotted a few notes from our many walks. *Claudia's words*:

> *"My father taught me the way you walk through a country. You follow fresh animal track. That's where the water will be. You learned the name of every animal plant and bird."*
>
> *"Your ranch eggs have those big, high yokes...green grass makes a dark egg yolk."*
>
> *"We had a bulldozer out here. It hit a nest of rattlesnakes. We came out the next morning and there were five hundred rattlesnakes climbing all over that bulldozer."*
>
> *"Drinking and women and good horses are a man's entertainment out here."*
>
> *"I think there's a mountain lion eating the wild pigs down in the river near the barn."*
>
> *"I close that front gate and lock it and leave the world behind me. I'm tired of people telling me how to live."*

Claudia Russell is a woman who speaks in direct Western tongue – unfettered with the idle jargon of the Internet age. She sleeps outside on the porch in summer, on an old iron bed. A gun at easy reach. Mountain lions have come near at night – almost nibbling on her toes and as they drank water from the pool a few yards away.

The work goes on. Through lean years and dry years. Los Angeles is two hundred miles and a century away. There were times when Claudia had to take a job in town at a *Burger Barn*. Rising at four in the morning for ranch chores, off to work, then back for ranch chores as the sun went down. She still takes occasional work as a cook for brandings, rodeos, and other wild Western affairs. She's a damn good cook. In the old style.

That wood stove in her kitchen belonged to her grandmother. It came across the country in the covered wagon of a frontier traveling salesman. A hundred thousand biscuits have risen-up in the cast iron insides.

Claudia ranched alone for years. But the task edged into the realm of the impossible. Cows bogged down in the mud. Bears. Runaway steers. Broken fence. Federal laws. Finally her son Jubal moved back in, to help out and raise a family with his wife Lauren. They all work together now – balancing the ranch work with odd jobs taken out of necessity. Cows are still cows. Grass is still grass. They pray for rain.

A hard life a long way from town. In a country where bear lard still makes good piecrust.

II The Basque Wood Stove – Rosalie Sorrels

We drank the rivers, we rode the twisters
We stumbled down to the ground
But we'll rake and ride, we'll spend our glory
On our last go round.

— **Rosalie Sorrels,** "The Last Go Round"

They say she left Idaho with a guitar in the late 1950s, fleeing an abusive husband. She hit the road with her folk songs, long dark hair, and *give 'em hell* attitude. She stormed Greenwich Village. *Rosalie Sorrels*. Fifty years later we were sitting in the cabin on Grimes Creek which her father had built. Rosalie was reading a poem from Lew Welch as she checked the pork roast. She continued reading as she reached down and tossed another chunk of split-oak into the little Basque stove in the kitchen corner.

Lew Welch had been a friend of Rosalie's. A Beat poet from the San Francisco scene in the 50s and 60s. One day he drove his car up to a back road in the High Sierra, left a note on the dashboard, grabbed his gun, and waltzed forever into the wilderness. *Gone.* Lew had been a cab driver, jack-of-all-trades, and fine poet. I named my first record album after his book of poetry: *Ring of Bone.* The drinking and depression caught up with him. They never found the body. Rosalie wrote a fine song for Lew Welch called "Going Away Party." I was thinking about Lew, and the song, as I stared at the Basque sheepherder's stove.

We were twenty odd miles out of Boise, Idaho – up a canyon off of Grimes Creek. Rosalie had a old dog named Lenny Bruce and a thousand or more books on the shelves and photos from her long, eventful life on the road. *Folk roads*. Hard traveled. That Basque sheepherder's stove fascinated me. She told me she'd bought it off an old trader, who'd inherited it from a Basque sheepherder who'd kept it in his sheep wagon as he rolled through the back hills of Nevada, following the slow moving herds.

This little stove is another linch-pin in my vision of the historic West. It connects back to the Spaniards, and in this case the Basques from the North of Spain. The herders were brought over to handle the migrating sheep. The *"Bascos"* had the ability to spend months and months alone with no one to talk to but a few sheep dogs and God. Their descendants built Basque restaurants in towns like Reno, Winnemucca, Elko, and even Fresno, California. And that Basque stove connects me to my visions of Rosalie Sorrels.

Recently I drove by the *Basque Hotel* in downtown Fresno. It has an abandoned *Jai Alai* court attached onto the side. Basque itinerants, in town for a few days rest, could open their window and watch a *Jai Alai* match directly below them. Imagine that. A drink of Spanish brandy in your hand – shouting out bets to your neighbor in the next room. The Basque hotel dining rooms were (and still are) family-style eateries – serving large plates of lamb shoulder, pork chops, beefsteak, Basque beans, rabbit, and a Basque cocktail called *Picon Punch*.

Up on Grimes Creek I looked into that Basque stove and told Rosalie I was reminded of an old folk song called "Spanish Johnny," which was built around a Willa Cather poem. It involves a rather homicidal Spanish cowboy named *Johnny* who liked to *sing to his mandolin,* after he'd butchered a few *compadres*:

> *Those dusty years, the bitter years*
> *When we pushed the big herds through*
> *I'll never forget the miles we spent*
> *But Spanish Johnny knew*
> *He'd sit beside a water ditch*
> *When he was drunk on gin...*
> *And those were golden things he sang*
> *To his mandolin.*

In the end, the boys hang Spanish Johnny...because *that hand so tender to a child, had killed too many men.* The bury him and ship his mandolin back around the horn to his folks in Spain. Yes, *Spanish Johnny* and little round Basque stoves that sing and sizzle. We're never that far away from Spain. Or deep song. *Cante hondo.*

Rosalie Sorrels continued reciting verse to me, that night, in the glow of the Basque stove. *Such a night.* I recall one morning in a railroad hotel in Toronto, Rosalie was sitting across from me in the restaurant and we were talking about drinking, and the ups and downs of survival on the road. We were both hung-over after a long night on the transcontinental train. Rosalie cleared her throat and declared:

"I told a friend once, 'I'm not an alcoholic. I'm a drunk. There's a difference.'"

"I'm with you," I said. I'd caught her full meaning.

I recall another night when I was on stage in New York City, singing Townes Van Zandt's great song: "Snowin' on Raton." A voice came out of the audience and leaped into the second verse. It was Rosalie.

Rosalie has recorded dozens of great records, collected traditional music, and chronicled the songs of the Mormon Cowboys. She's a living piece of folklore. Like that Basque stove. She's written one of our best modern Cowboy songs: "The Last Go Round," – inspired by a Ken Kesey novel about the Pendleton Roundup in 1911. Kesey was another of her friends.

I think of Rosalie Sorrels and that cabin on Grimes Creek and I find myself reaching out for the warmth of that Basque stove as my friend reads poetry. That stove represents, in an odd way, this woman's life: the deep traditions of the west, the rugged personality of objects collected from the journey, and the splendid isolation of living apart from the tribe – with a Basque wood stove for companionship, and a dog named Lenny Bruce.

I remember the pork roast was tender that night and the poems were recited between every course – from the salad and bread, on down to the cake and final brandy. The poems issued forth from earmarked, small-press books in cluttered shelves above the Basque stove. Poems written by her friends.

As I drove back into Boise I sang the last verse of a great cowboy song – Rosalie's song:

I have stumbled lost and wild
Onto sacred ground
I have loved just like a child
On my last go round...

III The Goddess at the Gates of Fear: Patricia McCormick

*The doctor in Ciudad Acuña said: 'take her
back to her own country to die.'*

— **Patricia McCormick**

Only bullfighters live their life full up...

— **Ernest Hemingway**

I have a small, brown-tinted photo that I keep in my writing office. A picture of a pretty 20-year-old American girl in tennis shoes and rolled-up Levi's. Her dark hair is cut what they might have called a *flip* in the 1950s, or a West Texas *pageboy*. The girl stands erect. *Muy serio!* Grave and sober beyond her years. She's holding a ragged cloth, draped over a stick – a simulated bullfighter's *muleta*. The pass she's executing is *The Pass of Death*, or a *Manoletina*, invented by the great Spaniard, Manolete.

Charging through the cloth is a Mexican boy with a Donegal cap turned backwards on his head. He's offering up a set of bullhorns, simulating a fighting bull running towards the red cloth. The year is 1950. The boy and the girl are *"practicos,"* practicing the *torero* trade. The girl's countenance indicates that she may know where the serious play will hopefully lead her – into the top bullfight rings of Mexico. Her name is Patricia McCormick and she remains a woman of legend in the North American *torero* world.

I was born in the City of Angels around the same time this young girl was practicing with slaughterhouse steers in Juarez. Manolete had been dead three years. Killed by the bull *Islero* in Linares, Spain. Patricia was on her way into the minor bullrings of Mexico. Anthony Quinn, Gilbert Roland, and Orson Wells were drinking wine from goatskin bags at the *Tijuana Bullring by the Sea*. Those days and that sort of border romance have vanished – gone up in old cigarette smoke, political correctness, and drug wars. The bullfights, dog races, the Jai Alai games, *the world's longest bar* with fifty cent margaritas – it's all just an old Mexican postcard now.

I grew up and collected books on the bullfight. I loved to look at the photos. I attended amateur *torero* classes in Mexico and Spain. I stood before brave fighting cattle (small ones) waving my *muleta*. I got knocked over. I never forgot the photo of that young girl in the

Juarez stockyards who went on to become a legend. Time moved forward. The Monumental bullring in Juarez was torn down to build a Wal-Mart. Where do all the old bullfighters go? The one's who lived?

Sixteen years ago I found Patricia McCormick's mailing address when she was living in Pebble Beach, California. Retired from teaching art. She was approaching eighty years of age. We began to write letters back and forth.

Do people write letters anymore? Letters such as these? This woman's letters were small masterworks. She'd been trained as an artist and has drawn and painted most of her life. The letters were often illuminated with her sketches of bulls and horses and *conquistadores*. Her words were always succinct and tinted with an elegant formality. She knew a hell of a lot about bulls, fear, *duende*, and the Spanish history of the West.

Here are some highlights from our letters: (*My questions in italics.*)

A question: How does a girl from the 1930s Midwest end up a bullfighter?

"I grew up in Kansas, Illinois and Missouri. Moved to Big Spring Texas when I was thirteen. Became a Texan. I was 20 years old, in 1950, when I first seriously wanted to become a professional bullfighter. I was attending Texas-Western University in El Paso. I saw my first bullfight in 1937, at the age of seven, in Mexico City, while vacationing with my parents.

"They said it couldn't be done. I was a U.S. student from the other side. No money. No contacts. A female. An Anglo Saxon (*no temperament!*) and I didn't speak Spanish. And so I turned to the biographies of matadors to find a common denominator that could possibly offer a solution. The biography of Rodolfo Gaona was the answer. He was a poor Indian boy from the *pueblos* who had nothing but desire and fortitude. He went to Mexico City to stay – he hung around until they finally gave him a few lessons and discovered he had talent. The rest is history."

I found another early photo of you from 1950 titled: "Passing a range steer in the Juarez stockyard." The steer is almost as big as you are. I'm fascinated by a young girl practicing on slaughterhouse range steers. In a Juarez stockyard.

"It was probably a Hereford. The range cattle included everything that could be rounded up for the meat market. I only fought once in the stockyards and that's when the picture was taken. Never again. The cattle didn't want any part of us. Tin cans were thrown at them to get them to charge out so we could make a pass."

What about fear...in the bullring?

"The bullfighter takes with him two kinds of fear: the fear of the unknown, and the fear of failure. There is another kind of fear – a deep inward insecurity. Rodolfo Gaona was asked once in an interview what he feared most. 'That one bull, usually smaller and less brave, that can destroy in one afternoon everything you worked hard for, and leave your career in shambles.' It always struck me like a pending nightmare.

"I have the utmost respect for those magnificent animals. Their intelligence is above the average bovine species. Active, alert, fast moving with an aggressive instinct to charge anything that threatens, or what moves. This is the first concept in fighting the *bull de lidia*: It will charge what moves, rather than what is stationary."

You were gored and received the last rites of the Catholic Church in Ciudad Acuna, Mexico?

"I was facing small six year old bulls (very old for the ring) that knew "Latin" with lots of *"genio"* (temperament). Very difficult. They learned very fast and hooked on both sides. I made a mistake. A miscalculation in distance. A chance I took!

I don't recall receiving the last rites. I was unconscious from the sedation. They told me about it later. The nurses saw my religious medals, and a rosary laid out on the hospital end table. They thought I was a Catholic and sent for a priest. The time was well after midnight. He came and remarked, 'I don't know if she's Catholic, but it can't do her any harm,' and he administered the last rites.

There were two operations: One in Villa Acuña, Mexico, and the other one in Del Rio, Texas. The doctor in Acuña said: *"take her back to her own country to die."* It was midnight. There was no ambulance available to take me across the river, so a hearse was used instead – accompanied by a police escort with sirens on a car-clogged bridge. If you can imagine that one!"

I'm curious about how and when the breed of Spanish fighting cattle arrived in the New World. We know that Columbus and Cortez brought horses and beef cattle. There were records of bullfights in Mexico as early as 1526.

"Cattle came into Mexico after the conquest because the Spanish soldiers demanded to eat beef. They were tired of eating wild turkey, corn, beans, tortillas and chili... and drinking *pulque*! They wanted wine. Grapes for wine. Wheat for bread. And olive oil. My understanding is that fighting cattle were brought in for protection rather than entertainment, but later there were accounts of bullfights from horseback in the later *haciendas* and *ganaderias*.

These haciendas were half-deserted, but acquired their own legal system along with their own armies, and local life revolved around them. Bulls were watchdogs. The notion was that no one would dare cross the territory where these bulls were kept."

The Spanish poet, Garcia Lorca, wrote several treatises and lectures of the concept of "duende" with relation to dance, flamenco, cante hondo (deep song), and bullfighting. What's your concept of 'duende'?

"The *duende* is an unexplainable mystery. I don't think even the Spaniard's know exactly what it is. It's hard to define. Lorca refers to it throughout his writing and it is referred to often in bullfighting and applies to the other arts as well. I describe *duende* as the inner core of a person. A presence, a rare quality, that is capable of communicating itself outward, through a talent, like a spontaneous revelation. It thrills! It ignites! Like the passionate intensity of the flamenco dancer with all the *salero* (grace.)

"John Steinbeck called it *'the power and the glory'* when he reached it in his writing. Jo Mora, the writer from Carmel, describes the unexplained phenomena in his book on cowboys, *Trail Dust and Saddle Leather*, as 'that natural God-given *something* that's born in one and seldom acquired,' like the way some cowboys handle cattle – like magicians. Can it be acquired? I don't know. But it cannot be faked."

And there you have it. *Some of it*. Patricia McCormick died in Del Rio Texas in 2013, the year I'm writing this. She'd fought three hundred professional fights and was gored six times. She died on the border, very near that bridge she'd crossed in a hearse sixty years ago, gored and given up for dead by Mexican doctors.

IV Our Lady of the Canyons: Katie Lee

Life is a river to me.
And if I'm going to be on that river, by God I have to check out what's going on, with me, and with total observation, finding out who I am, what the river is, what the side canyons are, what's in the rock – all that.
I have to know about that, or I don't know about me, and I sure don't know about the river...

— Katie Lee

The Chapel of the Holy Cross sits up on a high red rock mesa outside Sedona, Arizona. A fine place to rest the spirit and contemplate eternity and the desert. My last visit was on a summer's day. Clouds floated across the high windows and the background music out of a little speaker in the rafters was Gregorian chant. The chapel sits on the rim of the canyon – glass and wood jutting up towards the heavens. The architects knew how to perch a structure within the landscape, without offending the terrain or violating the earth spirits.

I sat in that chapel, a few years ago, and followed the clouds and allowed the ancient chants to pass through me. A time to talk with the God of the desert, the rivers, and the canyons. The God of the Hopi and the white man. The God of cowboy songs. The God of wild things. And I thought about Katie Lee.

A few leagues away from the chapel is the town of Jerome, Arizona. In this old mining town, on the edge of another canyon, is the home of Our Lady of the Canyons, Katie Lee. I've given her that title. Maybe it's too reverent. What the hell. For the purposes of this essay I might call her: *Our Lady of the Adobe and Dynamite Boxes*. She's a force of Western nature.

Katie Lee was the second woman to run the Colorado River (1953) – an award winning author, cowboy-folksinger, film actress, photographer, videographer, and wilderness adventurer. Like the Sedona chapel, Katie seems part of the high desert landscape – a living being whose presence in the West is ornery, and yet holy and monumental. Like a ninety year old saguaro. Or a non-denominational church perched on a cliff.

These cliff dwellings abound out West. I'd visited Katie Lee in a house, which seemed to tilt and sway on the canyon's edge – Noah's Ark balanced on the Mount, after the floods subsided. The house was full of books, guitars, and photos of old friends. There was an early photo of Katie, naked, stretching her hands up toward the heavens above Glenn Canyon – perhaps she was dreaming back to when the canyon and the river were still wild. Before the dam. It looked like an Alfred Stieglitz photograph. She was melting into the rock and sandstone.

This particular afternoon Katie greeted me from her writing cave below the house. She's always working on a book, song, opera or epic. Katie Lee, at the time, was 90 years old. That was a few years ago (as I write this) and she's still going strong. Who's counting? She looked maybe sixty-eight. *If that.* She owes it all to the right food, exercise, yoga, and a dollop of vodka at nightfall. Amen.

She emerged from her writing cave and gave me a hug and a kiss. She was as lusty as ever. This was the woman (the *only woman* I think) who'd recorded my song "Gallo del Cielo," thirty years ago. That song about the one-eyed fighting rooster. She had the guts to take that one on. And nail it.

She's been singing since the 1940s – with folks like Burl Ives and Josh White and a hundred others. On TV, radio, and records. She's written three or four books on the West, including *Ten Thousand Goddamn Cattle*, a definitive and personal history of cowboy song.

Rumor around the canyon says Katie rode a bicycle naked through the streets of Jerome at age 80. She says it's true, but she wasn't celebrating her birthday. She was riding in honor of an old friend who had died. We laughed about it as we stood out on the porch, looking down on a lush garden of trees and shrubs from around the world. These were planted an nurtured by Katie's companion, Joey, a Dutchman she met in Australia when she was backpacking around the world thirty years back. When she was in her 60s.

Joey is a whole other story: a man who can make exotic and non-indigenous trees and plants grow anywhere. He also works in wood. An artist of the old school. My visit with Katie was sidetracked with trip up the side of the mountain to visit a house Joey was caretaking. The house had once been a Mexican Presbyterian church, built in 1939 out of old dynamite boxes that were discarded from the local mine. The current owners, over the years, had spread adobe over the boxes, and now the house is a weekend retreat filled with antiquities from around the world. *Adobe and dynamite boxes.*

I shared lunch with Katie that afternoon and we talked about the legendary cowboy singers and songwriters she'd known. In her words:

"Real Cowboys and good songwriters are seldom looped in the same *riata* –any more than real poets and good singers. I can name some good writers of cowboy songs, but that doesn't mean they were real cowboys. I'll tell you two older ones that I've actually ran into. One was Romaine Loudermilk *(rumored to have written the music to The Strawberry Roan)* and Gail Gardner *(Tyin' a Knot in the Devil's Tail).*

"Probably the best one that I never ran into was Curley Fletcher. Later on I knew Travis Edmonson, Buck Ramsey, and Tom Russell. In my opinion the best Cowboy songs have been poems put to music by somebody else. Cowboys? Well maybe. Badger Clark and Henry Herbert Knibbs were the turn-of-the-century best.

"My favorite old songs are 'The Town of Old Dolores,' 'The Border Affair (Spanish is A Loving Tongue),' and 'The South Coast.'"

We talked about songs for a long while and then both of us stared silently out across the deep canyon, toward the high desert rocks on the far rim.

"If you don't love the desert," said Katie, "if you don't understand it, didn't grow up in it, or know how to live in and with it, stay the hell out of it and leave room for those who can. If you aren't careful, it can, and will, kill you."

"Indeed," I said. Then we both agreed there were too many damn people out here, and stucco houses and fake gurus and fast food joints. And that set her off again.

"The West, eh! Our poor, poor over-trodden, developer-ridden, over-mined, over-logged, dammed, toxic dumping ground, wasted, Wild West! Filling up with humans that have no sense of place. People who are actually fearful of open space. Folks who don't know how to conserve the main thing that keeps them alive. Water!"

"Water," I repeated. She was on a roll.

"I'm most proud of the fact that I've had the stamina, the energy, the will to accomplish what I set out to do, using the limited talents I've had to do it with. The fact that with my music and books I've been able to turn a few heads toward an appreciation of natural things and places."

We chatted awhile longer. We stared at the desert. We said our goodbyes. I drove out of that canyon hearing Gregorian chant in my ears, and "The Strawberry Roan," and "The South Coast," and I thought of Katie Lee's house and the Chapel of the Holy Cross and all of it – perched, tilting, on high rocks. The living West seen at odd and marvelous angles. Vodka at sundown. Adobe and dynamite boxes.

Katie Lee.

Another El Dorado Sunrise (Coyote & Raven Prayer) #2

Out Where the Horses Were Tied...
Living Inside the
Greatest Cowboy Song Ever Written

Out through the back door of Rosa's I ran
Out where the horses were tied
I caught a good one, he looked like he could run...
Up on his back and away I did ride

— **Marty Robbins,** "El Paso"

I   The Jukebox at Rosa's Cantina

And at last here I am on the hill overlooking El Paso
I can see Rosa's Cantina below....

— **Marty Robbins,** "El Paso"

Almost every afternoon, around happy hour, an old gringo gentleman used to walk into Rosa's Cantina carrying a foam beer can holder. Koozies they call them. This particular koozie had a saddle bronc rider on it and advertised an amateur rodeo in Fabens, Texas. It was a fixed part of the old man's drink ritual. His personal beer holder. An extension of his arm.

The old man sat at the corner of the horseshoe bar and ordered the first can of ice cold beer and jammed it down into the foam holder. Then he got up and fed three or four dollars into the jukebox. He played Marty Robbins' "El Paso" at least five times. The old gringo nursed his beer and listened deeply. He closed his eyes. He was feeling close to God. The God of great cowboy songs.

I sat there with him on three or four hot afternoons. Nodding and smiling at the song. We didn't talk. It would have been rude and ignorant to interrupt Marty Robbins and this epic cowboy story. This was church. This was the movies. This was art. This was Rosa's Cantina. The old gringo's eyes were glowing each time the song began. He knew what was coming. We both knew what was coming. It was the high point of our day. The coins dropped into the slot and the lights blinked on the side of the box and a Spanish guitar lick rolled out like a reata and danced across the room. Then that voice flowed out of the speakers:

Out in the West Texas town of El Paso
I fell in love with a Mexican girl
Nighttime would find me at Rosa's Cantina
Music would play and feline would whirl...

Marty Robbins. It was the voice of a cowboy-opera singer. A huge, vocal instrument cutting to the heart of the gunfighter waltz. A corrido in English. Here we go with that classic story: A cowboy walks into a border bar and falls in love with a Mexican dancer. Or is she a whore? Love is blind on the frontier. The Spanish guitar licks are pushing the lyric along. Trouble coming. Guns flashing. Horse hooves pushing off against hard desert scrabble. Murder. Remorse. Retreat.

That first verse always raises hair up across the back of my neck. The Spanish-Mexican guitar intro, played by Grady Martin, and Marty's voice, and the poetry of his well-writ epic. It all makes very clear sense at five in the afternoon in a dark cantina in the Chihuahua desert. And the beer is cold. And the waitress is pretty and doesn't talk too much. And that cantina you're sitting in is the same cantina as mentioned in the song, the lair of the lovely Felina.

If you should walk over to the front windows and squint out through the iron bars, into the hard sunlight, you might be able to see that famous hill where the last verse of the song plays out. That hill of fate the cowboy rides down, in a hail of gunfire, only to die in Felina's arms. You can see it out there. Unless the dust is blowing.

Go back to your bar stool. Close your eyes and listen. It's happy hour and you're living inside the greatest cowboy song ever written.

Rosa's Cantina. It has a ring to it, eh? Spanish is the lingua franca here, and El Paso is one of the only songs on the box sung in English. As it should be, amigo. The coins are dropping into the slot, again, and the lights are flashing. Forget the year 2012. Wipe it all out. It's 1959, before life and romance kicked the hell out of all of us, and Marty Robbins' "El Paso" is on the top of the country and pop charts, and all things are possible again. Love is worth fighting and dying for, and there are fast horses outside the door ready to carry us away to safety, into the badlands, where a man can live off rattlesnake meat and the memory of that senorita back in the cantina. Felina.

Yes, 1959. Back when all the border ladies were beautiful, the drinks were strong, the horses were fast, and your knees didn't ache. That's why we write cowboy songs. To escape into the ageless, overly romanticized dream.

Rosa's Cantina rests in a half-acre gravel lot near the desolate tail-end of a street called Doniphan Road, near the horse track in Sunland Park New Mexico. Rosa's is actually located within the city limits of El Paso, but this is a small corner of wild geography which embraces Mexico, New Mexico, and Texas. In the space of a quarter mile a man could drink at Rosa's, place a bet at the New Mexican horse track, and cross over the wrong way into Juarez, Mexico.

Johnny Cash sang about this very matter in "Wanted Man," a song he co-wrote with Bob Dylan. "I went the wrong way into Juarez with Juanita on my lap..." The real trouble began when Johnny crossed back over into El Paso. October 5, 1965. He was busted. But that's another story. Involving a large quantity of pills.

I don't mean any disrespect to Mr. Cash, who not only recorded several of my songs, but allowed me to sing "Peace in the Valley" with him in Switzerland once. He sang it into my ear and it came out of my mouth, and I sounded like a Johnny Cash ventriloquist dummy, singing about "lions lying down with lambs," to ten thousand Swiss country music fans. Johnny Cash was a great man, and a friend, and I wish we could have enjoyed a beer together at Rosa's. Cash understood this mean as hell frontier. He stared out at it all through the bars of the county jail.

This is my country. Mi Tierra del sol. The Pass of the North. The beginnings of our cowboy cultures passed nearby our hacienda near the Rio Grande. If you understand the history and the terrain, then that cowboy song on the juke box takes on greater meaning.

II The Pass of the North – the Mean As Hell Country

Nobody cared if I died or moved to El Paso...

— **Raymond Chandler**

In the year 1568 Don Juan Onate crossed over the Rio Bravo on his tall, stout Andalusia horse. Onate declared all the land north of the river the property of the Queen on Spain. Then his expedition – made up of soldiers, priests, pilgrims, one songwriter, cattle, fighting cattle, and horses – sat down and celebrated the first thanksgiving in the United States. No, the first thanksgiving wasn't near Plymouth

Rock, amigo. That was a few decades later. This feast by the Rio Bravo was the first cowboy thanksgiving.

And now place your gunfighter ballad into the historic and geographic context on a wild frontier that has never been tamed. Imagine those Spaniards and Mexicans, riding the giant horses – the men covered with armor in 110 degree heat. These men were a breed apart. When the Aztecs saw a man on horseback they thought it was a mythical beast, like a Minotaur. The odds were stacked against the Natives.

The Spanish horses were sturdy, and the saddle bags held Spanish wine and dry chorizo. The Onate expedition followed a trail they titled El Camino Real, the true road, though a land they named the horno del muerto – the oven of death.

Rosa's Cantina fits into this landscape. We toss around the word "frontier," but this is truly the last frontier. The edge of history. The brink. The border. The badlands. Most folks lay no claim to having been in El Paso. It's the end of the line. The middle of nowhere. If you tell people you live in El Paso, and they usually respond: "Why?" Or they might say: "I was there once. In the army. Went to Juarez. Got drunk. Got thrown in jail." Or maybe: "I passed through there one time and kept going..."

This is a country best summoned up by writers such as Cormac McCarthy, or even Johnny Cash, in his recitation: Mean As Hell. In Cash's poem the Devil is asking God for disposable land to build a new hell:

The Lord said: "Yes there's a plenty of hand
But I left it down by the Rio Grande
The fact is, ol' boy, the stuff is so poor
I don't think you could use it as the hell anymore...
The heat in the summers are hundred and ten
too hot for the devil too hot for men..."

Welcome, pilgrim. Carry water. And dry chorizo. Let's say you happen to fly in here from Phoenix, Los Angeles, Denver, or Houston. Maybe you have business here. Or relatives. Or a wish to find Rosa's Cantina. A few years back, when you walked down the stairs from your arriving flight, the first stop on your right was the "Marty Robbins' Bar," which featured a fake gold record and a few pieces of memorabilia.

There was a mayor's award for Marty, a plaque that said

something akin to: Dedicated to Marty Robbins – the man who put El Paso on the map. The bar is gone now. It's a wine bar with a Starbucks Coffee joint facing it. Go grab your luggage. Vamoose. You'll walk beneath a huge mural depicting General Black Jack Pershing chasing Pancho Villa through the Chihuahua Desert. Pershing is using horses, mules and bi-planes. They never caught Pancho. He was later assassinated by his own people. His last words: Don't let it end like this, tell them I said something.

Outside, beyond the parking lot, sits the largest equestrian statue in the world. Don Juan Onate on his colossal Spanish horse. The horse is rearing up, welcoming you to the frontier. The steed's features are anatomically correct. Spanish Conquistadors and Mexican Charros ride stallions, amigo. Don Juan is waving his sword in the air, appropriating land for the Queen. Land God declared not fit for a hell.

Drive straight out of the airport and you'll end up in Juarez in ten minutes. Not recommended these days without an armored vehicle. The nightclubs where Sinatra sang, and the five star hotels and divorce mills are long gone. Bulldozed during the cartel wars. The Plaza Monumental bullring has been torn down and replaced by a Walmart. There's your shifting history.

Better turn right on Highway 10 and aim for downtown El Paso. This is the town which, until the 1960s, used to have live alligators in the town square fountain. The gators were staring up at The Plaza Hotel, built by Nicky Hilton, who shared the penthouse with his wife Liz Taylor. Liz, in turn, stared out at Juarez, where Marilyn Monroe once divorced Arthur Miller. Marilyn then proceeded to the Kentucky Bar and bought the house a round of Margaritas. This is the hearsay. Some folks say the Margarita was invented in Juarez. The best fresh-lime margaritas are still served at The Kentucky Bar. Don't turn your back to the front door. That's gunfighter wisdom. Let's cross back into El Paso.

Back in El Paso my life would be worthless
Everything's gone in life, nothing is left....

Viva El Paso! This is the town where John Wesley Hardin set up his law practice, after his prison time. He claims to have shot 27 men. Mas or menos. Hardin stated: I never killed a man who didn't need killin'. He was eventually shot in the back by Sheriff John Selman, then his body was drug out into the street, so the townsfolk could gawk at the dead outlaw-lawyer who always cheated at cards. Hardin is buried in the historic Concordia Cemetery, next to the Chinese graveyard where the railroad workers are interred. Another quote from Johnny Cash:

> *Right through the swinging doors John Selman came with a blazin' gun*
> *Wes Hardin chug-a-luggin' red eye, John got him in the back of the head*
> *John Wesley Hardin fell dead – Hardin wouldn't run*
> *Hardin Wouldn't Run*

Across the street from the graveyard is the L and J Café, in my opinion it's the best Mexican restaurant in the West. L and J is near Fort Bliss, one of our largest Military facilities, and history tells us that soldiers once trained a mule to walk down to The L and J and fetch a bucket of cold beer and then bring it back. The story is written there in the menu.

Within this cowboy-mythical terrain the song El Paso fits perfectly, and Rosa's Cantina sits in the heart of our west. Let's head back over there. We'll take a drive along Alameda, the old road which snakes along the border. The fence is up now – high black mesh, topped with cameras – but a few years ago this was open territory. You could almost reach out to those Juarez poverty shacks as you whistled that Bob Dylan line:

> *When you're lost in the rain in Juarez*
> *And it's Easter time too...*

> — **Bob Dylan,** "Just Like Tom Thumb's Blues"

III The Last Bar on Earth

> *I'm sittin' here drinking in the last bar on earth*
> *And out in California she's takin' off her tight red skirt...*

> — **Dave Alvin and Tom Russell,** "Out in California"

> *Maybe tomorrow a bullet may find me*
> *Tonight nothing worse than this pain in my heart*

> — **Marty Robbins,** "El Paso"

We're back at Rosa's. It's August, 2012. Rosa's white stucco flesh is peeling off in the brutal heat, and the crimson-red letters of the fluorescent sign have turned a dusty, faded pink. There's a side entrance for beer deliveries with a screen door decorated with a cast iron rose entwined around a horseshoe – an image from a song that will never fade.

Rosa's front windows stare up at that rocky hill called "Mount Cristo Rey," where a giant cross of the Jesus Christ lures the faithful and the sick-of-heart up a switch-backed, five mile trail of rock and sand. Penitent souls crawl up there on their knees, asking for healing and forgiveness from a merciful God.

This country around Rosa's is now an isolated desert patch of closed copper refineries, gravel pits, and forgotten bars with great jukeboxes. Freight trains wind their way around the mountain and border patrol trucks chase illegal ghosts through the agave and cactus.

The dark interior of Rosa's is dotted with card tables and folding chairs and one big old wooden horseshoe bar that curves into the back wall. The Wurlitzer is filled with records by Little Joe y Su Familia, Vincente Fernandez, Los Tigres del Norte, Ana Gabriel, Freddy Fender, The Rolling Stones, and Marty Robbins. I peer into the box, on occasion, and marvel about how many songs the charro singers have written about horses.

We have very few songs about horses in English. But the Mexicans are enamored with them. The horse is the hero and the center of hundreds of long ballads. This is a damn good place to hear those horse corridos, especially when that old grandmotherly cook is firing up the enchiladas and refried beans, and chopping fresh salsa.

The kitchen opens at 5pm and runs all day on Saturdays and Sundays. The one page menu features two types of cuisine: "Mexican Marty Robbins," and "American Marty Robbins." On the Mexican side are the standard tacos, enchiladas, burritos, and nachos.

The American side features "The Marty Robbins Burger," and "Felina's Fries." A burger and fries will cost you six bucks. Then there's the beer. Might I recommend Tecate? Corona? Pacifico? Victoria? And maybe a backing shot of Siete Leguas tequila, named after Pancho Villa's favorite horse. Okay, they're out of that one. Pick anything that's 100% agave.

If my memory serves me – "El Paso" is number 1101, or maybe 2011, on the juke box. I believe it's been on that box since the early '60s, a few years after Marty Robbins drove through here. Rosa's would have been located on the old road before Highway 10 was completed. Marty drove by and the muses began to sing into his ear. There's the hill outside, which used to be called Mule Driver Mountain. The very hill the cowboy rode down to his doom. Yes, Marty was here all right.

Marty Robbins was quoted as saying he drove through El Paso at least three times, when he was touring in the mid 1950s, but never stopped at the bar. He made note in his head about a song called "El Paso," because he thought the name of the city had a romantic ring to it.

That bar may, or may not, have been called "Rosa's" in 1957-8. It doesn't matter. Great songwriters are short on facts and long on mystical yarns about connecting to the songwriting angels. This is art, not science. Marty was here, inside Rosa's. Or his soul was. He's still there. Every day at happy hour. Let's leave it at that. Great songs destroy the notion of time. Which came first, the song or the bar? Who cares? Art trumps details. Art is forever.

"It just came out," said Marty. "I was waiting to see what was going to happen. It came out like a motion picture...it's cowboy music and it's got a little mariachi type music in it and the Mexican border sound."

The combination of Spanish guitar licks, great singing, and an epic story drenched in detail – make the song work. If we boiled it down – it's a song about a whore-mongering murderer and horse thief with a death wish lust for a Mexican dancer. All bent into a five minute horse opera.

Let's go back to the 1950s again. We have the West Texas badlands geography pegged now, but what about the musical atmosphere – the world of American pop culture back then? How did a gunfighter ballad emerge out of the 50s Rock and Roll ether and become a pop hit?

IV Murder Ballads, Whores, and Hanging Trees

Hang down your head, Tom Dooley
Hang down your head and cry....

— **Tom Dooley,** folksong

In 1958 I was going to a Catholic grammar school in Los Angeles. I was an altar boy. I played right field on the little league team. I was an American kid. I stole my brother's Tijuana guitar and strummed folk songs in my room. Secretly. The number one hit on the Billboard charts was "Tom Dooley," an old folk song based on the 1866 murder of a woman named Laura Foster in Wilkes County, North Carolina.

"Tom Dooley," as sung by The Kingston Trio, topped the Pop and Country charts, and then worked its way around the world. The song was first collected from an old time Appalachian banjo player named Frank Proffitt. I played the song on my gut string guitar. It was easy. Only two chords.

The song seeped deeply into this culture. Little kids were singing it all day. Dogs were howling along with it. My Swiss father-in-law still sings it and he doesn't speak English. My father took to calling me Tom Dooley in the 1960s. You couldn't get away from this song about the woman-killer, Tom Dooley.

Around that same time Marty Robbins had a hit with the "Hanging Tree," the title song from a classic Gary Cooper movie. Marty didn't write that one. He was just getting warmed up. He was driving across the desert, working on his masterpiece, "El Paso." A while later Columbia released a 45 version of "El Paso," and it topped the country and pop charts for a long while. It went up and never came down. No one thought radio would play a long song – so the record company released an edited version, on one side of the 45 rpm single, and the complete version on the other. The longer version was the one which took off.

A Tex Mex gunfighter ballad. Blood and guts. It pierced the heart of America. Grady Martin played those fast and flawless Mexican licks on his steel string Martin guitar and the Glaser brothers sang backup. It remains one of the finest recorded tracks in the history of Country-Western music. And America was ready for it.

In the late 50s there were at least a dozen prime time television shows featuring cowboys and the Wild West: Gunsmoke, Have Gun Will Travel, Wyatt Earp, Maverick...it was all black and white. Good guys and bad guys. Floating the song El Paso into this outlaw atmosphere was perfect timing.

El Paso was included on the LP Gunfighter Ballads and Trail Songs. The entire record was recorded in one day – an eight hour session at Columbia Records on April 7, 1959. There were seven traditional songs, including "The Strawberry Roan," "Billy the Kid" and "Utah Carrol," and four originals by Marty Robbins – "El Paso," "Big Iron," "In the Valley," and "The Master's Call."

"The Master's Call," a tale of a stampede and the born-again transfiguration of a cowboy, could have been the follow up to "El

Paso," but Marty flubbed one word – he pronounced performed as pre-formed, and he wouldn't allow it to go out as a single. He was a perfectionist.

Listening to this album now is like hearing an opera by Verdi – it's unimaginable that this entire record was recorded in one day. It's akin to Van Gogh knocking out ten paintings in an afternoon. It sounds like it was recorded yesterday. It's a big, lush sound, with a perfect election of songs. It'll knock you out.

The success of "El Paso," and the western-themed album, prompted Marty to record at least six more long-playing western records. Marty also wrote "El Paso" follow-up songs about Felina, and a new take on "El Paso" called "El Paso City," in which a modern day cowboy flies over El Paso and dreams he's a re-incarnation of the cowboy in the original song.

El Paso City, by the Rio Grande
Could it be that I could be
The cowboy in this mystery
That died there in that desert sand so long ago?

Maybe so. You'd have to study the entire set of these lyrics to understand how a writer like Marty could concoct such epics along the lines of cowboy mysticism and Greek Tragedy. He explores the deep mysteries of re-incarnation:

Can it be that man can disappear
From life and live another time?
And does the mystery deepen' cause you think
That you yourself lived in that other time?

Who knows? He ponders the big questions. He pulls it off with that voice. He makes you believe it. And where did he get his yen for cowboy stories? Let's take a quick gander at his biography.

Marty Robbins was born in Glendale, a suburb of Phoenix, in Maricopa County, Arizona. The Sonora Desert. The land of the great saguaro and organ pipe cactuses. He grew up idolizing Gene Autry and picked cotton at a field ten miles away to earn money to see Gene Autry's newest film. When he got there he would sit in the first row "... close enough so I could have gotten sand in the eyes and powder burns from the guns. I wanted to see the cowboy simply because Autry was my favorite singer. No one else inspired me."

Marty was also enamored with the cowboy songs of Bob Nolan, who wrote the classic Sons of the Pioneer songs like "Cool Wate" and "Tumbling Tumbleweeds," and he heard true-life outlaw yarns spun by his grandfather, Texas Bob Heckle, a former Texas Ranger. The desert scenario, the cowboy-outlaw stories, the wonderful Autry and Bob Nolan melodies – all left their mark on young Marty Robbins.

Marty joined the Navy and was stationed in the Solomon Islands, where he picked up a guitar and learned Hawaiian songs. You can hear that influence in his beautiful melodies, and his ability to hit the high notes. He later appeared in movies and TV series like The Drifter, was also an accomplished NASCAR driver. The song "El Paso" remained his creative monument.

Marty Robbins died from heart problems on December 8, 1982. He had a long string of hits. Rosa's Cantina was quiet the day after his death. The old Mexican gentleman who owned the place was quoted as saying he didn't know how he could honor Marty. He kept shaking his head: "We have to do something in his memory. He was the man who put El Paso on the map."

Marty's old LP covers went up on the wall and the song remained on the jukebox. The burgers, eventually, were named after the man who wrote the greatest cowboy song of all time. Old men arrive at sundown to worship at the shrine.

V   Old Cowboy Songs Don't Fade Away....

From thirty thousand feet above
The desert floor, I see it there below
A city with a legend
The west Texas city of El Paso
Where long ago I heard a song
About a Texas cowboy and a girl
And a little place called Rosa's
Where he used to go and watch this beauty whirl.

— **Marty Robbins**, "El Paso City"

I went back to Rosa's on a recent afternoon. It never disappoints me. It's on my official historic tour of El Paso/Juarez. It's a destination for a memorable happy hour. The problem is – when I take friends to Rosa's they never want to leave. They want to listen to "El Paso," over and over, and drink beer or margaritas, and look at Marty's album covers, or stare out at Mt. Cristo Rey. They want to live inside the song. Forever.

The old gringo with the foam beer-can holder is long gone. He only spoke to me one time that I remember. After listening to El Paso five times in a row, he turned to me, with his eyes closed, and stated: "That's a song, my friend."

And I answered: "Yes, sir, it surely is."

The Wild West in Europe

Buffalo Bill is the only one who gained the permission to lead real Red-Skins, the only one who could assemble real cow-boys and he is the real Buffalo Bill, the king of scouts and pioneers!

— *Le Figaro*, Italy, 1905

I was running through the streets of snowy Turin, Italy, trying to catch a train north back to Switzerland. We'd played a folk club the night before. My path led through a long, winding, antique book market, snaking beneath the arcades in the old part of town. I noticed a cardboard advertisement for tobacco featuring an Indian in full headdress. It was a yellow placard about a foot high. Colorful as hell. The vendor said it was from 1916, so I bought it. *Thirty euros*. Cash. *Cruwell-Tabak from Belefeld*. Natural fine-cut tobacco from the Brother's Cruwell. It's a beautiful piece of deco art – an Indian smoking a peace pipe stuffed with German tobacco.

I ran on toward the station but kept noticing Western images on comic books, the covers of Karl May novels, old etchings of Indians, cowboys on cigarette and match packs, and other Western offerings. I wished I'd had the time to look into it all. You cannot escape the American Wild West in Europe. It's a lingering vision. A war drum beating softly through an Italian afternoon.

I ended up running into the train station beneath a neon sign over the entrance: *Wild West Tex Mex Bar*. I'm sure they had *Texas T-Bone Steaks*, and *Apache Cheeseburgers*, and *Pancho Villa Sangria*, served by buxom Indian maidens from Milan. No time though, boys.

Years back I played *Cowboy and Truck Driver Festivals* in Germany and Switzerland – odd music carnivals where folks walked around dressed like Buffalo Bill, Wyatt Earp, Hopalong Cassidy, or Sitting Bull. Or that's what they *thought* they looked like. In England I've seen Civil War re-enactments and Tombstone shootouts.

Europeans are fascinated with the American West. They travel to America and visit all the National Parks and famous Western Towns. They want to see Tombstone and Rosa's Cantina and maybe drive down Route 66 for a capper. They have the thirst.

A few years ago I did a concert in Berlin and the promoter gave me a book titled *Polish Poster Art and The Western* – classic American cowboy films that were dubbed in Polish. The introduction by Edward Buscombe and Kevin Mulroy gave detail to the Wild West and Native American penetration of Europe. I've added my own points to their loose chronology:

1616: Pochohantas is brought to England to visit The Court of St. James.

1840s: George Catlin carried his Indian paintings to London for a large exhibition which attracted 32,000 customers. Caitlin had a dozen real *Iowa* Indians hanging around for color – they were brought over by P.T. Barnum. Charles Dickens gave the show a nasty review. Dickens didn't dig Indians.

1887: *Buffalo Bill's Wild West Show* appeared at Earl's Court in London. The Queen was there. Cody's show drew 83,000 people on Easter Monday.

1890: Buffalo Bill is pictured in a gondola in Venice Italy accompanied by four Sioux Indians – *Black Heart* and *Rocky Bear* are two of them.

1893: The German writer Karl May's latest Western novel, *Winnetou,* appears. It's a blockbuster. May reinvents his own American Wild West and sells a million copies.

1939: Gene Autry is mobbed at a street parade in Dublin, Ireland.

Sliding forward into the present:

2012: Reenactments of *Buffalo Bill's Wild West Show* are installed at Euro-Disney in Paris.

December 18, 2013: 100 American Indian artifacts go on sale at the Drouot auction house in Paris, including items from the San Carlos Apaches and 24 pieces held sacred by the Hopi Tribe. The Annenberg Foundation of Los Angeles successfully buys up most of the Hopi artifacts and plans to return them to the tribe.

We could add detail and color to this list, but I can boil the European fascination with the Wild West down to two major characters and their influence: Buffalo Bill Cody and the German novelist Karl May. Western films, TV shows, cowboy songs, and Western art were influential, but the enduring shadows of Cody and Karl May loom large. Throw in a chorus of *Tom Dooley,* in German, and you've got the mix.

I   **Buffalo Bill's Wild West Sails to Europe**

Buffalo Bill is the most romantic figure in American history, the idol of every man and boy. Book tickets now while his name is on every tongue....

— Promotional Flyer
(Probably written by Cody himself)

It is often said on the other side of the water that none of the exhibitions which we send to England are purely and distinctly American. If you will take the Wild West show over there you can remove that reproach.

— Mark Twain to Buffalo Bill

The year is 1887. Imagine being a wrangler onboard one of two ships transporting Buffalo Bill's Wild West entourage across the Atlantic Ocean towards Europe. The troop included 200 cowboys, cowgirls, and *vaqueros,* as well as 97 Native Americans, 18 buffalo, 181 horses, 10 elk, 4 donkeys, 5 Texas longhorns, 2 deer, 10 mules, and one *Deadwood Concord* stagecoach. Hang and rattle, boys. Tonight we ride. These days I find it hard enough to negotiate a European tour with two guitars and a rental car.

The show was aiming for the 1897 World's Fair and the special *American Exhibition.* Cody's troupe toured England for the next six months, returned the following year, and continued visiting Europe until 1892. For European audiences, Buffalo Bill and his Wild West show not only represented the West, but all of America.

A brief update: Buffalo Bill was born William Frederick Cody on February 26, 1846. He lived until January 10, 1917. Cody grew up on the frontier and loved the cowboy life. As he got older, some of his titles he earned included: buffalo hunter, U.S. army scout and guide,

Medal of Honor winner, and Wild West showman, as well as Pony Express Rider, Indian fighter, actor and author.

In 1883 Cody launched *Buffalo Bill's Wild West Show* in Nebraska. Cody was the star of the show and the hero of all historic re-enactments. At the turn of the twentieth century Buffalo Bill Cody was known as *the greatest showman on the face of the earth,* and he dominated the Wild West show business. It would appear Cody learned much from circus owner P.T. Barnum about the art of promotion – back in the 1800s promotion was occasionally termed *humbug,* and Barnum was the spin-master.

It didn't take much prompting by Mark Twain and others for Cody to consider a tour of Europe. Cody knew he'd be lionized. He could provide foreign audiences with a living re-hash of the Wild West, with himself as a major player and hero.

II *Tableau Vivants*, Cycloramas, and The Rough Riders of the World

> *It was like being at a pitched battle without the real terror of anything happening to you, but it was happening all around you with startling clarity and realism...These were real Indians. They were not using real bullets, but the sound and the action was all the same. And the men lay there dead...as on a real battle scene. But they got up and everyone cheered, and then she could see it all again the next day....*
>
> — A French Girl's Recollection of The Cody Show
> Black Elk Speaks

The initial Buffalo Bill show in Europe was based on a spectacle titled: *The Drama of Civilization.* The structure was a series of *tableau vivants* (living pictures) in which actors stood like statues against theatrical backdrops as the action took place in front of them. The backdrops where grouped into four *epochs: The Primeval Forest, The Prairie, Cattle Ranch,* and *Mining Camp.*

Act I, *The Primeval Forest,* ended with a fight among the Indians. It was followed by an interlude featuring Native American dancing, then a demonstration of Lillian Smith's sharp shooting. Lillian was a young rival to Annie Oakley who was also on the show. Lillian didn't possess the shooting chops of Annie but dressed loud and talked a good game.

Annie Oakley usually outshot Lillian and all the male sharp shooters as well. (Fast forward in time, to Broadway and Irving Berlin's score in 1945, of *Annie Get Your Gun*, starring Ethel Merman. Songs included "There's No Business Like Show Business," and "You Can't Get a Man With a Gun.")

Act II, *The Prairie*, included a buffalo hunt by the Indians, the passage of a train through *hostile land*, a prairie fire, and a stampede, followed by *cowboy riding, roping, and bronco busting*.

Act III, *The Attack on the Mining Camp*, starred Buffalo Bill defending a cabin against *gunfire and screaming Indians*, followed by Cody and Annie Oakley performing a shooting act. The last act, *Mining Camp*, featured the Pony Express, an attack on a Deadwood stagecoach, and *a cyclone*. A cyclone? Trains? That's what the program said.

Eventually a fifth act was added: *Custer's Last Stand*. After the dramatized massacre Cody entered and circled the arena on a horse, while the warning *Too Late!* was projected onto the *cyclorama*. The *cyclorama* was a panoramic painting – a lavish backdrop – which gave the viewers the sensation they were inside the scene.

The dramatic conclusion suggested that Cody had been near the Custer battle scene, but had arrived too late to save the day. That wasn't exactly the case in real life – Cody was far away. What the hell, Buffalo Bill wasn't above creating his own mythical twists to Western history. *There's no business like show business.*

Imagine those huge theatrical gimmicks: the *tableau vivants* and the *cyclorama* – the lavish backdrops for the action. In front of these settings came marauding Indians, cowboys on bucking broncs, *vaqueros*, the stagecoach, the burning cabins, and the small herds of buffalo, deer, and elk. Then Buffalo Bill himself, bigger than life, well mounted and firing his six guns. Who needed a Western movie? You were riding with Buffalo Bill, inside the action. It was *live*, and you could smell the blood, smoke, and horse dung.

And it scared the hell out of the Queen of England. Europe was hooked forever.

Bill Cody had renamed the official title to: *Buffalo Bill's Wild West and Congress of Rough Riders of the World*. This enabled him to expand on his vision and use horse-culture groups from around the globe: Turks, Gauchos, Arabs, Mongols and Russians, as well as their *distinctive horses and colorful costumes*. They rode alongside the

Indians and cowboys. The opening parade was spectacular.

Cody, like Barnum before him, brought the goods. Irving Berlin later captured Cody's spirit in the show-biz song from *Annie Get Your Gun*:

The cowboys, the wrestlers, the tumblers, the clowns
The roustabouts that move the show at dawn
The music, the spotlights, the people, the towns
Your baggage with the labels pasted on

The sawdust and the horses and the smell
The towel you've stolen from the last hotel
There's no business like show business
     ...Like no business I know

Amen.

III Black Elk Speaks

It is in the darkness of their eyes that men get lost.

— **Black Elk**

Most of the Native Americans in the show were from the Sioux tribes, including Black Elk, second cousin to Crazy Horse. Black Elk would live until 1950 and record his history in a narrative written down by the poet John Neihardt, who then published the classic *Black Elk Speaks*. Carl Jung, the prominent psychologist, urged that the book be published in German – which it was in 1953. One of the chapters deals with Black Elk's tour with Cody.

Black Elk lived a full-up *Western* life. He took his first scalp at age thirteen at the Battle of Little Bighorn and later survived the Wounded Knee Massacre. Buffalo Bill sometimes dreamed himself into the center of key battles of the old West – but Black Elk didn't have to create any forked-tongue myths about history. He was *there*. From the great Indian victories, to the final historic massacre of Indians fomented by white soldiers, to the Wild West shows. He was also a respected medicine man.

Young Black Elk rode in the mock Indian raids and met the Queen of England. This transpired because Cody had invited the Prince of Wales, (who later became King Edward VII) to a private preview of the

Wild West performance on May 5, 1887. The Prince of Wales was impressed enough to arrange a command performance for Queen Victoria on May 11.

The Queen enjoyed the show and wrote in her journal about meeting Cody, Annie Oakley, Lillian Smith, Chief Red Shirt, and Black Elk. She also recorded her fright of the Indian war dance, saying: *they danced to a wild drum & pipe, it was quite fearful, with all their contortions & shrieks, & they came so close!*

Black Elk said of Victoria: *she was little but fat and we liked her, because she was good to us.*

IV Turn Away Business in a Drizzling Rain!
The Towel You Stole From the Last Hotel!
An Insider's View of The Euro Wild West Tour...

Within two minutes from our main entrance
you could take a trip, to heaven, hell, the North Pole
or any old place for four cents...ours was
the big show and everything in it was proclaimed American.

— **Charles Eldrige Griffin**

In 1908 Charles Eldrige Griffin published *Four Years in Europe with Buffalo Bill*. Griffin was a magician, fire-eater, hypnotist, illusionist, sword swallower, and newspaper publisher. He'd also worked in the Ringling Brothers circus and married a snake charmer named Olivia. *There's no people like show people!* Griffin was approached to work the Wild West show and sailed aboard the Cunard ship *Etruria* in 1903. He performed magic and sideshow acts with the troupe.

As a companion piece to Black Elk's later reports, Griffin provides us with an inside view of the tour with Cody. He begins with his ocean journey aboard the *Etruria*. It appears the passengers were well fed:

I ate my regular six meals a day...breakfast at eight, bouillon and sandwiches at eleven, luncheon at twelve, tea at five, dinner at six and supper at eight o'clock.

Onward to the show:

We opened the season on 1903 at Brook's Bar, Manchester, April 13, to turn away business in a cold drizzling rain, which turned to snow. At the opening performance Colonel Cody was thrown from his horse, or rather the horse stumbled, severely straining one of the Colonel's ankles, consequently he was unable to ride during the three weeks engagement at Manchester, but was driven round the area in a carriage at each performance.

— ***The New York Times,*** April 14, 1903, reported Cody's horse reared up and fell over on top of him.

At Birmingham, June 7, there was born to Chief Standing Bear and wife Laura (Sioux), a squaw papoose, the only one ever born in Great Britain...the little stranger was christened Alexandra-Pearl-Olive-Octavia-Birmingham-England-Standing Bear...after the birthing the mother walked across to our dining pavilion and ate a hearty meal...two days later manager, Mr. Parker, had them on exhibition in the annex...they proved a potent attraction...

The first fatal accident occurred at Bristol, July 23, Isadore Gonzalez, one of the Mexican riders, was thrown from his horse and instantly killed. He was buried at Bristol...

Shortly after leaving Paris, glanders broke out among the broncos...forty two horses were taken out and shot in one day...when we closed the season at Marseille we only had about one hundred broncos left to give the performance, two hundred having been killed during the season...when the show was over it was decided to kill the remaining hundred broncos and burn all the trappings, being the only way to stamp out the plague, we would import new broncos from America for the next season...

Griffin wrote a long article about the shooting of the horses for the American press (he called it a *French Tragedy*), but the manager of Cody's show concluded: *The less said about this the better.* The story was squashed. *Glanders,* an infectious equine disease of the lungs, has since been eradicated in America and Europe.

Onward they went, wintering in Marseille, then performing in Rome, Genoa Vienna, and Budapest. Sipping espressos, posing in gondolas, learning local customs, flirting with the French girls. Griffin's book includes a blurred photo of at least fifty Sioux Indians posing inside the Rome Coliseum.

Griffin, in the end, declares his utter exhaustion at trying to make himself understood as a sideshow magician because he'd encountered sixteen different languages during his tours. But he concludes that *Buffalo Bill's Wild West Show and Congress of Rough Riders of the World* left a long shadow across Europe, which would last for centuries. The shadow endures.

V   Karl May and his Alter Ego: *Old Shatterhand*

I have given my mind and soul an earthly garment, called a novel...this garment is the only body, in which it is possible for the people inside me to talk to my readers, to make themselves to be seen and heard.

— **Karl May**

In an antique store in a small farm town in Switzerland, I came across an entire shelf of Karl May novels. I bought one titled *Der Shatz im Silbersee* (*The Treasure in the Silver Lake*). The cover painting is of an Indian in full headdress standing up in a canoe on a lake. He's saluting the mountains and the sky. In Karl May's world Indians walked around in full headdress, raising their hands in salute. Urging peace. The Noble Savage rides again.

On the back of the book there's a photo of Karl May (pronounced *My*) where he resembles Buffalo Bill. May sports an Old West style mustache beneath a large *sombrero* hat. There's a coyote or wolf skin (or a German Shepherd pelt) draped over his right shoulder. May was also known to walk around in a suit of stitched buckskins, sporting a ring of bear teeth around his neck. This was in his mansion in Germany in the 1880s.

The Treasure of the Silver Lake was later made into a film – the first of the so-called *Kraut Westerns* or *Black Forest Westerns* of the 1960s. The film, in German, starred American actor Lex Barker as *Old Shatterhand,* and a Frenchman, Pierre Brice, as *Winnetou* – the noble Apache Chief. The plots of Karl May Winnetou books are akin to *The Lone Ranger and Tonto* type setups – leaning heavy, as always, on the myth of The Noble Savage.

I was trying to figure out Karl May as I began writing this in the Wild West of Switzerland. My wife and I slip over here when the weather in El Paso hits 115 degrees. Every morning the farmer next door herds his Simmental cows into the field below me. Another farmer up the road raises Galloway cattle and Swiss *warm-blooded* draft horses. The clanging of Swiss cowbells and the *clop clop* of draft horse hooves was my soundtrack as I wrote about The West in Europe.

Down a village street is a Western store called *Cheyenne*. A Swiss-German man sells kitsch American Indian art – feathers, beads, statues, jewelry – the stuff you see in gas stations along Highway 10 in New Mexico and Arizona. *Made in China*. But it's the *symbols* and the Native American *images* which endure here. And cowboys. Much of it has to do with the ghost of Karl May and his novels.

The town of Segeberg, Germany, features an annual Karl May Festival that draws up to 300,000 people. Karl May's romantic-western novels have sold over one hundred million copies. They continue selling. Karl, in his travels, had never been West of Schenectady, New York, but he led people to believe he'd ventured far and wide, spoke Native American languages, and was even the living embodiment of his main character *Old Shatterhand*. He was a dreamer who heard voices, and those voices spoke out through his Western fiction.

In April, 2012, *The New Yorker* magazine published a lengthy article on May titled "Wild West German," written by Rivka Galchen. The subtitle was: "Why do Cowboys and Indians so captivate the country?" The enduring popularity of May's Western novels might be baffling to American readers and historians. It takes an understanding of the German temperament and their yen for exotic and romantic yarns set in the shoot-em-up West. Deeper than this lies the mystery of who in hell this Karl May *was* and how did he dream the stuff up?

May was born in 1842 in Saxony, one of the fourteen children of an impoverished weaver. May claimed he was blind from birth and then miraculously cured. Karl May claimed *a lot of things*. He was known for what the New Yorker article called his *confabulations*. That's a fancy word for *harmless, multifarious bullshit routines*. For the sake of art.

May grew up a juvenile delinquent, in and out of jails, eventually doing four years in prison for stealing furs. He worked in the prison library and read a number of books on the American West, no doubt familiarizing himself with James Fennimore Cooper's *Leather Stocking Tales* and *The Last of the Mohicans*.

In his 30s, Karl May began to write pulp fiction and make a living as a writer. In 1893, when Karl was 51, he published his first *Winnetou* and *Old Shatterhand* novel, and this one took off. Winnetou was an Apache (sort of) and Old Shatterhand was a German-American immigrant and railroad surveyor who becomes Winnetou's friend. Together they ride across the West, righting wrongs and promoting peace.

When Buffalo Bill brought his Wild West show to Germany there could have been an historic meeting of the two minds, but Karl May avoided meeting Cody and the Indians. May didn't speak English well (nor the Native American languages he claimed to know) and he surmised Buffalo Bill was mistreating the Indians. He didn't think Cody was the real deal.

There wasn't room enough on one Wild West stage for the showbiz egos of Buffalo Bill and Karl May. Karl probably didn't want to look into the eyes of a real roughrider or an Indian. Black Elk might have scared the hell out of him. No matter. Karl retreated to his German mansion, donned his bear tooth necklace, summoned *the voices* and pumped out another Western yarn. His readers gobbled it up.

It's easy for myself, as an American, to deride May's Western novels, but May was a decent writer who'd done research and effectively implanted a love for the American West and Native America into the hearts of his German speaking readers. In *The New Yorker* essay the author, Rivka Galchen, states that while she was living in Germany many Germans asked her why there was a museum of Holocaust in Washington, D.C. but no museums about slavery or Native American genocide. Good question.

With few exceptions, May hadn't visited the places he described, but compensated for his lack of direct experience through a combination of creativity, imagination, and documentary sources – including maps, travel accounts and guidebooks, as well as anthropological and linguistic studies. Readers took it all as fact.

Here's the kicker and maybe the key to May's ability to dream up his own *West*. While digging through articles on Karl May (your cowboy reporter breaking into sealed vaults in the dank basement of a long-shuttered Berlin library) I came across a research paper published in 1994 by a Dr. William E. Thomas later titled: *Karl May and Dissociative Identity Disorder*. Eureka! I micro-filmed the article and fled through a fire exit, guard dogs yapping at my heels.

Dr. Thomas surmises Karl May's traumatic early life (parental abuse and prison time) led to a personality disorder. I won't bore you with the heavy lifting in this article. You've heard the routine. The messed-up, early psychological conditions which breed killers, misfits, and pissed-off artists.

The Doc's conclusion: *When faced with traumatic situation, from which there is no physical escape, a child may resort to going away in his/her head. It is a dissociative process which is a highly creative survival technique.* The abused kid learns to disassociate, and different personalities rise up and split off. The kid creates his own world and goes into a *fugue state*. Bring on your Bach's, Beethoven's, and Billy the Kids. And novelists. They hear *voices*, and turn the voices towards profit. Or plunder.

Enter *Old Shatterhand* and his sidekick *Winnetou*. *I have given my mind and soul an earthly garment, called a novel,* (wrote Karl May)...*this garment is the only body, in which it is possible for the people inside me to talk to my readers, to make themselves to be seen and heard.*

Karl May actually believed he'd **lived through** these Western experiences and was the living embodiment of *Old Shatterhand*. So be it. Hitler and Einstein and fifty million other readers were fans, and a Karl May Native American Museum now exists in Germany. As I write this, a Native American tribe in Canada is asking for the return of a sacred skull and other artifacts housed in the museum. The West rolls on and on.

VI Coda: A Swiss Girl's Wild West

Hängen Sie Ihren Kopf, Tom Dooley
Hängen Sie Ihren Kopf und schreien...

— ***Tom Dooley*** (GermanVersion)

Ten years ago I met my future wife in a Swiss cowboy bar called *The Dream Valley Saloon* located in the mountains near the Swiss city of Bern. The proprietor had a small ranch near the saloon and two fairly tame buffalo he kept in a stout corral near his house. He said he bought the Buffalo in Geneva. His saloon served steaks, burgers, and BBQ ribs.

Fast-forward a few years later. I married my Swiss gal in Elko, Nevada, at the Cowboy Poetry Gathering. Our honorary best men: Ian Tyson and Ramblin Jack Elliott. An ongoing Western Romance story, which begins in Europe and keeps spinning round and round.

I learned back then that my wife, and her mother, were quite familiar with The West and Tex Mex music. My mother-in-law is a lifelong fan of legendary outlaws, Indians, and the Old West. Here was an opportunity to ask a living person how she learned about cowboys as a young gal growing up near Basil, Switzerland.

A few snippets from Silvia:

> When I was about seven or eight we watched Bonanza on television. Those brothers who came riding up on their horses while the music played. It was dubbed into German. Then when I was ten or eleven we read Karl May in our school and also the priest's house had a library with a lot of Karl May. Everyone read Karl May...priests, my parents, everyone. The whole country.
> Every afternoon when we got out of school we ran to the forest. We threw our books down and played Winnetou and Old Shatterhand...he was the friend of the Indian. We also had Indian caves in the rocks...

> When I was about eight or ten my brother was always singing "Tom Dooley" with his guitar. He sang it in German. There was a German version by The Nielsen Brothers that was a hit song here...everyone sang Tom Dooley...they're still singing it.

Karl May, *Bonanza*, and *Tom Dooley* – a hit song in America, recorded in a half-dozen languages across the globe. The Kingston Trio recorded the first popular version. 1958. One hundred years back, Laura Foster had been murdered by a Confederate veteran name of Tom Dula. Dula, Foster's lover and fiancé, was convicted of her murder and hanged May 1, 1868. Then came the folksong. *Dula* became *Dooley*. Change one syllable, add just two chords, and you have a hit.

I was always curious about Tom Dooley's wide popularity – a *hanging ballad* – and I wrote and asked Bob Shane, the only living original member of The Kingston Trio, why he thought the song was so popular around the world. Even in Switzerland.

Bob was kind enough to write back:

> A fellow once said to me that if you had a public hanging in Madison Square Garden, it would be sold out overnight. Hate to say it, but that's probably part of the reason of the song's success – meaning, it's a story that intrigued people in that

kind of macabre way. Also, at that time, American music was all bubble gum (think "Itsy Bitsy Teeny Weeny Yellow Polka Dot Bikini") and I think the public was ready for something different. Also, the song had 2 chords and was very catchy, with lyrics that were easy to follow and a pleasing melody.

Hang down your head, Tom Dooley.

****

So be it. A grand-entry parade of Western voices echoing across Europe for the last century and a half: *Buffalo Bill, Annie Oakley, Black Elk, Karl May, Old Shatterhand, Winnetou, Tom Dooley...* and whatever happened to *Alexandra-Pearl-Olive-Octavia-Birmingham-England-Standing Bear?* Remember the little Native American baby who began her life as a Western sideshow exhibit in Birmingham, England? And where in Bristol might we find the grave of the Mexican vaquero and roughrider, Isadore Gonzalez? There should be a *corrido* written for him.

I'm finishing this essay in our hacienda in El Paso. I can hear my wife practicing her Swiss-German accordion. It sounds like she's playing *Tom Dooley*. Tex-Mex style. Maybe she'll yodel. Yodeling was used in the Swiss Alps by herders calling their stock in Alpine villages. The earliest record of a yodel is in 1545, where it is described as *the call of a cowherd from Appenzell*. And Swiss German accordion music was picked-up by Mexican musicians and formed the foundations for *Norteno* and Tex Mex accordion styles. The circle spins 'round again.

Ole! Hang down your head. Hold fast. Hang and rattle. *Auf wiedersehen!*

Hemingway in the West

Before I was 16 I bucked out anything there that was in the shoots (chutes) with a bear trap saddle when I needed 100 dollars...

— Ernest Hemingway
Letter to Charles Scribner
From the *Finca Vigia*, Cuba
July 19, 1950

I was sitting in my writing office in El Paso across from Ian Tyson. We were engaged in the thorny business of attempting to co-write a modern cowboy song. What's left to say? At some point in our bantering back and forth Ian changed the subject and stated, out of the blue: *You know Hemingway met Will James once. In the basement of a ranch in Montana. They hated each other. I think they were both drunk on their asses.*

End of anecdote. No more information.

I asked Ian where he'd heard that, but he couldn't recollect. A Montana rancher might have told him. And maybe somebody had told the Montana rancher. A modern Western rumor.

I thought about it for a few months, but couldn't track or trace that Hemingway-Will James meeting down. Ian's remark placed Hemingway in cowboy country, meeting a well-known Western writer and artist, and I was interested in seeing if I could essay up something called *Hemingway in the West*. So what was this Will James deal?

We don't normally connect Hemingway with the West. Or the cowboy lifestyle. Hemingway *died* in the West, of course. At the wrong end of a Boss shotgun balanced in his own hands. That was Ketchum, Idaho, 1961, where he'd lived his last few years.

We tend to associate Hemingway with the locations of his best known stories, novels, non fiction books and essays: the boyhood summers in upper Michigan, the European front in WWI, Bohemian Paris in the 20s, skiing in the Austrian Alps, bulls and the Civil War in Spain, African safaris, and big game fishing in Key West and Cuba. And finally Idaho.

In my mind he invented his own *semi-fictional West,* where the hunting and fishing were always good, the country was wild and beautiful and ever changing, and there was a Spanish bullfight every Sunday within driving distance. He possessed a western *spirit.* He performed his writing chores with strict discipline (in the good years), and the rest of his days were given to outdoor sport, food, travel, camaraderie, wine, hard spirits, and love or war, whichever one was in the cards that particular season.

But what of this meeting with Will James? Was it *apocryphal?* What would they have talked about? Will James was a curious, self-made character who'd reinvented himself in the West. He became a writer and visual artist who inspired thousands of boys (including Ian Tyson and Ramblin' Jack Elliott) to follow the cowboy trail.

I have a few pieces of Will James *memorabilia* – a letter he sent from the Algonquin Hotel in New York, and a cancelled check made out by Will to the Triangle Drug Company of Hollywood, for two dollars, on January 14, 1941. A pint of bourbon? A box of pencils? His legend is an enduring one in the world of Western writers and artists. I also have a lifetime interest in selected pieces of Hemingway's writing, so this Hemingway-Will James conflict interested me.

I wrote my friend Allen Josephs, a Hemingway scholar who teaches in Florida, and has published many fine books and essays on Hemingway, Spain, and bullfighting. Allen pointed me towards the published collection of Hemingway letters gathered by Carlos Baker. There were two references to Will James in the index.

We were on the trail.

I Will James and Ernest Hemingway: The True Gen

I have met Will James...and he is a sort of
Dog-eared, moth-eaten, shifty eyed, fake
imitation of old C.W. (sic) Russell, who was
a real cowboy artist...

— **Ernest Hemingway,**
Letter to Archibald MacLeish,
1930, from Billings Montana

Hemingway didn't meet Will James in Montana. He met James in publisher Charlie Scribner's office in New York, probably in the late 1920s. Both men were published by Scribners. James had written his first six books, which included the classic, award winning, *Smoky the Cow Horse* (1927). Hemingway at that time had published the novella *The Torrents of Spring* (some considered it a weak, nasty parody of Sherwood Anderson's writing), collections of poetry and short stories, the Pamplona novel, *The Sun Also Rises* (1926), and the WW1 novel *A Farewell to Arms* (1929). These last two were triumphs. He was on his way.

A chance meeting in Scribner's office was probably the only time the two men met. It would not be unusual for Hemingway to take a dislike for someone he figured might be trespassing in his own literary territory – outdoor life, male adventure, the *last good country*, etc. And Will James sold a *helluva* lot of books. Maybe competitive tempers flared up. Too many cocktails for lunch? The boys were both world-class drinkers.

Hemingway would later be involved in a punch-out with Max Eastman in Scribner's office, so he was territorial there. Maybe Hemingway smelled a rat, or found out the "true gen" on Will James – that James wasn't born on a ranch in cowboy country. James was born Joseph Ernest Nephtali Dufault, in 1892, in Quebec, Canada. He'd learned to cowboy from a French-Canadian wrangler and was later arrested and did jail time, twice, for cattle rustling. Later he'd do a turn as a horse wrangler in a prison in Nevada.

This French Canadian kid, Dufault, changed his name and taught himself to cowboy, draw horses, and write Western yarns. And steal cattle. He then fictionalized his cowboy roots. But, hell, almost every cowboy in the West had re-invented himself. A lot were Easterners, or Europeans, who were headed West, *out where the bullets fly, to follow the cowherds 'til the day I die*. To quote the old song: "The Hills of Mexico."

What about that James-Hemingway *Montana* connection? The answer is in the Hemingway letters. Hemingway was in the hospital in Billings, in 1930, recovering from a fractured arm acquired in a car wreck. He welcomed visitors, but was tired of the locals continually name-dropping Will James. James was well known in Montana, and owned property in Pryor Creek and Billings.

Hemingway wrote from his hospital bed to Archibald MacLeish:

*This is Will James country out here. Anybody
who comes into see you...talks about Will James...
the next time anybody comes in, I'm going to claim
to be Will James himself, and present them with an
autographed copy of* **Smoky**, *that classic for boys.*

Papa Hemingway apparently never got over his competitive grudge against Will James. It kept simmering on the back burner for thirty years. In July of 1950 Hemingway was getting shelled by the critics for the novel *Across the River and Into the Trees* and he fired off a letter to publisher Charles Scribner from *The Finca Vigia,* his home in Cuba.

Hemingway was irate at the tidal wave of critical reviews of his novel, and the continual backhanded shots at his manhood. He raged on and on in the letter. At one point he proclaims his expertise as a cowboy, and this boast flies out of nowhere:

*Before I was sixteen I bucked out anything there
that was in the shoots (chutes) with a Bear Trap saddle
when I needed 100 dollars...you probably know
what a Bear Trap saddle is from having that phony
Will James work for you...on the second buck the horse
throws you because of the twist he makes. In a bear trap
saddle he can't throw you. You are with him for keeps.
But it's 20 to 1 he breaks your back.*

There isn't evidence that Hemingway rode broncs for wages. But what the hell. He was trying to best Will James at his own game. But why? Apparently Charles Scribner was fond of Will James, and Hemingway demanded full attention and reverence from Scribner. How could Hemingway out-cowboy a man who'd gone to prison twice for cattle rustling?

By 1950 Hemingway was starting a slow, downward mental spiral and swinging wildly at old shadows. The aged heavyweight champ defending his reputation in round fifteen, trying to last until the final bell. And then, two years later, he fooled the naysayers and came back with one last knockout punch: *The Old Man and the Sea.* It won the Pulitzer Prize.

The critics were hyenas circling the meat, waiting to move in on a wounded lion. You can't blame the old man's defensive stance. Ernest Hemingway was, and remains, a big target. Because he was a *big writer*. He re-invented the American sentence and wrote at least four monumental novels, dozens of classic short stories, and well-crafted essays and magazine pieces. And then there's *that lifestyle*, which writers from all corners of the globe have made unwise attempts to emulate or lampoon. Hemingway's work stands above the fracas.

We may never solve the final riddle of his passionate dislike for Will James. I've gone down that trail. It's only a rope trick to look at the Hemingway's Western years. Let's move further West in the game. Hollywood.

II Hemingway in Hollywood

The best way for a writer to deal with Hollywood
is to meet the producers at the California state line:
You throw them your book, they throw you the money.
Then you jump into your car and drive like hell back
the way you came...

— **Ernest Hemingway**

Will James died from the effects of alcohol in Hollywood, 1942. James was working with scriptwriters and producers who were adapting his stories. Script collaboration was often frustrating, demeaning work for writers use to working alone. Will would flee Hollywood and hide out on a dude ranch in Apple Valley, or in a bar on the high desert. He died in the Presbyterian Hospital in Hollywood. No comment from Mr. Hemingway.

Hemingway only visited Hollywood one time, in 1937, when he gave a speech to collect money in support of the Republican side in the Spanish Civil War. Eight Hemingway novels and several of his short stories were made into films, including: *The Sun Also Rises, A Farewell to Arms, For Whom the Bell Tolls, To Have and Have Not,* and *The Old Man and the Sea*

Hemingway didn't care for the manner in which Hollywood handled his stories – most serious writers do not. But he liked the money. The other literary lion of that era, William Faulkner, had a sour taste for California after working for the film studios. He insisted on transporting his daughter's pregnant riding mare back to Mississippi, so the horse wouldn't foal on California soil.

Hemingway's old Paris cohort, F. Scott Fitzgerald, lost what remained of his soul by working for the movies. Scott drank. Deeply. What Fitzgerald called *going on the wagon* was a case of beer a day. He gave up the booze finally, but died in Hollywood, aged 44.

Hemingway wasn't made for script adapting. He left that to others. He was given $80,000 for the rights to *A Farewell to Arms* (1932), a large amount for the adaptation of a novel back then. In 1958 Warner Brothers gave him $150,000 for the rights to *The Old Man and the Sea*. In the 40s and 50s, Hollywood put Hemingway's name up on the marquee, since he was the most famous *living* writer in the world. He received equal billing to the star actors.

Hemingway had many friends among those famous actors and actresses: Gary Cooper, Ingrid Bergman, and Marlene Dietrich, were a few of the *names,* and they traveled to Key West, Havana, New York, or Idaho to hang out with him. He didn't care for the Hollywood social scene, or in fact *any* scene that did not revolve around himself, hunting, fishing, the bulls, betting sports, and drinking bouts in his favored haunts.

From 1939 on, Hemingway split his time between Cuba and the fall hunting season in Sun Valley, Idaho. Idaho was *the last good country.* The story of his final move out West begins in Cuba, where I once had the opportunity to step inside the Hemingway house. I climbed through the living room window and felt the ghosts rising above the half-empty gin bottles.

III Cowboy Nights in Cuba

The branches of the mango trees shook
and snapped in the wind and its heat burned
the mango flowers until they were brown
and dusty and their stems dried...the winds came in
Lent...there was a local name for them, and bad writers
always became literary about them. He had
resisted this...

— **Ernest Hemingway,**
Great News From the Mainland, A Short Story set in Cuba

In 1932 Hemingway bought a vintage colonial house in Key West, Florida, and lived there with his second wife Pauline, on and off, until

1939. The house featured the first indoor plumbing on Key West. Here he wrote *The Snows of Kilimanjaro, To Have and to Have Not* and *The Green Hills of Africa*. Cuba was across the Straits of Florida and he began to retreat there to write and fish.

Hemingway enjoyed the old Cuba, before Castro. The wild, corrupt, mafia-controlled Havana of bars and sporting clubs. There was cockfighting, Jai Alai, sports fishing, bird hunting – all of it within a short drive. His third wife-to-be, journalist and war correspondent Martha Gellhorn, found the property called *Finca Vigia* (Outlook Farm) in a village a few miles from Havana. A farmhouse and fifteen acres of flowers and fruit trees.

Hemingway eventually bought the place and they moved in with 5000 books, phonograph records, art, bullfight posters, and wild game trophies. Gellhorn went off to work as a war correspondent, and the marriage went on the rocks. Hemingway stuck around Cuba and later lived in *The Finca Vigia* with his fourth wife Mary. The guests arrived on a regular basis.

An average night might begin with the absinthe ritual, or a martini or two, a bottle of red wine with dinner, cognac, and then a chauffeured drive into Havana for the *pelota* matches (*Jai Alai*) and sojourns to the preferred bars. They watched the matches in a fronton called *Horno Verde*, the green oven. Hemingway's favorite bars were *La Bodequita* and *El Floridita*. He wrote a declaration on a piece of butcher paper, framed on the wall in La Bodequita:

My Mojito in La Bodequita.
My Daiquiri in El Floridita.

He still holds the record in *El Floridita* for imbibing 16 straight double rum Daiquiris. Don't attempt this. The world record for writers goes to Dylan Thomas. Dylan's last coherent statement, after drinking at The White Horse Tavern in New York, was:

I've had 18 straight whiskeys –
I believe that's the record.

Good night, sweet ladies. He went into coma and died shortly after.

Hemingway's spirit endures in Havana. His drinking stool stands in *El Floridita*, inside a velvet rope which keeps the tourists off. In the corner is a full size bronze of Hemingway standing at the bar. Monuments to a man and a lifestyle.

In 1999 I visited Havana under the auspices of doing folk music research for a record I was working on. In truth I also wanted to visit the Hemingway house, and I accomplished this. The day after the visit I wrote out a summary of my visit on five pages of stationary at the old *Hotel Nacional* in Havana. Excerpts from those notes:

> *We took a taxi to the edge of Havana, about five miles out, into a little village called San Francisco de Paula. Street vendors sold canned soup and cheap cigars and gaunt, skeletal dogs yapped and whined as they limped away down dead-end alleys. Somewhere up the road was the Old Man's house, Finca Vigia.*
>
> *Around a dusty corner there it was – a large tropical bungalow hidden in the overgrowth of palm trees, orchids, jasmine, avocados, hibiscus and bougainvilleas – 26 varieties bougainvilleas. Lush and decadent. The old farm. Decaying in the wet heat.*
>
> *Castro allowed Finca Vigia to stay much as it was when the Old Man handed over the keys and walked away. The valuable paintings are gone, including a Miró (which Hemingway took), two by Juan Gris, a Klee, and a Braque. Miro's painting, "The Farm," now hangs in The National Gallery in Washington D.C.*
>
> *Once we exited the taxi I noticed the empty swimming pool, where he swam laps every afternoon after writing. His fishing boat, The Pilar, was dry-docked poolside, next to four little graves for his dogs: "Negrita," "Blackdog," "Linda," and "Neron." Blackdog was his favorite, killed by Batista's troops. The Black Dog," was also the term he used for the deep depression which would eventually choke him. You weren't allowed inside the house, but a woman guard approached and offered to let me go in for a five-dollar bribe. No one else was around. She pocketed the money and held her finger up in warning: "Three minutes. You no touch nothing. I watch."*
>
> *I climbed in a window and walked around. Eerie it was. The half-empty gin and whiskey bottles on a small table next to his reading chair. The ten-foot high bullfight posters. His bedroom with the typewriter where he stood to write every morning at first light. The books and magazines. Frozen in tropical time. The pencil marks in the bathroom where he marked his blood pressure.*

There were hundreds of books and, unlike the libraries in most people's homes, these volumes looked like they'd all been devoured. Chewed-on. The covers were tattered, rotting in the wet heat. They matched the feel of the place.

It was the house of a writer. He'd been gone for fifty years. Yet he wasn't gone. There was enough gin left in one of the bottles, and I felt he could whirl out of there at any moment and throw a few jabs.

I climbed back out of a living room window. As we drove out through the bougainvilleas, we had the taxi take us to Cojimar, where he used to dock his boat, Pilar. We ordered rum and lime Mojitos and they tasted perfect that afternoon. Sweet and sour, like the Old Man's life.

IV Last Stand in the West: Idaho & The Vanishing Frontier

The critics waited for him to write a bad one.
Then they clobbered him. But when the Old Man
couldn't throw the fast ball, he threw his heart.

— **Raymond Chandler** (on Hemingway)

I think he was in search of the vanishing
frontier...a place where he could have some
anonymity, where the hunting and fishing
were still good. And he found that in Central Idaho.

— **Marty Petersen,** The University of Idaho

Ernest Hemingway made his final stand in Idaho, where he'd been hunting and enjoying the outdoor life for several decades. In 1958 he and Mary Hemingway purchased a chalet on a hill with a view of the Big Wood River and the Sawtooth Mountains.

Hemingway's time in Idaho dated back to 1939, when Union Pacific Railroad chairman Averill Harriman invited Hemingway and other celebrities to Sun Valley. Hemingway hunted, fished, and drank in the local bars with Ingrid Bergman and Gary Cooper. In the fall of 1939, he worked on his novel *For Whom the Bell Tolls* in suite 206 at the Sun Valley Lodge.

Photos of Hemingway's last years in Idaho reveal a man who has aged rapidly. Confusion, paranoia, and doubt drew him inward. He'd survived two plane crashes in the African bush, but the concussions and internal injuries left a deep mark on his health. Those who wrote about him in his last years sway between two tacts: *papa was my good hunting pal* types, and the sycophants who charted his mental downfall.

I came across one noteworthy article written by the young Hunter S. Thompson for *The National Observer* in May, 1964. The title: *What Lured Hemingway to Ketchum?* Hunter would go on to write the outrageous drug and drink addled American classic: *Fear and Loathing in Las Vegas*. He later killed himself in the manner of Hemingway.

Thompson was influenced by Hemingway, both the writing and the lifestyle, and Hunter understood the pressures of worldwide fame on an American writer. Hunter might also have been the only writer who could have matched the old man drink for drink.

Hunter Thompson wondered why Hemingway had moved to Ketchum, and Hunter concluded that Idaho was the only place (in contrast to Spain, Cuba, Paris, Africa etc.), which had not changed since *the good years*. A place where the old man had come since 1939 to hunt, fish, and drink in the bars with the locals. The past was used up and written. All the *good country* was ruined and the shadows were closing in on Papa Hemingway. He was in retreat.

V The Bottom Line: Seeing it Clear and As a Whole

If you ride and if your memory is good
you may ride still through the forest of
the Irati with trees like drawings in a child's
fairy book. They cut those down. They ran
logs down to the river and they killed the fish...

— **Ernest Hemingway,**
Death in the Afternoon, Final Chapter

We've placed the old man in the West where he clawed out his last days. In the end, why should we give a damn about Hemingway? Let's get to the core of the deal. *The writing itself.* The poet Charles Bukowski, with whom I shared a correspondence for twenty years, once wrote me: *Hemingway is better when you're young.* The truth is that Bukowski *is better when you're young.* Much of Hemingway can be revisited with pleasure.

To get to the heart of Hemingway, proceed to the last chapter of *Death in the Afternoon*, his 1932 non-fiction treatise on Spanish

Bullfighting. Trust me. Forget the rest of the book, for now. It's a bit outdated, and chances are you aren't interested in the history of the bulls or the art of *toreo*, or your wife, husband, kid, or girlfriend might run up your nose at such politically in-correct fare. Ignore them.

Follow me. Go to the last chapter, in which he talks about everything which was left out of the book. There, succinctly in nine pages, you'll find the writer Hemingway and his ability to summon up the country, *any country*, and make you feel it, and enable you to carry it away with you.

He was a master at landscapes, at the changes in the country, and how the seasons revolve and work. Against this backdrop were the local characters and Hemingway's affinity and practiced eye for painting their faces, gestures, and manner of dialogue: bootblacks, bartenders, hotel keepers, whores, bullfighters, chauffeurs, and wine merchants. He possessed an ear and an eye, and a writer's heart.

Here he speaks of the things he's left out, and finishes with the hard earned wisdom that we cannot achieve it all in one book.

He begins this way:

> *If I could have made this enough of a book*
> *it would have had everything in it. The Prado,*
> *looking like some big American college building*
> *with sprinklers watering the grass early in the*
> *bright Madrid summer morning...*

And then he moves on to the miniature scenes left out of the main body of the book. In this chapter we find Hemingway. The well-hewn, matchless force of his writing. Forget the critics, and the putdowns and parodies. Forgive him his petty jealousies and drunken rants.

Here, in scattered settings, we are with him: on a Spanish train, with the closed window blinds blocking the sun, as the breeze blows against the blinds. The boy with the wicker basket of wine samples who shares the wine with everyone on the train, as the country rolls by, and the whole train, including Guardia Civil officers, becomes drunk.

A high mountain turn on a back road in Spain, where pine trees and blackberries come into focus by the roadside. And then Pamplona, which is already changing in 1932, as he writes:

They have built new apartment buildings
out over the sweep of plain that runs
to the edge of the plateau, so that now
you cannot see the mountains.

What would the old man now think of a Pamplona that has been ruined for a good fifty years, partly due to Hemingway imitators and their fixation with the running of the bulls in *The Sun Also Rises*, and the ruination of culture brought on by the Euro and European Union?

The scenes roll on and on in this chapter: swimming in the Irati river, and the gradual coldness of the water at different depths, and how the water felt as you sunk down into it. The shadow of leaves on the side of a horse. Clouds coming fast, moving in shadows over a wheat field. The loops of twisted garlic, the smell of olive oil, and the pitchforks made of natural wood, *the tines were branches*. The earthen jars of wine, twelve feet high, set side by side in a dark room.

He possessed the eye of a painter. He'd worked at it. He wrote, in *A Moveable Feast*, that when he was starving in Paris, he learned to write by visiting the Louvre Museum, standing in front of the Cezanne paintings for hours. He wrote in a painterly way. He *saw* and felt the country and distilled it down into a poetic language which makes us feel and see as well. But his language is never obtuse, or hard to decipher.

There's damn good reason why there have been more books written about Hemingway (and Jack Kerouac for that matter) than Twain, Faulkner, Fitzgerald, Steinbeck, and all...because of the overall effect Hemingway (and Kerouac in his own way) have had on American culture, the American lingo, and the American creative mind.

In this final chapter of an early bullfight treatise, you understand the honed-force of Hemingway's writing and his ability to carve out poetry from small scenes he experienced and then forged into his writer's memory. In this he is matchless. We read lines that roll out like folkloric verse.

Lets steal a short paragraph, refigure it, and create a poem called *In the Cafes:*

In the cafes where the boys are never wrong
In the cafes where they are all brave
In the cafes where the saucers pile up and
the drinks are figured in pencil
on the marble tops among the shucked shrimp

In the cafes of seasons lost and feeling good and
Everyman a success by eight o'clock
If someone can pay the scores in cafes

Yes, indeed. *If someone can pay the scores*. Ending this final chapter, he leaves us with the job of a writer:

We've seen it all go and we'll watch it go again.
The great thing is to last and get your work done
and see and hear and learn and understand; and
write when there is something to write that you know;
and not before; and not too damned much after.
Let those who want to save the world if you can
get to see it clear and as a whole. Then any part
you make will represent the whole if it's made truly.

There lies the goal. The heart of the creative task. *To see it clear and as a whole*...And that's what the old man did. Lived it. Drank it up. Wrote it. When he was on his game. And when he couldn't do it anymore he checked out. He died in the West. He remains a *Western* writer, because of his love of *country*: the trees, rivers, mountains, wild game, and an affinity for the everyday folk within these landscapes.

And the bulls. OK, the bulls. The bulls are missing from American history books. Fighting cattle came over on the first Spanish ships with the beef cattle, horses, conquistadores, wine, distilled spirits, and priests. The bulls were fought in the old ranch rings of Mexico, Texas, and California. They fought grizzly bears at *fiestas*.

This is our West, and Hemingway's West, and it winds back through Mexico, to those Spanish ships, and then Andalucía and back further to the Moors. Bulls in the pastures. Wine in the barrels. Men horseback. Death in the afternoon.

Hemingway knew all that. And bulls are still being fought in ritual, bloodless festivals in Texas and California. It rolls on.

Coda: Far out Past Where We Can Go: Facing Eternity

Ernest Hemingway won the Nobel Prize for Literature in 1954. After the two African plane crashes he wasn't in shape to travel to Europe, but he recorded a short speech and sent it in. Here's a part:

Writing, at its best, is a lonely life. Organizations for writers palliate the writer's loneliness but I doubt if they improve his writing. He grows in public stature as he sheds his loneliness and often his work deteriorates. For he does his work alone and if he is a good enough writer he must face eternity, or the lack of it, each day...It is because we have had such great writers in the past that a writer is driven far out past where he can go, out to where no one can help him.

Hemingway took the writing *far out past where he could go*, far past where anyone could help him. Throughout his lifetime he didn't join writer's clubs, teach writing classes, or move to Hollywood to write scripts. It wasn't his style. He was an outdoorsman who rose up to write at first light every morning of his working life. As long as he was able.

No matter, now, the Will James conflict, the bear trap saddle, and the inconsistent opinions of wormy detractors. The writing holds up, for all eternity, and his grave lies out West.

In the last good country.

When the Wolves No Longer Sing
Ian Tyson & the Re-invention of Cowboy Song

Empty house, children grown,
Old man rides these hills alone
How long? How long would it take
To find me?

— **Ian Tyson**
"Love Without End"

Winter. Elko, Nevada. 2005. Midnight. Holed up in a parked rental car. The windshield wipers are scooping away wet snow, and the fabled Montana poet, Paul Zarzyski, is sitting shotgun beside me. Wiping his eyes. Zarzyski being the bronc-riding poet from Great Falls, Montana, by way of Northern Wisconsin.

We're parked with the engine running and the music blasting. Two old high school football players in cowboy hats, caught up inside a deep Nevada winter. There's a fifty-foot concrete Polar Bear rearing up above us, pawing at a neon casino sign. Clawing at the frozen moon. Ice is falling off the beast's snout.

The statue is a monument to White King, the world's largest polar bear. The old boy himself is on display in the coffee shop, forty feet away, inside Elko's Commercial Hotel and Casino. The stuffed bear stands 10 feet 4 inches and weighed in at 2,200 pounds, before they shot, gutted, and stuffed him. He keeps a glass-eyed vigil on the old ladies at the slot machines. Elko is a long way from Vegas, baby.

The car heater hums and whirrs up against Ian Tyson's song "Love Without End." Love's gone way bad and the cowboy in the song rides away. Disappearing into the hills. The soul of a man is dying. How long will it take to find the body?

Work it out, it don't take long,
suddenly you're strong.
But I don't know what you do,
about the lonely.

"Damnit, I'm gonna cry," Zarzyski says.

"I know," I say. "The lonely."

"Goddamnit that's sad. Great song."

"Yeah," I say. "Chilling."

Chillingly bleak. Sad to the core. Too close for comfort. I know about the old man's personal life, you see. The man who wrote the song. Hell, it's about *all* our personal lives. Most cowboy songs don't go to that place in the heart. Cowboy *aloneness* is something you ride away from and become a night guard on a trail herd. Or you sign on to wrangle cattle in Mexico and bitch about your gal who ran off with a Philadelphia lawyer.

That's the way the old songs went down. *I've got no use for the women.* Or maybe: *Her parents didn't like me, now she's gone the same, if I'm writ' on your book love, just blot out my name.*

But what about the raw truth of Tyson ranching alone in that far Northern country, Alberta, a landscape he's declared unfit for anything but buffalo? The frozen earth goes eight feet deep and winter lasts forever. The dog has died. The best horses are gone. Sold. Twenty-year marriage falling apart. Kids won't talk to you. Lover disappeared. The divorce money is "hemorrhaging out of the bank." The Cowboy poetry scene has become a "petrified forest." No country for old men, gunsels, or grousers.

Try writing about *that*, amigo. Well the old man summed it up pretty damn good. "Love Without End." Could be a Tom McGuane story. But this one rhymes and rings through your bones. It invades the comfort zone. It questions the tired poetic maxim that love might last forever.

This was Ian Tyson circa 2005. The record is *Songs From a Gravel Road.* The gravel road runs between the main Tyson Ranch house and the stone cabin where Ian writes. The road is Ian's walking think-tank. Discarded song lines fall and weave themselves into the gravel. Crumbs for magpies.

Songs From A Gravel Road portrays a veteran cowboy-songwriter in his late 70s, *facing eternity or the lack of it every day,* to quote Papa Hemingway. Or shall we site Williams S. Burroughs, who surmised: "there was only one way out, I had to write my way out." This was after old Bill shot a cocktail glass off his wife's head in Mexico City, in a "William Tell experiment." Bill missed. Killed her. Went to Mexican jail. Became a writer. Love without end.

Ian Tyson. His friends, or those who use the word "friend" in the classic cowboy way, they all want him to be the legendary cowboy songwriter. No one yearns to talk about the personal crap. The closest shrink is in Calgary – forty miles away. And cowboys don't go to psychologists. Naw. They chew on it and spit it out into an empty tomato juice can. They ride off into the hills like Kirk Douglas in *Lonely Are the Brave*. They talk to themselves, and finally get run down by a toilet-fixtures truck on a rainy highway. They die like Kirk, talking to their dead horse. Alone. Brave. Clawed up inside. Roll the credits.

Back to that Elko winter's night in a rental Chevrolet. Another slab of ice falls off the polar bear's snout and Zarzyski is rubbing his eyes, moved to tears by a song. This was a moment when I understood once again what a great song is able to do. Make us cry. Or elevate our souls. Slap us around. Three minutes of truth serum, straight to the heart.

Lawrence Ferlinghetti, the esteemed Beat poet, now over 90, recently wrote: *Woody Guthrie, Bob Dylan, Johnny Cash and you songwriters are the true popular poets of America...voices moving everyone more than poets in books, the printing press having made them so silent.* It took guts for a famous poet to say that. The songwriters, the good ones, inhabit permanent rooms in people's souls, while out in the literary world poets and novelists get the grants and suckle on the tired teat of the University system. *If you can't write, teach.* Old Indian dictum.

But I'll give a nod to W.B. Yeats. "Love Without End" rings with the feeling etched in lines from Yeats' "A Prayer for Old Age":

God guard me from those thoughts men think
In the mind alone
He that sings a lasting song
Thinks in a marrowbone

Great songs don't issue forth from the mind alone. The arise from deeper wells. Love or sorrow welling up in the blood and marrow. Foaming over. In the Elko rental car Tyson is moving onto the next song.

I passed over Raton, stood there alone
Staring into the heart of the night
Across that dark plain to El Paso...

Tyson looks down from Raton Pass and envisions the lights of Las Cruces and El Paso. Fragments and scenes from a desert evening. A panorama of images. Across that great Chihuahua Desert plain, *The Queen of El Paso*, sleeps alone in a distant house. Dreaming. Out of reach. Cattle on the desert are milling around. The horses in Tyson's trailer *will not stand*. Mexican illegals are moving up from the border, underneath the wire and through the ditches, headed up the brutal escape route the Spanish called *El Camino del Muertos*. The Highway of the Dead.

It's a Breughel painting. Muted oils and starlight. Hidden Mexicans, sleeping beauties, trailered-horses, and an elegant melody pushing it along. A modern cowboy waltz. With guts and grace.

At the line of desire
Seven strands of barbed wire
To hold back the on-rushing tide
Many dreams have been brought to the border
Down in the canyons, down in the culverts...

The cowboy in the song has poetic night vision. He sees into culverts filled with ditch water, hubcaps, and hidden Mexicans. A desert wind is building. Something is coming at us. Something else is out of reach. Much of it is behind us. We move on.

Tyson gets back into his truck and drives over the high pass of Raton and closes the door on it all. Enters another scene. Another song. The melody drifts away, but the images do not fade. Who the hell mentions culverts in a song?

This is songwriting.

I recall Tyson turning to me once in his stone house and declaring: *I fell in love with the English language at age 50.* That was it. You have to love the lingo. Taste the weight of words. Ride the slang. Steal from tradition. Then pray for the muse to intervene.

Art, I guess you call it. Sleight of hand. Everything is beautifully out of reach and persistent in memory. But forgive the witty hogwash. Leave it to music critics. Songs need to be absorbed and enjoyed, not torn apart. The good ones stick with you. Forever.

Back, one last time, to that Elko winter night. The music rolls through the rental car. Zarzyski is shaking his head, staring at the lights across the parking lot at The Stockman's Casino. White King's marble eyes shine through the fogged-up Commercial Hotel window. An old lady lights another cigarette. Retired waitress. Insomniac. Flat-hat buckaroos stagger from bar to bar. The whorehouses are heating up and the Basque Cafés are closing. Tyson's opera continues. He's seen all this.

A last slab of hard ice falls off the polar bear. The windshield cracks. The record ends.

II Stories He'd Tell

All along the shoreline,
Arbutus trees do grow
And watching from their red limbs,
Kingfishers come and go
And their secrets of hidden coves,
As they call cross the bay
Late in the afternoon on salt rocks
Where we lay

— **Ian Tyson**, "Stories He'd Tell"

Above are the well-carved lines from an early Tyson song, "Stories He'd Tell." Ian is a kid, sitting on rocky shoreline with his father. They're staring at a wilderness bay in British Columbia. Tyson's father is asking his boy what he intends to do with his life, and Tyson hasn't figured it out yet. Young Ian is still caught up in his *aimless ways*. He's enthralled by his father, George Tyson, who'd emigrated from Liverpool, England in 1906. A man who knew horses and had fought in The Great War.

Was his faith so strong,
had he doubts that didn't show?
Seeing life and death,
had he learned what I don't know?

That song always took me to a place that the literature of my youth could not. *Huckleberry Finn, The Catcher in the Rye,* or *To Kill a Mockingbird.* I love those books. But the loss of innocence rang through Tyson's "Stories He'd Tell," sailing on a vocal instrument that hit all the high notes. Not the same Tyson who, sixty years later, would end up on that gravel road. Voice half shot. Women gone. No way out but *through*. Dead wildflowers on the kitchen table next to a bottle of vodka. Still writing his way into a deeper understanding of what went right or wrong, and how the country was. Enduring the heavy weather. Making it rhyme. Reinventing cowboy music. Wondering what old Irving Berlin might have said about all *this blowed out country* and love gone bad.

Ian's first thirteen albums were recorded as one half of the groundbreaking folk group (and country rock pioneers) Ian and Sylvia. The 1960s. While my father and older brother were drawn to the rodeos, racetracks, and Los Angeles Horse and Mule Auction, I was sneaking into the back door of The Ash Grove, a folk club on Melrose in Hollywood, where I first saw Ian and Sylvia. I was a teenaged wanna-be songwriter, bone dumb in the ways of the music business.

Ian met Sylvia in Toronto in 1959. They recorded a dozen albums. They were the real thing. Their concerts weren't peppered with *shtick* jokes about tuning guitars, or the *faux seriousness* and moral righteousness of protest songs. When Bob Dylan picked up the electric guitar and the protest movement was all but over. Protest songs had a *shelf life*, to quote Sylvia.

When Dylan walked onto that Newport Folk Festival stage and sang "Maggie's Farm" backed up by the Paul Butterfield Blues Band (with the feral screaming of Mike Bloomfield's Stratocaster guitar) Pete Seeger began to weep. Literally break down. Sylvia Tyson told me that one. She was standing right next to Seeger. Bye-bye protest movement, hello Rock and Roll.

Dylan wasn't deaf to the overwhelming impact of The Beatles. In the next eighteen months Bob Dylan would record three albums filled with over thirty songs which changed the shape of modern music. Tyson sang up arbutus trees, but Dylan sang of *haunted frightened trees* and a *windy beach of crazy sorrow*. He was absorbing Arthur Rimbaud and Allen Ginsberg.

The first snare beat of Dylan's "Like a Rolling Stone" was the shot heard round the world. Most songwriters of that era were drowned in Dylan's wake. Tyson observed and stuck to his own game.

But hold on. A few years earlier Bob Dylan writes "Blowin' in the Wind" and then walks into a Greenwich Village bar and sings it to Ian Tyson. Tyson thinks, *hell, I can do that,* and retreats to his manager's apartment to write "Four Strong Winds." Sylvia Tyson, not to be outdone, goes to the Earl Hotel, sits in the bathtub where the cockroaches can't get her, and writes "You Were on My Mind," a hit for the group "We Five."

It's unimaginable, today, that these big songs were being written right out of the box. These folks hit the ball so far out of the park no one ever found the ball. "Four Strong Winds" was later voted the most popular song ever written in Canada.

Tyson remarks:

> *Damned if I know what the four strong winds are. It was basically the first song I'd written.*
> *It came real easy...when I got the first check I went and bought a big cattle farm East of Toronto...when I got the first big check for 'Someday Soon' I bought the adjoining farm...*
> *I started getting seriously into breeding*
> *cutting horses.*

Horses. The code. Dylan broke the code. As did Ian and Sylvia, and few others. In search of *the code* I ended up, much later, writing songs with both these folks. Ian and Sylvia. It's a helluva' way to grow up and become a writer, sitting across from your idols, trying to contribute something that doesn't ring off their *built-in bullshit detectors*.

Songwriting school. Bring you lunch, dinner, and a bedroll. Hold fast.

III The Bars Along Main Street and The Code of Tradition

> *So I'll work on the towboats,*
> *With my slippery city shoes*
> *Which I swore I would never do again.*
> *Through the grey, fogbound straits,*
> *Where the cedars stand watchin'...*
> *I'll be far off and gone like summer wages.*

— **Ian Tyson,** "Summer Wages"

Back history: Ian Tyson was born on Vancouver Island, did a turn of bronc riding in the 50s, and took a degree in the graphic arts. He broke a leg on the broncs and, recovering in the hospital, picked up the guitar. He read Kerouac and Hemingway. He's a voracious reader to this day. If he has one piece of advice for young songwriters it's: *read, read, read.* How many other cowboy singers subscribe to *The New Yorker?*

I've seen him peruse *Bartlett's Familiar Quotations* for hours and then look up at me and declare: *Old Tennyson sure knew a few things about love.* He's a fan of Toronto poet/ novelist Michael Ondaatje (*The English Patient*) who crafts sophisticated love poems like "The Cinnamon Peeler":

If I were a cinnamon peeler
I would ride your bed
And leave the yellow bark dust
On your pillow.

In the late 1950s Ian played with a rockabilly band, *The Sensational Stripes* in Vancouver, B.C. They opened once for Buddy Holly. He gigged in the rugged bars along Main Street. Twenty years later I paid my dues in those same bars on Skid Row, Vancouver: The Gulf Club, The Commercial Hotel, and The Smiling Buddha, where in the 1970s, there were still separate entrances for men and women. The whore and knife bars of Apache Pass.

Hastings Street, near Main St. in Vancouver, is the first known Skid Row (or Skid Road) in history. The term connects back one hundred and fifty years to the logging trade in Vancouver. Tyson later wrote about it all in "Summer Wages":

In all the beer parlors, all down along Main Street
The dreams of the season, are all spilled down on the floor
Of the great stands of timber, just waiting there for falling
And the hookers standing watchfully, as they wait there by
    the door.

The trained visual artist in Tyson allowed him to paint western landscapes into the song lines. Cedar trees, magpies, hidden coves, fogbound straits, and Main Street hookers. A touch of Maynard Dixon, Charles M. Russell – an urban dash of Edward Hopper. The word paintings are built atop a solid foundation of old Scots-Irish folk music. As Bob Dylan revealed recently, his (Dylan's) song ideas can be traced back to folk and blues music. Ditto Ian Tyson.

Sayeth Dylan:

> *These songs didn't come out of thin air. I didn't just make them up out of whole cloth...It all came out of traditional music: traditional folk music, traditional rock & roll and traditional big-band swing orchestra music.*
>
> *I learned lyrics and how to write them from listening to folk songs. And I played them, and I met other people that played them, back when nobody was doing it. Sang nothing but these folk songs, and they gave me the code for everything that's fair game, that everything belongs to everyone.*

Code talkers.

Another anecdote: It's the late 1950s. Tyson's driving an old Dodge down from B.C. to visit a beautiful Greek gal-friend in L.A. The car breaks down on the Grapevine Hill, outside of Bakersfield. Tyson puts on his beat straw cowboy hat and sticks out his thumb.

Sam Peckinpah, then working on the TV series *Gunsmoke,* stops and picks Ian up. He asks Tyson if he can ride horses. Tyson boasts: *Hell, yes, I can ride anything.* Pecikinpah gives Tyson a business card and says he can get him cowboy film work.

Later Tyson gets kicked out of his girlfriend's joint and hightails it back to Canada. Forgetting Peckinpah's offer. Years later he meets Sam, on the set of *Pat Garret and Billy the Kid.* Dylan's in the film and also composing the music. The two code talkers. There's more of Tyson's influence on Dylan in Suze Rotolo's book – *A Freewheelin' Time.*

"There hasn't been a Bob Dylan in cowboy poetry," said Tyson in his book *I Never Sold My Saddle,* "The Bob Dylan of cowboy music has been me."

The 60s faded into the 1970s and Ian and Sylvia broke up. Tyson moved out West. Re-married and bought a ranch near Calgary with money from Neil Young's cover of "Four Strong Winds."

There was a great record from the 70s – *Old Eon* – but it was a time for Tyson to reorganize. He couldn't relate to Nashville networking or the Cosmic Cowboy scene down in Texas. He edged deeper into the cutting horses and his ranch. Part one of his career was fading behind him. The music biz passed him by, and he didn't seem to give a damn.

IV The King of the Mood Swings

Walking on a gravel road
Trying to think of higher things
Trying to shift my heavy load
I'm the king of the mood swings

— **Ian Tyson,** "This is My Sky"

There was an old Irish horseshoer that frequented Tyson's Ranch in the early 1980s. A man named Neil Hope. He shoed Tyson's horses and always asked Ian to sing a song or two. Tyson would pull out the guitar and sing old ballads like "Rambler Gambler" and "The Streets of Laredo."

"The Streets of Laredo" can be traced back hundreds of years to "The Unfortunate Rake," a song about a man dying on the street outside a syphilis clinic in London. Singing the traditional cowboy standards in the kitchen gave Tyson the yen to record *Old Corrals and Sage Brush* in 1983. He covered one of my first songs: "Gallo del Cielo," at a time when no other backslapper had the guts to take a shot at it. A seven-minute song about cockfighting? Tyson could relate. We began corresponding about co-writing and met in New York, traded ideas, and came up with "Navajo Rug."

On the third record, in his 1980s resurgence, Tyson hit the groove, dead on, with *Cowboyography*. He never looked back. *Cowboyography* embodies at least five Western Music classics: "Fifty Years Ago," "The Gift" (about Charlie Russell), "Cowboy Pride," "Old Cheyenne" (a reprise), "Navajo Rug," and "Claude Dallas." I co-wrote the last two.

Still the student.

Fast forward three decades to present and at least a dozen records of finely crafted, soulful songs, and more Tyson classics: "Will James," "M.C. Horses," "Blue Mountain of Mexico," "The Rockies Turn Rose," "The Road to Las Cruces," "Blue Mountains of Mexico," "This is My Sky," and others – take your pick.

Over the years we co-wrote "Navajo Rug," "Claude Dallas," "The Banks of the Musselshell," "The Rose of the San Joaquin," "Heartaches are Stealin'," "Ross Knox," "When the Wolves No Longer Sing," and a few more. I kept learning from the master. Let's open a window, back in time, into that cabin where we used to write.

V Songwriting School, Bring Your Bedroll

Nashville has a stranglehold on radio, and I don't relate to what they do. They don't want to play sixty-year old guys, they want to play twenty two year old guys...these writers and their songs about 'personal relationships.' They can't write knife and whore songs like Tom Russell.

— **Ian Tyson,** "I Never Sold My Saddle"

The cabin stood in the foothills of the Canadian Rockies. *The rocks* the old man called them. There was a small knotty pine kitchen with a coffee machine. An icebox filled with beer and soft drinks. We brought a large thermos of coffee from the main ranch, thirty miles away. There were sandwiches for lunch. Ham. Cheese. Tuna. Roast Beef. This was in the late 1980s.

The nearest neighbor was a mile off. A woman who kept goats. The cabin shelves were filled with books on the West. Western prints on the wall above Tyson's working table. The tools were set down there in strategic places, next to a writing pad where he wrote fragments and lyrics, left-handed, in strong script.

He put the words down with the firm hand of a sketcher. He did not trifle with words or ideas that weren't strong enough to be committed to the white sheet. The hands of a graphic artist who'd once designed the label of Resdan Dandruff Shampoo.

More tools: Pencils and pens. A metronome for practicing guitar grooves and strict musical time. A small cassette tape recorder with melodies and ideas. And the reference books: Dictionary, Bible, Thesaurus, *Bartlett's Familiar Quotes*, and a road atlas to look up place names.

It was that eternal quest for the big song. Tyson signed a book for me back then: *Friend Tom Russell, may we always quest and chase the big one.* Then he drew a buffalo skull in the spirit of Charles M. Russell. The search for the big one. The reaching back for the code. A prayer for the alchemy.

Ian and I would drive out to the cabin every morning after chores and work on songs most of the day. Tyson might leave me up there for the night, to contemplate wolves and bears, as I supped the red wine. To work the songs all evening. A twenty-four hour gig. One afternoon he handed me Teddy Blue Abbott's book, *We Pointed Them North*, and said:

Here. Try this. There's got to be a song in here about a kid on a long trail drive. Riding toward the Musselshell River up North. See if you can suss one out. That's your assignment.

I read the book that night, drank the red wine, and found inspiration for a bundle of odd lines to show Ian. I learned a hell of a lot about the Teddy Blue Abbot's West that night, and where Larry McMurtrey got many of his ideas for *Lonesome Dove*. Tyson added more lyrical elements which later became "The Banks of the Musselshell."

Songwriting school. You couldn't beat it.

In the early years I was the gunsel who jumped out of the truck to open the gates. He called me *the king of the whore and knife ballads*. I called him *El Viejo*, the *old one*. As friends we've had our ups and downs. Battles on the road. Minor stuff arguing about sound and song. The backside of the music world. I'll toss out a quote from Dr. Hunter Thompson on the foibles of the music biz:

The music business is a cruel and shallow money trench, a long plastic hallway where thieves and pimps run free, and good men die like dogs. There's also a negative side.

It all worked out. I ended up getting married to a lovely Swiss gal. The ceremony took place in Elko, at *The Happily Ever After Wedding Chapel,* and Ian Tyson was our best man. Ramblin Jack Elliot sang "The Rake and Rambling Boy." I was in the presence of my heroes.

It felt like I'd graduated from song school.

VI When the Wolves No Longer Sing/Full Circle

The old songs are forgotten
Gone with the raven on the wing
And love no longer matters
And the wolves no longer sing

— **Ian Tyson and Tom Russell,**
"When the Wolves No Longer Sing"

Seven years ago, in the midst of his vocal and romance troubles, Tyson was in El Paso and we were going head to head on a song idea. I studied his face. We were both hung over and edgy. Acrawl with nerves. He was hurting.

Tyson grabbed his guitar, went out and sat under an Elm tree and strummed away for an hour, searching for an idea and a melody. Singing to the doves, high up in rotten limbs. I watched and listened through the window. He summoned up the old ballad, "Lord Lovel." Beautiful and weird. Singing away his pain and searching back through *the code* and the magic, and a new way out of the darkness.

> *Lord Lovel stood at his castle gate*
>   *combing his milk white steed...*
> *"On where are you going Lord Lovel?" she said*
> *"Oh where are you going?" said she.*
> *"I'm going, my dear Lady Nancy Bell*
> *"Strange countries for to see."*

Tyson returned spouting about *strange countries* and *milk white steeds*. From the shadows of that Elm tree he'd arrived a modern variation on "Lord Lovel." It concerned our friend Ross Knox, the muleteer, being fired from his pack train job with the Arizona Park Service for refusing to wear a crash helmet instead of a cowboy hat.

We repaired to the main house, where Ian's old bottle of Grey Goose vodka sat in the freezer. It's been there for six years and gone through two refrigerators. We'll move it up to Santa Fe and make it available when we've both got another song idea.

Enough. *Don't always try to be Tolstoy, Russell*...Ian yelled at me once. Everything isn't a whore and knife ballad. You have to cough up a little tenderness.

A week ago, as I write this, Ian sent me a dub of his fine new record: *Carnero Vaquero*. The record takes Tyson full circle – starting with the traditional "Doney Gal," then a nod to Ian and Sylvia ("Darcy Farrow"), an older Tyson classic ("Will James"), and a co-write with myself: "When the Wolves No Longer Sing." Plus new Tyson gems.

The strongest might be "The Flood" – true tale of the Alberta flood, which wiped out far more than the landscape. Acts of God and shattered marriages. The album is a keeper and a fitting addition to the Tyson canon.

Okay, Tolstoy, sum up the re-invention angle. If we were to consider the top Western songs of all time they would fall into loose categories: the traditional classics, the poems turned into song, the gunfighter ballads, the film songs, the tin pan alley gems, and modern country and pop takes on The West.

What does Tyson bring to the table? A link to the past. An eye on the future. A love of history and literature. An articulate outlook on the West, coupled with a deep honesty about the personal life of a cowboy who's lived with love, and then alone the past years. A re-invention without the clichés. But there's more.

Tyson re-emerged in 1983 with cowboy material. Starting over with traditional songs. But he'd been there before. (He sometimes forgets this). Twenty years earlier, in 1963, he'd written one of the biggest cowboy songs of all time: "Someday Soon." A Western standard.

Ian and Sylvia had written and recorded: "Someday Soon," "Four Rode By," "Short Grass," "Barney," "Lonely Girls," "The Renegade," "Wild Geese," "Old Cheyenne" (the original) and others. Their first albums covered traditional gems "Rambler Gambler," "Spanish is the Loving Tongue," and "Old Blue." They'd digested of *the code* Dylan mentions.

The bars and coffee houses in early 60s Greenwich Village (and the world) rang with the songs of a few cowboys and Indians – Ian Tyson, Ramblin Jack Elliott, Harry Jackson (later a renowned Western sculptor), Derroll Adams, and Peter La Farge ("The Ballad of Ira Hayes"). The cowboy song has been with us over one hundred years.

Ian Tyson's artistic endurance, deep catalogue, and continual re-invention of Cowboy song entitle Ian to a statue outside The Cowboy Hall of Fame – much the same as Casey Tibbs' on that bronze bronc in front of The Rodeo Hall of Fame.

These are people Oliver LaFarge called *Seldom Men,* men the likes of whom we may never encounter again.

But our good times are all gone
and I'm bound for movin' on
I'll look for you if I'm ever back this way...

— **Ian Tyson,** "Four Strong Winds"

Gallo del Cielo
The Journey of the One Eyed Rooster

Gallo del Cielo was a rooster born in heaven,
So the legends say,
His wings they had been broken
He had one eye rolling crazy in his head...

— Gallo del Cielo

His name was Augustine. He was originally from Toluca, near Mexico City, and he'd been around the frontier forever. Fixing rooves, hanging rain gutters, cleaning yards, planting pecan trees. Mucking out horse stalls and all the odd, bottom line jobs of the horse trade. He was a good man. At least three quarters good. There was a certain part of him always working on an angle, and the angle usually had to do with pumping a few more dollars out of you. He was one of those characters who was a jack-of-all trades and a master of the sudden dire warning. *Cuidado!* Action was needed at once, because something was about to collapse or blow up around the hacienda. Horses were bound to stampede and pipes might burst, and if that thing wasn't fixed immediately we were all in trouble.

That *thing* usually entailed another three to five days of work. If Augustine was painting your front porch, he'd indicate to you that the porch was soon to collapse if he didn't build a new wood frame to prop the roof up. Then the new frame needed to be painted. And the roof itself should be replaced soon or it might cave in and kill you while you were sleeping. You get the picture. Augustine was a good man. But a hustler. That's how he survived. And prospered. On the frontier.

Here's the deal. One day, several years ago, I left Augustine in charge of the yard while I went out on tour around the U.S. He had the keys to the front gate and the number of my cell phone. He was going to keep an eye on things, you see, and keep the yard clean. *No problema.* That's another issue. Augustine didn't speak a word of English, and my Spanish has grown sketchy, but effective in the clench. With hand signs and bad grammar I get the job done. *Mostly.* A lot of dialogue on this border gets lost in translation, like a tequila dream. There's a universal sign around here of holding up your hands, elbows bent, palms up and out, pointed away from each side of your body, then shrugging your shoulders. This means: *I refuse to accept responsibility for any actions – past, present, and future.*

Okay, so I'm gone a week and Augustine calls me up in a panic. Something to do with *gallos*. He kept shouting the word over and over.

"*Gallos?*" I yelled back. "*What Gallos? Roosters?*"

"*Gallos,*" he kept saying. The connection was bad and I was in the middle of a sound check.

"*Gallos,*" he yelled, following it with a long string of speed-talking street Spanish I couldn't make out.

"You mean my song, *Gallo del Cielo?*" I was kidding him.

"*Si, si, gallos! Gallos!*" He kept running on about something to do with roosters.

"Okay, Okay." I said. "*Todo bien.* Whatever..." Maybe he had to build a high fence to keep the neighbors roosters out. Or maybe he wanted another one of my cowboy records to give to a friend. Because of my *Gallo* song, which Augustine loved. *Quien sabe?* Another scam.

Thirty years ago I'd written that eleven verse song, a *corrido* in English, about a fighting rooster with one eye. The rooster from heaven. *Gallo del Cielo*. It had become a hit among cowboy audiences. That rooster kept raising its one-eyed presence my life. Maybe Augustine had translated it into Mexican street Spanish. To *record it.* Make a million. Whatever. Maybe he wanted the publishing. I believed this guy was capable of hatching anything. But I was busy. I hung up.

Two weeks later I drove up to my front gate. I got out of the truck and reached out for the lock and I noticed odd motion inside the fence to my right. There were three circular cages lined up in a row, and inside each cage, perched on a stick running through the wire, sat three roosters. *Fighting* roosters. *Gallos de pelea*. There was no mistaking the high arched necks, crimson feathers and cocky demeanor. They were also hooded to keep them calm. Warriors. A fighting rooster operation. On my property. All within easy view of the front road, where farmers and ranchers and moms taking their kids to school could evidence what that crazy-assed songwriter was into now. *Chicken fighting.* No wonder he wrote that depressing song. He's a *cockfighter*! There goes the neighborhood. Bring out the tar and feathers, etc. Soon they'd be marching up the streets with their signs. The humane society backed by the Salvation Army Band, followed by *Mothers Against Cockfighting*.

Augustine and I had strong *palaver* about this deal, an hour later.

It was all a big misunderstanding, he said in *Spanglish*. He threw his hands up, palms pointed to the side, in the universal gesture. He and his partner only needed a temporary place to keep the roosters. They were planning to move them any day now. They were waiting on something. He stood out there near the cages, gesticulating wildly. Then he proposed to make me a partner in the operation. A third party. Probably *the investor* I was thinking. They were going to win a lot of money. He pointed down to the evil looking cocks. The *gallos* were ready to tear each other's eyes out. The roosters were champions, he said. We would all make out. *Millionarios*!

"*Basta. Basta.*" I kept saying. "*Finito.* Get them out of here. Illegal!"

"No!" Augustine said. "No! In Chaparral. No *illegal*! *No, no, no.*"

Okay. Cockfighting was actually legal in New Mexico at this time (a few years ago), and the New Mexico State line was just up the street. And maybe it wasn't illegal to actually *to own* these roosters in Texas, but I wanted them gone anyway.

The palaver and sign lingo went on and on, and I finally agreed that they could keep the roosters on the property for two weeks, provided they moved the operation to my back field. Out of sight from the main road. This they did. Augustine introduced his partner, a little man in a cheap straw cowboy hat, long sideburns, and pointy-towed boots with silver tips. He looked like miniature version of the *charro* singer Vincente Fernandez. *Chapo*, I believe his name was. He died his long sideburns and mustache with boot polish. A *puro macho caballero* in cheap boots. A *cockfighter* right out of a grade-B Mexican movie.

They trained the birds every afternoon. *The partners.* Training entailed the boys swallowing a half dozen beers while sparring the roosters. A battery operated radio played *narco-corrido* songs and *rancheras* from an AM radio station over in Juarez. They'd pull the birds from the cages and hold the beasts by the tails and face them off, then allow the roosters to thrust at each other without making contact. It built endurance. Like sparring.

The roosters looked pretty damn *game* to me, but I wasn't investing. It made for an entertaining happy hour. I would pour a cold beer or hefty glass of *Rioja* and go out back to watch the birds work and listen to the music. Colorful as hell. The boys were planning on their first fight in Chaparral, a nearby New Mexico town. Chaparral had two official gaming pits, with organized cockfights every Saturday. The boys showed me the little program cards, which were printed with ornate fighting-cock graphics and *Tecate* beer advertisements on the back. It looked official alright.

Augustine kept humming *Gallo de Cielo,* trying to entice me into the deal. I was never getting away from that damn chicken song. It was taking over my life. I had to sing it every night on the road. All six minutes. It took a good deal of concentration. You had to remember the names of all the California towns where Carlos Zaragoza fought his rooster, until old one-eye met his match. It was a good song, sure enough, but now I had these *gallos del pelea* in my back yard. It was the curse of the one-eyed rooster.

The whole matter was resolved a few days later when a pack of wild dogs ravaged the neighborhood, wiping out three of my neighbor's guinea hens, a peacock, two turkeys, and all three of Augustine's fighting roosters. *Well two and a half.* One *gallo* staggered off into the apple trees and hid in there a few months, his spirit broken. He was found face-down in an irrigation ditch. He couldn't take it anymore. Game over. We suspected suicide. Augustine disappeared for a few months, muttering about trying to raise money to buy a broken down race horse in Santa Teresa.

Since then my neighbor has been fond of citing verses from *Gallo del Cielo.* He keeps mentioning the time I was almost in the fighting rooster business. You have to endure these jibes when you've written a cockfighting *corrido.* But allow me tell you a few more stories surrounding *El Gallo.* The anecdotes are becoming as legendary as the song, and the song might be more legendary than the songwriter.

II The Wild Dogs of Mexico

> *Carlos Zaragoza left his home in Casas Grande*
> *When the moon was full*
> *No money in his pocket,*
> *Just a locket of his sister framed in gold.*
> *He headed for El Sueco, stole a rooster*
> *Called Gallo del Cielo...*

I wrote Gallo del Cielo in a garage in Mountain View, California in 1979. I'd been in the music business about eight years and quit for awhile to tend bar in San Francisco. I was trying to write novels and concoct better songs. I worked at a comedy club called *The Holy City Zoo,* where Robin Williams dropped by to hone his routines. He helped me pour beer. During the week I wrote songs in an empty garage down the peninsula. I had a few notes made in Mexico, and an idea for a long tragic story with a *corrido* form, like a gunfighter ballad, but I have no full recollection how this Gallo saga was created that morning in the garage. Townes Van Zandt used to call them *sky songs*, because they seem to fall out of the heavens. *Gallo del Cielo*. Rooster from heaven.

A *corrido*, in English, about cockfighting? The *corrido* is a long, running story in rhyme. From the Spanish word *correr*: to run. *Corridos* sung during the Mexican Revolution link back to similar stories sung by the Moors when they invaded Spain. The Moors invented much of what has colored our deep West – from horsemanship to *reata* braiding. And cockfighting was an ancient blood sport which had been blessed by St. Augustine of Hippo, who thought God directed the action of the great fighting roosters. Maybe I absorbed this through my fallen-away Catholic bones.

Okay. I'm in the garage with a bunch of song notes. Fragments about Pancho Villa. About three years before I'd taken the Chihuahua-Pacific train from Chihuahua, Mexico, up to a little town called Creel in the Sierra Tarahumara. They called this the *chicken train* (of course) because it stopped at every station along the mountain line, and old ladies would come up to the train windows and sell tamales and quesadillas and mangoes and things I couldn't identify, let alone be stupid enough to eat. It was a wild, hot ride – twisting and switch backing up the Sierra.

We arrived in Creel, a few hours from the rim of the Copper Canyon, and I stayed at an old inn owned by an old man they called *The Professor*. The whole scene was right out of the movie: *The Treasure of the Sierra Madre,* or that Sam Peckinpah film: *Bring Me the Head of Alfredo Garcia*. Creel was a fly-blown village where *mal hombres* on bony, spavined horses clattered through the town square and rabid little rat dogs snarled at you 'round ever corner. I've been back since. It hasn't changed. It's the *wild west*, amigo.

Creel is a crossroads for lumbermen, drug dealers, beggars, and Tarahumara Indians selling rough wooden carvings and blankets. The French poet Antonin Artaud went crazy around here eating peyote with the Tarahumara. If you should research the town of Creel on your computer, you'll find that almost every recent news item and film involves a major gunfight, with automatic weapons, between drug families. It's a quaint little town all right. Perfect for the beginning of any *narco corrido*.

Back to 1976. This hotel *Professor* took me on a little tour, out to one of the Tarahumara caves. An Indian woman with a serape around her head sold me a toy violin she'd made. These were an ancient people. Corn planters, goat herders, and cave dwellers. They had a wise look behind their milky eyes, as if they were waiting for western civilization to rot. They'd survive up in their caves. The husband was off running through the mountains. The Tarahumara are known for their ability to run long distances without tiring. In fact they're considered the greatest long distance runners in the world. The *Professor* filled me in on all this.

I could go on and on about Creel, but the point here is that once *The Professor* had my ear, he bent it with Pancho Villa legends. All the way back from those caves he told me stories. Pancho Villa will never go away in the mind of the people, or in the songs of the West. His image is on the pack of tortillas I bought in Switzerland this summer. The truth of Villa's history is complex; the myth of Villa outlives the facts. He was a slippery old ghost. Pancho invaded Columbus, New Mexico in 1916, and the U.S. sent Black Jack Pershing after him, with a young George Patton in tow, but they never caught him. He was finally assassinated by his own people. His last words were: *don't let it end like this, tell them I said something.*

It was *The Professor* who told me Pancho used to ride through the mountains, during the Revolution, and take over the big ranchos and haciendas on behalf of *the people's revolutionary cause.* If one of the large landowners had a beautiful daughter, then Pancho would offer to marry the daughter, on the spot, in exchange for letting the landowner keep his land. I guess there was a priest travelling with the boys. Pancho married quite a few young women in this manner. *Dozens at a time.* So sayeth *The Professor.*

Villa didn't drink. He liked cigars, American ice cream, good horses, and pretty women. One of my favorite Villa corridos is *Siete Leguas*, the song about Pancho's famous horse. The steed could run seven leagues without tiring. I suppose I was beginning to dream up my own *corrido*, like *Siete Leguas*. A historical action ballad, seeped in Spanish culture.

Back to the young Mexican women. That Villa marriage anecdote stuck in my mind, and I used the idea, later, in the refrain of *Gallo del Cielo*. Carlos Zaragoza steals the infamous one-eyed rooster, wades across the Rio Grande, and plans to fight *Gallo* up the California coast, in order make enough money buy back the land Pancho stole from his father. Carlos is promising all this in letters home to his sister back in Mexico. She was probably the ugly one. The spinster that Pancho didn't marry.

Now back to that garage in Mountain View.

I polished up the song in a few hours then went into the house and sang it straight through to my first wife. She got up from the table, with tears in her eyes, and told me I'd written my first great song. Now I must say, at that particular point in time, there was a question (among my in-laws) of whether this songwriting deal was going to work out for me as a viable career. ("*When is Tom going to face reality?*" Etc.) *Gallo* solved all that, and in fact the old rooster took off down the road and got me involved in situations I would have never dreamed up. That's the great thing about songs. They have a life of their own. Like your children. Some leave the house and become doctors and lawyers. Some go to prison. All are God's children.

I'd written the song. All I had to do now was hang on. And *remember the words.*

III The Asphalt Jungle

Hola my Theresa I am thinking of you now
In Santa Barbara
I have fifteen hundred dollars and the locket
With your picture framed in gold
Tonight I'll put it all on the fighting spurs
Of Gallo del Cielo...

Two years now after I'd written the song I'm in New York. The asphalt jungle. Trying to make ends meet. Driving taxi cabs twelve hours a day and working on a novel for The William Morris agency. The novel is going nowhere. The cab driving is killing me. Twelve hour shifts. Six at night, 'til six in the morning. Bad dudes in mirrored sunglasses in the back seat, staring at my neck. Guns in their socks. Or so I imagined. This was the early 1980's New York of graffiti-ridden streets, muggings, and murder.

One night I'm driving down a dark avenue at two in the morning and a group of dangerous looking Puerto Rican gents are blocking the middle of the street, flagging me down. Six of them. The cab company boss told me never to stop in those situations. Cab drivers were in season that year for robbery and murder. So I jammed the gas pedal down and scattered these *cabrones*. I passed them and they screamed and cursed. Then my cab seemed to explode. It flew up into the air and crashed down in a blast of scraping metal, yellow sparks, and doom. I assumed they'd tossed a hand grenade under the car and I whispered a *Hail Mary*, threw my money under the seat, and reached for a tire iron.

These guys ran up to me, shouting something like: *"Que paso? You okay? What you trying to do, loco? We were trying to warn you, hombre, 'bout that hole!"* Indeed. *The hole.* I got out of the car and there was a ten foot deep chasm in the collapsed street. About fifteen feet wide. The car had flown over it, hit the far edge, rose up again and skidded a few feet beyond and was now *totaled*. Game over. There goes my job, I thought. I left my Puerto Rican pals and walked a few miles back to the cab station. Ready to hand in my license. But the owner of the company didn't fire me, or even charge me for damages. He was a songwriter too, you see. A country singer on the weekends. We use to play music together. His favorite song was *Gallo del Cielo*. The one eyed rooster saved me again.

I took a month off cab driving to work as an *Urban Cowboy* singer in a Puerto Rican carnival, and *Gallo del Cielo*, was the most requested song. Cockfighting is the national sport of Puerto Rico. The song was continuing to save my life, except that one of the security guards took issue with me over the last few verses. He didn't like the rooster dying at the end. *Losing*. It depressed him. It shamed the national pride of Puerto Rico, or something. *It would not end that way*, he kept moaning. Angry about it. One night I made the mistake of leaving my guitar in the dressing room, and I'm sure it was this gentleman who shot a hole in the back with his service pistol. That guitar, a 1946 Martin D-18, is sitting right behind me as I write this essay. Bullet hole intact. It's the guitar I wrote *Gallo* on. Rooster memories surround me.

I went back to New York, and back to the cabs. Dreary business. One night, around midnight, I picked up Robert Hunter in front of a theater in Rockaway Beach, Queens. He had a guitar case and a glass of Jack Daniels in his hand. He also had a long cigarette holder, with a lit cigarette in it. Right out of a movie, this guy. His name was up on the theater marquee: *"Robert Hunter Tonight! Songwriter For the Grateful Dead!"* Hunter had written Dead classics like *Truckin'* and *Friend of the Devil*, and was inducted into the Rock and Roll Hall of Fame with them in 1994. He also co-wrote most of the songs on the last Bob Dylan record: *Together Through Life*. A master poet of rock and roll.

He stepped into my cab and gave me the address of a motel in Jamaica, Queens, and we took off. I struck up a conversation with him. Told him I was a songwriter too. I blurted it out. Now you might expect a famous songwriter would scoff at that. Or ignore you. Not Robert Hunter. He said something like: *"Oh Yeah? You're a songwriter? Cool, man. Sing me a song, then."*

The chips were down. I pulled out my strongest card. *Gallo.* Started singing it accapella.

He stopped me after the first verse and made a few comments. Then he apologized. *"Hell, I'm sorry. It sounds interesting. Sing me the whole song. I'll be quiet."*

I sang the whole thing. Every cockfight in every town. I finished up and checked the rear view mirror. He was staring at me.

"You wrote THAT?" he said.

"Yeah," I said.

"Sing it again, man. *Sing it again."*

And so I did. The cab meter was up to over a hundred bucks, but time seemed to stop. We were both wrapped up in the journey of the one-eyed rooster. The money was on the table.

> *Hola, my Theresa, I am thinking of you now, in Santa Clara,*
> *Yes, the money's on the table,*
> *And I am holding to your locket framed in gold...*
> *Tonight I'll put it all on the fighting spurs of Gallo del Cielo...*

Robert Hunter loved the song. He demanded a tape. *Immediately.* That very night. So we drove back in the opposite direction, fifteen miles to my house, and I crawled under the bed and found a cassette demo of the song. I gave it to Hunter, who was now promising to play it for the *New Riders of the Purple Sage.* He said *they had to* record it. I drove him back to the motel. The tab was maybe two hundred bucks. He paid in cash, and I never expected to see him again. I already thought it had been a damn fine evening. But, hell, he'd forget about it.

He didn't forget. He called me a week later and said the *New Riders* had lost their record deal. But he was coming back to New York for a show at *The Bitter End.* I should come down and hang out. I was thrilled. Fast forward to that evening in Greenwich Village. I'm drinking *Jack Daniels* in Robert Hunter's dressing room before the show. Excited. Then he gets up on stage, and about twenty minutes into the show, he starts a story: *"You should hear the song I heard from a cab driver the other night...but hell, let's just get him up here to sing it himself."*

I gulped. Felt a bead of sweat run down my back. I hadn't performed in a few months. I was rusty and the song was demanding, even if you're sober. Which I wasn't. I got up on stage, in front of a packed house. Hunter handed me his guitar and split. I looked down into the faces of hundreds of reverent Dead Heads waiting for the magic song Hunter had promised them. All eleven verses. The room was silent. I started, hesitantly, but the story took over and I melted into the song and let the rooster do the work. I finished the song to rowdy applause and looked around for Robert Hunter. He'd vanished. Somebody yelled out: *Do another one, man.* And I did two more. I'd regained my footing and my confidence. I was back in the music business.

Hunter appeared back on stage and, later that night, offered me a gig opening for him at the old Lone Star Café in New York. I've been working full time in the song-trade ever since. I thank Robert Hunter. And the one eyed rooster. I've made *Gallo* a solemn promise that I'll never forget the words. And never change the ending. Shoot another hole in my guitar, *amigo*, but the story stands.

IV Midnight in the Palace of Milkshakes/ Sundown on the Rio Grande

> *Do the rivers still run muddy,*
> *Outside of my beloved Casas Grande?*
> *Does the scar upon my brother's face, turn red*
> *When he hears mention of my name?*
> *Do the people of El Sueco, still curse the theft*
> *of Gallo del Cielo?*

After the taxi cabs I lived in a boarded-up storefront in Brooklyn for ten years. An artist's garret, with a loft bed and a desk, and little else. I wrote songs and played honkytonks in Manhattan and Long Island during those *Urban Cowboy* days. Up the street from my bunker there was a little Cuban/Dominican joint called *The Palace of Milkshakes*. They specialized in Cuban sandwiches and huge milk shakes. On weekends they covered the windows with cardboard and held illegal cockfights. No *gringos* allowed. This was my neighborhood. I was living inside that song.

Around that time, early 1980s, I sent a cassette tape of *Gallo* to the cowboy-folk legend Ian Tyson. I'd been a huge *Ian and Sylvia* fan in the 60s and I'd written Ian letters over the past years. He had a solo career and a television show in Canada. He loved *Gallo* and recorded it on an album which put a spark back into cowboy music and resurrected his career: *Old Corrals and Sagebrush. Gallo del Cielo* was on the record.

Ian and I began a co-writing relationship with songs like *Navajo Rug, Claude Dallas, The Rose of the San Joaquin, The Bank of the Musselshell,* and others. Ian's record: *Cowboyography* stands as one of the most important cowboy records ever recorded, and it turned the Western genre around. We've since recorded *Gallo* and *Navajo* as duets on several of my own cowboy records.

Yes, *Gallo* took off down the road and stuck its one-eyed head into every little nook and cranny of the music world. Katie Lee, now ninety years old, and one of the first ladies to run the rapids of the Colorado River, recorded the song back in the 1980s. The most passionate version yet recorded is Joe Ely's, on the record *Letter to Laredo.* Joe nails the song. A wild flamenco guitar rolls through the track. His version took the song into the rock community, where it landed at the feet of Bruce Springsteen. *The Boss.*

I drove home from a gig one winter's night in New York; must have been in the early 1990s. I recall it was a snowing. Wet streets. Tough going. Two hour drive. I made it back to my artist garret and collapsed into a chair, leafing through the damp mail that had been shoved under the door. One letter came from England. Scrawled inside on hotel stationary was a note about *Gallo del Cielo.* It was from Bruce Springsteen, on tour in England. *"When Joe Ely played me that song I said, man, who wrote that? It's a great song...thanks. We'll get together..."* The Springsteen connection gets weirder now.

Clarence Clemmons, Springsteen's great saxophone player, passed away recently. He published a book a few years ago titled: *Big Man.* There's a scene in the book in which Kinky Freidman, Clarence Clemmons, and Bob Dylan are talking about Dylan seeing Joe Ely play in a roadhouse:

"Joe did a hell of a song tonight," says Dylan. *"A Tom Russell song. It's about a fighting rooster. It's called 'Gallo del Cielo.' It's good. And I'm hard to impress."* Who knows how or whether this scene actually transpired? But it's in the book. The rooster works in mysterious ways. His fame and journey continue to impress me. Onward he rolls. There's now a famous cutting horse stud named *Gallo del Cielo,* and also resort cabins, pit bulls, and fried chicken recipes.

Enough anecdotes.

Some nights at happy hour I pour a glass of *Rioja* and watch the sundown reflect back on the Franklin Mountains in El Paso. The high rocks near the summit turn a crimson red, then roan-grey and finally dark brown. I sip the Spanish wine and wonder if Augustine is out there somewhere training a champion rooster or pumping illegal vitamins into an old racehorse. I miss his schemes. And the old *Professor*, up in Creel, must be long gone.

In the end, I don't know where this rooster song really came from. Or where it will go next. It was crafted from fragments and journeys and the memory of blood rituals. Maybe it passed down from one of my past incarnations, when I was walking around in the desert with the original St. Augustine, before Christ was born. According to his *Confessions*, St. Augustine of Hippo understood the cockfight*: "to be divinely endowed as a visible sign of an invisible reality...every motion in these fighting animals, who are unendowed with reason, is graceful and brave, and guided by a higher power."*

Amen. The rooster and his song were born in heaven...*so the legends say.*

Gallo del Cielo
A Song by Tom Russell

Carlos Zaragoza left his home in *Casas Grandes* when the
    moon was full
No money in his pocket, just a locket of his sister framed
    in gold
He headed for *El Sueco*, stole a rooster named
    Gallo del Cielo
Then he crossed the *Rio Grande*, with that chicken nestled
    deep beneath his arm

Now *Gallo del Cielo* was a rooster born in heaven, so the
    legends say
His wings they had been broken, he had one eye rollin'
    crazy in his head
He'd fought a hundred fights, and the legends say that one
    night near El Sueco
They'd fought *Cielo* seven times, and seven times he left
    brave roosters dead

Hola, my Theresa, I am thinking of you now in San Antonio
I have twenty-seven dollars and the locket of your picture
    framed in old
Tonight I'll bet it all, on the fighting spurs of *Gallo del Cielo*
Then I'll return to buy the land Pancho Villa stole from
    father long ago

Outside of San Diego in the onion fields of
    Paco Monteverde
The pride of San Diego, he lay sleeping on a fancy bed of silk
And they laughed when Zaragoza pulled the one-eyed
    del Cielo from beneath his coat
But they cried when Zaragoza walked away with a thousand
    dollar bill

Hola, my Theresa, I am thinking of you now in
    Santa Barbara
I have fifteen hundred dollars and the good luck of your
    picture framed in gold
Tonight I'll bet it all on the fighting spurs of *Gallo del Cielo*
Then I'll return to buy the land that Villa stole from father
    long ago

Now the moon has gone to hiding and the lantern light
    spills shadows on the fighting sand
Where a wicked black named *Zorro* faces *Gallo del Cielo* in
    the night
But Carlos Zaragoza fears the tiny crack that runs across his
    rooster's beak
And he fears that he has lost the fifty thousand dollars
    riding on the fight

Hola, my Theresa, I am thinking of you now in Santa Clara
Yes, the money's on the table I am holding now your good
    luck framed in gold
And everything we dreamed of is riding on the spurs of
    del Cielo
I pray that I'll return to buy the land that Villa stole from
    father long ago

Then the signal it was given, and the roosters rose together
    far above the sand
Gallo del Cielo sunk a gaff into Zorro's shiny breast
They were separated quickly, but they rose and fought each
    other thirty seven times
And the legends say that everyone agreed that *del Cielo*
    fought the best

Then the screams of Zaragoza filled the night outside the
    town of Santa Clara
As the beak of *del Cielo* lay broken like a shell within
    his hand
And they say that Zaragoza screamed a curse upon the
    bones of Pancho Villa
When Zorro rose up one last time, and drove *del Cielo* to
    the sand

Hola, my Theresa, I am thinking of you now in
    San Francisco
There's no money in my pocket, I no longer have your
    picture framed in gold
I buried it last evening with the bones of my beloved
    del Cielo
And I'll not return to buy the land that Villa stole
    from father long ago

Do the rivers still run muddy, outside of my beloved
    Casas Grandes?
Does the scar upon my brother's face turn red when he
    hears mention of my name?
Do the people of *El Sueco* still curse the death of
    Gallo del Cielo?
Tell my family not to worry, I will not return to cause
    them shame.

Blue Rooster

Margaritas with Monte Hellman, The Modernist Western, and a Nod to Jack Nicholson, Warren Oates, and Harry Dean Stanton

*Hellman was effectively reinventing the western...All told it's a visionary strategy...*The Shooting, *and* Ride in the Whirlwind *could both be set on a post Armageddon plain, and their characters could be the last people on earth. But they're westerns.*

— **Michael Atkinson**

I like to work on a film where it's continually opening up its secrets to me. I think any work of art, not just a film, is a mystery. I think it was Jean Cocteau who said it should reveal its secrets slowly.

— **Monte Hellman**

Harry Dean Stanton, approaching ninety years of age, is sitting on his back porch above Hollywood. Cigarette in hand. The presumed drink is off camera. Across from him is renowned film director Monte Hellman – interviewing Harry Dean as a follow-up to a new Criterion DVD re-release of Hellman's *visionary* Westerns from the 1960s: *The Shooting* and *Ride in the Whirlwind*. Harry Dean played the outlaw "Blind Dick" in the *Whirlwind* film.

The movie opens on long shot of Blind Dick, with eye patch and crushed fedora hat, sliding down a steep hillside on foot, ready to mount up and rob a stagecoach. Next shot – Blind Dick slips behind a sagebrush to relieve himself. Welcome to the modernist western. His sidekick is complaining of *carbuncles* and Blind Dick states: *you ought to attend to that.*

In the recent back porch interview Harry Dean surmises that he learned the secret to natural acting in this early Hellman western. Jack Nicholson told him: *Let your wardrobe do the character.* Harry and Nicholson were once housemates. You can imagine the parties.

Then Harry Dean pauses, pulls on his cigarette, and squints. Trying to recall something lodged in the deep, cowboy past.

"Didn't I go to jail one night out there in Utah? For resisting arrest or something?" He scowls and can't remember. "Might have been another movie."

The interview fades on that note.

A few years ago I got a call from Monte Hellman's office. Mr. Hellman was looking for me. I was hiding, under the radar, dug deep into the trenches across the river from Juarez, dreaming up a *frontier musical*. Painting blue cows. Pondering the death of literature and song. I'd never had the honor of meeting the esteemed director.

I was aware Monte had worked with Roger Corman on early Jack Nicholson horror flicks and Westerns, and that Hellman's *The Shooting*, and *Ride in the Whirlwind* were groundbreakers – considered the first *modernist* or *acid* Westerns.

Those two were followed by *China 9, Liberty 37*, starring Warren Oates – this third western was considered more traditional, but it vanished from view. Copies are extremely rare. Monte also directed Charles Willeford's adapted novel *Cockfighter* – again, starring Oates.

I hadn't heard of Monte Hellman since his classic 1971 film: *Two Lane Blacktop*. That's the one where James Taylor, singer-songwriter, and Dennis Wilson, original drummer for The Beach Boys, drive a hopped-up vintage Chevy across the USA, racing a cranked-up goon in a leisure suit named *GTO*, played by Warren Oates. The boys were racing for pink slips.

You might wonder if James Taylor and Dennis Wilson could act. They didn't have to. Not with Warren Oates in the film. Warren always commanded total screen attention. Because he was real. He tore it up – whether a sidekick in a TV series, a lead in a Monte Hellman film, or a half-dozen roles for Sam Peckinpah. Warren Oates leaped over the edge, whilst spouting humorously appropriate lines.

I'd recommend Monte Hellman's *Two Lane Blacktop*, or Sam Peckinpah's *Bring Me The Head of Alfredo Garcia*, for a savage dose of Warren Oates. In *Garcia* Warren drives around Mexico, drunk on tequila, talking to the severed head of a Mexican *bandito*. The head is rotting in a bag (flies attached) on the car seat beside Warren. I'm a big fan of Warren Oates.

Warren Oates was Monte Hellman's best friend.

I did a little research and learned Monte had since produced Quentin Tarantino's *Reservoir Dogs,* and taught for eleven years at California Institute of the Arts, in the graduate film-directing program.

I finally got ahold of Monte. He had all my records – wanted me to write songs for his new project, a baffling noir film full of ghosts, airplane wrecks, and gunfire. *A film within a film.* No horses. I picked up my guitar and hit the A minor chord.

I was hoping to meet up with Monte in person so I could chat with him about his early Western films, and get the lowdown on Jack Nicholson, Warren Oates, and Harry Dean Stanton, a trio of classic actors who owe much to Monte Hellman's first films. Mr. Hellman was a vital part of Western film history. But first I had to write the song.

I   The Road to Nowhere

> *Well the ditches are on fire*
> *And there ain't no higher ground*
> *You were a prince in the City of Angels, kid*
> *Now you're pawning your clothes in a railroad town*
> *Well, forgiveness is the killer of snakes, amigo*
> *In the gardens of anger and despair*
> *Keep your mind in the middle, little brother*
> *Out on the road to nowhere*
>
>   — **Tom Russell,** *The Road to Nowhere*

Fast forward. Slow motion. Our film essay comes into focus on a mountain road somewhere above Hollywood and Vine. The radio is blasting a Warren Zevon song: *I saw a Werewolf drinking a Pina Colada at Trader Vic's...and his hair was perfect!* We're climbing backwater canyons which sucked the creative blood out of Faulkner and Fitzgerald. Screenwriters on the dole. Whiskey in the bottom drawer. *No literary art, please, boys.* I can hear Norma Desmond in Sunset Boulevard: *I AM big. It's the pictures that got small...*

My wife and I on our way to the top of the canyon to visit Monte Hellman. Monte's invited us up for drinks and dinner, and he's offered to screen the film – the film I wrote songs for over the last year. Monte's first feature in twenty-one years.

I was thinking a German houseboy might open the door and Monte would be lounging by the pool, sucking on a cigarette holder. He'd call us over to him with an arrogant wave of the hand. He'll trash my song and offer my wife a bit part. I was wrong. Monte opens the door. His hair is combed straight back, then curves up around his skull in wild arcs. The Einstein look. He's not even trying to be eccentric. This cat is real.

Any twisted notion I harbored that Monte might be bullshit or *Hollywood* vanished. He pulls us into the kitchen overlooking the requisite empty swimming pool (*It's being refurbished. The goldfish are dead and the mortgage is due.*) Nathaniel West couldn't have made this up. The struggle never ends. *The Day of the Locusts.*

He begins mixing three classic *Monte Hellman Margaritas. Healthy* margaritas. He uses Xylitol to sweeten them. No sugar additives. We feel better for that. Fresh limes. And 100% agave tequila. Just what the doc ordered. Naturally, being Monte Hellman, there would be no additives. He's of the Samuel Beckett school, and carves all nature down to its core. I was pleasantly amused at the stark presumption of the drinks (to steal from James Thurber.)

Spinning with good tequila, we're aimed towards the screening room. Which is also Monte's bedroom. Three director's chairs propped in front of his bed and a wide screen in front of us. There's no escape. What if we don't dig the film? No way out.

Two hours later we came out of the bedroom, *reeling*. I'm still trying to figure out this movie. A filmmaker falls in love with his lead actress, who in turn, seems to be melting back into the woman whose part she's playing.

Many months later we're invited to the premier on Hollywood Boulevard. More Xylitol Margaritas were served. Monte introduced us to everyone. Bit actors, screenwriters, and semi-stars. We sit through the film again, on the big screen this time, and the beauty and mystery revealed a few more secrets. I'm proud to have written the theme song.

The film would go on to gain prestige notices in Europe, and Quentin Tarantino awarded Monte a *Palm D'Or* Lifetime Achievement Award at the Venice Film Festival. Thus began my friendship with Monte Hellman, the man who, along with Sam Peckinpah, has been hailed as the visionary who brought the cowboy film into modern times.

II *The Shooting* and *Ride in the Whirlwind*

> *Heavies are closer to life than leading men. The heavy is everyman – everyman when he faces a tough moment in life. It's the heavy that has to do with the meat of life.*
>
> **— Warren Oates**

> *There were forty Western TV series, and I went from one to the other. I started out playing the third bad guy on a horse and worked my way up to the No. 1 bad guy.*
>
> *I have a face like two miles of country road that you're never gonna get to the end of...*
>
> **— Warren Oates**

In 1962 Roger Corman, the 50s and 60s king of low budget exploitation films, invited Monte Hellman to lunch at the old Brown Derby in Hollywood. Corman told Monte he wanted him to direct a Western themed film, and while he was at it he might as well knock out two – two on the same location might prove cheaper in the long run.

Both films were eventually made for under $75,000 each. Twenty per cent of the budget was spent on the horse wranglers, who were members of the Teamsters Union. Their boss was a legendary cowboy named Calvin Johnson, who provided the livestock and scouted the Utah locations.

Monte directed both films, and Jack Nicholson co-produced, wrote and acted in *Ride in the Whirlwind*. Carole Eastman wrote *The Shooting*. The films were shot around Kanab, and many of the locations later disappeared under water after the government created Glenn Canyon Dam.

Let's think of Monte Hellman as a man, on one level, who filmed parts of our American landscape which don't exist anymore – the terrain flooded by that giant dam, and the picturesque roadhouses and gas stops along Old Route 66 in *Two Lane Blacktop*. Inside those lost terrains Monte Hellman re-imagined the West.

Monte learned an editing trick or two from Corman about cutting frames out on each side of a scene – which saved money and tightened up the film. Monte also cut out unneeded dialogue in order to tell the stories visually. Samuel Beckett rides again.

Samuel Beckett's literature of minimalism and absurdity was a reaction to James Joyce's florid, *throw the kitchen sink in*, approach to literature. To summon up Beckett in his own words:

> *I realized that Joyce had gone as far as one could in the direction of knowing more, [being] in control of one's material. He was always adding to it – you only have to look at his proofs to see that. I realized that my own way was in impoverishment, in lack of knowledge and in taking away, in subtracting rather than in adding.*

Monte Hellman's penchant for Beckett-like Westerns might have been a partial reaction to the John Ford school of full-on plot, sensible dialogue, lush landscapes, and predictable endings. The first Hellman westerns were termed, by critics, *modernist westerns* that express a bleak, minimalist, quality that didn't sentimentalize the Wild West.

Jack Nicholson and Monte rented an office to polish the scripts in the Writer's Building in Beverly Hills, next door to Fred Astaire's office. Monte skipped up the stairs and Fred Astaire danced down. In *Ride in the Whirlwind* (a phrase taken loosely from the Old Testament) Nicholson based his story on a book of bandit histories he'd found in the L.A. County library. Nicholson loved the films. He carried the finished reels around in a cardboard box as he travelled to foreign film fests.

Recently Monte had Criterion send me the new DVD editions of *The Shooting* and *Ride in the Whirlwind* – with updated commentaries by Monte, and actors Harry Dean Stanton and Millie Perkins. There's a great chat with the horse wrangler who found the locations, Calvin Johnson. There's plenty of horse yarns.

I jammed the first film – *The Shooting* – into the machine and sat back on a Mexican blanket. I tried to resist reading the comments on the back of the package about the *gritty, dreamlike* nature of the films, and Monte's penchant for *deconstructing genre*. I didn't want to think of terms such as *acid western, existential,* or *modernist*. I didn't have a real clue anyway. I flunked college philosophy, and Sartre bored the hell out of me. I just wanted to watch the film.

Both films involve a hunt. In *The Shooting,* Jack Nicholson plays a hired gun and Warren Oates is a bounty hunter. The men are working for a woman who's tracking someone. You're along for the mystery ride into the wild sandstone terrain, as the characters sling heated half sentences back and forth.

It unfolds with a collage of odd camera shots of tired horses and red-bluffed desert, and with a sonic landscape of horses hooves, wind, bird calls, whistles, gunfire, and odd orchestral fragments. And the fractured cowboy dialogue.

From memory – here's a string of dialogue samples:

Just tell me what yer tellin' me...be calm and tell me.
His face all spittered out, spilling into his coffee...
I'm so hungry I could chaw off my own lung...
Your brain's gonna fry out here, you know that?
Why you shoot him for (the horse) *there ain't an unsound bone in his body?*

At least I *think* that's what I heard. Cranky half-conversations by folks who seem to draw questionable conclusions, and shoot before they think. Or maybe they think too much before they shoot. Or maybe they don't think at all. I've hit on the partial formula of the *modernist* Western.

It's like walking into a bar and catching scraps of disoriented, angry dialogue from an isolate oddball at the end of the bar. You wonder why this human is so pissed off, but if you engage them in conversation you've made a grave mistake. You've bit into a ragged, poison chunk of humankind. That's why Monte's films make sense when they don't make sense.

Ride in the Whirlwind also involves a hunt – a group of lawmen tracking down a trio of cowboys mistakenly thought to have robbed a stagecoach. The original gang leader is the above-mentioned *Blind Dick*, played by Harry Dean Stanton. They hang *Blind Dick* early on. He has no final words. Nobody does. They die. They stare into the abyss. And spit.

In these 1960s Monte Hellman westerns, we're treated to actors Jack Nicholson, Warren Oates, and Harry Dean Stanton, working on their craft in the early years. Jack Nicholson and Warren Oates are messing around with character sketches, acting chops, and facial ticks they'll use successfully in later films. Harry Dean Stanton seems to have had his persona down for the duration.

Here is Harry Dean again from the extended Criterion Collection, fifty years after the filming:

*This film (*Ride in the Whirlwind*) solidified my approach to acting. If you're playing an authority figure you don't have to do anything – just be yourself. You can be indecisive or gay or anything...just be yourself and it's real.*

I asked Monte recently about his perceptions of Jack Nicholson and Warren Oates, in the early part of their careers.

Monte:

Warren Oates was the closest I found in an actor to represent me in my relationship with the audience. I guess I see myself as an antihero, and he embodied that. He also conveyed the classic western traits of honor, quiet strength, few words, and a softness beneath the hard exterior.

Monte on Jack Nicholson:

I was lucky to catch Jack before he discovered which of his personal mannerisms audiences were attracted to. He was always able to force the character to become him, but the "him" was multi-colored and multi-shaped. Even though he played more varied characters later in his career, the variations were more pronounced in these early films.

Jack said:

All I could see in the early films, before "Easy Rider," was this desperate young actor trying to vault out of the screen and create a movie career.

A note from Warren Oates:

Hopalong Cassidy and Ben Johnson have rubbed off on my life. That's about all I have to say...I don't intentionally set out to be a villain. I do what is given me to do and from there I evolve my attitude and comment.

Jack Nicholson went on to stardom. Warren Oates and Harry Dean Stanton were never fully able to shed the over-the-top, *bull-goose-loony,* sidekick personas which kept them from big time starring roles. They were deep characters with real ticks and grins. But we loved them all the more.

III Peckinpah and Hellman and A Quick-Draw, Rough Guide to Western Film

All right, I'm coming out. Any man I see out there, I'm gonna shoot him. Any sumbitch takes a shot at me, I'm not only gonna kill him, but I'm gonna kill his wife, all his friends... and burn his damn house down.

— **Will Munny**
(Clint Eastwood), *The Unforgiven*

Ah, the consideration the Western film. The funded "scholars" blather on about *the solitude of the lone rider, the loyalty of his horse, and the unspoken code of the West* ...scholars living high off their grant money, as they chortle and foment footnoted lists of crap in scholarly journals about *investigating subjects of nature, ethics, identity, gender, environmentalism, and animal rights...* they concoct this in cluttered offices of East Coast Universities. Mostly. They get paid for this.

Meanwhile directors like Hellman and Peckinpah defied the system, the scholars, the expectations of the masses, threw back the agave juice, and shot from their gut. That's the way art is created in the cultural wasteland. The *genre inventions* and arch terminologies are constructed, after the fact, by those who overthink everything that should be digested and experienced by the individual. Pay your money at the box office and come up with your own conclusions. Critics be damned.

A wise man once declared that there are only two real story lines in the history of literature. *One*: A man goes on a journey – see *The New Testament* or Homer's *The Odyssey. Two*: A stranger rides into town – see almost every Western film, book, or song ever created. Consider *Shane*.

Cogitate on the classic movie *The Oxbow Incident*, directed by William A. Wellman, based on the Walter Van Tilburg novel. The film was made in 1943 and starred Peter Fonda. Monte Hellman was deeply influenced by this one.

Fonda and a partner ride into a desolate town. As Fonda gets down from his horse he declares: *This place is as deader than a Paiute's grave*. Minutes later the barkeep pours the whiskey and tells Fonda that the only available woman is *an 82 year old blind Paiute woman.* The boys decline the offer and join up with a posse that eventually hangs an innocent man.

All the elements are here that Hellman will later pare down into his own vision of the raw West. Monte strips away the obvious and never overplays the emotional element or easy love angle.

The modernist approach often doesn't fly well in Middle America. Lots of viewers crave an obvious plot and structure, and a happy love story, cause they ain't gettin' any at home.

European audiences are not so demanding. They welcome the intangible. Tough-talking cowboys who ride into town and bark out quatrains of hard-assed, confrontational cowboy slang. Armed to the teeth. Black hat, white hat, no matter. Bang, bang. Ride away.

If you're an electrician in Munich this is the stuff of daydreams and dime novels. And then there's the Italians and French, who invented futurism and cubism. They see matters at odd angles, in cracked poetics. They also drink more per capita wine then we do.

Europeans are forever enchanted by the Western landscape. They're obsessed with old Route 66, The Grand Canyon, Mesa Verde...all of it. If you visit a National Park in summer you're gonna run into more Germans than Americans. The foreign tourists want to see the Cowboy and Indian terrains of their childhood daydreams.

Monte Hellman fits into their picture. He thinks globally and was never afraid to buck the odds, the stock formulas, and the studio moguls. He loved the music of horse hooves and wind. The *Palm de Ore* from the Venice film fest d'or sits on his mantle. The director's chairs are in the screening room, next to his bed. Margaritas await you in the blender. The swimming pool is filling.

But what about the history? What can we sum up about the Western, and Hellman and Peckinpah – without sounding like an obtuse academic?

My Texas friend, and authority on film, W.K. "Kip" Stratton, has authored books on film, rodeo, boxing (Floyd Patterson), and is also a fine poet. He's now immersed in a book on Sam Peckinpah's *The Wild Bunch*, a movie that usually makes everyone's "ten best cowboy films" list.

I asked Kip about Monte Hellman and Sam Peckinpah, and the evolution of Western film. I wondered if he could do it in four sentences. It ran a little over four, but it's concise and as enlightening as a mini-course in Western film. And you don't have to sit in class and snore.

In Kip's words:

> *Okay you had John Ford and also Howard Hawks. Next came a group of directors who upped the "art" ante in the Western movie: George Stevens and "Shane" – there was more realism, particular in how violence is portrayed. Then came Anthony Mann and the psychologically driven Western,* The Naked Spur, Winchester 73, *also Fred Zinnemann,* High Noon.
>
> *And Delmer Daves – Westerns simple on their face, yet symbolically rich, particularly his use of nature and natural settings as symbols. Then Budd Boetticher, especially "branding" his "Ranown" Westerns with an auteur's touch, also presenting bad men as characters we feel some sympathy for.*
>
> *Those guys were transitional. They made the Revisionist Westerns of Monte Hellman, Sam Peckinpah, and Sergio Leone, possible.*

> *My four sentences (or so): Monte and Sam did their best work free of the studio system, so they didn't have to adhere to the story conventions that Ford, and others, had to... such as the mandatory love story, which sunk so many Westerns.*
>
> *They were free of the conventions of the Western mythology itself. They were able to, and did, deal with existential themes (Ford would have thrown-up upon hearing the word existential).*
>
> *They were able to portray a West that was dirty and unethical, where nice guys often finished last, where flies crawled on horses, where women had **boobs** and **fornicated**, where dying wasn't pretty. One final thing: they both steered clear of the stereotyped portrayal of Indians within the cowboy/cavalry vs. Indians context.*

(* The above words **in bold** were substituted by this essayist to protect sensitive readers.)

It's best to remember one thing I learned from painter Wayne Thiebaud. Art (ditto film, literature, song) doesn't evolve along straight, progressive lines. Technology be damned, films are not necessarily better or more artful then forty or fifty years ago. And no one's writing better songs than Bob Dylan, or those traditional cowboy songs like "Old Paint." All the great classic novels were written before 1970. Art erupts in individual, out of time, Van Gogh giggles. Visionaries are well-needed.

IV A Final 10 Questions at Twenty Paces (or eight Hundred Miles) with Monte Hellman

I have nothing against happy endings, even though my movies rarely turn out that way.

— **Monte Hellman**

I haven't seen many films for a while.
The last year and a half, the only thing I've had time for was my own dailies. I did catch (Monte Hellman's) Two-Lane Blacktop, *and loved it. I thought* The Last Picture Show *was a piece of shit, except for Ben Johnson. Apparently, I'm in a minority on both opinions...*

— **Sam Peckinpah**

1. **Monte, what's your intellectual aim, as the critics might ask?**
   My aim always is to move the audience. Jack (Nicholson) is possibly more intellectual than I am, so in Ride in the Whirlwind *I remember a conscious awareness of trying to break with audience expectations: not having a character read a letter from mom, hopefully to make us care about him...no taking the girl to the barn to inject a little sex. We tried to blur the colors of the white hat and the black hat.*
   I tried to make the images engaging, so it didn't matter what the characters were saying.

2. **In your words...what's the Beckett connection?**
   I directed the first L.A. (and fifth in the world) production of Waiting For Godot. *It was a life-changing experience. I'm sure it had an effect on all my subsequent work.*

3. **There's plenty of mention of the oft-misused term *existentialism* in critical regard of your work.**
   I was interested in Sartre's writings on the subject, and never understood what critics meant by applying the term to me or others. Sartre made it very clear that his philosophy when applied to drama meant that although his characters were free to make choices that could alter the course of their

lives, more often than not they would do what their heredity and environment had conditioned them to do.

So that, although "existence precedes essence," the characters we have become at any given point in our lives will dictate the choices we make 90% of the time. The critics seem to be referring to harsh reality, and confusing existentialism with naturalism, a la Steinbeck.

4. **Filmic Influences?**

I think my westerns owe more to previous movies The Oxbow Incident *and perhaps* Greed, *than they do to any literary category or philosophy. I think the biggest influences were* The Virginian *(c. 1930),* Stagecoach, My Darling Clementine, *and* Shane. *As to why, I think these were the ones we admired most. And they also represented some clichés we were trying uncliche. I have nothing against happy endings, even though my movies rarely turn out that way.*

5. **Jack Nicholson loved those films, eh?**

Jack took both pictures to Cannes, and in cardboard boxes. The usual metal cases were too heavy to cart around that way. He still looked like Willy Loman, with one box held by its rope wrapping in each hand.

6. **Final thoughts on Harry Dean Stanton, Warren Oates, Sam Peckinpah, and Jack Nicholson?**

Harry frequently expressed resentment at my casting him as second banana to Warren. In Ride *he appears without Warren, and he's top banana in his band. On his (Criterion) interview he tells he learned from Jack how to let the wardrobe do the acting, so he claims this movie was a turning point for him.*

Warren was a sane version of Sam Peckinpah. Warren wasn't afraid of his soft side, the poet inside. Sam was constantly trying to hide it. You were never in danger of getting shot if you went to visit Warren. Warren and I played chess, invented new cocktails, and he even got me to eat the rich Southern food that eventually killed him. He had a lot of charm, but nothing like the magic that took over him when the cameras were turned on.

I was lucky to get Jack before he became JACK. He was always a movie star, because he always knew he was inside. But he hadn't yet learned the tricks he relied on once he found what it was the audience liked. He'll always be one of the greats, but he could have been so much greater.

7. **Why, in these westerns, did you pick that particular area of Utah to film?**

    Because we were doing two movies, with radically different requirements, we scouted all the traditional western locations. Kanab was the only one that worked for both pics. Each location becomes a character in its scene, and landscape is second only to casting in importance. The trick for me is making the landscape, as with all other elements, invisible. If you notice it, it's bad.

8. **I've heard Antonioni mentioned a few times as an influence. In the 60s I loved his movie *Blowup*.**

    Antonioni had a huge effect on Jack and me when we did the westerns. He was much more groundbreaking to my generation than Orson Welles was. Orson was just doing what I had grown up with on radio. Antonioni shook us up. I loved Blow Up. *Now I'm a little critical of his dealing with British youth, disco clubs, etc. But all the core of the movie still holds up.*

9. **What changes have you seen in Hollywood and the film world?**

    I sometimes stay locked in my castle for a few days at a time. Then, when I go back down to the Strip, everything has changed. Buildings have disappeared. New ones have sprouted up. The kids have begun hanging out at some new place.

    As for Hollywood, the big change is the corporate ownership. There were once moguls, who, for good or bad, could make decisions on their own. You could actually meet with a person and make or break a deal. Now there's no such person. There's no human touch. A reader who's paid fifty bucks to read a script becomes the basis for decisions made by a group of ten fearful people. It's always safer to say "no."

10. **Last question – is your swimming pool still empty? Is it okay to mention that you now operate a B & B in your house to makes ends meet? So you can make more films!**

   I just filled the pool, but didn't have the plumbing ready for a couple weeks. So the algae grew fast. Now I'm waiting for fish, animal and plant-friendly stuff to make it clear again. No more chlorine, back to eco-balance. Yes, please mention the B & B. We have no business protecting people from the realities of life.

Thank you, Monte Hellman. Good night.

Iron White Man

Fritz and Georgia: Indian Not Indian

I believe a good painting...you can sense it a mile away. The minute you walk across the room, it either grabs you and knocks you down and kills you, or forget it....

— **Fritz Scholder**

In the late 1940s an eleven-year-old South Dakota kid named Fritz painted images and stamps on blank letter envelopes. His own concoctions. A boy-dreamer from the Badlands. The kid sent these art envelopes off to famous folks like Albert Einstein and Prince Feisal of Iraq, among other luminaries. He asked Einstein and the boys if they'd put their signature on his hand-made envelopes and return them in the mail. I'd imagine that the famous ones were amused at the kid's presumption and gravitas. Most of them signed the envelopes and sent them back to South Dakota, postmarked from different countries. Instant collectibles. Even King Feisal complied. Two days before he was assassinated.

Welcome to the keen mind and artistic career of young Fritz Scholder – quarter blood Luiseno Indian, three quarters German, and son of an Indian school administrator. Fritz would become a world-famed painter: major collectors of his art being Robert Redford and Ralph Lauren. *Among others.* And myself. Though I don't own any originals. Just posters and prints. For many years I've been intrigued by Scholder's stormy career, his technique, and his colors. He was a man who painted Indians in the abstract and pushed the outsider boundaries of what we know as Western art.

Fritz Scholder (1937-2005) was part Luiseno Indian, but later in later life he looked *full-blooded* Indian, with his long black hair and a bemused scowl on that mug worthy of Red Cloud or Sitting Bull. He possessed Indian bearing. He attacked the canvas in that manner. Like a warrior – paintbrush in one hand and a rag in the other – painting a line or a figure then wiping out and smearing his lines and images. Pushing the limits of color and under-coating. He called it *covering up his tracks*. Bob Dylan records might be blasting on the stereo as the paint flew. Dylan and Scholder seemed to be in touch with parallel, untamed muses. American visionaries.

I don't need to detail Scholder's early years, the schooling, and the awards. Fritz fought his way up through the ranks of American art. *Quickly.* He studied under various Native American artists, including Oscar Howe, but as he moved on, his major influence was his teacher Wayne Thiebaud – the Sacramento master known for his colorful pop realism of objects like cakes and pies and donuts, and depictions of the farming delta around Sacramento California.

Scholder was also influenced by Richard Diebenkorn's *under painting* technique. The secret here being to paint over one color with a different shade or tint, and keep layering the paint so that remnants of the older coats show through in spots. This creates a multi-dimensional, color-textured background.

Finally, and most importantly, Scholder was caught in the rum-drenched sway of Francis Bacon, the Irish painter who depicted wildly distorted images of human subjects: ghoulish popes and poets. Bacon had also used a rag to smear and distort faces.

Francis Bacon's studio was so outrageously cluttered with rags and cans and paint tubes and brushes that, when he died, the studio was moved into a museum. *Intact.* It was a monument to fanaticism in art technique. Our man Bacon liked to drink and gamble in Monaco. And throw paint. Fritz picked up on all that passion and process and brought it to his Indian images. Fritz abstracted the West, but the message beneath was deeply realistic.

II   Into the Mystic: The Fetish Maker

The power of art in anyone's life is a must.
Every society has some form of religion and some form of art.
It seems to me to a basic activity of putting down one's marks that you were here.

— **Fritz Scholder**

My interest in Scholder's paintings is centered in his depictions of Indians – as well as the few cowboy images. I won't analyze or discuss at length his vampires, devils, martyrs, and pyramids. Leave that to the critics. I like the Indians. We're centered in the West here. It's the Indians that drew the world's attention to Fritz, and it's the Indian paintings that created controversy.

Scholder's work has drawn me to it. Yanked me by the neck. He called himself a: *"Painter, print-maker, and fetish maker."* He said: "I revel in being able to produce statements in various forms, because in today's world art and magic are greatly needed." This word *fetish* is at the heart of understanding Fritz Scholder and his art. A fetish may be a *fixation,* or a *thing evoking irrational devotion or respect. A charm, amulet, talisman, totem."* (Quote: *The Oxford Pocket Dictionary.*) Scholder was a medicine man. A conjurer in paint, print, and clay. He even carved his own fetish dolls. It's an Indian thing.

Scholder denied feeling "Indian" or being a purely "Indian painter." But it was in the blood history. His heritage is outlined in an interview in 1995 with Paul Karlstrom of the Smithsonian Institute. To quote Fritz:

> "The Scholders were an old pioneer family of San Diego County. My great-great grandfather had come over with two brothers from Wurtenberg, Germany. He decided to walk across this country. He ended up in Fort Apache (*in the Eastern part of Arizona*) and was mustered into the army there, because they were trying to catch Geronimo. After he got out, with some kind of injury, he continued to walk toward California.
>
> "He was just about dead out there and laid down under a big Oak tree to die. But he woke up and found he was in an Indian village...and he married an Indian woman. The tribe I'm affiliated with is called *Luiseno,* after King Luis of Spain. They were one of the Indian tribes that were forced to build the missions. They were chained to pillars at night so they wouldn't run away – another chapter in that particular history of the West. And my dad saw Pancho Villa once, riding around. And he shared a stage with Will Rogers."

Later, when Fritz went to seek out his Indian heritage in California, he found only ill-kept graves behind Missions, littered with *"old salt shakers and broken soda bottles."* The Indians built the missions and then were buried behind them – in unmarked graves with trash littered on top.

There's a more personal angle to my interest in Scholder – I began painting about ten years ago. I walked into an abandon studio here in El Paso and painted a cow. The cow looked more like a dog or a pig, but what the hell. I was on my way. Some call it *naïve art.* Others might call it regressing to a childish state. I call it *starting from scratch*. Somebody eventually bought that first painting. They thought it was a horse. Welcome to the world of art. I never gave up my day job as a songwriter.

I now have my art in many galleries and a book of my paintings is on the market. Not to brag. I'm a beginner. I have a long road ahead of me – and my biggest influence is Fritz Scholder. I would consider him, along with Georgia O'Keefe, two essential artists who brought a modernist view to Western painting – a magical way of looking at our landscape and Western character. We can toss around these artsy and spiritual notions like *magic* and *mystical*, but you have see the paintings yourself and gauge your own reaction, in your mind, gut, and heart. It's about the same as listening to a song. You can look or listen again and again and always take something different away.

Black river rocks. Cow and horse skulls. Drunken Indians. Fritz and Georgia O'Keefe. *Western fetish makers*. I got to thinking about them one day and wondered if they'd ever met. Then I stumbled upon that manuscript from the Smithsonian Institute interview. In sixty-eight pages of deep dialogue, Scholder lays it all out: his life, his teachers, his passion for painting, his friendship with Ralph Lauren, his meeting with Picasso's wife, the controversy surrounding his Indian paintings, and on and on... and a weird and wonderful dinner with Georgia O'Keefe.

Let me begin, though, with a short tale of my journey to one of Scholder's studios. Halloween afternoon in Galisteo, New Mexico – and the goblins and trolls were lurking in the shadows of his art.

III Halloween in Galisteo

> *You read about this lion - he killed a man with his paw*
> *Sampson he got his hands around the lion's jaw*
> *And he ripped that beast till the lion was dead*
> *And the bees made honey in the lion's head.*
>
> — **Reverend Gary Davis,** *Samson and Delilah*

It was a Halloween afternoon and the road out of Santa Fe twisted down south, aiming for Mexico, which was three hundred miles away. The journey led through a Southwestern landscape broken by adobe villages, abandoned trailers, tumbleweeds, and vacant mom and pop grocery stores. We drove onward through crippled cottonwoods and across dry creek beds – through dust-devil cyclones of autumn leaves. Deep into the forgotten West.

Galisteo was down here somewhere, where Fritz Scholder and his wife Romona owned a house and painting studio, before Fritz moved on to Scottsdale and onto his third and last marriage. Romona was still here. I was driving and thinking of that film: *Something Wicked This Way Comes*. It was a carnival movie based on a Ray Bradbury story. A carnival was setting up on the edge of town. The leaves were turning the color of a Halloween pumpkin. Autumn was the time of witches and ghouls and primitive harvest rituals. And carnivals. Fritz Scholder territory. The day had that feel to it.

Romona had kindly invited us down to see the house and studio. She met us at the church and led us down the road to the two hundred year old adobe fortress. Outside, in the back courtyard, we could see the tip of Scholder's large sculpture of a man fighting a lion beneath a Mesquite or Cottonwood tree. I thought of the Reverend Gary Davis song about Samson fighting the lion, ripping it apart, and then the bees making honey in the lion's head. Fritz must have known the song.

There was another statue of a martyr. Or was it a vampire? These figures danced beneath the falling, harvest leaves. *A ballet for The Day of the Dead.* We entered the kitchen and front room of the old adobe. The spirits were here: Native American pots, skulls, baskets, votive crosses, shrunken heads, voodoo dolls, Scholder paintings, and a small Maynard Dixon painting. Art everywhere. Tastefully arranged. A dozen more objects I couldn't focus on.

Five years earlier I'd travelled to all three major Scholder retrospectives: Santa Fe, Washington D.C., and New York City. I was on a pilgrimage. I'd stood and faced a hundred paintings, but that experience couldn't match standing in his studio, or in the front room of this adobe, feeling Fritz's ghost in all the images and objects and art. We were now inside Fritz's head. *The fetish maker.*

Romona patiently described all of it. Romona is a successful practicing psychologist and knew of my interest in Fritz's work – and here we were. Trying to absorb. In my mind you cannot glean truth from the essays and exhibition folders writ' up by art historians and critics. These folks are always telling us *what we're seeing* and *what the artist was feeling* and what *we should be feeling* and the *rudiments of the era when it all happened.* The context, you see. It doesn't work that way. Art escapes time and explanation. Here we were, in the midst of the man's mind – something here we could not describe. Like seeing a movie that altered you, but later you couldn't explain the plot.

Here was a part the collection of the kid who'd sent those

envelopes to Albert Einstein and the Royalty of the Middle East. I asked Romona about Fritz meeting Georgia O'Keefe and the legendary dinner. "Yes," she said, "He came home reeking of garlic." That was it. She smiled. Remained silent.

We walked out thought the back courtyard to his studio. I recall pictures of Fritz in this very studio – squatting down on a Navajo rug as he contemplated works in progress. I've seen a film of Fritz, in this room or another studio, pulling unfinished paintings out of a stack and destroying them. Slashing the canvas with a bowie knife. The art was either good, in Fritz's eyes, or it was gone. He was passionate and dramatic even in the process of destruction.

We looked through a large stack of Scholder's lithographs, chatted awhile, and it was time to head back to Santa Fe. We walked out of the compound. Across the road a bent mesquite fence toppled over itself, snaking up the lane – running away into the early sundown light of oranges, reds, and yellows.

Ramona Scholder said goodbye, then she took a step closer and looked me in the eye – like she was about to reveal the secret to all of this. She spoke softly.

"Did anyone ever mention to you where Fritz is buried?"

I hesitated a second. "No," I said. "Where *is he* buried?"

"I wouldn't know," she said. "*I have no idea.*"

She looked me in the eye. I looked her in the eye. On the other side of the adobe wall, behind us, a sculpted man was fighting off a bronze lion and martyrs were weeping. Weird magic afoot. Little witches were dawning their costumes in houses across the haunted West.

I had no idea where Fritz was buried. Nor did Ramona. Curious end to a Halloween afternoon. Fritz was laughing about all this, somewhere out beyond the dust-red sunset.

"*I have no idea,*" kept running around my head as we drove north, back to Santa Fe. He was buried *everywhere,* is my guess. In every painting and curious collected object. In all those dolls and crosses above the adobe fireplace. The master fetish maker had *become his art.*

As I glanced back at the adobe compound two chubby Indian kids, a boy and girl, were walking down the road with trick or treat bags. I thought of Fritz and Georgia O'Keefe. One of the little boys even *looked like* Fritz, and I suppose it was. The old trickster and shape shifter.

The Indian kids were yelling *trick or treat,* and I hit the gas before the little Fritz monster could grab me and inform me where he'd been buried, before he'd crawled out of the grave with his trick or treat bag. I reached into the glove box and brought out an old Paul Siebel CD and jammed it into the player. I turned it up loud, as we flew though that Halloween afternoon – back towards Santa Fe.

But the Fritz necromancy wouldn't give up. The old Luiseno fetish maker had hold of my soul. Paul Seibel sang these lines from the song: "Then Came the Children":

Well come gather around me friends of mine,
While I sing to you about a minstrel band
Of children in their witches hats,
Painting pictures with the pipes of pan...

IV Fritz and Georgia

"...to live on paper and canvas
what we're living our hearts
and heads."

— **Georgia O'Keefe**

For traditional Western painters I favor Edward Borein and Charlie Russell for their depictions of cowboys, vaqueros, bony steers and horses. True West. Their drawings and paintings exuded raw character and knowledge of the cowboy soul. A horse felt like a horse. If the horse had wintered poorly, that's how the boys painted it. Remington, for my taste, was too polished and removed. He was a fine illustrator, but I couldn't read where his heart lay.

I like Maynard Dixon for his skies, and I have seen those same rolling cloudbanks on many an afternoon in West Texas. They certainly exist as wonderment of the Great Spirit's work. Maynard had them down. I loved Tom Lea, because he *knew* the country and *knew toros bravos* and I was honored to have lunch with him once, when he was 90 years old and blind, and we talked about the bullfighter, *Manolete,* and about how to distinguish between dozens of varieties of cactus and other varied Western matters. Tom Lea's lunch that day consisted of three bowls of Peppermint ice cream. I loved all these western painters.

Then there was Will James. I have odd Will James memorabilia – a cancelled check from 1931 and a letter sent to a friend from the Hotel Algonquin in New York, asking the friend to send Will's drawings back. Will (or *Bill* as he called himself) was fond of drawing broncs on cocktail napkins in back street Hollywood bars. I wish I had one of those.

But Scholder knocked me over. His Indians anyway. And I'd been an admirer of Georgia O'Keefe since I was a kid. She was a desert rat. So was I. Obviously when you speak of this thing called *art magic* or Southwestern *fetishism* or plain-old *Southwestern art*, you arrive at the bottom line. Georgia O'Keefe.

No need to dissect her life here. She has been well writ-up, and her landscapes, florals, and bone paintings are featured in a thousand sets of calendars and greeting cards. *An American icon.* Georgia's shadow snakes across the modern Southwest, and it's a long one. No other female artist, with the exception of Frida Kahlo, has empowered more women to strike out into their own isolate, artistic territories. Her spirit circles around Taos and Santa Fe and Silver City and anywhere someone is bent over an easel or a potter's wheel. She was a hard act to follow.

Georgia had seen the bright lights of Times Square, painted depictions of the Empire State Building (as did Fritz) and then turned her back on those Eastern lights, trading them for the magic blush and glow of the Southwestern deserts. She retreated to New Mexico. *"She went away inside her own country,"* a critic remarked. She re-invented herself and flourished for over ninety years. She had immense mettle. Plenty to spare.

Georgia *became* the Southwest she loved. Arid, cere, silent, portentous – at times poisonous. A wizened human-agave with long thorns. She was a minimalist in work and personality. There was no bullshitting her, and she preferred her own company. She liked smooth black river rocks and ocotillo fences and ancient Indian baskets. She loved to cook, and her hands seem to have been transplanted from an olden Spanish statue – long veins running down fingers that were elegant and knowledgeable in the dough. Always *in the dough*, or the clay or the paint. Or *thinking up* the paint.

Fritz Scholder knocked on Georgia's door one day, out of the blue, half-expecting to be thrown off the premises. Georgia was in a gentile mood that afternoon and invited him in. He sat at her feet and listened to her talking about "Frankie" (Frank Lloyd Wright) and how she missed not stretching her own canvases, and the sorry fact that you couldn't find a good wine in Santa Fe.

"It's always dangerous to meet one's heroes," Scholder said in the Smithsonian interview. "...because you can, of course be very disappointed. O'Keefe especially had developed a persona, and when she opened the gate I first was struck by just realizing she looked like her pictures. It was shocking. She'd developed a persona that I'd never seen in anyone else, and as we crossed the patio with the famous black door, she said something to me I'll never forget. She said, 'There are times when you must spend an afternoon with one whom one will never see again.'" *(Scholder laughs)* "And I knew what she meant. I'd caught her at the right time. She was lonely."

"She spoke in poetry," Scholder continued, "And she floated as she walked. She talked around her art, but never *about* it.

As the late afternoon shadows moved across O'Keefe's face, Scholder witnessed her shape-shifting between a male and female spirit. She seemed androgynous, basked in the red-yellow glow. She rocked in her chair and occasionally reached down and ran her hands across the smooth river rocks, which were arranged in a flat Indian basket on the floor.

"At one point," said Fritz, "she was talking, her eyes were closed, and she stopped in mid-sentence. And I looked up and it was quiet and I waited. *Nothing.* And I thought, *'God, Georgia O'Keefe has died on me.'* She was sitting there and it seemed like an eternity. But all of a sudden she started right where she left off. She had been waiting for the precise word, and if it meant that I had to wait and she had to wait, that was fine. She had self-integrity that wouldn't stop."

One night, when Georgia had become more comfortable around Scholder, she invited him to a dinner party at the adobe. There were at least eight courses of gourmet food served. The courses changed when O'Keefe rang a little bell for her Spanish maid. When everyone was full, out came a giant bowl of salad, and Georgia served up large portions for all. The guests choked it down politely. Nobody crossed Georgia.

"I took the first taste of that salad," said Fritz, "and I almost fell off my chair, because she'd put every garlic in the world in this salad. This salad would have walked off by itself. It was incredible! And I knew I had to eat it."

"At that point, Georgia looked up at all of us with a little smile on the corner of her mouth, and she said: 'Well how do you like the salad?' And like school kids, we said in unison, 'Great Georgia.' *(Fritz laughs)* And she said, 'Well that's nice because we have enough for seconds.' And she rings the bell and the maid comes *(Fritz laughs again)*...and I don't know to this day if this was some little joke of hers or what, because when I got back to Santa Fe that evening I was *green*, I was told. And I *felt* green too. And I couldn't look a garlic in the face for five years."

And on it went into the night. Georgia was the spirit and sainted presence hovering over the energy of the room. And who wouldn't have loved to have been a lizard or a fly on the wall above a basket of black river rocks – that night when the garlic salad was served?

The desert West is the territory you aim for when you've had enough of faculty meetings, grant applications, faux social scenes, and art openings where the cheap Chardonnay is served in plastic cups, and no one really *looks* at the art, or feels it. You *go away inside your own country*, out yonder to the desert, and reinvent your ability to talk to God through your art. You spice the salad any damn way you wish.

Fritz had met his match.

V Indian/Not Indian

> *Fritz Scholder was the preeminent Native American artist of the twentieth century, whose work speaks of contradiction and the unexpected. Characterized by psychological complexity, Fritz Scholder's work led the way to a bold, new kind of Indian art and enriched American art history...*
>
> — **Ralph Lauren,** *Indian Not Indian*

In the year 2008 the Smithsonian Institution, in league with the National Museum of the American Indian, staged a double Fritz Scholder exhibit in New York and Washington D.C. The exhibition (and the book which followed) were titled: *Indian Not Indian.* I would recommend the book for anyone interested in Western art. I favor the Indian and cowboy images. I've established that above. But in order to understand this man's life and work you'd have to cast an eye on the dark stuff – the vampires, martyrs, monsters and fallen angels.

As I leafed through that Smithsonian interview I discovered that Fritz was a friend of the late songwriter John Stewart. Stewart had been a member of the Kingston Trio and later enjoyed a successful solo career. I'd worked with John several times and some folks have compared my singing voice with his – dark and low. I'm honored. He was a damn good songwriter with a huge following in the Southwest.

I called up John Stewart's wife, the singer Buffy Ford, and learned a few more details and amusing anecdotes about Fritz and his penchant for collecting odd objects, and painting unsettling subject matter. I was a given another insider view.

"Fritz was light as a person," said Buffy, "but dark as an artist. He was scared of death. But in his house he had this death room with mummies and coffins! One time he came home with this real voodoo doll from New Orleans. He brought it in a plastic sack, and when he got out of the car his dog attacked the bag and ripped it apart. Fritz had to put the doll in a glass case."

"One day my husband John and I went over to Fritz's house and Fritz showed John the voodoo doll. In the glass case. John felt instantly sick when he got close to the case. We had to leave. That's the kind of stuff Fritz had around."

"Another time Fritz brought out this little sliver of wood. He said it was an authentic piece of *the true cross*. The cross Jesus was crucified on. A little sliver. He handed it to John, and John drops the cross! They're both down on the floor looking all around for a long time. They never found it. Fritz was such a nice man. He never used profanity or anything. But he had all this dark, weird stuff. And he always wore these red shoes. Like magic slippers or something. He was a magician. So was John."

Here was the doubled-sided nature of the artist who painted the martyrs and vampires. And those Indians. *Monster Indian, Portrait of a Massacred Indian, Drunk Indian in Car, Indian With Beer Can* – Scholder seemed to be scratching and smearing the paint, in order to reach the voodoo beneath it all. And the message. The pain embedded within Native American history.

"I knew," said Fritz, "that when I started the Indian series that it was a loaded subject. It was a no-win subject and it was national guilt. So it was a subject that had tremendous baggage with it. And for me to abstract the subject...well..." It was a dangerous move.

Fritz continues: "But I was surprised at the outrage, immediate outrage, especially in Santa Fe, when I started the Indian series. The gallery literally had to have armed guards at the door because of the reaction of the militant Indian groups. And for a number of years in Santa Fe there were armed guards at my openings. Art is very powerful.

"With the Indian thing I was intent on going past the clichés and pushing people's ideas about the subject. I once did an Indian standing in front of the Eiffel Tower, and people might have thought that I was using my imagination. I wasn't. There were old photographs of Indian chiefs being photographed when Buffalo Bill's Wild West Show arrived in Paris."

The current world of Western art, at times, slides into a *greeting card* view of the West. Cowboys on hills gazing at the stars. Stage coaches in rainy frontier towns. Images of male and female Indians dressed up in buckskin finery. They usually look like well-tanned, white, Hollywood actors. Movie extras. Scholder saw the other side of the coin. Fritz had been to Gallup, New Mexico on a Saturday night after the bars closed down. He'd witnessed *the parade of the walking wounded*. That outsider territory of our West where a Navajo might hawk his best silver or *Two Grey Hills* rug – and go on a bender. Staggering towards the next bar.

"Non Indian painters," said Fritz, "had been painting the Indian for decades as a noble savage in a very romantic way, coming up with paintings that looked like Italians squatting by the bonfire sharpening their arrows. And then there were a lot of Indian artists from the Indian school who had been caught in a tourist pleasing cliché – painting colorful paintings for tourists. Being in an art colony can be an albatross around the neck of any town."

So be it, Fritz.

There are deep mysteries embedded in the history of our Western art. We're reminded of that by peering at old Kachina carvings, antique Navajo rugs, Mimbres pottery, and such. And the images of certain fetish makers and painters like Fritz Scholder and Georgia O'Keefe. It's strong stuff. Like a salad spiced with an overabundance of garlic. You may not like it – but you'll never forget the experience. And the mind of the person who served it up.

That Halloween afternoon in Galisteo swirls around in my memory, and the Paul Seibel Halloween song. In that same song Seibel wrote:

Somewhere in the distance
you and I have fought
the monster to a draw...

Fritz Scholder looked the monster in the eye and fought it to a draw. He painted what he saw. And felt. The quarter blood Luiseno gave us an abstract-expressionistic eye for viewing the Indian West. Fritz and Georgia expanded our Western vision, even if they tossed the odd dark image, or a chunk of raw garlic into the mix. They both *went away inside their own country* and left their mark by putting on canvas what they lived inside their hearts and heads.

Thanks to: Romona Scholder, Gary Brown, Eric Temple, and Buffy Ford.

Through the Looking Glass with Ramblin' Jack Elliott

*Did you ever stand and shiver,
just because you were lookin' at a river?*

— **Ramblin' Jack Elliott**
912 Greens

I **Four Scenes from a Rough Script...**
The Makings of Ramblin' Jack

Scene One:
Picture a four-story Victorian Brownstone apartment in Brooklyn. Around 1939. Up in a high window there's an eight-year-old boy peering down onto Ocean Parkway, the wide promenade running from Prospect Park to Brighton Beach. The kid in the window hears the roar rising up from nearby Ebbets Field. One of the Brooklyn Dodgers just hit a home run. It's a Flatbush summer's day. It's an American moment. The kid is all ears.

Later the boy will mimic and re-create that roar with a hurricane, windy-sound rolling out of his throat and over his lips. He will tell you it's the sound of the crowd at Ebbets field on a July day. You will believe him. He will tell you this long after Ebbets field has been torn down and the Dodgers have moved to Los Angeles.

The kid will be an American *raconteur*. A spinner of long remembered dreams. The boy will be able to summon everything that ever happened to him. Every moment in his event-filled life. How the weather was, and what the girls were wearing. In elaborate and charmed detail.

Now the magic moment is at hand. The turning point in the kid's life. The boy looks down and sees a cowboy riding a horse up the Parkway below. *Imagine that.* Out of the blue. It's one-horse parade advertising the rodeo at Madison Square Garden. A cowboy riding through the streets of Brooklyn. The boy in the window is hooked. *Forever.*

The kid runs down four flights of stairs and follows the cowboy to the edge of the Belt Parkway – miles away – to Coney Island. Out to an old rent-horse stable near the beach. The kid wants to talk to the cowboy. The following week he will command his parents to take him to the old Madison Square Garden in New York City. *To the rodeo.* He will hear Gene Autry sing. Next year they will return to the rodeo and hear Roy Rogers. The kid will buy a cowboy songbook and learn *Red River Valley.* He will read all of Will James' novels. The boy is now a cowboy. *In his imagination.* He will saddle-up his dream and spur wild his buckaroo fantasy. *Forever.*

The boy's name is Elliott Charles Adnopoz. His father is a doctor.

Scene Two:

A few years later. Around 1945. The teenaged boy has run off with the rodeo. He's got a job cleaning stalls and grooming trick horses for Colonel Jim Eskew's outfit. The kid has a guitar. He's learning chords and songs from a rodeo clown named *Brahma Rogers.* The cowboys and wranglers call the kid *Poncho.* And later *Buck Elliott.* His parents, back in Brooklyn, are dead-worried. There's a *missing child* flyer nailed on telephone poles all over Brooklyn and New York City. I've seen this flyer reproduced:

"Wanted: Elliott Charles Adnopoz...age sixteen...
gold rim glasses...carrying a small brown
    canvas bag...
probable destination a ranch...Parents not opposed to him
staying on a ranch."

Exactly like that.

Scene Three:

1957. Paris. The kid has grown up. In his 20s now. He calls himself *Ramblin' Jack Elliott.* He *is* Ramblin' Jack Elliott. This thing he has become. The myth fully formed — spurred and broke to ride. He's learned guitar from Woody Guthrie out in Coney Island. He's memorized Woody's repertoire — including all the cowboy songs. He's now busking (singing on the streets for donations) with his friend Derroll Adams. *Rake and a Ramblin Boy, Buffalo Skinners, Muleskinner Blues, Old Blue, Billy the Kid.* They're bringing cowboy music to Paris, Rome, Brussels and London. They ride Vespa motor scooters with wives and girl friends and guitars and wine bottles strapped on the back. Bohemian cowboys. *Boulevardiers.*

Ramblin' Jack Elliott will busk on the London subway platform and Mick Jagger, later of *The Rolling Stones*, will see the cowboy with his guitar and he (Mick) will decide then and there to become a singer and quit art school. *Imagine* the musical history involved here. The conjunction of artistic spirits.

But wait.

Somewhere, high up on the Mesabi Iron Ore Range of Minnesota, a young kid named Robert Zimmerman will borrow a Ramblin' Jack Elliott LP from a friend. He will study Ramblin Jack's guitar styling, his drawl, and his manner of presenting a song. This kid, up in Minnesota, will later change his name to Bob Dylan. He will, in turn, concoct his own personal myths and histories which will include tales of carnivals, circuses, reform schools, playing piano in rock and roll bands, entertaining at Colorado strip joints...and the like. Some of it true. Some of it fiction. The Minnesota kid will pioneer folk songwriting.

Scene Four:

2008. Elko Nevada. The National Cowboy Poetry Gathering. I'm getting married to a lovely Swiss gal, in a backstreet wedding chapel – a light snow is falling. *Wylie Gustafson. Paul Zarzyski. Dick Gibford.* The room is filled with cowboy singers and poets. The *crème de la crème.* Ian Tyson is our best man, and he sings a song with lines such as: *What does she see in this old cowboy*? Ramblin' Jack Elliott is also honorary best man, and he's now hopping around and singing endless verses of *Rake and a Ramblin Boy*. It's like Jack's theme song...and mine, in a way.

It's a wedding song on this occasion.

Well I'm a rake and a ramblin' boy
There's many a city I did enjoy
But now I married me a pretty little wife
And I love her dearer than I love my life...

Ian keeps elbowing me: *"Is he through yet? Is he through yet?"*

But Jack ain't never through. He's dancing and singing. His mind was carried off by that rodeo cowboy riding up that Brooklyn Boulevard. Almost seventy years back. Jack's life is enveloped in a never-ending biographical rap which issues forth from his musical tongue – a long bending story or song – footnoted in the ever changing moments of Jack's mind. *Living folk history.* American Poetry.

Roll the credits. For *now.* Our experimental cowboy script has no end...the stories go on and on. Let's take a closer gander at Jack's early music years.

II Buskers, Boulevardiers, and Basket Houses

Jack treats his guitar like a human being...
his (first wife) June told how when they first got married
Jack wanted to keep the guitar in bed with them...
June would make sure that Jack had his finger picks
and that he knew what songs he was going to sing
and that his hair was
combed and that his fly was zipped up...
and after he got through she would pass the hat around
and then they'd go somewhere to eat, and she would portion
out the money...(To Jack and Derroll)...

— **Shel Silverstein,** 1957

What does this *Ramblin' Jack Elliott* have to do with the vision of our West? *Plenty.* The West is a land of ongoing reinvention, fashioned by artists, writers, showmen, flim-flammers, snake oil salesmen, range bums, saddle tramps, and outlaws who altered their personal histories and re-christened themselves with a more colorful handle: *Billy the Kid, Mark Twain, Will James, Buffalo Bill Cody* and such....Jack's contribution? Ramblin' Jack Elliott created his identity in those early Wild West shows out East, grabbed a guitar, learned traditional cowboy songs, and then took this music back to the old country, in much the same way that Buffalo Bill took buffalos, broncs and Indians across the Atlantic. Europe never got over it. Then Jack returned to America and made cowboy music legit among the new-folk crowd.

I'm damn fascinated by Jack's "early period" when he sang on the street with that Portland banjo player named Derroll Adams. On the avenues of the old world they call it *"busking,"* from the Spanish verb *buscar: to seek.* (Ramblin' Jack told me that.) It's an honest trade that goes back to Homer and *The Odyssey* on down to Zossimus in Ireland. The *sung-news* accompanied by drum, lute, mandolin, or guitar. For a begging basket the boys had a cowboy hat turned upside down on the sidewalk. Derroll and Jack played for food and wine, and maybe a pallet on the floor. Wandering bards. Folk blood brothers.

> "We'd put out our hat on the streets of Paris," said Jack, "and play 'til we made enough for a hotel room and a meal. Other people might play all day, but Derroll and I were not all that greedy. Maybe we shoulda' been. Ha!"

They eventually recorded an album called: *Ramblin Boys*. Another called: *The Cowboys*. They yodeled and drank up their busking money and cris-crossed the continent. In a short time they were European legends. When Jack had his fill of busking through Europe he caught a freighter back to America. He was welcomed as a hero in Greenwich Village. Folks began to steal his style and guitar licks.

Derroll Adams never came back.

He established himself as a folk presence in Europe and married a pretty Belgian woman, Danny. ("*The most decent human being I've ever met.*"). He settled in Antwerp and created a banjo style he called *Up-Picking* and *Back Picking*. In the next three decades he'd read a thousand of books, paint a thousand pictures, and occasionally appear in the smoky Belgium folk clubs and festivals all over Europe. Not so much a *renaissance man* as Zen-Cowboy throwback.

Derroll was part of the Beat scene in Topanga Canyon, California, in 1954. He met the actor-botanist Will Geer and also had his first encounter with Ramblin' Jack Elliott. Jack does a fine imitation of Derroll at that historic meeting:

> "*I hear you play the banjo.*" *says Jack.*
> "*Yup,*" *says Derroll.*
> "*You wannna play a song?*" *says Jack.*
> "*Guess so,*" *says Derroll.*
> "*You got a banjo? Says Jack.*
> "*Nope,*" *says Derroll.*
> "*Maybe we could borrow one from Bess Hawes,*" *says Jack.*
> "*Yup,*" *says Derroll.*

The first song the boys learned together was *Muleskinner Blues*. Says Jack:

> *Derroll Adams was the closest thing to a Muleskinner I had ever met at that time...he had been a lumberjack choker-setter and a windfall bucker. But Derroll had something extra. He had a Chinese kinda' beard, and he had sorta' Japanese calligraphy written on his banjo. It was some kind of hip statement that Jack Kerouac wished he'd have wrote.*

In 1958 Derroll and Ramblin' Jack performed at the Brussels World Fair billed as *The Cowboys*. Then Jack split and there was Derroll, happy to scratch out a living as the only banjo-playing cowboy on the European continent. Derroll Adams died in Antwerp Belgium February 6, 2000.

One magic afternoon in Antwerp, after Derroll had passed on, I was allowed to step back into his life. I was invited for coffee at his old apartment. I was sleuthing Jack and Derroll's busking years. I sat in the kitchen with Danny Adams, Derroll's wife. I don't like the word *widow*. It connotes spiders and death and loss, and Derroll was still hovering around us. Frailing the banjo.

Those old Antwerp rooms were crowded with *the things Derroll left us*, as Danny whispers. *The things Derroll left us*. A grand bohemian disarray of an underground life lived well. Tea kettles, coffee cups, and jelly glasses with Burgundy stains. Stack of his original paintings. The aroma of red wine, candle smoke, old books, oil paint and kerosene. Two of his banjos sat propped-up on the couch.

Nothing was moved since Derroll passed-on. I strummed a G chord on one of his banjos and got the chills. I pictured him riding his old bicycle down to the river in Antwerp – sitting there with a sandwich and a bottle of wine. Playing banjo or painting all day. Matisse in a cowboy hat. Now he's moved to higher ground. I thought of that Ramblin' Jack line: *Did you ever stand and shiver...just because you were lookin' at a river?*

Jack's still here. I closed my eyes, strummed another G chord, and thought back to when I first heard Ramblin' Jack *live*.

III Visions of My Folk Childhood

I've heard a lot of wonderful stories about myself.
Enviable – I wish I could've done it.

— **Ramblin' Jack Elliott**

I used to hang out at a folk club in Hollywood called *The Ash Grove*. Early 1960s. If I was broke, I snuck through the back door. I saw Lightnin' Hopkins, Mississippi John Hurt, Doc Watson, Dave Van Ronk, Ian and Sylvia (best folk group ever), and Ramblin' Jack Elliott.

One night Jack pulled up in a big telephone truck he was living in with his dog Caesar. Jack would later say, on stage, that Caesar drove the truck. Caesar would only drive at five miles per hour. You had a choice when you listened to Ramblin' Jack – you could close your ears in disbelief or pretended boredom, or you could listen and believe *Ramblin' Jack's Never Ending Garden of Verse, Riddles, Bullshit, and Whole-Hog Fairytales*.

That rap, which is the essence of Jack, is like going down the rabbit hole with *Alice in Wonderland*. If you survive the story – with all its beatniks, abstract painters, brahma bulls, mad hatters, ex-wives, cow dogs, Presidents, mustangs, wooden boats, sailing ships, 18 wheeler trucks, rope horses...and who drank *what* and *when* in *whatever* town...then you become an *aficionado* of a man who has changed the face of this music we call "folk."

Sometimes Jack would step off the stage at the Ash Grove and walk around the room, stopping at your table – playing his fingerpicked Martin guitar right in your face. It was spine tingling for this kid. *Wondrous. Epiphanious.* Is that a word? Hell, I wanted to become a folksinger. A songwriter. I wanted to ride down the trail with Jack. And Bob Dylan. And Ian and Sylvia. The minstrel road. *Hand me my wild harp, sire, I'm bound for the land of song.* But I didn't have the guts. Yet.

But Jack! What a guitar player. I am presenting Jack here in fragments because Jack can only be *understood* in fragments (like his rap), and not in straight-time biographical detail. You must understand Jack *in the abstract*. Take what you will. Like his guitar playing. It seems to combine a little Woody Guthrie with tricks from the old rodeo clown, Brahma Rogers. And then throw in some jazz – say Freddie Green and the up-picking banjo styles of Derroll Adams, all mixed in a blender of guitar swaps from long nights on the road.

Ian Tyson has a take on Jack's guitar style:

> *I heard Jack when he came back from Europe, in '63 or '62, and he was with Cisco Houston at Gerde's Folk City, and I had never heard anything like it...his style went back to the Gib Tanner stuff, the really early stuff, but I didn't know anything about that coming from Canada, cause the guitar styles we knew came from Wilf Carter, and it was a great style. And I heard Jack, and it was very syncopated. And he blew me away with his early stuff. But Jack had all the pyro-technics. He'd been blowing away all those young Mick Jaggers, and AC/DC and all... but, yeah, it was great to hear. I've never figured out if Jack knew what the hell he was doing or not.*

Let's attempt to peer a tad deeper into Jack's soul and dig into one of his few original songs – *912 Greens*. Inside this *folk-rap-song* or *talking blues* you catch a glimpse of the oft-cultivated, deep furrows of the man's memory. Jack keeps turning the sod over and coming up with newly discovered relics, bone fragments, and fossils...relating to a journey sixty years ago.

IV 912 Greens

> *We met a banjo picker with two different eyes.*
> *One eye was looking at the audience, and the other*
> *was oogling the girls backstage...I wished I could do that.*
> *He made that banjo sound like a train coming in and out of*
> *a tunnel. It was a **Kay** with a resonator on the back...*
>
> — **Ramblin' Jack Elliott**, *912 Greens*, 2008 Version

Jack Elliott has written only two or three songs that I know of: *912 Greens* and *A Cup of Coffee* are two of' 'em. But that's enough. The rest of his repertoire consists of chestnuts visited and revisited through dozens of records and a hundred thousand performances – from the Paris streets to Carnegie Hall to the saloons of Winnemucca. Cowboy songs, truck drivin' songs, Woody Guthrie songs. But those two originals give us a slanted glimpse of how Jack's creative mind works.

A Cup of Coffee, originally recorded with Johnny Cash on Cash's record *Everybody Loves a Nut*, is another spoken word sort of deal. In the narrative Jack drives his semi-truck up to Johnny's house to say hello. Coffee is prepared. Later Johnny is pouring whiskey in Jack's coffee, *to cool it off*, and Jack passes out on the couch (leaving his clutch foot on the floor) – but only after a long, humorous Ramblin' Jack dissertation on trucks. And Jack knows *all about* big-rig trucks. (And wooden boats and schooners.) *Ask him*. He'll take you through every gear. I later recorded the song as a duet with Jack on one of his records. We also recorded a song of mine: *The Sky Above the Mud Below*. Quite an honor for this kid.

But *912 Greens*.

The song recreates a trip Jack took to New Orleans in 1953. *912 Greens* (*greens* as opposed to *blues*) has to do with the address, *912 Toulouse Street*, the destination of the journey. *Sorta*. That's where the party took place – the central focus of the song. The bohemian pad of banjo-picker Billy Faire.

> *Round about 1953 I went down to New Orleans...*
> *perhaps I should say – many years ago...we sang*
> *and busked our way through the Smoky Mountains*
> *and on down to New Orleans...*

Onward it rolls like a road story from the best of Jack Kerouac. Finally, at about the seven minute mark, Jacks eases to a close...

> *Stayed around three weeks in New Orleans...*
> *never did see the light of day...and I've never*
> *been back since.*

Then Jack lays-in the closing line – the only rhymed couplet of the song:

> *Did you ever stand and shiver,*
> *just because you were looking at a river?*

Sort of a Zen question. The end of that three week party where Jack drank Billy Faire's wine, danced naked in the rain around a banana tree – with a ballet dancer, raced a three legged cat up the stairs, stared at the Mississippi River (*The Missus Miller* river he calls it), and sat in a chair where Jack Kerouac had once sat. And plenty more. It seems like nothing happened. It seems like *everything* happened.

I've heard Jack sing the song a dozen times, and there are various recorded performances, and each one is vastly different. A version in 2008 deals with the first part of the trip, with a stop in Asheville to meet several famous banjo legends, and Jack describes the color of the shirts each was wearing.

Other versions sing up: *smoke clouds of sugar blowin' off the French donuts* (*beignets*) in the Cafe du Monde in New Orleans, and the smell of chicory coffee, and a long ramble about Jack hearing someone in the car singing *South Coast*, and it's the first time Jack's heard that great cowboy song, and the guy (Frank) would only sing the song if it was raining, and later Jack would learn it and sing the definitive version. Stuff like that.

912 Greens accomplishes what Jack Kerouac attempted in *On the Road*. The *U.K. Guardian* said of Kerouac: *He had a remarkable ear for the cadences of a phrase...the sense of how to register in words the sheer, sweet flow of things.* Kerouac considered all his novels to be one long series of books which detailed the *Proustian* history of his life.

That might be a high-flown way of trying to unravel Jack's continuous rap. The stories are *Proustian. Kerouac-ian. Ramblin' Jack-ian.*

If you'd recorded every story Jack has ever told – in the last fifty years – you would arrive at that monumental 100 volume *prosaic thing* Kerouac and Proust were after. *The Remembrance of Things Past.* Welcome to Jack's life – through *the looking glass* and down that rabbit hole you might never return from. Carry water. Or whiskey. And a bedroll.

But I digress. It goes with the territory.

V This Train is Bound for Glory

> *Nobody I know – and I mean nobody – has covered*
> *more ground and made more friends and sung more songs*
> *than the fellow you're about to meet right now. He's got a song*
> *and a friend for every mile behind him. Say hello*
> *to my good buddy, Ramblin' Jack Elliott.*
>
> — **Johnny Cash,** The Johnny Cash Television Show, 1969

I could rave on and on. Casting chunks of paint on the canvas and attempting a raw portrait of Ramblin' Jack. But it comes out all *cubist* and fragmented like a middle period Picasso. I could tell about the time in Switzerland, when I was touring with Jack, that I watched him talk to a caged Cockatoo in a hotel lobby in Zurich. Jack talked to the bird for half an hour and the bird seemed to be talking back. You'd expect this.

Or I could tell about the premier of the film: *The Ballad of Ramblin' Jack*, in a grand old theater in New York City. The film was made by Jack's daughter. I was sitting behind Jack – who was slumped down in the seat, hiding beneath his cowboy hat – painfully having to watch this film in which three of his ex-wives, and his daughter, are trying to pinpoint and come terms with Jack's *wanderabo* personality and the *irresponsibility* of his rambling ways. Good luck.

Later on Jack and I ended up in a New York joint called *The Rodeo Bar*. Singing, laughing, and drinking away the weirdness. We were but a few blocks away from where the old Madison Square Garden used to sit. The very spot where young Elliott Charles Adnopoz saw Gene Autry and Roy Rogers sing – *horseback*. This night at The Rodeo Bar Jack unleashed his rendition of the roar the baseball crowd after a home run at Ebbets field, circa 1939. *Whooosh...*

Or consider the time, at The White House, when Jack received a lifetime achievement award from President Clinton, and Jack whispered in Clinton's ear: *lets sneak out the back door and go down the street and see Bob Dylan...he's playing down there.* And Clinton whispered back, grinning: *Jack, I only wish I could...*

I was stuttering towards an end to this piece when I ran across a live tape. A song workshop in a train rolling across Canada. Tom Russell, Ian Tyson, and Ramblin' Jack Elliott. The year was 2007. A series called: *Roots on the Rails*. Roll the tape. Ramblin' Jack just got on in Winnipeg. He hasn't slept in a few days. It's around noon. Jack orders a bourbon and water. Ian orders a Chardonnay. Then another. Myself, I'm on my second coffee, hanging on for dear life, sandwiched in between two of my heroes.

Jack and Ian launch into stories and songs. You shoulda' been there. Two legends feeding off each other and telling it *like it is* and *was*. Everything I've been trying to capture about Jack is evidenced in that one hour.

Briefly:

Jack*: The idea of being a Cowboy from New York is somehow atrocious for people to understand...Well, it came to me just a few weeks ago, that the stork that was carrying me, was supposed to deliver me somewhere near Miles City, Montana, and he was flying over...and he looked down and he saw Will James, and Will James looked up and he saw the stork with me, and he beckoned the stork to come down and have a drink. And one drink let to another. And after about 4 drinks, the stork finally said: "I gotta get out of here," and he took off. Thanked Will for the drink. Got me all secured in his beak...but he was a little off in his navigation. He dropped me in Brooklyn by mistake. Supposed to drop me in Miles City, Montana. That's my story and I'm sticking to it.*

Then Ian tells a good one about Will James and Ernest Hemingway meeting in the basement of an art gallery in Montana. Ernest had two broken legs from skiing in Idaho. Will and Ernest are drinking. Hard. They hated each other. There are words between them....end of story.

Back to Jack*: Well...My dad's nurse, Katherine, gave me a Christmas present when I was 12 years old, of a book by Will James, called: "Lone Cowboy, My Life Story," I read that very carefully. And then I read almost every other Will James book that I could get my hands on.*

Jack and Ian sing a duet of Tyson's *Will James*. Ragged and right.

Jack goes back into a rap: *How does a Cowboy every come from Brooklyn? It's not known for any cattle...but I saw some cows when I was a kid. My grandpa had cattle. My father was born on a farm in Connecticut, and his daddy had some cows. And I was chased by a bull when I was about 4 years old on grandpa's farm. That might have been some of the inspiration that made me later on wanna' ride bulls. I'm kind of what you call a* **slow bloomer**. *I was 47 before I ever got on a bull. And I was 47 when I* **quit** *bull-riding. But at least I got a chance to see of what it feels like to sit on one of them. That was the main thing, just to sit on one to say I'd been there.*

The train stops and starts moving slowly backwards. Ian remarks that we'll never arrive in Vancouver. But we are literally and figuratively backing-up into western Canada and into real folk history. The stuff that lured me into the game. The boys break into *Muleskinner Blues*. Guitars wailing.

John Graves, the Texas essayist, defined history as: *that scattered, paper parchment, half reliable racial remembrance, where people make tales, since not much of history is reliable.* Indeed. I prefer the folk tales of my childhood heroes, a few of whom are still out there, bent over a guitar, spinning the yarns, creating ballads, and *legendeering* on down the road. It's a noble task.

Basta! Enough. Long live the minstrel boys. And that Brooklyn kid who followed the one-horse parade towards Coney Island. On towards Colonel Jim Eskew's rodeo, and further onward to the boulevards of Paris, and the basket houses of Greenwich Village, and on up to The White house and back out on the road. Fingerpicking. Flatpicking. Rapping and a rambling. Out of the bucking chutes and down that rabbit hole. Through the *great cowboy looking glass*.

Ramblin' Jack Elliott has left his spur marks in the America Grain.

The Falconer
A Journey into the Western Outback

GoHawks were psychic, like red setters, and rage was contagious between unconscious hearts.

— **T.H. White**, *The Goshawk*

We were seated for dinner. The table was set with a large bowl of freshly chopped salad and a sizeable pot of homemade *posole*. Southwestern-style *posole*. Mexican stew with wild pig meat and *frijoles* and I don't know what all. The cook was Libby, an archeologist, mountain climber, musician, and chef. Four feet away, the Peregrine falcon was perched on the gloved arm of her husband, the falconer. The bird watched us with its sharp, raptor's eyes, and then began tearing away at chunks of frozen quail which the falconer held out with his opposite, ungloved hand. The chunks of quail flew across the dinner table. We covered our plates and reached for the Mongolian vodka.

Outside we could hear the baying of coursing hounds, *Russian Tazi's,* as the moon floated up over red mountains. Welcome to Mongolia. My wife's father, visiting from Switzerland, was sitting across from me. He has abandoned his trepidations about hounds, falcons, flying quail meat, bears, and the Wild West, and had fortified himself with the Mongolian firewater. His eyes glazed over with the drink and the promise of medieval spectacle. We were getting that all right. Full dose. The stories were flying now and that falcon kept staring us down, in between its attack on the quail meat.

Yes, we could have been in Mongolia. True enough. Riding across the steppes on a Mongol pony, a giant eagle on our arm, hunting for a wolf hiding up yonder in the low rocks. Our hosts had certainly been there. Hunted with the Mongols. Drank the vodka. Wrote the book.

Time to uncork the wine. Truthfully, for a sober moment, we are in Magdalena, New Mexico, a half hour from Socorro, and two hours from Santa Fe. It's exotic enough. The West goes on forever and connects with the Moors and Mongols and falconers and all of it. Ancient hunters and mounted hordes. We've come to visit the falconer, Steve Bodio. I was tipped off by the renowned Western photographer Jay Dusard. He said Bodio was a man I should meet. I might like his writing.

Dusard told it true. I have enjoyed and learned much from the books Bodio has written: books on the Southwest, falcons, eagles, hawks, pigeons, coursing dogs, hunting, and on and on. Eight books and numerous articles for *Sports Illustrated, Atlantic Monthly, Grays Sporting Journal* and such. He is not only one of our foremost "nature" or "sporting" writers, he's a top level American writer. Period. Now he was sitting across from me with a Peregrine falcon on his arm, and the raptor is slewing chunks of meat across the table. Pass the wine, please.

To draw a bead on this falconer, consider the words of Annie Proulx, in her introduction to Bodio's new history of eagles – (*An Eternity of Eagles*):

> *Bodio...was a man who collected insects, raised pigeons, and hunted with falcons and hawks; collected rare books on the natural world, was vastly well read in history, paleontology, archeology and climatology; knew about ancient horses, the history and habits of the dog, and Egyptian mummification process...*

And on and on.

We'd stopped in Magdalena at the tail end of a Western journey in which I was determined to show my Swiss father-in-law a portion of this still-wild Southwest, and the remarkable characters who inhabit it. The trip would take ten days through the back country: from West Texas, through Arizona and New Mexico. From the Chihuahua desert into the Sonora desert, and back. A one week odyssey where I had to sandwich-in four music concerts. After all, I earned my daily bread as a troubadour. This was a working vacation.

II The West Still Wild and Wild Again

> *Leave the ponies to run free, far as the eye can see*
> *I'd ride the range forever, just to see them once again.*
> *Let the wild, flying things, soar above me on their wings*
> *The stars fill up the night sky and the moon light up the plain...*
>
> — **Mary McCaslin,** *Prairie in the Sky*

We left El Paso at sunup. Myself and my wife, master guitarist Thad Beckman, and Rudolpho, my father in law. We call him *Poppi*. Poppi doesn't speak English. Okay, he knows one phrase that a wise guy up in the Alps taught him: *F*** you, cowboy*. I don't think Poppi knew what it meant. I tried to warn him, through my wife, the interpreter, of the consequences of muttering that phrase in a cowboy bar in Tucson, Tombstone, or Flagstaff. Or *anywhere*. I think he understood, but I didn't like the gleam in his eye. We were not in Geneva anymore, Rudolpho.

You want trouble, Poppi? The West was still wild enough. Juarez was just over yonder and all the bullets you might wish to catch in your teeth. In fact stray bullets sometimes fly across the Rio Grande and hit the courthouse in downtown El Paso. The Mexican Revolution never ended. Poppi wanted to visit Juarez, but we talked him out of it. I asked him to clean up his English before we hit Tombstone. So he started singing the first line of the chorus of "Tom Dooley." *Hang down your head, Tom Dooley.* Over and over. Poppi's a funny guy, alright.

We took the back roads west, out of El Paso, and rolled down Highway 9 into the desert towards Columbus, New Mexico. Columbus is the town Pancho Villa attacked in 1916. The U.S. sent Black Jack Pershing, with young George Patton in tow, into Mexico – chasing after Pancho with horse soldiers and bi-planes. They never caught him. Funny thing about Villa. He attacked the United States, but everywhere in this desert border country are cafes, cantinas, and state parks named after the old bandit. There's a giant statue in a downtown park in Tucson. The Villa legend outlived his blood history. We kept running into his *bandito* specter.

On we drove, westward, through blown-out, ghostly towns like Hachita and Animas, where hard core desert rats made their final stand in trailers, cabins, and adobe hovels. Off the grid. We hit Arizona and turned south towards Douglas. Deep Apache country. We stopped at the monument commemorating *Geronimo's Surrender* and squinted up towards Skull Valley, where the Apache chieftain rode down carrying a white flag of truce. He regretted it.

The government shipped Geronimo to Pensacola, Florida, and he was finally moved to Fort Sill, Oklahoma. In his old age he became a celebrity. He appeared at 1904 World's Fair in St. Louis, where he rode a roller coaster and a Ferris wheel, and sold souvenirs and photographs of himself. He learned to print his name in block letters. The image of Geronimo on a Roller Coaster is as American as you can get. I wish I had a photo of it. I'd like to paint that one.

The old warrior died after falling off a horse in 1909. *Cowboy'd all to hell.* His last words were: "I should have never surrendered. I should have fought until I was the last man alive." So be it.

In Douglas I showed the crew the Gadsden Hotel lobby, and the vintage cowboy watering hole: *The Saddle and Spur Bar.* Outside the bar, in the grand lobby, there's a historic chip in one of the Saltillo tile stairs. Pancho Villa again. He rode his horse into the hotel and up the stairway and took a chunk out of the architecture. Maybe Villa was riding *Siete Leguas,* his favored mount who could run *seven leagues* without tiring. There's a fine *corrido* about it. Your local mariachis will know it – in fact there's dozens of songs about Villa. As I've said, there's no escaping Pancho's ghost.

Next stop Bisbee. The deep, open copper pit mine. Renovated miner's shacks shimmering across high desert hills. A winding, historic main street with decent restaurants and art galleries. I owned a cabin here once, but the town got too *discovered.* We were performing a concert that night in Bisbee for a writer named Bill Carter, who wrote a fine book on salmon fishing in Alaska (*Red Summer*) and another on Copper Mining in The West (*Boom, Bust, Boom.*) There are damn good Western writers and artists all over this Arizona country – J.P.S Brown is down in Patagonia, and Jim Harrison has a place there. The legendary photographer Jay Dusard lives near Douglas.

I'm a desert rat by nature. I travel all over the world but never feel at home until I return to the arid regions, flying into El Paso over a beige, sandy landscape pocked with mesquite and *Palo Verde* brush. The land below looks like the scorched top of a *crème Brule.* But we're in Arizona now, and this area of the Sonora desert is richer with desert plants: agaves, *Palo Verde's, cholla, saguaro,* organ pipes, yucca, prickly pears, barrels, creosote, devil's claw, Mormon tea, Queen on the Night...and more.

A peculiar form a human character is drawn to this parched land. There's always something to learn from the resident buzzard in a desert café or *cantina.* I recall running into an old guy once in a bar in Douglas who told me his grandfather packed camels for the U.S. Army. In the Arizona desert. *Camels.* He said their hooves couldn't adapt to the difference in sand density in our American deserts. I thought he was pulling my leg. Until I read up on it.

The U.S. Camel Corps was created by the Army in the 1850s. It was an experiment in employing camels as pack animals in Florida, and also the Southwestern deserts. Almost one hundred camels were shipped over, in two loads from *Smyrna* (now Turkey). The camels worked out for awhile. They could travel long distances on little water and cross inaccessible terrain. But the army horses and mules were frightened of the foreign-looking beasts, and the camels had *unpleasant dispositions.* They spit, bit, kicked, fought, and even killed each other during the rutting season.

One of the head camel drovers was a man named Hi Jolly (*Hadji Ali*), an Ottoman citizen. After his death in 1902, he was buried in Quartzsite, Arizona. His grave is marked by a pyramid-shaped monument topped with a metal profile of a camel.

With the outbreak of the Civil War, the Camel Corps was dismantled. Camels were sold off to private owners and zoos, and the rest escaped into the desert. The bones of a famous white camel, named *Seid,* wound up in the Smithsonian Institute. Feral camels were sighted in the Southwest through the early 1900s. The last reported sighting was in 1941 near Douglas, Texas. Imagine being hung-over one morning, out hunting jack rabbits in the desert, and your field glasses draw a bead on a feral camel. Or how about a jaguar? Sobering desert moments when you figure you'll cut back on the tequila.

Camels. And that's right, *jaguars.* Spotted leopards. Near Douglas, Arizona, a few years back, a rancher out hunting mountain lions with his dogs came across a large Mexican jaguar, thought to be extinct in those parts. The big cat was up in a tree fighting off the dogs. Unlike mountain lions, jaguars will turn and fight. The Mexican jaguar is the only extant North American wild cat that *roars.* Jaguar sighting keep reoccurring in Arizona.

The west is still wild and wild again. Cowboys, jaguars, and feral camels. But we've got to keep moving towards our final destination. The falconer's adobe. Hundreds of miles away.

We were now driving deep into *Saguaro* country. The mystical cactus trees appeared on each side of the road out on the passing desert. *Poppi* wanted to stop every time we saw a huge one. Europeans consider the giant cactus an iconic symbol of the American West, as much as a cowboy on a bucking horse, or an Indian in full headdress. The Saguaro's are almost exclusive to the Sonora desert of Arizona and Northern Mexico. They grow as tall as seventy feet, take seventy five years to grow an arm, and live up to 150 years. Gila woodpeckers, purple martins, house finches, and gilded flickers live inside the saguaros.

The saguaros are protected by law, but that doesn't stop thick-headed amateur gunslingers. In 1982 a man was out firing away at

Saguaros, knocking them over, when a one hundred pound cactus arm fell down and impaled him. Our tom-fool hero was pin cushioned, crushed, and killed. *Desert justice.* Hard way to die. You don't mess with the mighty *Saguaro.* They have a long memory and a short temper. They are well armed.

Time to return to the back roads, heading due east now, through towns like Payson and Show Low. Aiming for New Mexico. Somewhere on a high pine grade in Arizona we stopped for a coffee at an isolated gas station. One of those places where the coffee, milk cartons, sandwiches, tuna cans, and even the jokes – have all exceeded their shelf life.

The owner was persuaded to make us a fresh pot of coffee, as my father in law, *Poppi,* kept mumbling to my wife that this looked like *bear country.* Were there any bear around? He asked in Swiss-German. He wished to see a bear.

I translated this for the gas station owner, a big 'ole rough cog in a Pendleton shirt. A *Paul Bunyan* type fellow. He hesitated, coffee pot in and hand, and looked toward Poppi. He spit out: *"Tell your father in law to tie a pork chop around his neck and go sit out in the woods. He'll see plenty bear."*

We thanked him for that advice. I was glad Poppi didn't use his one English sentence in reply. Things could have gotten *western.* We walked out into the parking lot and spit out the bad coffee and drove the truck down the long grade, into New Mexico. Poppi had gotten over his yen to see a bear. He kept his mouth shut. Next stop, Pie Town, New Mexico, population 25. A slice of pie was now required. A western tradition in this country.

We found a small joint and slid up to the counter and eyed the goods: boysenberry, blackberry, blueberry, apple, and mixed berry. Grandma-style thick crust. The great vanishing American dessert. Homemade pie. Hot coffee.

There was an old codger sitting there who looked like a regular. Maybe he was the mayor. Long white beard and coveralls. Might have been age eighty-five or one hundred and ten. The old gent was working on his dinner, which consisted of a large bowl of clam chowder into which he'd crumbled at least a dozen saltine crackers. For *bulk.* He was chopping away and refining the mix. I figured he knew all the deep mysteries of Pie Town, but I didn't want to disturb his meal. Pie Town is one slice away from turning into a ghost town.

We left 'ole Pie town and traversed *The Plains of Augustine,* with its *planetary observation dishes,* and finally came down into

Magdalena, New Mexico, as the light was dimming. It was that time of day when the desert turns a light red, like the colors the old Hopi carvers put on traditional Kachina dolls. There is a mystical, late afternoon light which washes across the deserts of New Mexico. It's a different tint then the sunset colors in West Texas and Arizona. A peculiar New Mexican glow, reflecting off red sand and rock, filtered through the spiny plants. That late afternoon light which attracts painters and poets to Santa Fe.

Magdalena could have been used by Sam Peckinpah as a location for *The Wild Bunch*. One main street and backstreets of adobes and cabins. A cowboy bar. We found the Falconer's red adobe, on an unpaved back street, and knocked on the door. Steve Bodio peered out at us. His Russian coursing hounds were barking behind him. He opened the door a little further, to welcome us in, and we spotted the hooded falcon on its perch. Poppi looked scared, but he kept his mouth shut.

Soon we were imbibing the above-mentioned Mongolian vodka

III Hunting Wolves with Winged Dinosaurs

> *My mother showed me a photo, in some lost magazine, that I never forgot: a dark man in a spotted fur coat and shaggy hat, seated on a horse, holding on his arm an immense black eagle...the story of my life-long pursuit of that image is told in my last book,* **Eagle Dreams.**
>
> — **Steve Bodio**

All I knew about falconry at this point was maybe a half verse from the old Yeats poem, *The Second Coming*. You know the one: *The Falcon cannot hear the falconer*. The blood dimmed tide was loosed and a mythical beast, like *The Sphinx*, was slouching towards Bethlehem. Quite a poem. We studied it in high school and I visited Yeats' grave in Ireland, with a line of his inscribed across the stone: *Horseman Pass By!* That was the title to Larry McMurtry's first novel, which became the movie: *Hud*. The West goes on forever.

I did a little research before our trip. I wasn't aware that falconry was practiced much in America. And I was ignorant of the rich history. I'd imagined it something from the Middle Ages. I found a standard definition: *Falconry is the hunting of wild quarry in its natural state and habitat by means of a trained bird of prey*. OK.

Somewhere I came across a mention that Golden Eagles have been used to hunt wolves in Kazakhstan. I couldn't believe that. It sounded like a tale from an old children's tome about the exotic Far Orient.

Then Steve Bodio sent me his book: *Eagle Dreams: Searching for Legends in Wild Mongolia*. On the cover was a hunter mounted on a pony, with a three foot tall Eagle on his right arm. This was not eight hundred years ago. *This was now.* Kazakhstan, the largest landlocked country in the world. Still inhabited by nomadic horse tribes. *Tonight we ride, boys.* Bodio and his wife Libby had been there and written about it. They'd ridden with the Mongols, drank their vodka, and heard their primeval legends and stories. They'd witnessed an eagle taking down a fox, and heard tales of eagles going after deer and wolves.

The whole enterprise sounded pretty damned *cowboy* to me. I'm always interested in the roots of Western culture, but up 'til now had focused my attention on Mexico and Spain. Never thought about Mongolian horsemen. And hunting horseback with eagles. There was a long, wild, historic strain running through our horse culture.

That image of a man on a horse with an eagle on his arm is haunting. Years before I'd heard of Steve Bodio, I'd purchased an antique wooden statue – a Mongol horseman in a Chinese antique store in New Mexico. In The 1960s I'd also bought five small horse bits in a street stall in Northern Nigeria. They've been carbon-dated at an estimate of six hundred years old. They're probably Mongol pony bits. But let me tell you about that Mongol statue.

IV The Mongol Cowboy
(On the Trail of the Ancient Horse)

In terms of square miles, Genghis Khan was the greatest conqueror of all time – greater than Alexander the Great. His success was the result of unparalleled leadership and mobility. There was simply no mounted force able to hold its own against him. His were the world's best riders on the world's best horses.

— *True Appaloosas*, Ranch Brochure

A few years ago I stopped for a double espresso in Deming, New Mexico and noticed and anomalous looking little store across Spruce Street: *Xian Antiquities: Cultural Antiquities of the Northern Buddhists*. Peculiar. Out of place in this roadside, desert town.

I went over and entered a crowded little room filled with ancient Chinese antiquities. The owner had brought them over from China, where'd he taught school for many years. Up on a high shelf I spied a Mongol horseman on a small pony. An ancient wood carving. The surface was patched with reddish-white hues and the wood was notched and molted from the centuries. He took the statue down and handed it to me.

The horseman had a secret door carved into his back where prayers and small charms were stashed. *Homage to the ancient spirits of the horse? The first cowboy song?* I bought the carving for a few hundred bucks. It reached out to me. I carried the little Mongol horseman back to El Paso. The proprietor wrote out providence for me – a sheet of paper which told the history or the statue:

> *"I collected this piece at a village market in the North China Village of Tai Shan in the late spring of 1968. It is carved of fir or poplar in the first or second quarter of the 18th century, about the year 1730. It depicts a Mongol ancestral figure and was probably displayed in elaborate home shrines. These are known as effigy images. It was originally covered in colored paper."*

Maybe it was Genghis Kahn riding across the Asian steppes. An ancient-day Pancho Villa. The carved Mongol could damn sure sit a horse. I am a man who comes from horse culture – my father was connected to *his* grandfather through the family business: "*Russell and Sons: Horses and Livestock for Sale,*" back in North-Eastern Iowa. It was horses that got my father's blood moving and it was the betting on them that brought him down. My brother, Pat, is a renegade horse trader. The blood of all true horse traders goes back to the Moor and the Mongrel. I was surmising this. It all leads to that little prayer door carved in the back of my Mongol rider.

One day and I pried open the carved prayer door on the back of the Horseman. Out popped a miniature fossilized *sea horse* and a paper scroll with Chinese writing on it. I'd like to surmise it was an early Chinese version of the *Streets of Laredo* or *The Alleys of Shanghai*, but I've yet to have it translated. And the sea horse? The horse image keeps reappearing in our search.

Consider this conundrum: the first horses originally came from the Americas. Most of the evolutionary development of the horse (54 million years ago to about 10,000 years ago) actually took place in

North America, where they developed the strategy of grazing.

At some point the ancient horse crossed into the Old World via the Arctic-Asia land bridge. Then, suddenly, around 10,000 years ago, the horse disappeared from North and South America. No one knows why. The horse was gone from the western hemisphere. The horse didn't appear back on its native continent until the Spanish explorers brought horses by ship in the sixteenth century.

What's it all mean? Something tells me the answer might be on that prayer scroll in the back of my Mongol rider. At least that's what I was vodka-day-dreaming about as I was peering at Steve Bodio's photos of his far flung adventures involving Mongol ponies, nomadic horse tribes, and hunting with eagles in Kazakhstan.

Which brings us back around to Magdalena, New Mexico.

V Happy Hour in the Shadow of the Peregrine Falcon: Magdalena

Cast a cold Eye
On Life, on Death.
Horseman, pass by!

— **W.B. Yeats**

In Steve Bodio's words: "*Magdalena started as a town in the 1870s after the Apaches were pushed back. It was first a mining town, but soon became the greatest cattle shipping terminal in the United States. More cattle came out of it than even Dodge City – it was at one point the biggest town in Socorro County, bigger than Socorro, over 10,000 in population...all that's gone. We're down to one bar. Our house is one of the oldest in town. Not really adobe. Underneath is stone...*"

Now, in Magdalena, we were drinking ourselves back through a crack in space and time, and found ourselves in that Mongolian scene I was speaking about at the beginning of this essay. We were invited into the kitchen, where Steve's wife Libby was cooking that very large pot of *posole* made from fresh wild pig. Five little shot glasses on the table were filled with very cold Mongolian vodka from the freezer. It was an old Mongol tradition to welcome people into the house with a shot of distilled nectar from the potato plant.

The vodka changed the course of the evening. The look of apprehension was wiped off Poppi's face, replaced by a wild grin. I had him perform his only sentence in English, because I felt we were among friends. Everyone laughed. Except the falcon. (A few weeks later Steve and his wife informed me they had to sell this particular falcon. They knew the falcon *didn't like them* and its presence in their front room was becoming uncomfortable. Evidently some falcons are friendlier than others.)

I picked up assorted bits and pieces as I stared at the Falcon and wondered if they ever went for your eyes. Steve informed me that birds of prey will usually not peck out your eyes. *Initially*. The danger lies more in the tremendous power in their talons and feet. If they grab you on your opposite, ungloved hand, you will soon discover deep religion and the ability to make deals with God. *It hurts*. Since the Falcon sits on your gloved arm, with a tether attacked to that hand, if the bird were to get disturbed and jump to your ungloved hand you might experience what Bodio called *handcuffing*.

In his words: *I've been "handcuffed" a few times. Gloved to bare hand by a goshawk – ouch! The eagle with concrete-blunted talons who cracked my hand went all the way through a glove – they can exert hundreds of pounds of pressure.*

We chatted on and I picked up a few details: there are more than 2500 Falconers nationwide and several associations, and one big club: *The America Falconers Association*. There are state laws and rules dealing with becoming a legitimate falconer. There's a wealth of falconry history, and much can be gleaned from Bodio's books. I'll leave it at that.

Then it was back to a horse discussion, and Bodio's observation that some Mongol ponies have Appaloosa markings. Bodio said: *"Appaloosas! Of course the actual breed was defined in the Palouse and descends from Nez Pierce Indian horses, or so I am told, but the classic Appy pattern – spotted behind – is not rare in Mongolia, and I have seen photos in ancient Chinese paintings as well. So how did this pattern get from Asia to Spain to Indians?"*

My head was too filled with Mongolian vodka to figure that one.

Bodio showed us more photos, saying: *"Imagine this photo an old Chinese Mongol hunting party – with horses, hawks, and Tazi dogs. The men are wearing Snow leopard hats."*

Enough. The vodka and wine were distorting my sense of time and place. The dogs were hungry and the falcon was giving us the evil eye.

Besides his eight books, Bodio has also written introductions for a series of archetypal "sporting" books published by The Lyons Press in the late 1990s. These books, most of which he sent me, opened a back door into another world I was not only unaware of, but, to tell the truth, was not even the slightest bit interested in. Until I read the books.

Rat Hunting in England? Shark hunting off the Scottish Isles? Ranching in the 1800s in Patagonia? And, at the top of the list, T.S. White's wonderful tome: *The Goshawk*. The books are sporting classics. What unites these books is the unique, wild subject matter, mixed with plain old *great writing*.

T.S. White went on to write *The Once and Future King*. *The Goshawk* is an early book in which White is holed-up in an isolated cottage in the British Isles and orders a young Goshawk from Germany. He intends to train to the bird to hunt. What follows is a "storm of emotion which blows between man and bird." A damn good read. Recommended.

At midnight we drove out of old Magdalena. I felt confident we had shown Poppi a wild West soaked in legend, myth, saguaros, Mongol ponies, feral camels, Russian coursing dogs, and falconers. Then Poppi suddenly sprung loose with a new English phrase he'd rediscovered. The vodka had unleashed it. *Your light is not on.* The first time he'd been in the U.S. he'd been pulled over by a Florida highway patrolman, because Poppi's headlights weren't on. Poppi memorized what the cop had yelled at him. *Your light is not on. Your light is not on.* This now amused him.

I told Poppi to chill out or I'd find an all-night grocery and buy a pork chop and tie it around his neck, then I'd drive back to Magdalena and set the Peregrine falcon and Russian dogs on him. Poppi laughed hysterically, then fell asleep singing *Tom Dooley*. We drove into Socorro and found a motel.

We were almost home. And the West was still wild and went on forever.

A White Horse Named Tequila

Drunk from tequila
I carry drunkenness in my soul
see if I can heal this cruel melancholy...

— **Alfredo D'Orsay,** La Tequilera

When I first moved to West Texas there was a widow lady, Rose, down the road, who owned a white horse named *Tequila*. Her late husband once worked as a ditch rider for the water department. He rode *Tequila* up and down the canals, opening and closing water ditches into ranches and farms. Tom Lea, the great painter and author, once told me the Mexicans called the Rio Grande: *la madre acequia* – the *mother water ditch*. And I was honored to become the *alcalde*, or mayor, of our little ditch.

By the time I had settled-in, the old ditch rider had passed away and his horse, *Tequila*, hung on through a few more winters. He looked to be about thirty years or more. He possessed one milky eye and stood all day 'neath a Globe Willow. Only his ragged tail moved, picking up the winds out of the Southeast and Juarez.

I asked Rose how the horse got his name and she informed me her husband was fond of white tequila. Which I took to mean *silver, plata,* or *clear* tequila, as opposed to gold, *anejo, reposado,* or the more brown-yellow varieties. She said the old man gargled with white tequila every night to keep away throat infections and evil spirits. If I wanted to understand Mexican life and border culture, said Rose, then I must understand tequila and horse flesh. These things were at the center of the old Mexican songs.

I promised Rose I'd do my homework, which led me to the bars and liquor stores of *Ciudad Juarez*, across the Rio Grande river. I hung out in the historic *Kentucky Club*, sampling the *agave* juice and listening to jukebox *corridos* about horses by such luminaries as Antonio Aguilar and Vincente Fernandez. I went to the frontlines. These two ideas, horses and tequila, would come into clear focus a few years later in Guadalajara, in an airport liquor store, when I ran across *Siete Leguas*.

I   The Horse Pancho Villa Most Esteemed

Siete Leguas, el caballo
Que Villa más estimaba,
Cuando oía silbar los trenes
Se paraba y relinchaba,
Siete Leguas, el caballo

Seven Leagues, the horse
that Villa most esteemed,
When he heard the train whistle
He stood up and whinnied,
Seven Leagues, the horse
That Villa most esteemed

— Siete Leguas

It was fifteen years ago, *mas or menos*, and I was connecting through Guadalajara, flying back to Juarez. I may have been down to language school in Guanajuato or amateur bullfight class somewhere in the interior. I disremember the exact circumstances. I had a few hours layover in the Guadalajara airport and there was a well-stocked tequila store in the terminal. I was in the Mexican state of Jalisco, the center of the tequila industry.

In the shop I studied the bottles and labels with their fine *Mejicano* art depicting *agaves, charros, sombreros, caballos,* and other symbols of Mexican drinking culture. The proprietor spoke *Spanglish*, and we chatted for a while about the goods. I asked him his favorite, normal-drinking tequila, and he picked up a bottle with a black horse on the label. *Siete Leguas* silver. Then he whipped an open sample bottle up from below the counter and poured me a shot. He winked. Folks like to wink at you when you're headed down the rabbit hole.

There were no limes or any recommended ritual. I poured it down and let it scour my throat, and in a moment the fumes came whispering up through my nose. The *tequila nose*. Lasted half a minute. The proprietor smiled. Then he told me a few stories about the horse Pancho Villa most esteemed, *Siete Leguas*. A caballo that could run seven leagues without tiring. A league is an approximate measure of distance that a sober person on foot can cover within an hour. About three miles. *Siete Leguas* is sung in every *cantina* in Mexico.

I bought the bottle. It was 100% agave, which basically all I knew at that point – you have to consume only 100% agave tequila. I'd learned that the hard way, ruining perfectly good Saturday nights with *gold* blends and cheap Margarita mixes. In one special moment in the Guadalajara airport I'd connected with the tequila, which in turn connected with Mexican *corrido* about a famous horse. I was on the right track. I would have told Rose, but Rose had moved to a rest home and the white horse named *Tequila* had vanished from the shade of the Globe Willow. Rest in peace, white warrior.

II The Stone that Cuts & the Nectar of the Petrified Octopus

Tequila after midnight drives the loneliness away
Makes strangers all around you look familiar...
And they say Tequila kills you, if you drink too much
Well, I hope they make tequila long enough.

— **Dee Moeller,** *Tequila After Midnight*

Tequila is a conundrum. A beguiling spirit distilled from the juice of the *petrified octopus*, which is what the Spanish poet Garcia Lorca called the *agave*. Tequila, in the oldest *Indio* sense, means *the stone that cuts*, and its manufacture comes from the state of Jalisco, Mexico. *Mostly*. That's where the town of Tequila is situated and the surrounding countryside and *ranchos* represent the center of the trade. Tequila is the national drink of Mexico.

The Aztecs discovered how to draw the fermented honey from the many varieties of the *maguey* or *agave* plant. The Spanish added the distillation process. The West was thus conquered by mounted horseman and distilled alcohol. My neighbor lady, Rose, was right on the beam.

The most common, non-distilled, alcoholic beverage deriving from the *maguey* or *agave* family is *pulque*. This is the juice of the *agave* pineapple which, when fermented, becomes milky white and *beerish*, with a raspy twist. Welcome to the ageless Mexican establishment titled the *pulqueria,* with adobe walls and dirt floors, and maybe a few *borrachos* passed out in the corner. At least in the bygone days.

I've never tried *pulque*, that I can remember, but I drank palm wine in West Africa, so I get the idea. These drinks are difficult to regulate for purity when they come straight from the tree into an old kerosene jar. After a night on palm wine I once bowed down once to the mother of all African dysenteries. I don't want a re-ride.

Here's a description of *pulque* from one of those out-of-print, politically incorrect tomes on Mexico from the 1930s, *Bright Mexico*, by Larry Barretto:

> *Now pulque is a Mexican national drink and as such deserves a few words since you are never far out of the sight or smell of it. The drink is made by drawing it from the plant in ways usually unsanitary – often by sucking it through a tube – and it is then fermented.*
>
> *As it ferments rather slowly artificial means are used to hasten the process. These consist of putting in pieces of rope and worse until a proper degree of ripeness is reached...it is then marketed in cans open to all the dust and germs that fly.*
>
> *It is mildly intoxicating and pleasantly stupefying...it has also certain nutritive qualities to it and for this reason is considered as much food as drink.*

This recipe sounds much like Teddy Blue Abbot's description of *Injun Whiskey* in *We Pointed Them North*. All that's missing is the strychnine. Those were the old days. I assume *pulque* is safer now.

Mescal is the next step up. It's distilled from many varieties of the *agave* plant. Some of these bottles have the famous *agave* worm, sunk dead at the bottom. The old adage is: you may gain a certain mystical knowledge or sexual prowess when you reach the bottom of the *Mescal* bottle and eat the worm. Good luck. I tried it one time, thirty years ago, in a Brooklyn apartment. Your reporter on the beat.

After reaching the bottom and eating the worm I thought my chair was dancing the *cumbia*. I toppled over backwards, spun a few times, and passed out. I was ushered into a long and nightmare-laden sleep, broken only by the sounds of six a.m. garbage trucks at first light, and the smell of bagels steaming up from the shop below. I was alive. There were no mystic revelations in the journey. No Aztec maidens or *curanderos* named *Don Juan*. My tongue felt like it had swept the bottom of the Sonoran desert. Lesson learned. From the worm.

There's also an agave drink called *Sotol* from the plant of the same name – which hails from Northern Mexico. Then there's the mysterious *Bacanora*, which is not readily available. I've never encountered it. I had a bottle of *Sotol*, encased in a fancy wood box, sitting in my kitchen for ten years. I tried a shot the one afternoon. I coughed. I spit. I thought to myself – *I might drink this stuff if I was snowed-in beneath an avalanche in the Yukon*, but it lacked any hint of smoothness or bottom. It was all fire, with a medicinal taste.

I was prepared to dismiss *Sotol* when a man who works for me, *Cuauhtémoc*, brought me another bottle from Juarez. *Cuate*, as I call him, is named after the Aztec King who was executed by Cortez during the Spanish invasion. This was a top-end bottle of *Sotol*. Cuate also brought me a great collection of Mexican horse *corridos* on tape and disc. Homework material.

The booklet on the bottle's neck stated that the Tarahumara Indians created this *magical drink* to celebrate their rituals and religious ceremonies. The Tarahumara are an ancient tribe in the Sierra Madre known for their ability to run hours on end without tiring.

Sotol is 100% *Agavacea*. The plant is still harvested in the wild, as opposed to Tequila which is harvested on private haciendas and plantations. This particular *Sotol* was USDA organic and Kosher, and aged from six months to one year in new French Oak barrels. *Sotol* and *Mescal* have now become sophisticated cousins to Tequila.

Agavacea is a plant that grows only in the high desert near Chihuahua – a few hundred miles from my hacienda. Encouraged by a yen to support local products I broke the seal and gave *Sotol* a second chance. I tried a shot. Good indeed, and smoother then I expected, though still lacking the depth and finish of its big brother, Tequila. The taste remains wilder. Any port in a storm. Onward towards the top shelf.

Finally we've arrived at Tequila itself. The trickster. What the hell is it? All Tequilas are *mescal* but not all *mescals* qualify as *tequila*. Sounds like trying to figure out mules. Only liquor that's distilled from 51% of the *Weber Blue agave* may be *officially* termed *tequila*, from distilleries in the state of Jalisco. Only true tequila can carry the pledge of *100% Agave* and a seal from the Mexican government. That's the official story.

I try to avoid the cheaper blends and bottles with the plastic sombreros on the top. That's the stuff they send to Germany for truck driver festivals. I've played those festivals. You're sandwiched in between bluegrass bands from Poland who play twenty-minute versions of *Country Roads* while fans, dressed as cowboys, Indians, and Confederate soldiers, fire blank pistols. No amount of bad tequila will get you through the gig.

Let's take a side-step and look at the Margarita.

III Consider the Margarita

A woman walks into a bar in Juarez,
Stop me if you've heard this one before,
She says, "Build me a drink, Panchito,
I survived the divorce wars."

"Make it taste like Arthur Miller and Monroe,
Tequila, lime juice, and a dash of Cointreau,
salt on the rim, shake rattle and roll,
You can call it a 'Poison Mosquita...'
Or name it after me, they call me 'Margarita.' "

— **Tom Russell**, *The Margarita*

A bartender named Pancho Morales said he invented *The Margarita* over in Ciudad Juarez, in 1942, at Tommy's Bar. He moved to El Paso and became a milkman and passed away in 1997. His son said the old man *didn't even like the drink.* Pancho's story: A lady came in and ordered a *Magnolia,* and he'd never heard of that one, so he played it by ear. Salty, sweet and sour. Tequila, ice, Cointreau, fresh lime juice, a cocktail shaker, and a thin drinking glass, shaped like an upside-down *sombrero,* with salt on the rim. Necessity is the mother of drink inventions.

Other sources say the Margarita was invented at the *Tail O' The Cock* Restaurant in Beverly Hills, or a bar down in Taxco, or Hussongs Cantina on the West Coast. My bet is on Juarez. Tequila was first imported into the United States in 1873, and it came right through here, on the El Paso/Juarez border, following the old Spanish Camino Real. All things deeply Western have crossed this historic frontier, where the first troubadour, carrying a Spanish guitar, crossed over with Don Juan de Onate in 1598. Don Juan sits atop his iron horse in front of our airport now – the largest equestrian statue in the world.

Lime juice and Cointreau were a way to introduce Tequila to border gringos because it masked the taste of the *maguey* burn. I've often sat in the old Kentucky Club bar and ordered a two-dollar Margarita while looking up at the picture of the great boxer Jack Johnson, who fought in Juarez, and photos of old Mexican baseball players and bullfighters. There is still a tile *spit canal* 'neath the bar stools, where a steady stream of water carries away the chawing tobacco, cigar butts, and contraband. They say Marilyn Monroe waltzed in one afternoon, after divorcing Arthur Miller, and bought a round of Margaritas for the house. This is a good place to drink. I rate it, along the cowboy-historic scale, equal to Rosa's Cantina in El Paso.

The Kentucky Club, as I mentioned earlier, used to have a great jukebox laden with *charro corridos*. There is no one more accomplished at *going on a bender* than the legendary and mythical Mexican *charro* of song, movie, and soap opera fame. He's often depicted with a fancy charro sombrero on his head, black mustache, cigar, knife-wound on his cheek, and a half-empty bottle of tequila at his elbow. Our hero is contemplating love and mayhem.

A back country cowboy, they say, may remain sober for years, and then all of a sudden, perhaps from a romantic setback, jump out of his chair and shriek: *AI YI! I'm Grabbing onto the bender!* He falls off the edge of the world and drinks tequila for a solid month. Until? Until he achieves transcendence, death, or sings his way through the historic catalogue of traditional songs, which heal him or lead him to a psychological breakthrough. Or *breakdown*. Then he eats *menudo* for a few mornings and walks the earth like a Tequila Lazarus who has seen the bottom of the pit and has returned to tell the story in yet another *corrido*. Something which might translate:

> *You have broken and stepped on my heart*
> *With your cruel and diabolical unfaithfulness*
> *I will spit on your memory with one thousand drinks*
> *To rid me of the screeching sound of your voice, you wench.*

> *If I had a gun I would have killed you many times*
> *And your family as well, and all their livestock*
> *But now your face is washed from the mirror of my soul*
> *By the cleansing waters of this tequila.*
> *Rot in your own hell, for I will live on...etc.*

You get the picture. Mexican songsters have a deeper resort to the dark poetry which washes through the tequila-sodden music of revenge. It's a long way from Nashville, folks, and thank God for that.

IV The Heart of the Agave – The Heart of the Matter

*Like coffee and love, Tequila is irresistible,
demanding and powerful.
Like coffee and love, Tequila is not
for the half-hearted*

— **Vicente Quirante**

I wanted insider information from somebody who *knows* tequila. There's a thin line between holy water and poison. Hype and history. I've seen a dozen Tequila books filled with pictures of men chopping agaves, and rooms with shiny steel distillation tanks, and those dark chambers with ancient clay ovens where the agave pineapples are roasted prior to the distillation process. Then there's the *rap*. Tequila has now become so popular and dignified you have these characters carping on and on about complexity, depth, elegance, and balance. Steer clear. Do your own research. Carry water.

Lawrence Osborne, a world traveller who writes about drinking better than anyone, has written fine observations on wine (and spirits) – he surmises that, in the end, your memory of a great wine or spirit has much to do with the situation, your love life, the food, the weather, the waitress etc. I'd recommend his book on wine: *The Accidental Connoisseur: An Irreverent Journey through the Wine World*. There's no pretense to it. This gentleman is fearless in his research. Last I heard he lives in Bangkok. Enough said.

Complexity and depth? It depends. I think I *get it*. One night I entered a drinking joint in Naco, Mexico – a dark little hole of a bar with no seats or tables or stools. Just a sinister room with grim walls stained with patches of slaughterhouse green and maudlin blue, layered with a century of cheap tobacco smoke. A ready-made tomb. The one-eyed bartender fed me shots from a bottle of silver Herradura tequila. One dollar per shot. A man in a baseball cap stumbled in, waving a *machete* above his head, howling and hissing. Threatening the ghosts of his romantic past. He circled the room and walked out.

Four shots and six jukebox *corridos* later the walls turned from smoky green to crimson and gold. The man with the *machete* returned swinging the blade, and the bartender told me not to mind him: *that's my brother in law, his mind is rotten from bad tequila and bitter feeling concerning his mistress. If he is swinging a shotgun then it can become very dangerous.*

The situation and circumstances were adding plenty of depth and complexity to the evening. Some of these components might have issued forth from the Tequila. That's my observation. And so I've judged Herradura Silver to be an *intriguing spirit*.

I was considering a trip down to Jalisco, a journey into the tequila heartland, but fate intervened. My friend Brian Kanof, a former Special Forces officer, started his own tequila brand. He partnered-up with Dianna Offutt, a certified wine *sommelier*, and also Kinky Friedman, the legendary Texas song man who's now in the runoff for Agricultural Commissioner in Texas. Kinky has written dozens of successful detective novels, and also composed a batch of the most irreverent songs in the American canon. The Tequila is called: *Man in Black* and it is a good one. Available only in Texas.

Brian travelled down into Mexico, in search of the truth about tequila, into the very belly of the beast. He arrived at my front gate with samples of his stock. We retired to my private cantina to talk Tequila. And imbibe.

V   Conversations with a Tequila Magnate

> *A computer lets you make more mistakes faster than any creation in human history – with the possible exception of handguns and tequila.*
>
> — **Mitch Ratcliffe**
> (via Gary Brown)

Brian's first trip down to Jalisco was an odyssey to find a distillery that would produce a tequila for his newly launched brand. He wanted the top shelf. His Tequila is made by *Industrial de Agave San Isidro,* in Tepatitlan, the company which bottles *Don Ramon,* arguably the best selling premium Tequila in Mexico.

Brian brought me a g*lorifier* he'd made. I'd never heard of this object. This is a *presentation stand,* or bottle holder, or *altar,* for bars and cantinas. Brian hammered this one out in his studio. The idea was to make your brand stand out from the others. Standing tall inside the metal glorifier were three grades of *Kinky Friedman's Man in Black Tequila*, plus another dark bottle on the side. Brian sat the glorifier on my bar. School was now in session. We would see about the strength and courage of his product.

"Look," he said. "I learned what I know from Mexicans. Not foreign snobs who drink holding their pinky fingers in the air, making long, running descriptions of what they don't know. The basics are smell, taste, and finish. I've been drinking tequila since 1963, when I crossed the border into Juarez with my high school buddies. This is the best tequila in America."

"Simmer down," I said. "I ain't one of those snobs."

"Good. Americans tend to do with distilled beverages what the French do with wine, and it rubs me the wrong way. I don't give a damn about that. To rate it too much or equate it with some fruit or spice is for journalists, not tequila drinkers. I drink it straight. Not with lime. Not with salt. Not cold, the exception being *plata,* which I occasionally put in the fridge for a few hours."

"What about Margaritas?" I thought he'd wince in disdain. Or shoot me.

"I love 'em. It's like drinking coolaid. I love the way they taste."

"How does your brand differ from Mexican Tequila? That stuff that they don't import over the border?"

"Mexican tequila varies in proof, but is usually less than 80 proof. That's why some people think it's smoother. The exported tequila to the States is *80 proof.* We went down there and ended up working with Don Jorge at *Don Ramon.* We tasted twenty varieties and picked four."

I told him my ranch employee, the Aztec King, *Cuate,* just brought me a bottle of *Don Ramon* from Juarez, with a tax stamp on it. He'd walked it across the border.

"Good man. That's the best drinking *reposado* in Mexico, my friend. Exactly the same tequila as ours…there's a lot of alchemy involved in good Tequila, you know."

"Such as?"

"Don Ramon won't harvest in an odd-numbered year. *Superstition,* I suppose. The process involves praying to the gods and following the growing phases of the moon. It goes back to the Aztecs. He has a scale model of the Sistine Chapel on his property…he covers all the mystical bases. His *plata* is called *Cristenos* and the "t" on the label is a Catholic cross."

"Let's get down to the tasting," I said. "The mountains are turning crimson and happy hour is at hand in the Land of the *Charro.*"

There were three bottles of *Man in Black* sitting in *the glorifier*. *Plata*, *Reposado*, and *Anejo*. There was a fourth one on the side, a dark, squat bottle holding the *Extra Anejo*. The big boy. The top of the line. One hundred and ninety bucks a bottle.

"All our tequila," said Brian, "has to be distilled twice to reach 80 proof."

He picked up the bottle of silver, or *plata*. *Unaged* tequila. We poured a half shot and drank it down.

"First of all," Brian said. "It smells like a great tequila. Right?"

"It doesn't smell like Kerosene."

"It's smoother than most. Our *Plata* is twice-distilled from the *Los Altos Weber Blue Agave*. First distillation is in stainless steel, the second is in copper. The agave is harvested after 8, 10, and 12 years."

I noticed I wasn't getting much of that tequila nose. The after-burn.

"It has a long finish for a *plata*. This is a very smooth silver."

He reached for the next bottle. *Reposado*. The literal English translation would be *rested*.

"Aging changes everything," he said. "The *Reposado* is aged for 8 months in virgin American barrels that are first smoked in a smoker for three days before being filled. Barrels you might age whisky in. The inside of the barrel is never charred. The smoke comes from burning the waste *agave* fibers after the juice has been extracted. It's like a Texas brisket. The smoky taste."

"It's spicy," I said.

"Peppery," Brian said. "At first. That's the smoking process. The barrels. But that smooths out after ten seconds or so, eh?

"Definitely." I would have agreed with anything at this point.

"Most Mexican men prefer *Reposado*," he said. "The old story is if you're buying a friend a shot of *plata* he thinks your a cheapskate. If you try and show off and order *anejo* he thinks you're arrogant, or have money. So you aim for middle ground. The *reposado*. It has character, without being pushy. That's what we're talking about, here. *Character*.

He moved his hand to the right and pulled out the *Anejo*.

"*Anejo*. Aged fourteen months in French Red Oak barrels. You don't get the pepper taste with this one. Smoother, darker. Long finish."

We stood awhile and looked up at the old film and bullfight posters from Juarez. There was also an original Tom Lea drawing of a bullfighter, and the prints Tom had signed for me. But now Brian was opening the *Extra Anejo*. The little jug with the heavy price tag.

"Aged for over five years in French Oak, and a sixth year in Port wine barrels."

"It picks up the Port flavors?"

"I'd say so. Some of the distilleries use old Jack Daniels barrels."

We tasted. We toasted Tom Lea and Manolete, and the movie placard of Bette Davis, who starred in the film: *Juarez*. We toasted a signed photo of Anthony Quinn and Antonio Ordonez's parade cape, given to me by Sylvia Tyson. Gilbert Roland, the Mexican actor, gifted it to her. Ordonez was Hemingway's favorite matador. Hemingway wrote about him in *The Dangerous Summer*.

This *extra anejo* was dark, smooth, and enduring. It tasted like a expensive brandy.

"You could substitute this one for any great cognac," said Brian. "And sip it as you smoke your cigar."

"I'd get spoiled," I said. "I can get by on *plata* and *reposado*."

"I agree," he said. "There's not too much of this *extra anejo* around."

He looked at all my Tequila bottles. "There are over 1,200 different Tequila on sale in the United States," he said. "Frequently, when a brand grows and begins to become popular, it is purchased by a large spirits corporation. Tequila has become a mainstream spirit over the last three decades. The idea of aging tequila in oak is an American innovation. *Extra Anejo* Tequila is strictly American, brought to market first by a Texan named Neal Williamson."

Brian keeps his large tequila inventory in a warehouse in Laredo. "You have to manufacture it by the container load," he says. "It's like getting plastic kazoos out of China. You have to buy a container load to justify all the trouble and expense."

Kazoos from China? I was losing the thread.

No matter. Worship was over. He packed up the *glorifier*, grabbed the *extra anejo*, left me a bottle of *plata* and disappeared, driving towards the mountains and a gig somewhere with Kinky Friedman.

VI The Old Agave Bar, The Eisenhower Sauna, and The Pass of Death

"Tequila is a pallid flame that passes through walls
And soars over the roofs to allay despair.
Tequila is not for men of the sea,
For it fogs the instruments of navigation."

— **Alvar Mutis**

When I started my tequila studies I decided the safest way to enjoy my happy hour research was in my own bar. So I built a small cantina in my *hacienda*. I was a bachelor back then. I knew enough about mental health to surmise it wasn't wise to drink alone, so I bought an antique dummy and put a *sombrero* on him. I named him Pancho Morales, for the inventor of the Margarita. Here was my bartender. He worked cheap and I'd assumed he'd keep his mouth shut. I was wrong. *Tequila wrong*.

One day Pancho insulted me, after many shots of *Siete Leguas*, and I knocked his block off and sent him to the trash barrel in a beer carton. The next morning I arrived at the realization that I needed to slow down, or contemplate detoxification. What the hell, I purchased a used sauna. It works for the vodka drinkers of Finland, doesn't it? My own private detoxification unit – a sauna torn out of Fort Bliss, Texas – a wooden room which had once been the think tank for Generals Eisenhower and Bradley. I was awarded this plaque from the company that restored the sauna – it's hanging on the wall near the glass entrance door:

> *This sauna was originally installed in the officers club at Ft. Bliss, Texas. It has been used by the likes of Dwight Eisenhower and General Omar Bradley. It has now been commissioned for service by Tom Russell...*

Ole! I savored that bottle of *Siete Leguas* for a few years and it sits, empty, in my bar in El Paso, beneath the stuffed head of a brave fighting bull (missing both ears.) On the bar are other oddball spirits from around the world, including *Carlos Arruza Anis*, *Manolete Anis, Sotol, Mescal,* and a brand of *Vincent Van Gogh* absinthe. I have not sampled the *Van Gogh*. It requires a mysterious ritual with hot flame and silver spoon and besides, Vincent ended up staggering around a French brothel, holding his ear in the palm of his shaky hand.

I'm still chasing the horse corridos. Every Saturday in July and August the local *Lienzo Charro* ring, near our house, has a *charreada*. A celebration of music, drink, food, and horsemanship. The events include *The Pass of Death,* where a *charro* jumps from his own horse to the back of an un-broke horse and rides it backwards until it stops bucking. The band bangs out *corridos*, beer cans are crushed underfoot, and raised tequila flasks glisten in the desert sun.

Yes, Rose, I am still doing the research, dancing in the shadow of the *Blue Agave*. Running my hand over *the pallid flame which allays despair*. Talking to the three-headed dog. I have learned to respect the mystical spirit of the juice of the petrified octopus. Two shots per day is plenty.

I'll leave you with a favorite tequila verse, by the late Hoyt Axton:

There's a great hot desert, south of Mexicali
If you don't have the water, you'd better not go...
For tequila won't get you, across that desert...
To Evangelina, down in old Mexico.

— **Hoyt Axton,** *Evangelina*

Dispatches from Patagonia
The World of J.P.S. Brown

Friend Tom:
I'm proud of the land and people I chose to record, so I ain't sorry about anything. I went all out and it is what it is. Remember, I'll always keep coffee and a pot of beans hot for you and your lady.
Hold fast,
Joe

Letter – J.P.S. Brown to Tom Russell
11/14

Patagonia was down there somewhere. The name kept badgering me. It was postmarked on a batch of letters on my desk. Not the Patagonia at the tip of South America, where a *gaucho* bucked off his mount might wander through the desolation, lose his bearings, and vanish forever. Not the far terrain of *The Last Cowboys at the End of the World.* Nor *the ancient land of the giants*, named by Magellan.

There was another Patagonia at the Southern end of Arizona and I kept chawing on that name. The eminent Western author J.P.S. Brown was living there, a few hundred miles south of my El Paso hacienda. Joe and I had corresponded, but I hadn't made the trip down there to meet him in person.

I'd read sundry outrageous stories and anecdotes, and heard so many rumors about the man and his colorful life, it was a lot to confront. Then there were the acclaimed novels. And those dispatches from Patagonia.

We'd exchanged letters every six months over the last five years. I would ask Joe a question, or just say *hello*, and Joe would fire-off random anecdotes and fragments of his cowboy life. A life never dull.

An example:

Jan 21, 2015
Friend Tom,

In 1948, for my HS graduation, my dad gave me a John Bean saddle. Made for quick, sure, free escape with as little abrasion as possible, it was flat as can be, no cantle, no swells...slick. It was rough side out, but had a foam rubber seat covered with tight buckskin with colored needlework. Very short in the skirts. I broke 25 colts every summer so that saddle wasn't made for it. Nevertheless, because it gave me such pleasure it made my ass laugh it was put to work full time. It was a roping and bulldogging saddle, so it got a lot to do for those two sports that I indulged myself in, from time to time. I used it to do a bulldogging exhibition at the "Congresso National de Charros" in Tepic in the 70s. My son has it now as a stuntman in the movies. I hated to give it up, especially to him, because he can hairlip and anvil and gives daily live performances of that.
Hold fast,
Joe

What, in hell, did *hairlip* and *anvil* entail in stunt riding? And I wondered why he'd sent me the saddle anecdote, then I remembered I'd written an essay on that same Johnny Bean, saddle maker and horseman, who'd been torpedoed on a ship transporting mules to Burma during WWII. There were sharks involved in the story. Johnny Bean survived. The mules did not.

I asked my cowboy brother and his stuntman friends about those terms, *anvil and hairlip*. Nobody had a clue. So I wrote Joe. He answered:

Feb 27, 2015
Friend Tom,
(Re: Hairlip and Anvil.)

It's Joe Brown talk about destructive cowboys. Give him a shovel and he breaks it before he finishes the job. Harelip and anvil? He could permanently scar or break anything he's given to handle, even put a harelip on an anvil.
Hold fast,
Joe

Each letter is signed *hold fast.* You'd have to hold fast to follow the sage, maverick insights and insider lingo. In four letters from 2010 Joe spoke of his time as a journalist at the *Herald Post* in El Paso, when he was 24 years old.

> *I worked full time at the Herald-Post and earned $62 a week. I became very dedicated to becoming a matador and spent every Saturday afternoon in Juarez, either practicing with a "capote" and "muleta" in the main Juarez ring, or doing the same thing with cattle in the stockyards...I really wish I had thought of being a rodeo clown, but I never considered it, because I aspired to be a matador, not a clown.*

Joe wrote of his wife's Alzheimers, which went on for 22 years, until she died in 2010. She required constant care and Joe wrote in the midnight hours after she fell asleep. He was as candid in his reports on their love and daily struggle as he was in his straightforward prose on cowboy life.

In December of 2014 I wrote and asked Joe his views on Spanish and Mexican horse traditions, which trail back to the Moors. Below his letter, which speaks to the historic core of what the hell may have happened to the Middle East, and why it's violently off kilter. Leave it to J.P.S. Brown. The trouble began when the Moors stepped down off their horses. Consider this, all ye smug world news commentators:

December 8, 2014
Friend Tom,

> *On the Moors: I believe that they founded an immortal horse tradition that began when mankind first mounted a horse. That was probably about Biblical times in Arabia between the Tigris and Euphrates rivers, was it not? Most of the tradition has been passed down to us through the Spaniards and the Mexicans. I have a limited edition book that was published in 1946 by a Mexican Charro for his colleagues that is full of the tradition. Some of the tales and folklore credits the Moors, some does not, but has surely been borrowed from them.*
>
> *Their mastery of horsemanship has never been equaled. How long did they keep Spain under their saddle blankets? Something like 300 years, until El Cid finally mounted his country on a horse and used what he had learned from the Moors to run them out.*
>
> *All of the Moorish and early Arabian folklore is a song to*

the horseman and to chivalry, valor, honor, dignity, and romantic love. What happened to the people who invented their own distinguished brand of that? What brought them so low that they murder their own kind by the thousands to kill a dozen infidels? They got off their horses and turned them loose, that's what. Even now, the Bedouin, who is still a horseman, keeps himself apart from the rest of the fanatics that today are called Arabs and other Muslims, like the Iranians and Afghans, mostly all city-dweller Moors without horses, now.

History sorted. Damn right. The letters are vital, plain-speak documents. Joe has a point of view and an unblinking knowledge of horse traditions. I'll roll back now to the point of time when Patagonia kept tugging at me. Before I shook hands with Joe Brown.

I kept sifting through those endless letters, articles, and anecdotes about Joe, the man who had herded horses and wild cattle up from Mexico. The *hombre* who'd flown low in small airplanes and scared hell out of every whore in every whorehouse in the Sierra Madre Mountains. The boxer who'd sparred with Rocky Marciano. Then there was the bullfighting, whiskey smuggling, knife fights in bars, heart attacks, and five marriages.

Somewhere in there he'd taken the time to write a dozen books chock full of the real Western deal. I'll ponder the details in a moment. Enough footnotes to fill a Western encyclopedia on living on the hellish, raw edge of the final frontier. Creating art out of it all.

The important news: Joe's now pushing well past eighty and still writing down in Patagonia, Arizona. It was time to meet the man. My wife and I loaded up the truck and drove across the bottom of New Mexico, towards Arizona.

I   Homage to Patagonia

The Patagonia, my friends, is a blue rock
pigeon. At first glance she looks like a big dove,
much larger than a mourning dove, a little larger
than a white wing. She's not a big-footed Indian,
as people wrongly believe...her eyes are red.

— That makes her a pigeon.
J.P.S. Brown

Patagonia, Arizona, is one of those Western places which exist under a veil of Eden. A land unto itself. We drove southwest across the spare reaches of the Sonora desert, past Columbus, New Mexico, where Villa's troops invaded the U.S. one hundred years ago. We crossed into Arizona. Onward past long miles of *cholla*, sand, and mesquite, past the canyon where Geronimo surrendered. Finally we drifted over a hill, looking down on green rolling ranch land. The change in landscape is dramatic.

Patagonia is tucked down in the valley of the Sonoita Creek, between the Santa Rita Mountains to the north, and the Patagonia Mountains to the south. A haven for ranchers, the rare Mexican jaguar, and writers and artists like Joe Brown and Jim Harrison. Men who prefer to carve out their art in splendid isolation, ignoring the vagaries of Hollywood and New York.

My wife and I drove into town and called Joe from the local phone booth, tucked next to the Post Office. In a matter of minutes a pickup truck clattered into the lot and out stepped Joe Brown, the man Lee Marvin termed *the wildest son-of-a-bitch who ever walked.*

His skin was coffee-colored, seared and sandblasted from years of riding the outback trails of the Mexican Sierra Madre. He stood barrel-chested and a trifle bow-legged, and as cowboy-fit as the man who faced Rocky Marciano. The old whiskey smuggler with a smirk. *Hold fast*, boys. The beans are on the stove and there's *lechuguilla* in the jug.

We followed his truck, winding up dirt ranch roads towards Joe's house, which was set back in a canyon, shielded behind rows of old rose bushes. These old soldier plants were high, wild looking shrubs with white and yellow petals falling down to the earth. We met his dog *Mike,* and Joe pointed off towards a far corral where his old racehorse *Mercy* was lodged. Joe tells us Mercy stands for: *Mercy, boys, let her run.*

Inside the house there was the eternal pot of beans on the stove, and a Notre Dame football game on the T.V. Joe graduated from Notre Dame in 1952 with a degree in journalism. He showed me a photo of the ring where he sparred with Marciano at Notre Dame. Later Joe was scheduled to spar with Sonny Liston in Las Vegas, but Joe fell ill, and while recuperating he began to write short stories.

I listened, and tried to juggle the Joe Brown timelines – writing, boxing, the Marines, marriages, the Mexican cattle trail, the movies. The whiskey. The flash of knives. The great books. It was coming at me from all angles. J.P.S. Brown was able to toss a deck of biographical cards at you, a poker hand where every card was wild. And when the cards settled on the floor they were fodder for his novels.

I asked Joe his about his writing ritual. When his wife was alive he worked between midnight and six. Patsy was a dancer, barrel racer, and the love of his life. She died a few years ago. He showed us their bedroom, with wonderful photos of Patsy, and then he opened a bottom dresser drawer filled with recent editions of his books. He pulled out three and walked into the front room to sign them for me.

Joe Brown signs his name in a measured, floral penmanship, taught by The Christian Brothers. He uses a fountain pen. He told me he went to town to buy ink and no one knew what he was talking about. *Bottled ink? Fountain Pens?* It's all disappeared and gone to hell since the Moors got down of their horses.

After a few hours and more stories we have to take off, and I tell my wife, Nadine, we've just chatted with one of the last great Western writers. The real deal. As we were leaving Joe handed me eight few pages of the oration he gave at his wife's funeral. Then he pointed out toward the fence post and told us the story of the Patagonia pigeon.

Joe and his brother-in-law were sitting out on the porch on a Saturday morning in May, 2010, and a Patagonia pigeon flew in and perched on the only bare limb in a grove of mesquite trees. Prior to this Joe had only seen the Patagonia's in (his words) *wild and reckless flight.* He had never seen one at rest.

The bird was only fifteen yards away and Joe studied her through binoculars. She had the red eye of the Patagonia. She was completely at peace. Then the phone rang in the house. The Patagonia sat there at rest, *preened and fluffed her feathers.* At that moment Joe turned and went inside to take the phone. He found out that his wife had just died, the very moment the Patagonia landed on that mesquite limb.

II The Wildest Son-of-a Bitch Who Ever Walked

Yes, I smuggled whiskey into Mexico to make money.
Yes, I stayed half-drunk for most of three decades. Yes,
I've had five wives, including the third, a Zapotec
Indian from Jalisco, who poisoned me with strychnine.
Irene was a working girl in a Mexican
whorehouse...she tried to bump me off. Twice.

— **J.P.S. Brown,**
quoted by Leo Banks, the *Tucson Weekly*

Joseph Paul Summers Brown was born in Nogales, Arizona, 1930, a fifth generation Arizona and Sonora, Mexico, cattleman. His father, Paul Summers, was part Irish, part-Choctaw, and *wild as a wolf,* according to Joe. His dad came from an Arizona cattle family, as did Brown's Irish-Cherokee-French Basque mother, Maggie Sorrells. Dad gave him his first swallow of *bacanora,* a Sonoran *mescal,* as a 5-year-old riding cow trails. Summers would tell the boy, "It freshens the horse for the ride back to camp.

After graduating from Notre Dame, in 1952, Joe was a commissioned second lieutenant in the U.S. Marine Corps. He was a heavy machine gun platoon commander in Fuji, Japan, 1955-1956. He also coached Third Marine Division boxing team and animal packing in the Marine Corps Mountain Leadership School. Joe would later box professionally in Mexico. He broke his hand 17 times.

When he was released from active duty in 1958 he wrangled and purchased cattle and horses in Mexico: Chihuahua, Sonora, Baja California, Coahuila, and Jalisco. He built the first dipping vat for the eradication of the fever tick in the municipality of Navojoa, where he was also a member of the Charro Association. Later he worked in Tucson as a member of the Teamsters Union Movie Wranglers, providing cattle, horses, stunts, and acted in bit parts in the movie business.

He ran with folks like Casey Tibbs and Slim Pickens:

> *I knew Casey and Slim very well during their final years. Casey and I wrangled* The Alamo, *the TV version that starred Jim Arness...Casey liked my books long before we ever met. I worked with Slim Pickens on the movie* Tom Horn *with Steve McQueen. I was the priest who spoke with McQueen in the jail and Slim was the jailer. Slim and I had a lot of mutual cowboy friends in the cattle and horse businesses and in the movie business.*

In Mexico Joe began to write stories that became his first novel, *Jim Kane,* in 1960. He admits to the influence of Hemingway, William Saroyan and Mickey Spillane. The protagonist of that first book, Jim Kane, buys cattle and horses in Mexico and sells them in the United States. Joe Brown's ability to write up the rugged Mexican Sierra Madre equals the scenery in B. Traven's classic: *The Treasure of the Sierra Madre.*

Jim Kane was made into the movie *Pocket Money* with Paul Newman and Lee Marvin in 1972. The script got out of hand, hacked together by re-write boys who figured it should have an overdose of lightweight humor. Foolish mistake. Much of Joe Brown's hard-edged knowledge of Mexico and the cattle business was lost in a sea of one-liners.

Jim Kane was followed by *The Outfit,* and *The Forests of the Night. Forests of the Nights,* the story of a man trailing a renegade jaguar through Mexico, was hailed by Sam Peckinpah as the best novel every written. Film promises were made. The script never surfaced.

To compose *The Forests of the Night,* Joe went to a ranch in the Mexican Sierra and completed the bulk of its 278 pages in 30 days. He wrote in longhand, barely eating or sleeping, fueling himself with *lechuguilla,* a rawer cousin of *mescal.* When he needed a boost, he'd dip his cup into the five-gallon jug underneath his writing desk.

Joe rode out of the Sierra Madre with his manuscript in a satchel strapped to the saddle and went on a two-week binge in Douglas, Arizona and Agua Prieta, Mexico. He kept the manuscript under his arm as he staggered from bar to bar. At the far end of the binge he woke up in a bed at the hotel in Douglas. His limbs were still attached to his body, but his manuscript was gone.

Joe's words:

> *Ten days went by and I woke up in my room at The Gadsden Hotel to read from my manuscript and couldn't find it. I was having too much fun to worry about it...*

Joe and his drinking buddies retraced their steps, back through the bars along the border of Arizona and Mexico. After a three-day search a cowboy friend found the manuscript in a trash barrel behind a poolroom called *The B and P Bar.*

I probably put it there for safekeeping and forgot about it, Joe remarked.

Much of Joe Brown's *walk on the wild side* life has been well documented by writers such as Leo Banks in the *Tucson Weekly* and Richard Grant, in his book on the Sierra Madre: *God's Middle Finger.* Recommended reading for those seeking more J.P.S. Brown color.

Joe filled Richard Grant in on the Mexican history which impacts cowboy culture.

> *That's where all the cattle traditions come from, not from the East or England. The Pilgrim fathers weren't known for their hospitality or their horsemanship or their generosity. They were more intent on punishing and killing people for their own good.*

The J.P.S. Brown books cascaded out in between turns to Mexico, the knife fights and the binges, the whoring and the coming home. Between the ranching, the settling down, and the losing of ranches. And the string of wives – until he found his true love Patsy. He never quit the writing.

The literature rolled forth: *Keep the Devil Waiting, The Cinnamon Colt* (stories), *Steeldust, The World in Pancho's Eye, Wolves at the Door, The Sprit of Dogie Long,* and others. There were essays, a screenplay on Ben Johnson, short stories and a still unfinished three-part autobiography. The well of Joe's cowboy material is fathomless.

He now lives alone and works in the afternoon, those moments when, as Hemingway stated, a writer *faces eternity or the lack of it every day.*

Here's Joe in 2010:

> *I sit down with three fingers of bourbon and write two hours or a thousand words every afternoon at 4. Two years ago I completed a novel about a boy who is found in an abandoned wagon by a trail crew driving a herd from New Mexico to California. They keep him and raise him the Cowboy Way.*
>
> *I don't cowboy so much anymore, but as a cowboy, I often knew the privilege of being way out alone in great country doing work that took risk, instinct and courage, and I wished everybody could know more about that aspect of a cowboy's life. Now I write more than ever about the Cowboy Way.*

The *cowboy way* is deeply carved into J.P.S. Brown's classic, *The Outfit*.

III The Outfit: A Cowboy's Primer/ A Runaway Horse Opens A Grave

The Outfit *is the best contemporary Western novel yet written.*

— **Ian Tyson**

Present time. March, 2015. Ian Tyson was visiting my office-studio recently and he spied my stack of J.P.S. Brown novels. Each one signed by Joe Brown in fountain pen ink. I asked Ian which ones he favored and he reached into the middle of the stack. He pulled out

The Outfit. He slapped the book down and declared it the best contemporary Western novel yet written. To rate *The Outfit* above Larry McMurtrey's canon and Cormac McCarthy and other Western writers is fulsome praise, and issues from Tyson, the man who reinvented the cowboy song.

The Outfit concerns the time Joe spent cowboying on the 1,300 square mile Nevada ranch owned by T.V. personality Art Linkletter. Linkletter bought the ranch thinking there were 1,400 cattle out there, but Joe and crew gathered 5,000. Four months later, the ranch was sold with the additional 3,600 cattle as part of the deal and Linkletter did well.

In Joe Brown's world the word *Outfit* is defined as a group of men or an entire ranch equipped to husband a herd of cattle from birth to market. The novel's format is distinctive. Chapters are headed with a Western term or concept which are explicated and jawed-on for a paragraph, then the action and the plot are carried forward. We have a Western primer melting into a novel.

Chapters begin with terms such as: *remuda, leppie calf, buckaroo, dogie, riding in a circle, rimming, querencia, tallow, hondo, remnant cattle, dally, horse poor, rimfire, houlihan, night loop, running iron, retozo* (a horse getting loose with the saddle on), *turned out*, and *maverick*.

You can explore many of these terms in compendiums like the Ramon F. Adams classics: *Western Words*, and *Cowboy Lingo*, which are fine resource books, but Joe Brown's take on the lingo is unique, and his personal insights work into the plot. He *lived* the concepts.

Here's a sample from *The Outfit*:

> A "querencia" is an individual animal's own abode...the place where he finds subsistence best for himself. The brave bull will often make a "querencia" of a certain area in the bullring and a matador feels he can do a better job of killing him if he can draw him out of his "querencia." An Indian is united with his "querencia" no matter how far away from it he finds himself and no matter who thinks he owns it. The Indian yearns to be in his own home ground in this life and the next. A cowboy's "querencia" is anywhere he finds the seldom and meager society of other cowboys, open country, and good horses for travelling it, feed and water and cattle and job to do with cattle.

Dead on. I learned about *querencia* in a few amateur bullfight classes in Mexico and Spain. Hands-on. I am reminded of the old bullfighter in Hemingway's time, Luis Freg, who was gored 72 times. His respect for *querencia* was obscured by bravery or extreme stupidity. Hemingway called it a *strange valor*.

For another angle on *querencia* I'd recommend Bruce Chatwin's *The Songlines*, in which Australian aboriginals walk across their *querencia*, singing up the land as they go. Each rock and riverbed has a distinct song.

Along with cowboy terms in *The Outfit*, Joe mixes in Mexican *caballero*-proverbs such as: *Al ojo del amo engorda el caballo* – under the watchful eye of his master the horse will prosper, and *Caballo encarrerado, sepultura abierta* – a runaway horse opens a grave. Joe's command of colloquial *espanol* lends even more depth and lyricism to the book.

In an updated introduction to *The Outfit:* Joe puts a final wrap on the cowboy deal:

> *I've always laughed when I heard people say cowboys are extinct...I knew the shoot 'em up cowboys were all dead before most people did. They killed themselves off in the big shootouts Hollywood staged over and over and over again...those cowboys died with their hats on wrong, wearing trousers too short, still packing baby fat, and nobody cared. I write about cowboys because I believe people should know the real animals, men, and women who make their living with horses and cattle, and the artful life they create for themselves, with no audience, no background music, and no ticket sale.*

Basta. Enough said.

IV Goin' Back Where the Bullets Fly

> *Oh, curse your gold and your silver too,*
> *And curse the gal that can't prove true;*
> *I'm goin' back where the bullets fly,*
> *I'll stay on the cowtrail till I die.*

— *The Trail to Mexico*
(As sung by Buck Ramsey)

All the J.P.S. Brown lore began to remind me of that old song "The Trail to Mexico," about a lovesick cowboy who vows to return to Mexico where the bullets still fly. I'm also reminded of Charles Goodnight, who lived 93 years. Joe Brown and Goodnight are kindred spirits. Along with Oliver Loving, Goodnight established The Goodnight-Loving Trail. He and Loving first drove a herd of feral Texas Longhorns up the trail in 1866. Goodnight also invented the chuck wagon.

In his younger days Charlie smoked up to fifty cigars a day, and in his later days, age 91, he married a 26 year old distant cousin named Corrine, who became pregnant with their child, but miscarried. His was a legendary life on the last frontier. Hold fast, boys.

And J.P.S. Brown? I think old J. Frank Dobie would have loved Joe Brown. Frank Dobie was a strong judge of character. Here's what he said about Goodnight, and it would serve J.P.S. Brown as well:

> *I have met a lot of good men, several fine gentlemen, hordes of cunning climbers, plenty of loud-braying asses and plenty of dumb oxen, but I haven't lived long enough or traveled far enough to meet more than two or three men I'd call great. This is a word I will not bandy around. To me, Charles Goodnight was great natured.*

Amen. Joe Brown is *good-natured*, truly kind, and *great* in the sense of Dobie's *cowboy great*. Joe's been up the mountain and slapped the elephant on the hind end. He's cowboy'd on the last wild edge of the border West – the cattle and horse trade, the whoring, drinking, and knife fights, which eventually faded into finding his true love Patsy, ranching and wrangling for the movies, and sharing all this hard won life experience with readers. Woody Guthrie said *all you can write is what you see* and J.P.S. Brown has seen plenty.

If there was any difficulty in writing this essay it was – where in hell do you start? We're confined now to the diminishing returns of worn out vocabulary and a dissipated language. Computers with short cuts to hell. Tweets and texts on phones. In essays we overuse words like *great* and *wild* until they're watered down and meaningless. And the local store doesn't know what the hell ink is. And there sits J.P.S. Brown. In spite of it all. A man who created a cowboy-lingo of his own by living it. How do you do a life like that justice?

The books are all you need for evidence. Here's one recent dispatch which manifests Joe's kind-heartedness toward fellow writers:

Friend Tom,

I've been reading and enjoying your stories in R&R. *They hit square at home with me...You are in a position that I always wanted to be in. I had an ambition to write a novel about a cowboy's first hand experience with every husbandman in the world. I'm 85 now and won't ever do it, but I sure like what you are doing with your knowledge of many of the people and places that I would have liked to write about. However, I'm proud of the land and people I chose to record, so I ain't sorry about anything. I went all out and it is what it is. Remember, I'll always keep coffee and a pot of beans hot for you and your lady.*
Hold fast,
Joe

A generous man. J.P.S. Brown may never make *The New York Times* best-seller list, because the real Western truth lies on a road that forks away from where Hollywood and Western dime novels have taken us. His work is imbued with the personal history of an educated, articulate, multi-lingual cowboy was has been in the trenches and still signs his name with a fountain pen.

The lingo which rings with truth. I've always enjoyed the introductory note from John Lomax in his first edition of *Cowboy Songs*, pertaining to the hard lingo and deep spirit of traditional songs:

> *To paraphrase slightly what Sidney Lanier said of Walt Whitman's poetry, they are raw collops slashed from the rump of Nature, and never mind the gristle...some of the strong adjectives and nouns have to be softened...there is, however, a Homeric quality about the cowboy's profanity and vulgarity that pleases rather then repulses...he spoke out plainly the impulses of his heart. But as yet so-called polite society is not quite willing to hear.*

J.P.S. Brown and his work. Poetic raw collops composed, carved-out, and slashed from the rump of Western Nature. Lived fully. Never mind the gristle. Joe Brown speaks and writes plainly from wise impulses of a cowboy heart. Hold fast, boys. Here comes another dispatch from Patagonia.

Red Desert (3)

Four Dreamers on a Western Landscape

Nothing happens unless first a dream.

— Carl Sandburg

I   Santa Fe Crossing the Mojave

All around the water tank
Waiting for a train
A thousand miles away from home
Sleeping in the rain...

— **Jimmie Rodgers,** *Waiting for a Train*

Chuck Steiner weighed in at nearly three hundred pounds. Bison-like. His face was shielded by a mouse-grey beard, which drooped down and splayed out over his gut. He didn't walk, no, he *rolled* toward an unseen spot on the horizon, or the corner of a honkytonk, where he'd turn and prop himself up against the wall, then slide down into his throne. Ready to face the world.

Chuck was there to hear real country music. If the band played anything Chuck didn't consider *true country* he'd raise up a fleshy index finger and declare: *Das is not da reel cow-n-tree music! No! No! No!* He'd shout in broken English and shake his huge head back and forth in rank disgust. Others shook their heads in unison.

Chuck liked most country music recorded between 1925 and 1965. Jimmy Rodgers, The Carter Family, Hank Williams, Lefty Frizzell, Porter Wagoner, Johnny Cash, Merle Haggard, Buck Owens, George Jones. And all the early cowboy music – Tex Ritter, Carl Sprague and such. Chuck was quick to remark that Carl Sprague's "When the Work's All Done This Fall" sold 900,000 copies in 1925. Chuck declared that after the late 1970s country music went all to hell and became disposable pop trash. I generally agreed with him.

This story begins in the West. West *Switzerland*. Chuck Steiner was the man behind the biggest country music radio show in

Switzerland. He created the set lists and pulled the music from his personal, extensive collection of LPs and rare 78s. He never spoke on the air. He sat propped in a corner passing the producer the music. They were handed over like sacred gold platters.

A fellow named Christolph Schweigler did the talking, with a deep, resonant voice. Chuck kept the music pure and he's credited with creating the audience for country music in Switzerland. This is no small matter, since Switzerland hosts at least five major country music festivals a year.

Chuck travelled with a driver-sidekick named Markus. Markus was a smaller version of Chuck. Probably weighed around 250. A quiet, round guy, proud to be Chuck's best friend. He nodded assent to each of Chuck's violent pronouncements on country music. He was a country *yes man* and he could fit behind a steering wheel.

Chuck and Markus enjoyed two passions – country music and trains. On weekends they repaired to a shed outside of Basel where they kept an elaborate model train setup. Here, far away from the ignorant, philistine, pop country crowds, they blasted *da reel cow-n tree music*, donned engineer caps, and ran their little trains through the miniature wild west. Dreamers.

Their favorite model train was the finely painted Santa Fe Freight train. Twenty box cars long. The boys fiddled with their train setup as Jimmie Rodgers spun around on an old 78 record, yodeling about life on the rails and in the hobo jungles.

What's this have to do with our American West? Plenty. The West was created, sanctified, and then mythologized by dreamers, and Chuck and Marcus had one gnawing, unfulfilled dream. They wanted to see a real Santa Fe Freight train crossing a real Western environment, like the Mojave Desert. They were obsessed with this vision.

As the years went on Chuck grew fatter, less healthy, and disgruntled with the state of modern country music. He was bitter. He gave up his job providing music for the weekly country music show on Swiss National Radio and spent hours and hours in the train shed, pulling switches and muttering. He was running the little trains too fast. There were unnecessary derailments. Markus was alarmed.

Markus decided the thing to do was go for the big one and splurge. Use their savings fly to California and photograph the great

Santa Fe Freight trains crossing the Mojave Desert. They could explore lost canyons, culverts, and old trestles where the Santa Fe engines might suddenly appear. God and Jimmie Rodgers would smile down from heaven.

One rainy May morning, thirty years ago, Chuck and Markus flew out of Zurich airport bound for Los Angeles International. They landed and picked up a rental car and, undeterred by jet lag and lack of sleep for 24 hours, they drove east towards the Mojave Desert.

Somewhere outside of L.A. they stopped and bought water, diet-Pepsi, potato chips, Ritz crackers, cheese spread, peanut butter, Oreo cookies, baloney sandwiches, and other vital American supplies. Maybe a map or two and an extra gas can. The vast Western Desert beckoned.

Did they cross the San Andreas Fault to see the historical Joshua Tree? Did they climb through the Tehachapi, San Gabriel or San Bernardino Mountains? Likely they had to. Did they see a Chuckwalla, a Fringe-Toed Lizard, Kangaroo Rat or Gila Monster? I never found out those details. They aimed toward a designated point, out on an isolated freight train line.

They stopped up on Cajon Pass, 3777 feet up, between the San Bernardino and San Gabriel Mountains, in the Mojave Desert. The boys located the rail lines and a strategic point on a back desert road. They sat inside their rental car to wait, cameras ready.

Chuck Steiner owned a Nikon camera with a giant zoom lens, and he loaded the thing and settled it on the dashboard, aiming it out at the freight train tracks. I assume they kept the car running with the air conditioner on. Maybe not. They would have run out of gas.

Can you imagine two obese Swiss men stranded, forced to crawl across the Mojave Desert in 110-degree heat? Gruesome. They wouldn't last long, I reckon. They spent the night in the high desert pass, and all the next morning. The car was filling up with empty water bottles and cookie wrappers. Trains passed by – nothing but Union Pacific's and Amtrak passenger trains. Not what the boys were after.

Finally, on the verge of giving up, they saw it. The great red and yellow diesel engine rolling down the line. A Santa Fe Freight train. Crossing the Mojave.

Chuck was ready. He fired off fifty frames. They laughed and ate baloney sandwiches and cookies. But they weren't finished. They decided to forge on to Canyon Diablo, Arizona, a ghost town on the Navajo Nation, then drive eastward to Abo Canyon, New Mexico, and Thoreau, New Mexico. Chuck carried extensive notes on isolated freight lines.

They were gone two weeks and went through mountains of potato chips and fifty rolls of film, then flew back to Zurich on a night flight.

I ran into the boys about two weeks later at a concert I was performing in a little dude ranch called *The Pony Ranch,* in Biel, Switzerland. Chuck was propped up in the corner of the bar, back on his throne, his dignity restored. By the look on his mug I could tell he wanted to show me something. There was color in his jowls.

He motioned me over to sit down. He pulled a 5 by 7 inch postcard out of his Swiss army bag. He presented to me as a gift. On the backside of the card, upper left hand corner, it read:

> *Four views of Santa Fe Freight Trains: Crossing Cajon Pass, Abo Canyon, Canyon Diablo, and The Continental Divide, near Thoreau, New Mexico.*
> *(Copyright: Charles "Chuck" Steiner, Basel, Switzerland. 1988.)*

His hands were wrapped contentedly across his gut as he watched me study at the card. He shook his head up and down and closed his eyes over the memory. Markus sat beside him, eyes closed in concert with his friend. They were back in Cajon Pass or Abo Canyon, cookie crumbs rolling down their contented faces.

It didn't matter now that modern country was a false-hearted imitation of the real thing. *Civilization be damned.* The boys had been to the top of the mountain and tracked down their great white buffalo. In the American West.

That night I sang a set of train songs from the 40s to the 1960s. Chuck held up his finger and I could read his lips:

Ya! Das was da reel cow-n-tree-muse-sic! Yah! Yah!

And that was the last time I saw the boys. I'd like to think they're over in that shed near Basel tonight, listening to Jimmie Rodgers, Johnny Cash, and Hank Williams. Moving those little Santa Fe freight trains across a desert that has become deeply real in their imaginations. Two characters bent over their model Western landscape. Yodeling softly. Lost in a diesel dream.

II Gunsmoke in Tucson

I was just a kid listening to my Uncle George's record prayer, while the great vinyl wheel spun 'round it's holy prayers...and the steel guitars in those Telecaster bars of San Joaquin towns...

— **Tom Russell**, *Mesabi*

I'm in between films.

— **George Malloy Jr.**

My Uncle George Malloy was the saloon piano player in the movie *Gunsmoke in Tucson.* You might have missed it. It was a hay-burner western shot on the backlots of Hollywood and released in 1958. Forest Tucker played the lead. The plot was basic B-Western, with a strong dash of the Old Testament. Two brothers witness the hanging of their father and they're forced to grow up alone in the Wild West. One becomes an outlaw. The other a Sheriff. You know the rest. Good and evil. Cain and Abel. Black hat verses white hat. Mule-shoe morality on a tight budget. Drive-in movie fare for Wichita Falls and Big Spring.

Some of the characters' names: *Slick Kirby, Clem Haney, John Brazos,* and *Notches Pole.* The moviemakers found my uncle on a union musician's list in Los Angeles. He'd been playing gigs in theater lobbies. In those days, when a movie opened, maybe a big musical, they hired a piano player to perform in the lobby, drumming up interest in the coming attraction.

I have an old press photo of my uncle from the 1938. He's dressed in a suit and tie and black and white dress shoes, perched in front of an upright piano in a theater lobby in Los Angeles. A poster to his right states that *Boy Meets Girl* is now showing. That was a 1938 *screwball comedy* (as they called it) with Jimmy Cagney and Pat O'Brian.

My uncle was employed to hype the coming feature: Irving Berlin's *Alexander's Ragtime Band,* starring Ethel Merman, Alice Faye and Don Ameche. The poster on top the piano reads: *this is not Irving Berlin's piano, but these are his memorable tunes. Don't miss the picture.*

My Uncle sat there and pounded out Irving Berlin classics. The film, *Alexander's Ragtime Band,* traced the history of jazz from ragtime through swing – following the story of a kid who scandalizes his family by playing ragtime instead of *serious music.* And here was my classically trained uncle playing in a theater lobby. A gig's a gig.

From theater lobbies to the big screen! *Gunsmoke in Tucson* called for a piano player to perform in a saloon scene while the gunfire blazed and the dance hall girls high-kicked the *Can Can*. My uncle knew he'd handle the job. He could sight read, had a great ear, and possessed a special Western piano trick he'd learned from the comedic pianist Victor Borge. My uncle could *shoot the keys*. He was ready to pull this trick out of his war bag.

Shooting the keys is of a Jerry Lee Lewis type piano-move which involves sliding the index finger down the keyboard, hitting all the white keys (usually the right hand down the treble side). At the end of the slide you cock your hand like a gun and shoot the final note with your index finger. Right in time. It's show biz. It's Western.

They dressed uncle George up like a saloon pimp, with derby hat, calico shirt, and sleeve garters. No cigar that I recall. My uncle said he shot the keys several times on camera, but they cut that part out of the film. They thought he was stealing the scene. That was my Uncle's final film. His part lasted about thirty seconds.

Fast forward – fifty years later. Uncle George is bent over a vodka tonic in Malachy's Bar, on 72nd street in Manhattan. I asked him about his West Coast cowboy movie career. He winced.

"I'm in between films," he said.

That was it. Then he sideswiped me with a sardonic look. A Jack Benny quarter-smirk with a raised eyebrow. *Anymore Hollywood questions?*

Here was the gunfighter pianist in winter. The keyboard wizard who could shoot the keys and break your heart with Chopin's *Heroic Polonaise in A flat*. One of our greatest American pianists. At least that's they way *I* saw it. He was a travelling musician, born in the West, conquering the world, and that's the life I wanted.

Uncle George, born in California in 1920, had become a New York character. An ex-patriot from *The Coast*, as he called California. At age 86 his life was revealed in nippy, verbal fragments, if he cared to talk at all. He was one of the guys at the end of the bar. One of the loners content to sit in the shadows and observe.

He played piano for vocal lessons, backed up a Gilbert and Sullivan Troupe for years, and did the occasional gig in opera piano bars. A large brandy snifter served as a tip jar. Malachy's Bar was his local hangout. His water hole.

In Malachy's nobody asked about your past, or your job, or where the ten-dollar bills came from. Nobody remembered *Gunsmoke in Tucson*. Old New York bars harbored taciturn compatriots of late afternoon oblivion. The boys knew your name, maybe, or your nickname, and the talk was kept basic, anecdotal, and humorous. No heroes or braggarts. No lights. No cameras. Little action. Just snippets and shards of the usual small talk, which went along with *the usual* drink.

"George, guy at the end of the bar just bought you a drink."

Bang. A wet napkin and a speed-rack vodka tonic shoved across the bar. A slow nod of thanks. Another ten minutes of contemplation. You return the favor and send the other guy, or old gal, a drink. Afternoon shadows move across dusty shades. The night bartender comes on. The clink of glass on glass. A hand tapping a cigarette ash into a tray. Back when you could *smoke* in bars. Back when people left you alone. Before the world got all snotty and politically correct.

Drinkers would show up daily for twenty years, then one day their place in the corner was vacant. Few questions asked. Two weeks later a new character arrives. It's a New York play written to protect shielded histories. There's seldom a great exit line. *See you tomorrow*, or an implied *maybe never see you again*. Malachy's regulars were stagehands, novelists, accountants and street sweepers. And the pianist who played in *Gunsmoke in Tucson*.

In between films.

Uncle George didn't show up one afternoon at Malachy's. Odd, but not unusual. At age 86 he was slowing down. Crossing 72nd street in the middle of the block, plodding slowly in a ragged diagonal line, honked at by Cab drivers and rich SUV dames. George was shuffling as modern times came speeding toward him. An old antelope limping at the back of the herd. Enter the hyenas. The New York streets and alleys conform to a Darwinian code.

Yeah, back in Malachy's they say *old age is a bitch.* Old folks fall down in the bathtub or shower and hit the head or break their hip and begin their slow descent back into the earth. Rest homes, hospitals, care facilities. Lights out. Paradise. Eternity. The drug companies, insurance agents, and quack doctors are waiting to take a huge slice of the old-age pie. Maybe they can sell a hip replacement or new knee before the old guy or gal croaks.

When my Uncle George fell they didn't find him for a day and a half. He was lying deep in the clutter of his rent-controlled apartment on 72nd street. He'd been living there fifty years.

He was ambulanced to Roosevelt Hospital where he agreed, or

was harassed into, a questionable eight-hour operation to possibly fix something that was pressing on his spine. He was conned, as the social workers moved his papers from drawer to drawer. The bills piled up. Was this anyway to treat the guy who played in *Gunsmoke in Tucson?* Where was the musician's union now?

The operation was a success, as they say, but the patient never got out of bed again. I was there when they wheeled him back from surgery. He'd survived. Barely. We gave him two weeks to live. He was resigned. The eight-hour operation had fixed his back, but exhausted his resolve to put his slippers back on. Roll the credits. Exit the gunfighter.

Back in Malachy's, around happy hour, the regulars eyed his empty stool. *George ain't been in for a few days.*

Silence. *Give me a double.*

He didn't end up in that full-care facility in Queens, where the doctors wanted to dump him. No. The old saloon piano player escaped back to the West. Trouble rides a fast horse. He was craving good Mexican food. He kept talking to me about *The Red Onion* in Inglewood, California, where he grew up. They had *the best tamales in the world.* I didn't have the heart to tell him that *The Red Onion* had been closed for forty years.

My sisters had flown in from the West, rescued him, and decided it was best to move Uncle George to Ogden, Utah, where my brother-in-law ran a senior care facility. George could spend his final weeks near family, that sort of thing. They could get him take-out Mexican food. I could sneak him a vodka tonic.

They flew him first class and wheeled him into a facility on the edge of Ogden. Fourth room from the parking lot. He never looked out the window. Never got out of bed. A funny thing happened, though. Uncle George didn't die. He survived fourteen months on chocolate milkshakes, root beer floats, and crossword puzzles.

He could finish four crosswords a day – starting with *The New York Times* down to the local rag. Then he'd work on a few *word puzzlers.* He adapted. Hell, he *flourished.* Sometimes I flew over and we'd listen to music all day – two road musicians chatting about life in the trenches.

My older sister, Nan, flew back to New York with her husband Andy and cleaned out George's apartment on 72nd and Broadway. Piles of dirty laundry, bookcases crammed full of music scores, crossword puzzle books, and an old refrigerator full of what we used to call *TV Dinners*. A huge black Steinway piano dominated the tiny living room.

Uncle George had been in this same apartment a half century. Alone. The paint was peeling off the walls and the radiators clattered all night. He was renting it four hundred a month and the owners couldn't wait for him to pass on. The location was worth a mint in rent. The vultures were ready to move in, refurbish the joint and jack the rent up to three grand a month. Or higher.

My sister dug into the closets and underneath the clothes and, as the family archeologist, began to unearth clues of George's life in the music business. A momentous career we'd never known much about.

Uncle George was a professional pianist, as I've indicated. An "accompanist." After his film career he'd traveled the world backing up the great classical singers: Todd Duncan, Camilla Williams, Roberta Peters, Eileen Farrell. *Giants*. He'd been to Australia, Africa, Japan, Egypt, Australia and the Philippines. The tour books were scattered about. The scrapbooks. The maps lined with red ink marking the concert trails. Can you imagine the cocktail receptions? Lord.

He'd brought back picture slides, exotic matchbooks, and a camel saddle. He collected hotel stationary from every hotel stop, and sent letters out on these exotic scraps for years and years. At Christmas he sent each of us four kids a check for fifty bucks, inside a piece of stationary from a hotel in Chicago, Tokyo, or Casa Blanca.

There were stacks of photos. Movie star Jeanette MacDonald signed a photo: *To My Buddy*. (My Uncle's nickname was "Bud.") Affairs with film starlets? We'll never know. There were letters from Nelson Eddy and other stars.

There was a hand-tinted photo of my uncle and my mother mounted horseback at Seminole Hot Springs, near Malibu, in the early 1930s. I showed him the photo – his cryptic remark: *The Hot Springs was run by my uncle Vern and aunt Anna...some movie actress used to go there to dry out...maybe it was Myrna Loy.* End of story.

When he was near dying we began to realize his "place" in American music. It was more than *Gunsmoke in Tucson*. He told my sister:

> *I was in the "Al Jolson Story," but I ended upon the cutting room floor. Al only came on the set once. I played the Hammond organ in "Unchained Melody," but I don't know if it made it into the movie.*

There was more.

George had performed at the White House during the Eisenhower administration. He'd been on the Johnny Carson and Mike Douglas TV shows. Then came a whopper. Uncle George was at the March on Washington in August, 1963, the most historic civil rights march in history, and the largest demonstration ever held in Washington D.C. 250,000 people attended.

He was sitting a row behind Marlon Brando, Burt Lancaster, and Judy Garland. Eileen Farrell was supposed to sing the "Star Spangled Banner," but she was caught up in traffic.

The eyes of the Nation looked down and landed on Uncle George. It was the bottom of the ninth in American history, and the coach went to the bullpen and went with my uncle. He was ready. Of course he knew the song by heart.

He was escorted to the stage to backup Camilla Williams who'd replaced Eileen Farrell. Uncle George pounded out the old warhorse, the "Star Spangled Banner," like it had never been played before. At least I assume he did. I don't know if he tried to shoot the keys. Not appropriate, I would guess. Then came Bob Dylan and "Blowin' in the Wind," and finally Martin Luther King.

In those last days in Ogden, Utah, we pieced together the anecdotes, the photos, the scrapbooks, and the tour maps, until he finally closed his eyes and moved on. It reminded me of that Guy Clark song, "Desperados Waiting for a Train," with the lines:

Then one day I looked up and he's turnin' 80
He's got brown tobacco stains all down his chin
to me he's one of the heroes of this country,
so why's he all dressed up like them old men?

Maybe someday they'll dig up the edited film outtakes from *Gunsmoke in Tucson* and the world can see him shooting the keys. For now you can go on *You-Tube* and see him playing behind Larry Adler, the greatest harmonica player who ever lived. Yes, Uncle George on the edge of history. Happy to serve. The guy at the end of the bar at Malachy's. The piano player in *Gunsmoke in Tucson*.

Don't bother him. He's *in between films.*

III Sharks and Mules

I think they call it progress, Tom.

— **Johnny Bean**

You can't say civilization don't advance ...
in every war they kill you in a new way.

— **Will Rogers,** *The New York Times,* Dec. 23, 1929

There's a *for sale* sign on Johnny Bean's horse ranch. I drove by there last week. A sad note. The sale of Johnny Bean's place marks a major blow to ranching and farming in our part of El Paso. The City government, in league with fast talking developers, rolled in a Trojan Horse they named *Smart Growth.* In fact the steed should be nicknamed *Ignorant Devastation* – developers selling cheap houses to middle and lower class Mexican families, then mortgaging the folks up to their eyeballs for the rest of their life, as the houses fall apart.

The ugly development surrounded Johnny Bean's horse ranch. A major truck route to Mexico was bulldozed through. Cheap catalogue houses lined up alongside the highway with backyards cluttered with broken trampolines, deflated swimming pools, overturned swing sets, and the requisite one-eyed pit bull. A man around here is now as tough, or stupid, as his yard dog.

Then cometh the "smart growth" strip malls with cheap pizza, fake burgers, and dollar stores. Will Rogers would have tossed out a witty remark for this savage decline, but thank God he ain't around to observe the disaster.

A few years back, when this *smart growth* began, I called up Johnny Bean. I asked him what the hell we could do about it all. Johnny was in his early 80s at the time. I could hear him breathing heavily. Thinking. Then he spat out: *I think they call it progress, Tom.* That was it. He hung up.

Johnny Bean died a while back. One day I walked into my local Postal Annex store, where I ship my paintings. It's owned by a fine cowboy and muleteer named Pete, and his wife Lettie. Pete knew Johnny Bean and told me a notable story Johnny had once shared with him. A mule story.

Johnny had served as a muleskinner during WWII and was in a

crew aboard a ship hauling three hundred mules to Burma. The ship was torpedoed and sunk by a German U-Boat. Johnny Bean and the crew escaped into lifeboats and survived three days before rescue. The mules were turned loose into the open sea.

The men sat in the lifeboats that first day watching as sharks went after the mules. A scene that would stay in your mind forever. An unnerving vision beyond any dark Peckinpah movie. Beyond *Jaws*. I'm tempted to turn it into a metaphor for El Paso *progress*, but I'll let that rest. Certain scenes defy the triviality of metaphoric tricks.

Pete and Lettie then shared with me Johnny Bean's obituary, which was posted on the wall of their store. I think it's worthy of including here, a short chronicle of a remarkable life in the West. Consider this:

The Obituary:

> *Johnny W. Bean, age 94, died peacefully at his home in Canutillo on Feb 12th. He was born 08/28/1918 at Crawfordsville, Ark. He left home at age 17 and joined the US Army. He served in the US Cavalry and fought in the Burma Campaign in WWII.*
>
> *While in route to Burma with a shipload of 400 mules, his ship was sunk by a German U-Boat. Johnny and his shipmates survived in lifeboats for 3 days until, they were rescued by the Indian Navy. While serving in Burma, Johnny and his fellow soldiers were supplied by airdrops and mule trains.*
>
> *At times when the US planes couldn't make food drops due to bad weather or combat with Japanese aircraft, Johnny and his comrades butchered and ate mule meat. When the war was over, Johnnie returned to Texas where he worked as a cowboy and horse breaker on several large Texas-New Mexico ranches.*
>
> *At one time he showed the famous QH stallion, "Sugar Bars." He became an excellent saddle maker and eventually developed a large horse boarding facility and equine surgery facility in El Paso.*
>
> *For many years he also owned and managed a saddle repair and tack shop in Ruidoso. Mr. Bean was recognized as an icon in the horse business. His Ruidoso shop was a gathering place for racehorse owners, jockeys, and trainers from all over the US. A memorial service will be scheduled at Sunland Park Race Track on a date to be announced.*

A Western Life. In capital letters.

And how to end this essay of four characters on a Western landscape? I'll set a scenario. Years ago I performed in a joint in Munich, Germany, called The Oklahoma Saloon. A loud dive. Tequila shots were delivered to the stage on the back of a model train coal car. The train ran from the bar and around the walls of the club, and carried drinks to the band. The drinks were needed to survive the gig. Trust me.

In my imagination, now, all the characters mentioned in this essay are in a bar in the Great Beyond. Chuck Steiner and Markus are the bartenders, sending drinks up to the stage on a Santa Fe model train.

Johnny Bean is up there singing: "I'm The Man Who Rode the Mule Around the World," the old folksong, and he's backed up by my Uncle George on the piano, who shoots the keys after each chorus. Chuck Steiner keeps yelling, *Yah! Das is da reel cow-n-tree music!* You get the picture.

Four characters on an eternal Western landscape. Dreamers. *Nothing happens unless first a dream*...Carl Sandburg said that.

James Joyce - The Dubliner

Muleteer on the Edge of the World

The Grand Canyon is not solitude. It is a living, moving, pulsating being, ever changing in form and color...pinnacles and towers springing into being out of unseen depths...among it's cathedral spires, it's arches and domes, and the deepest recesses of its inner gorge...it's spirit, it's soul, the very spirit of the living God himself lives and moves..."

— **R.B. Stanton,** 1909

*The Grand Canyon allows you no mistakes.
You screw up, you're gonna pay for it.
Man or beast."*

— **Ross Knox**

Ross Knox has been helicoptered out of the Grand Canyon three times. He's nearly died on a canyon trail with a fully loaded mule on top of him. He died on a heart-lung machine and came back. He's heard the angels sing "Streets of Laredo" and "Bury Me Not on the Lone Prairie." He harmonized with them. One morning I thought Ross was dying, on his knees, in my pecan orchard after a rough and rowdy night in Juarez with myself and the great cowboy songster, Ian Tyson. *Near Death* is Ross Knox's street address.

Ross is a *mulero*. A muleteer. A muleskinner. He's a pack rat, brush whacker, western poet and hardcore American cowboy. He looks all of these. His desperado visage was formed by the alchemy of sunlight, campfire smoke, and mule dust. The gods of terror have etched rings around Knox's eyes. He squints when he tells stories about psychotic muleteers and pack train wrecks, as if he's looking down into the abyss and hoisting the memories back up to the rim. He is Absalom, riding a mule under an ancient Oak tree, where death is waiting like a raven in the high branches.

Mr. Knox is not running the pony ride concession. At the time of this initial writing, Ross was packing supplies down into the Grand Canyon. He left at four in the morning on a daily basis – in the heat of summer and on the icy trails of winter. Ross does not call his mules "*Arizona Nightingales*" or "*Rocky Mountain Canaries.*" He makes good use of stronger lingo. The odd cowboy curse and *the great western expletive*. He tells it true. He shakes hands with Fear every morning, and is damn glad to be alive come happy hour. Again and again. Ride around slowly, boys, we're goin' down into the big ditch.

Below are my initial ruminations on *muleteer dread* after I'd spent a few afternoons talking with Ross Knox about his daily descent into the Grand Canyon:

> "Fear has many eyes, and can see underground," wrote Cervantes. Sixteen years on the back of a mule, descending into the Grand Canyon at dawn, six days a week, plays a hellish symphony on the nerves. A man atop a mule begins to see rocks tilting in the half-dark, roots reaching out, and the voices of dead muleteers calling from down below. At the bottom of the big ditch is The Valley of Empty Saddles. The Land of No Breakfast Forever. Mule packers, surviving trail wrecks, have been hauled up to the rim "mentally different," gaunt-eyed and gone.
>
> The face of the muleskinner begins to shape-shift in first light of the morning trail. A man's eyelids narrow down, searching for the edge. The eyes dart back and forth with the rhythmic click of a hawk or night hunting owl. The Grand Canyon packer calls upon whatever God or magic talisman will light the journey. Fear rides with him like a sidekick without a sense of humor.
>
> If you can't see danger, you can hear it or smell it. A packer's hearing grows sharper, straining to listen for the scrape of mule shoe sliding across ice – a mule in panic clawing at air, seconds before the snort and the scream and the horror of the pack train avalanche. Mules burning the breeze. Comes now the climactic moment in the terror symphony, when the world turns upside down and a man's vision turns blood red, then black. The next sound you hear is the whirring of medivac helicopter blades.

Thus were my poetic notes on *trail fear* and the life of a Grand Canyon muleteer. You can compose this sort of blown-out stuff when you don't have to actually *lead the mules* down there yourself. Trust me. The story is best related in Ross Knox's own words. In raw cowboy tongue. Ross is a fine cowboy poet, so the cadence and color of his speech is influenced by Oregon and Nevada buckaroo slang, mixed with Tennessee mule-breeder talk, by way of Charles Badger

Clark poems, by way of Robert Service, and on back to the verse of Rudyard Kipling. And then some. The rattle and the clatter and history of western rhyme.

When Ross recites "*The Cremation of Sam McGee*," he *inhabits* the poem. He *is* the dog sled driver who cremated Sam McGee in the belly of a Yukon paddle wheeler. The terrain Robert Service wrote about is Ross Knox territory. Trails that have their "*own stern code*," and sights that "*make your blood run cold.*" Ross Knox, like a lot of kids, left home at age seventeen to see the West. He descended into the myth and became the reality. Big time.

Muleteers are a breed apart. The Odd-Fellow fraternity of mule men may be traced back to the Spanish conquest: "*to the Aztec traders who, in Tenochtitlan, lived apart in a special ward, and had their own deities, customs, and dress.*" I am quoting the old mule historian Carlton Beals.

Ross Knox's story, the wonderfully rough-edged monologue which follows, may not be the cup of soup for animal rights folk, horse and mule whisperers, or tourists seeking the magic and colorful ambience of Arizona's Grand Canyon. The tourists who sleep on the fine mattresses of the Phantom Ranch, and sip the imported beer and dip vegetables into ranch dressing, may not really want to know how all that stuff got *down* to the bottom of the Big Ditch. Most likely Ross Knox brought it down on the back of a mule.

Dim the Coleman lantern. Let Mr. Knox, the muleteer, speak for himself.

"I've been packing supplies at the Grand Canyon for sixteen years. I start my coffee at 2am. My crew shows up at 2:30 and we'll drink coffee for half an hour then we'll hit it. I've got forty head of pack mules. You know, there's the Phantom Ranch there at the bottom of the Grand Canyon. Bed space for 115 people, then a campground that'll hold half again as much, so we'll roll pretty hard to supply it all.

"800 pounds of steak and stew meat a week, 80 cases of beer. Untold fresh produce. I've got to pack forty bales of hay per week just to keep up. I've got a hay barn down there that'll hold 350 bales of hay. In the wintertime we go pretty hard to fill that barn up, 'cause they hammer the hell out of us in the summer.

"Last month I packed two queen size mattresses down. It was a cool lookin' load. I had it on a mule called *Tugalong*, the biggest I have. I hung 'em with a barrel hitch, then came back and tied a double diamond over the top. Right down the trail we went. I've got a good crew and we can pack damn near anything.

"I'll load my pack mules carefully, 'cause them trails ain't too damned wide. I can't get too bulky and I have a tunnel to go through there at the bottom, so I can't pack real high, and there's a five foot suspension bridge crossing the Colorado River that's 440 foot long.

"So the alarm goes off. I coffee up and try to sear yer eyes open. Then we hit the barn. We'll make our loads up. Take us twenty minutes. Five loads per pack. Ten loads per day. 200 pounds per mule. I have two corrals there. In the afternoon I work the mules I want for the next day off into the back corral. So once we got our loads made, in the morning, we can close the end of the barn off and kick the door open on the other end and run the mules into the barn and catch 'em and saddle 'em.

"I don't use the same mules two days in a row. Not unless they make me mad. My older mules work one day on, two days off. My younger mules will go every other day. If they get to jackin' around they work harder. Hell, it worked for me as a kid! If I got into trouble, by golly, I worked harder and look at the sterling figure I've become. (*Ross chuckles. Spits.*)

"I've been here sixteen years and now my mules are a little gentler than they used to be. We get everything out of Tennessee from a man named Rufus, a mule broker back there. We've dealt with him forever. They'll ship 'em out and some of 'em will go to the dude string (*tourists that ride different, and safer, trails down into the canyon.*) Rufus will say: 'I'm sending you two mules that will have to go to the pack line. That's because they've had people problems somewhere in their past, and I'm the last thing between them and the dog food can. If they don't make it in my barn, their future is pretty damn grim.

"Over the years I've gotten some big ole feather-legged, nine year old mules that had flipped-out on quite a few people in the past. The mules had gotten used to it and they'd kinda' liked it. So we had our battles. I had a mule called 'Scrap Iron.' He got the name because he looked like he was put together with a bunch of scraps. He was an oddball son of a gun. Big and stout.

"The toughest mule I had to deal with was a big ole dun mule called *Yak*. I started him and he was pretty good. They get six years old and have 1300 pounds on 'em, and they get pretty hard to deal with. So I once had to use that mule 17 days in a row. I would load him 250 pounds goin' down and 200 pounds comin' up, and he's either gonna get good or he's gonna die, and I don't really care, cause he's tryin' to kill me.

"On day fourteen he threw a fit and tried to pass the mule in front of him. That mule knocked him off the edge. I had six duffel bags packed on him and he came down upside down on those duffels, and that's what saved his life. And then he went to rollin'. The big wall, what we call the Red Wall, with the big drop, was very close to him, but he ended up against a dead tree and my pack was sittin' straight up on him. Mac says to me, 'Boy you had that son-of-a-bitch *packed good.*'

"I unpacked him and I had to make him climb a wall. There's a man-made wall there, so I cut a sling rope off and tied it 'round his neck, then tied it to the tree on the other side of the trail, so I kinda' had a lifeline on him. Mac says, *'Build a fire under that son of a gun!'* and that mule finally jumps up and gets his toes hung up on the top of that trail, and just scrambled 'til, by golly, he was back up.

"Well one of his eyes is swole' shut, and there's a big gash down the side of his face, and a whale of a gash down his rib cage, and another one on his hip. Mac says, *'Hell, he's gonna be off for two weeks.'*

"I said, 'You know what? That son-of-a-bitch, if he can walk into the barn tomorrow, well, he's *goin'*. He was a stiff, sore, sun-of-a-gun too, and I put 250 pounds on him. On day seventeen I walked past him, and I just touched him on the hip and said *'Move over,'* and he didn't try to kill me, so he finally got a day off. Two weeks later one of my packers hit him with a tractor and killed him. I was so damn mad 'cause it had been so long where I could get this son-of-a-bitch where I could deal with him."

Ross takes a breath. I make a note not to be applying for this particular job. Ross continues.

"We can pack five mules and be out of there in 25 minutes. We're not supposed to pack more than five mules down. It's illegal. For years we did it, though. The most I left the top with was eight. But, boy, it's a long way back to the end, and mules are workin' on the honor system. If something happens back there..."

Ross stops. His eyes glass over. He's thinking of a past wreck, but he's not ready to talk about it. A man stares into the abyss long enough and the abyss begins to stare back. I think Nietzsche said that. *Or Will Rogers.*

"Two men go down," says Ross. "If I don't have any wrecks I can be sittin' down at The Phantom Ranch in two hours and fifteen. The minute it's light enough to see the trail I want to be on it. We used to be really bad about leavin' in the dark. *Shouldn't do it.* But we did. I never killed anything in the dark, but I just lost my nerve over the years. It's just too damn dangerous. So I got to where the only time I'd leave in the dark was if someone came to visit me and I wanted to scare the hell out of 'em.

"In the sixteen years I've been here I would say, conservatively, we might have killed 12 to 15 head of mules. The place allows you no mistakes. You screw up, you're gonna pay for it, man or beast. Doesn't matter.

"In the mule's case, the one who throws the fit, he's fine. He's gonna kill something else. He's gonna knock *something else* off the trail. The mule in front of him. As far as myself, they've flown me out of here three times. "One wreck, well a mule started buckin' with me. A man named Darrell Williams was out in the lead. It was a pretty bad spot. You could see the ridge goin' down there. It's called '*Heart Attack*.' I was gonna get her rode, so I squalled and called out, cause if I was gonna ride it out I wanted somebody to see it.

"So I squalled and Darrell looked back, and I'm gonna weather the storm. But one of the cinches or britchins broke off of my saddle, and shot my saddle off over hear head, and I came off on the edge side, and I got my hands out in front of me to keep from goin' over the edge, cause there was a major drop there, and I wasn't gonna like it, and it tore the palms outta both my hands, and I had a tendon in this right hand pop out, then the sow spun and kicked me in the back and bruised my kidneys and my spleen. So they flew me to Flagstaff..."

Pause.

"I was layed up and couldn't open or close a door for weeks. Then I was re-packin' a mule at Poison Point, a mule named *Perry*, who threw a fit. I spun back under her just to keep from her pushin' me over the edge, 'cause you don't come back from 'Poison Point.' And she comes out with a foot in my chest and one foot on the side of my head. Thought for a minute she killed me.

"The last wreck I had where they flew me out...the trail had caved off. I was sittin' there restin' my mules, and my hand mule, the mule in the lead, he's called the hand mule, 'cause he's *in-hand (the lead rope is in Ross' hand)*. He stepped on the edge of the trail, and the wall caved off and popped my dallies off my ridin' mule, and she come down upside down on top of me. I should have never walked away from that one. The packer that was with me thought I was dead. It knocked me out.

"When I come around, J.D. was on the radio sayin': '*Ross is down, and I think he's dead!*'

"It took me awhile to take stock. This left arm was fractured. I knew my left leg was bad, and my hip was real bad. But I was able to move my head and I raised it up and said, *'J.D. I'm not in very good shape, but I'm not* dead. So get me some help in here.'

"So they wheel me up to Mormon Flat. Park Service flew in there and took one look at me and called Flagstaff Medical, told them to bring their chopper. What was funny was when they wheeled me up there, they wheeled the gurney round Skeleton Point, where I'd just killed a mule, and they have me strapped down. They have a strap across my forehead so I can't move, and Skeleton Point's a *bad, bad place.* All of a sudden one of the rangers yells: *'We're getting' too close to the edge! We're getting' too close to the edge!'*

"I yelled, 'Get me off here, I'll *walk* to the damn helicopter.'

"Hell, that was the worst part of the wreck. So we hit Mormon Flat and I saw *two helicopters*, and I said, *'Man I'm not in very good shape, but I'm not in two pieces!'*

"There were at least three major wrecks, and I have a faulty heart valve. Which I've had all my life. They told me it had to be replaced. So about five years ago they replaced it, but I got a staff infection. It damn near killed me. They had to go back in and replace it again. They told me: *'Git your affairs right, 'cause you may not be comin' out of this one.'* And I believed 'em. Thought I was gone. But we got through.

"Somebody asked me the other day, *'Ross, when you gonna slow down?'* I said, the last time I slowed down the Grim Reaper was trimming my hair!' Next time the son-of-a-bitch is gonna surely be winded.

I asked Ross why one mule can't pull the whole line off the trail. Ross squints: "I've got 'em tied to a pigtail. I use bailin' twine. As long as they're not off balance, it'll break. But one time I killed three mules in one shot because they wouldn't break loose. First wreck I ever had. Two of 'em were good mules. The other one I would've gladly killed myself. They were off balance and they wouldn't break loose, and they all went over the edge. But that's the only time that's happened. Other times the string broke."

We pause to fill our coffee cups and take a breather. Ross has already detailed enough misery and mule wrecks to fill ten Sam Peckinpah movies. Walt Disney has left the building.

II Mule Intermission

*"Not the muleteers teach the mules,
The mules teach the muleteers."*

— Mexican Proverb

Let's allow Ross to catch his breath. What the hell *is* a mule? I'm trying to remember the details of the deal. Didn't Jesus himself ride into Jerusalem on the back of a mule or donkey? Was it a *Spotted Ass* or a *Grulla*? *Catalonian* or *Maltese*? *Majorcan* or *Sicilian*? And remember the *20 Mule Team Borax* soap? Damn good soap. You washed your hands with that coarse borax powder. It came out of a tin dispenser in every Ma and Pa gas station along old Route 66. That stuff made your hands feel like you were scrubbing with alkali and Death Valley sand.

But what about the crossbred animal science? A mule is a cross between a donkey stallion and a horse mare. *Usually*. A "hinny" is the offspring of a stallion horse and a mare donkey. Confused yet? I've been around horses most of my life, as an observer anyway, but never got to the bottom of the mule question.

Cowboys may be a *breed apart*, but mule men seem to be another *two breeds apart* from the cowboy. Mule men are a sort of biblical folk who can deal with stubborn, almost mythical animals. Mule men are much like elephant men. You have to know your animal's mind, or you're going to end up as flat as a Parisian crepe.

Most donkey breeds, horse breeds, cattle, and fighting-cattle breeds, can be traced back to the Andalusia province of Spain. All things "western," I would say, trail back down to Mexico City and then back across the waters to old *España*. *Andalucía*. From there you can follow the trail all the way back to the Moors, and finally into the bible and Noah's Ark. And somewhere there will always be an old muleteer carting the wine casks into town on the back of an *ass,* or a mule.

Consider these musings from a pamphlet on mules published in 1867:

> *The scriptures tell us that Absalom, when he led the rebel hosts against his father David, rode on a mule, that he rode under an oak and hung himself by the hair on his head... And He who came to save our fallen race, and open the gates of*

heaven, and fulfill the words of the prophet, rode a female of this apparently degraded race of animals, when he made his triumphal march into the city of the temple of the living God.

— *Mules* by **Harvey Riley**, 1867

Biblical history. Big medicine.

III Considerations on Mule Psyche

Let's talk disposition. *Temperament* is a core topic among the men who speak of mules. Temperament, attitude, and character. Ask Ross Knox about mule personalities and his eyes glaze over again. *Here it comes.* One more memory of a rank mule. A trail wreck. A bad day at Skeleton Point. The whirring of chopper blades. Unsweet oblivion.

Let's return to Mr. Knox:

"Worst mule I ever had? I mentioned *Yak* before. But I also had *Keno* and *Lone Star*. They were dangerous. *Dangerous.* But excellent pack mules. Once you got 'em on a string and out on the trail, they were excellent. But dangerous to be around on the ground. Sons-a-bitches could hurt you. Bad to kick. Bad to strike.

"*Keno* was a really bad striker. He could take the side of your head off if he caught you. I had another named *Ernest T.* who made a career out of kicking me. He'd kick me and I'd straighten him out, and that was just our routine. They told me to ship him, but I said 'No, he's either gonna kill me, or I'm gonna kill him. He's in for a life of hard labor.'

"I've learned about as damn much about mules over the years as I have about women. That is, there ain't no figurin' 'em. It took me a lot of years to learn you treat mules nothing like a horse. They don't *think* like a horse, they don't *act* like a horse. And once a man comes to that realization, you can deal with them a little bit better.

"I try not to get into a fight with a mule because they'll fight. I'll tell you something else, too. If a mule has a thrashing coming they'll probably take it. But if your start pickin' on a mule, and he ain't got it comin', he'll lay for you. I've seen it happen. Sooner or later you're gonna have your guard down, and that son of a bitch will hurt you. I've seen a lot of people who deserve it."

Ross is indicating that Mules carry a grudge. I've heard that before. A veterinarian friend of mine in Santa Ynez, California, put it this way: "If you understand mules, it will help you to understand women. You cannot yell at a mule. You cannot hit a mule. They don't forget. If you put a horse in a trailer and whip on him, he remembers the trailer. You put a mule in a trailer and whip on him, he remembers *you, forever.* He bides his time and he'll lay for you and he'll get you. Also, a mule has an 'on and off' switch, just like a woman. When it's off, it's off for good. Amen."

Back to Ross: "A mule can't re-produce, but they can sure *try.* So you gotta cut 'em. They have an odd number of chromosomes, which does not allow them to reproduce, with the exception of one in 20,000. Mules were tougher a long time ago. *Gosh, they were tough.* Now people are refining' em. They get these high powered mares and search around for a mammoth jack and I think they're getting' too much refinement. Big, good lookin' mules, but I think they bred out what they were lookin' for to begin with.

"Mules are good on the trail because they're creatures of habit more than any animal I've even seen. Not like the horse. You do the same routine on a horse everyday and he's gonna get burned out. He's gonna go sour. Mule is just the opposite. The mule *wants* that routine. If things change they don't handle it well. If there's a rock sittin' there on the trail that wasn't there yesterday, they'll throw a fit. They want the same exact thing, the same exact way, everyday."

Back to the Grand Canyon.

"So we go down into the canyon every morning. They feed us breakfast down on the bottom, and we load back up with trash and head back up to the top. I wanna be back on top by noon, 'cause it's so hot down there. If it's much past noon, it's because I had a wreck.

"If you've had a wreck they want you to fly the mule out of there, but anytime I've had a wreck there was no way to get a helicopter in there. You've got to quarter the mule. They've got to shut the trail down. It's a big long drawn out deal, *officially.* In the winter that trail's solid ice. We run tungsten-carbide shoes on mules. It's sheer ice and we gotta go down on the ice. The mules know. *They savvy,* but it's a horrible sound when you hear one of those mules slide. You better grab a hold.

"Nobody's ever been killed on a mule here, which is a phenomenal record. Guy before me got in a wreck and he was never the same. Nobody knows what happened. He's not mentally or physically the same. He was ridin' a mule called *Top.* He got into a whale of a wreck. He has no recollection.

"These trails ain't in good shape. There are fragile walls. One of my guys keeps sayin': *'I don't like this. Not at all.'* And I said back to 'em, 'Well if it goes, I only hope it goes with you on it, 'cause I have almost no time invested in you. Right now you're a liability, you're not an asset. And I don't wanna die.' But he didn't get my sense of humor."

Ross Knox yawns. It's early afternoon. I've got sufficient color and action about *muleteering* and western wrecks. *The real gen*, as Hemingway might put it. These blood details were rendered up by an honest man and a good cowboy. Ross has seen *the deepest recesses of the inner gorge* and shook hands with the living, breathing *gods of the big ditch*.

But Mr. Knox has had enough mule palaver. He ambles off to take a nap. Tomorrow morning it all begins again at 2 am. I hope his dreams are of wide trails and well-broke mules. I throw my pen into my guitar case and head out. The sun is going down over the rim of that wondrous red gorge, out there beyond the Ponderosa Pine trees. *The great canyon which allows no mistakes. Man or beast.*

As I drive away, I try to recall an old John Caldwell poem called *The Mule-Skinners*:

> *We never was rigged up pretty, of course, and we*
>   *Didn't talk too polite,*
> *But we led up that joltin' mule train,*
>   *To the trail end of every fight;*
> *We made a trail through the hostile lands and our*
>   *Whip was the victory's key.*
> *So why in the name of all that's fair can't we figger*
>   *In history?*

IV Coda

> *I have worn this silver belly*
> *For many a year*
> *It's truly a part of me*
> *That some damn bureaucrat*
> *Could abrogate a cowboy's hat*
> *Is rank absurdity*
>
>   — *Ross Knox* (song by Ian Tyson & Tom Russell)

Ross Knox eventually quit the canyon and moved on to Saguaro National Park in Arizona, where he worked as head Muleteer. I ran into him back then, at the old Congress Hotel in Tucson. He was just three days out of the hospital, having had a pacemaker put in to regulate his heart. He'd been bucked off a horse some gal had hired him to "*look good*" for a buyer. Ross had made it through his fifth near-death experience, fixed his heart, and went back to packing.

Then, after twenty years of livin' and near-dyin' in the mule trade, sliding down icy trails into the great ditches, defying fate, fear, and gravity, Ross Knox finally ran head on into his biggest nemesis: *Government bureaucracy.*

The National Park Service now required cowboy packers to wear *crash helmets*, instead of cowboy hats. That's where Ross Knox drew the line. He walked away from the job and the pensions and health insurance and all of it. He kept his cowboy hat on and retained his western dignity. I heard he's packing mules in the High Sierras of California. He's out there riding the rim, pulling a string of big, feather-legged mules. And he's damn sure wearing a cowboy hat.

True Grit and Hard Scrabble
Charles Portis & John Graves

>...the sounds and smells and the feel of the weather were known things, but with echoes. The rattle of black wasps flying out at your face to warn you from their nest, the slowing cluck of the rain crow...the steaming southeastern winds...and the clean hot ones out of Mexico.
>
> — **John Graves**, *Hard Scrabble*

"Language is deteriorating." The Flamenco guitar player spit out this declaration as he tuned his guitar.

"I agree," I said. "Writing, literature, songwriting. *Deteriorating*. I can't read modern fiction. Most of it. Can't listen to new songwriters. *Wallpaper*. Deteriorating. Nobody has a *voice*."

We were sitting in a dressing room in Switzerland. Full of pre-show venom and vinegar and making major pronouncements about the downfall of writing, song, human character, culture, and civilization. Idle conversation before a concert. Tongue-in-cheek babble. There was a fifty-dollar bottle of Spanish wine staring us down, but we wouldn't touch it until after the show.

I'd been telling the guitar player (*El Ciclon* – The Cyclone of Las Cruces) that I was reading Mark Twain's travel books on Europe, impressed with his expansive vocabulary. The choice of words. His command of the American language and lingo. The poetics, humor, and deft use of slang. The *writer's voice*. A distinctly Western American voice. And Twain wrote one hundred and fifty years ago.

Writers didn't seem to have that degree of access to the language anymore. Or the nerve to reach for it. Or anything *to say,* for that matter. *El Ciclon* and I agreed on that one. He played a fast flamenco run on the gut strings. Maybe, we mused, the culprit was the Internet age and cell phone communication, and twittering, tweeting, texting – the *character* of humans atrophying along with the language. People blurting out meaningless digital grunts. Books disappearing in favor of Kindle screens. I surmised aloud that reading a book on a

Kindle screen struck me about as exciting as kissing a blow-up doll. *El Ciclon* liked that one. (I'd used a stronger word than *kissing*.)

We were satisfied that we'd solved that big issue and walked out and performed the concert. We drank the wine.

This conversation took place a few months before I ran head-on into the work of Charles Portis and John Graves. I was late to the party. I consider them Western writers, since their finest material is based in the West. These two resurrected my belief in American letters and the power of the American writing voice. I tried to find everything they'd published, which is not a hell'uva lot.

True Grit lies at the center of all this. Three years ago I'd not read Charles Portis' *True Grit*. In my ignorance I'd assumed it might be akin to a minor Zane Grey potboiler on the Wild West, aimed at teenagers. A dime novel. An error in judgment on my part. I'd sidestepped an American classic. Two very good movies were made from the book – the first with John Wayne's Academy Award performance in 1968, and the recent remake by the Coen brothers, featuring Jeff Bridges. I had no idea who the hell Charles Portis was when these movies appeared.

Now that I've read and reread *True Grit* I believe, as other's do, it ranks with *Huckleberry Finn*, and to take it further – *The Catcher in the Rye*, *To Kill a Mockingbird* and, hell, throw *Moby Dick* into that pile and *On the Road*. Classics built around a narrator with a deep, one-off American voice. Make your own list. *True Grit* is a *tour de force* yarn – a fourteen-year-old gal's blood adventure in the last Wild West. Spinning out a tale of retribution which cuts deep into the reader's heart. The *True Grit* movies, as good as they were, don't rival the book.

First things first. Before I'd decided to read *True Grit* I stumbled on Charles Portis' third novel *The Dog of the South*. A fine place to start. The book that first rattled my cage, three years back.

I   The Dog of the South & Gringos

Beneath the deadpan humor of Portis's deceptively easy-seeming delivery moves the persistent threat that an atavistic wrath will burn away the farce and rise violently into the light of day.

— **Carla Rotella**, *N.Y. Times*

Charles Portis could be Cormac McCarthy if he wanted to, but he'd rather be funny.

— **Roy Blount, Jr.**

In 1984 a bookstore clerk up the upper eastside of New York City came across several large boxes of Charles Portis' 1974 novel *The Dog of the South*. The boxes were shoved into the back corner of the store basement. The book was out of print. All of Portis was out of print. The clerk read the book and was so impressed he set up a window display filled with copies of *The Dog of the South*. He was quoted as stating: *there isn't a false note in the book. The Dog of the South* became an underground classic in that part of town. Word spread out from there. When I came across that bookstore anecdote a few years ago, I sought out a copy.

I opened up the book and read the first paragraph:

My wife Norma had run off with Guy Dupree and I was waiting around for the credit card billing to come in so I could see where they had gone. I was biding my time...they had taken my car and my Texaco card and my American Express card. Dupree had also taken from the bedroom closet my good raincoat and a shotgun and perhaps some other articles. It was just like him to pick the .410 – a boy's first gun. I suppose he thought it wouldn't kick too much, that it would kill or at least rip the flesh in a satisfying way without making a lot of noise or giving much of a jolt to his sloping monkey shoulder.

Welcome to the world of Ray Midge. His wife has run off with her first husband and all the stuff above. Ray's car, credit cards, and gun. Midge is sitting in a dark apartment in Arkansas, shades drawn, plotting their journey by following the sequence of dates and locations on the credit card receipts. He tells us: *I love nothing better than a job like that.* Ray's an oddball, sure enough. He knows a lot about cars and guns, and not enough about women. He'll parlay his dogged innocence and muted sense of outrage down a lengthy, oft hilarious trek into Mexico and Central America. In search of his car and wife. In that order.

Midge will meet up with an eccentric coot, Dr. Reo Symes, who lives in a broken-down bus he calls *The Dog of the South*. Together Midge and Symes travel south, through the bottom of Mexico, down to Honduras. Hot on the trail. I won't give the rest away, but the novel is basted with comic eloquence and characters that speak their mind in batty, crackpot lingo. Pure Portis.

Charles Portis has written five novels: *Norwood, True Grit, The Dog of the South, Master's of Atlantis,* and *Gringos,* in that order. All are back in print, published by Overlook Press. *Norwood* was made into a film with Glenn Campbell, released after the first John Wayne film of *True Grit.* Campbell also acted in *True Grit. Norwood,* the book, is damn good, and *True Grit, The Dog of the South* and *Gringos* are great. *Masters of Atlantis,* a quirky tale of cults and wizards, I find unreadable. Four out of five ain't bad.

Overlook recently re-issued a Portis *miscellany* collection, edited by Jay Jennings, titled *Escape Velocity,* which includes a selection of Portis' newspaper and magazine articles, plus a rare interview, and one previously unpublished play. The highlights of this collection are Portis' essay on cheap motels in the Southwest: *Motel Life, Lower Reaches,* and another travel piece: *An Auto Odyssey Through the Darkest Baja.* In the later, Portis and a friend buy a 1952 Studebaker pickup and drive the length of Baja California, stopping every other day to fix the truck with ingenuity, raw nerve, and bailing wire.

Here you find the emerging Portis, the soon-to-be novelist who escaped the newsroom, his ear cocked and ready to hear the rants, raves, and fish stories of every off-the-grid character he encounters. Portis attained a profound understanding of the way real people talk when their guards are down. Dog chat. They step out of Mexican gas stations, old motels, trailer parks, and back street bars, right into his novels. Humans. Can't beat 'em.

A word about his last novel – *Gringos,* which rivals *The Dog of the South. Gringos* might be my favorite. I'm re-reading it now at Christmas. Here's the opening:

Christmas again in Yucatan. Another year gone and I was still scratching around on this limestone peninsula.

Jimmy Burns, the narrator and main character, is hanging out in Merida, Mexico, along with a disparate community of Americans. Burns once dealt in stolen Pre-Columbian artifacts. Now he's driving a truck and performing odd jobs, traipsing around the Mayan ruins and headed towards a violent showdown with a cult leader. Sounds offbeat, but the mastery is in the side characters and the dialogue. And a subdued violence that suddenly breaks through to the surface.

Portis makes us care about folks we might usually ignore, or even run from, should we encounter them on the street on in a bar. The ones that slobber on you, or whine and hiss, as they weep for their departed dogs or failed marriages.

I'll share this scene with you from *Gringos* – Jimmy Burns is having a conversation with an American lady friend who's castigating him for not settling down with a woman. She asks Jimmy what he's been up to and then unloads on him:

"Out at night drinking with your buddies, I suppose. Ike and Mutt are they? Those two you're always quoting?"

She meant Art and Mike, the inseparable Munn brothers.

"You're afraid of smart women, aren't you?"

She was right...I was leery of them. Art and Mike said taking an intellectual woman into your home was like taking in a baby raccoon. They were both amusing for a while but soon became randomly vicious and learned how to open the refrigerator.

These charged comedic scenes, laced with candid repartee, are what endear me to Portis. He never concocts a straw-boss narrator to woo our sympathy. Portis is not concerned with *the big issues,* political correctness, or people struggling to find their self-identity. These *people know who they are,* toting their off-kilter baggage across the West, or down into Mexico, knee deep in alligators, bad love, and quicksand. And car parts. And guns.

Roy Blount Jr. states above: Charles *Portis could be Cormac McCarthy if he wanted to...but he'd rather be funny.* Cormac surely ranks near the top of many critics' lists of American writers. No debate on that. And yet...Cormac seems to have created his own country, his personal *Grimm's Fairytales* that issue forth his fathomless mind. Humor? Not much. Gothic humor perhaps. And who are these people in his books? They emerge like zombies crawling out of his hand-dug well of a mind. Brilliant writing, but sometimes I crave a laugh.

Years ago I used to run into Cormac in El Paso and we'd swap small talk. I passed him by one day in an aisle at the local Home Depot store. He looked confused and was telling the clerk: *Look, you got to assume I'm from Mars. I don't know anything about this stuff.* Which was exactly how I felt. Dizzied from trying to figure out the subtleties of tile grout, pipe joints, and electric wire. *Mars.* We were writers and dreamers. Not handymen. Cormac and I would chat and go our own ways. Cormac is a private man who eventually had to escape El Paso for a gated-community in Santa Fe. Too many German fans were camping, uninvited, on his front lawn.

Portis' characters travel through the same gutsy Southwestern and Mexican terrains, but gain our sympathy from their tragic-comic resemblance to people we've known. And Portis himself is probably a *damn good* handyman. I'll bet he knows all about tile grout, gas refrigerators, car engines, and guns. He grew up in rural Arkansas, served in the Marines, and developed his writing chops as a novice journalist on the New York City police beat. Later he wrote travel features, observing the eccentrics in Mexican bars, motels, and auto-fix joints, where you tend to run into *plain folks*. Folks that talk and harangue and glue things back together.

But lets get down to the big one. *True Grit*.

II The Wicked Flee Where None Pursueth: True Grit

Like Mark Twain's **Huckleberry Finn**...
Charles Portis' **True Grit** *captures the
Naive elegance of the American voice...*

— **Jonathan Lethem,** novelist

*True Grit is the genuine article – a book
so strong that it reads like a myth.*

— **Ed Park,** *The Believer*

Charles Portis, all of a sudden, walked away from a lucrative journalist position In London, where he was bureau chief in the early 1960s. He declared he was going back to Arkansas to write novels. He *quit cold*, according to Tom Wolfe in the book: *The Birth of New Journalism.*

Portis left London, wrote Wolfe, and *after sailing back to the States on one of the Mauretania's last runs...he reportedly holed up in his version of Proust's cork-lined study – a fishing shack back in Arkansas – to try his hand at fiction.* In real life it was a shack behind a beer joint named *Cash McCool's.*

Soon Charles Portis published an acclaimed first novel, *Norwood* (1966). *Norwood* concerns one Norwood Platt, a mechanic and country singer from Ralph, Texas, who drives to New York to collect an old debt from an Army buddy. There's regional American dialogue here aplenty. *And food.* Potted meat sandwiches with mustard, baked beans, marshmallows, syrup sandwiches, and automat hotdogs. That ole Portis ear. Then Portis turns quickly around and publishes *True Grit* in 1968 – serialized first in *The Saturday Evening Post.*

For a man to walk away from a day job and go off, on his second book, and write one of the great American novels, is not only a bafflement but akin to Babe Ruth pointing at a spot in the center field bleachers, then hitting a home run directly to that spot. An American triumph of legendary proportions.

How does a man disappear, into rural Arkansas or Mexico, as legends will have it, and return with a book written from the perspective of a one-armed old spinster in 1928 – looking back on events which transpired when she was fourteen, hunting down her father's killer in the 1870s? A novel replete with finely carved cowboy characters, authentic western jargon, Old Testament quotes, and violent action of filmic proportion. Portis, upon completion of the book, wrote a friend and stated: *I think I've just written John Wayne's next movie.* And that is just what he did.

True Grit, according to novelist Ed Park: is *a book so strong that it reads like a myth.* Tom Wolfe, Portis' ole mate at the *Herald Tribune*, still couldn't get over it: *He made a fortune...in a fish shack! In Arkansas! It was too goddamned perfect to be true, and yet there it was.*

There are now two million copes of *True Grit* in print. Mattie Ross' voice slaps you in the face each time you crack open the book:

> *People do not give it credence that a fourteen year old*
> *girl could leave home and go off in the wintertime*
> *to avenge her father's blood...*
>
> *Here is what happened...I have never been one*
> *to flinch or crawfish when faced with*
> *an unpleasant task.*

Then she lays it down. And old lady looking back on the winter of 1873, when she vowed to avenge the murder of her father. She hires federal marshal Rooster Cogburn to hunt down the killer – hires Rooster because she believes he has *true grit*. Those two words have now slipped, forever, into our American lingo.

My guess is Portis was well aware of Thomas Berger's *Little Big Man*, which was published a few years before *True Grit*. Yet the film, *Little Big Man*, with Dustin Hoffman, wasn't released until *after* the film of *True Grit*. Berger's *Little Big Man* is a monologue by 115 year old year old Jack Crabb, an orphan boy who was adopted by the Cheyenne. Little Big Man (aka Crabb) meets up with Custer, fights at the Little Big Horn, runs into Wild Bill Hickok and Wyatt Earp, as he pulls us into this big windy story of the West – told in slang-driven Cowboy-Indian tongue. It's a damn good book.

Little Big Man was published in 1964. *True Grit* in 1968. Critics began speaking of a new era of *revisionist westerns* in the book and film worlds – with the good guy/bad guy plot turned upside down, and women, Mexicans and Native Americans given stronger leading roles.

Rooster Cogburn, in the original *True Grit* movie, was an ideal role for John Wayne, and Mia Farrow was the first choice to play Mattie Ross. Farrow balked at working with director Henry Hathaway and wanted the producers to hire Roman Polanski to direct. Imagine that. Boy, that might have been a freakish Western. Farrow was replaced with Kim Darby. Dennis Hopper, Robert Duval and Strother Martin also appear.

Mattie's voice moves the book from scene to dramatic scene. Here are several *Western* tastes from Mattie's narration:

> Tom Chaney rode a gray horse that was better suited for pulling a middle buster than carrying a rider. He had no handgun but he carried his rifle slung across his back on a piece of cotton plow line. There is a trash for you. He could have taken an old piece of harness and made a nice leather strap for it. That would have been too much trouble.

And:

> The Texas cowboys rode nothing but geldings for some cowboy reason of their own.

Or, when Rooster is trying to get young Mattie to try a shot of whiskey she replies:

> I would not put a thief in my mouth to steal my brains.

The character's breathe and snarl and bleed. Portis inhabits the voice and soul of this little gal growing up in the last Wild West and he yanks us along with her, right into a wicked finale – a snake pit filled with dead men's bones. Perfect for a *Saturday Evening Post* serial. Perfect for the silver screen. Much of the film dialogue was lifted intact from the book, though a good deal of Portis' sly humor is missing in the two movies.

True Grit is full of charmed, antiquated language. *Talk*. Portis came from a family of *talkers*. The old men, down in his native Arkansas, talked and smoked cigars and pipes, and the kid listened. Later, one of Portis' tasks on the *Northwest Arkansas Times* was to edit the reports sent by old lady correspondents in small towns. Portis states: *My job was to edit out all the life and charm from these homely reports. Some old country expression, or nice turn of phrase – out they went.* Portis regretted the task – he thought the old ladies were fine writers. And they wrote in perfect penmanship with pencil. He kept those edited anecdotes in the back of his head.

Around the same period that I delved into Charles Portis's work, I came across a fine essay by Gary Cartwright, in *Texas Monthly*, about writer John Graves. I had more homework to do.

III Ain't No More Cane on the Brazos: John Graves in Texas

> *Home after awhile, became a patch of rough and rocky country*
> *acreage... for the past forty years...*
> *building a house and barn and corrals and fences,*
> *the supervision of cows and goats and the other*
> *activities that functional rural life entails...the need*
> *to learn the hard way, and alone, and how you*
> *come to your own things in your head by working*
> *with them.*
>
> — **John Graves,** *Hard Scrabble*

In November 1957, John Graves and his dachshund pup, *Watty*, took a three-week canoe trip down the Brazos river, on assignment for *Sports Illustrated*. The river was to be altered by a dam project and Graves wanted to explore the last days of the historic waterway. The magazine rejected the story. Graves built it into a book.

Graves cobbled together his day-to-day river musings and added old pioneer's tales, Indian stories, folklore, encounters with odd characters, and hunting anecdotes. He turned the trip into *Goodbye to a River,* a classic that was nominated for a National Book Award. It's never been out of print.

Here's Graves on achieving his writer's voice:

> **Good Bye to a River**, *flowed like the Brazos itself...After a decade of deck clearing apprenticeship abroad...I slowly developed a degree of objectivity in regard to who I was and how to handle the language. After those years of trying, I had finally arranged to discern some subject matter that was right for me and, for better or worse, to attain my full voice as a writer.*

I took a break as I was writing this essay and reached down and opened up *Goodbye To A River* to a random page – page 191 – in the *Vintage Edition* paperback. And there, frank and bold, under a quote from Cervantes' *Don Quixote*, is John Graves waxing forth on the nature of the cowboy:

> *Are we going to redefine the cowboy? Give anew the lie to California's brave video-screen miracles of amorous, bellicose pig slop? Shall we pin-prick the rotund gassy fiction...and eat beans and biscuits and bacon, bacon and biscuits and beans, 'til we're loose with diarrhea and drum bellied with its opposite, and sleep four or five bug-crawling, dust coughing hours a night on the ground without being able to get the boots off our feet, swollen with heat and fungus itch...and worry about the Indians in the territory and at least get sloppy-sleepy drunk in Wichita...where a pasty whore will stash beneath her mattress our wages earned so pleasantly, and maybe in return give us a lasting souvenir?...*
>
> *Read Andy Adams if you want to see cowhands right; read Teddy Blue Abbott, and Frank Dobie, the groping-worded, utterly straight tales in "The Trail Drivers of Texas," and J.E. Haley's work on Old Man Goodnight.*

Ah, the nail bashed upon the very head! Graves is certainly in the league of Teddy Blue Abbott, J. E. Haley, Andy Adams, and J. Frank Dobie. Chroniclers of the true West. Telling it like it is, and was.

John Graves paddled his canoe down the Brazos, casting poetic fragments in our direction, as he detailed the dying Texas back country – the dirt and rain and heat, the tales of old traders with their *unfortunates thirsts*, and the Comanche's, whose oft-brutal raids matched the pitiless nature of the terrain. Hard country. Tough people. Eloquent writing.

I've gone over many of these paragraphs two or three times, allowing Graves' prose to sink in. He reflections are *Faulknerian*. At times you need to untie the knots that hold his sentences together, and then as you look closer the whole thing comes into focus and reads like a long ballad. Singing up the country.

Both Charles Portis and John Graves served in the Marines – Graves in WWII and Portis in Korea. A firm grounding. Portis arrived at fiction after a stint as a news reporter. With Graves it was the other way around. Graves originally wanted to write fiction, but found his voice in personal narratives based on his daily life. Graves only *fictionalized* names and places when he wished to protect folks' privacy.

John Graves was born in Texas, grew up in Ft. Worth, graduated from Rice University, served and was injured in WWII, and then hung around Europe for a few years, mainly in Spain. He was living the expatriate life, dancing across Hemingway's footprints. How many young writers tried follow Papa Hemingway's path – only to wind up teaching high school English, eventually tossing the failed novel into the wood stove or the storage shed? Almost happened to Graves.

Graves published a poorly received novel, *Spotted Horses*. Disenchanted, he taught high school English in Texas and other environs. Eventually he retreated to his home country, in central Texas, and started over.

With the proceeds from *Goodbye to a River* he bought a rugged patch of land in limestone and cedar country outside of Fort Worth and settled in to build his sanctuary. He called the place *Hard Scrabble*. Thus the title of his second book, which took fourteen years to complete. Graves surmised: *If I hadn't wasted so much time building and chasing cows, I could have written a whole lot more. But what the hell, that's how it was.*

Graves later published a fine piece of short fiction, *The Last Running*, about a group of old Comanches riding up to Charles Goodnight's ranch, long after the Indian wars are over. They ask for a buffalo from old man Goodnight's herd, so they can run the hunt one more time. The tale is attributed to an actual event.

With the exception of *The Last Running* and occasional short stories, Graves' work is centered on personal narratives imbued with the background history of the rural country south of Fort Worth. These are John Graves' notes from the trenches – hand carved by a one eyed ex-marine who dug in and learned his craft as he discovered how to live on the land.

Texas Monthly's Gary Cartwright visited Graves at his retreat in Texas in 2010. Graves was 90 at the time and recovering from a bad spill – he'd fallen down the back stairs of his office whilst relieving himself off the porch. *Watering the roses,* as we say. Ed Abbey once remarked that: *if a man can't piss in his own front yard he's living too close to town.* Graves was still working long days at his craft.

Cartwight described his friend Graves:

His trademark horn-rimmed glasses kept sliding down his nose, but that familiar twinkle of mischief was still backlighting his right eye – the left one has been glassy blank as long as I've know him, victim of a Japanese grenade on the island of Saipan in World War II. Tiny pieces of metal remain buried over his right eye, under one knee, and in his back... "I'm still here," he said cheerfully.

Graves, in 2010, said he didn't worry about publishing anymore. *Writing was it's own excuse.* John Graves, in the last fifty years, had not only written continuously, but also raised a family and built ranch houses, barns, and corrals, as the family raised their own beef, milled flour, grew vegetables, raised chickens, goats, dogs, hogs and horses. Ranch life. Near the end, when the weather was good, he slept out on the porch of his office – near his writing work. Says Cartwright: *Work is what he has left. Work is who he was, who he will always be.*

As Cartwright's visit neared the end, Graves mused about the dying old ways:

...when local people were a distinctive variety...but that's all been wiped out. It used to be that the differences among people were big, and all those differences interested me greatly. But now I find a lot of sameness. I don't like the way things are shaping up.

As I was finishing this essay, Tom McGuane was kind enough to send me a personal note on John Graves:

I knew John Graves through his books, our correspondence, fishing, and an event we did together at the Texas Book Festival. And in every one of these things, I had the same feeling and impression: that this was the most genuine and self-possessed man I had ever known. He's an example I can't live up to but won't go away, a beacon I guess.

Graves leaves us with a worthy assessment of the writer's journey:

I had discovered and then reported on the need to learn things the hard way, and alone, and how you come to own things in your head by working with them...
The kind of writing I have done has never made me rich...but at this late point that doesn't seem to matter much, because most of the work still seems to me to say more or less the things I wanted it to say when I wrote it, and it says them in my own way.

John Graves passed away July, 2013. Charles Portis is still with us, at age 80, living in Arkansas. He may have said his piece, or might be concocting another classic in that shack behind the beer joint. Both Portis and Graves have shown man as he really is – and have given us characters *of distinctive variety,* from a time when the *differences between people were big* – a time that is regrettably passing now.

It seems to my eye and ear that much of modern writing, and songwriting, is the empty *twittering of sparrows on a pile of manure.* To quote Anton Chekov. Chekov said all you need to write is a *decent pair of shoes and a notebook.* You walk out into the country and write down your observations and listen for interesting *turns of phrase.* Then go home and work at your craft fifty years. Good luck. Charles Portis and John Graves walked that long road. I'm damn glad I bumped into their work. It has lifted my spirit at a time when it needed lifting.

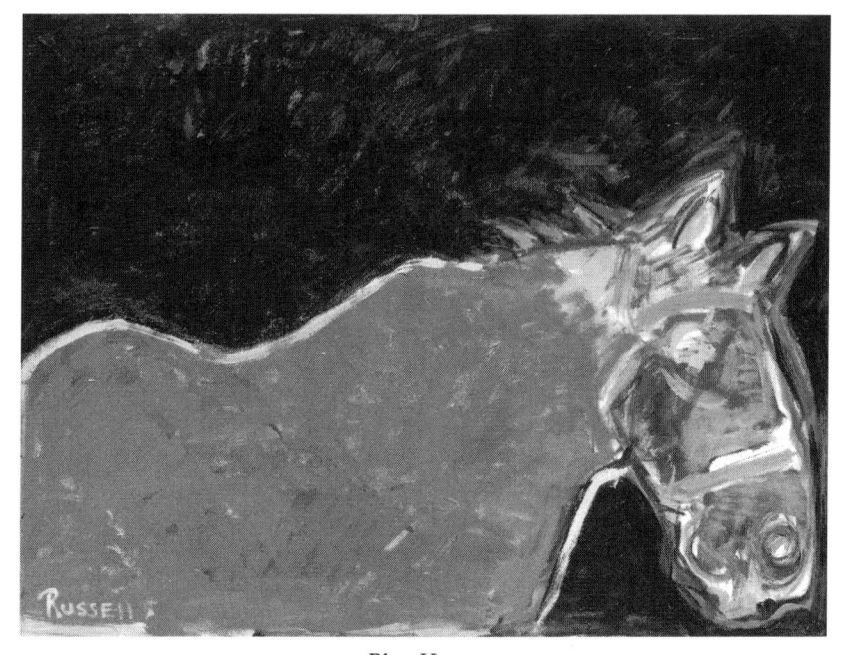

Blue Horse

The Strawberry Roan

*An' I spots the corral and a standin' alone
There I sees this caballo, a strawberry roan.*

— **Curley Fletcher,**
The Original Strawberry Roan

The first horse to run off with me was a roan. His coat was the color of strawberry milk with flies in it. *So I recall.* I was ten years old, and the scene of the action was an old rent stable called Fox Hills Academy, out on the edge of Inglewood, California. Fox Hills was near the Los Angeles International Airport where, in the 1920s, fields of wheat, barley and lima beans had been converted into landing strips. Then men started dreaming up freeways, and the freeways tore out the heart of the irrigated desert. Fox Hills is buried underneath the San Diego freeway. Rush hour traffic snaking across the horizon.

We've come full circle, when a horse in L.A. would be a faster mode of transport than a car. Ole Winston Churchill mused: *the substitution of the internal combustion engine for the horse marked a very gloomy milestone in the progress of mankind.* Agreed. But I wanted to tell you about that roan.

The stable was run by an old gal named Mrs. Kirby, who had a withered left arm and a helper named *Smitty.* Smitty was cowboy to the bone, and responsible for turning my brother Pat into a tobacco chewing, bull riding, bareback-bronc riding, bulldogging, horse-shoeing, horse trader, and all around western *character,* with a mouth on him like Slim Pickens. Smitty was the classic sidekick, with a yen for cheap red wine and a verbal battery of terse, off color western remarks. He delivered all his punch lines between spits of tobacco juice.

Back to the runaway roan horse.

I don't recall the horse's name, but he was one of those *special deals* my father picked up over at the L.A. horse and mule auction. Or he might have been a lead pony, gone bad, from the race track. My father had a line on sour horses from both venues. My old man was an Iowa horse trader who spent odd mornings playing poker with Hopalong Cassidy on the backside of Hollywood Park Racetrack.

Let's call this *special deal* horse *Roanie*. For the sake of poetry. Old *Roanie* had a few temperament problems. *Ticks*. This was the 1950s, before the age of horse whisperers and the gentler means of dealing with equine psychosis.

If he didn't pan out as a saddle horse, a misfit like this might be sold off to a second level bucking string in the San Fernando Valley. There were weekend rodeos at places such as Crash Corrigan's movie ranch. Usually a horse like *Roanie* wouldn't pan out as a bucker and end up running through fences with terrified amateur bronc riders trying to weather the storm.

I recall my brother Pat, whenever he was around somebody like myself who was being *run off with*, might yell: *Good luck, kid. Pick up the mail in Tucson!*

Humor gleaned from old Smitty.

Roanie's trick was to walk gently for a one hundred yards, then suddenly snort and make a savage U-turn, taking off, hell bent for the barn. If you were a neophyte rider dumb enough to hold on, Roanie would aim at the low beam hanging over the back barn door. *The great barn door equalizer.* He was a *head hunter* with worn-out brakes.

I was mounted on old *Roanie*, on this particular afternoon, when he made his U-turn and bolted. I was holding onto the saddle horn and *talking to the Lord* as the barn door beam came into sudden, looming focus. I had a vision of a scene in Washington Irving's *The Legend of Sleepy Hollow,* where Ichabod *Crane* is chased through the hollow by the *Headless Horseman.*

And now to the point. I was suddenly a character in one of my favorite songs: *The Strawberry Roan*. I was riding the horse *that could never be rode* – that *frog walkin'*, *sunfishin' beast* that *jumped up the east and came down to the west. The worse bucker even seen on the range. That pin-eared* monster who *screamed like a shoat. Oh that Strawberry Roan...*

I ducked my head down at the last minute and rode him through the barn and into history. My *personal* history. My memory of what happened to that horse has faded. But that old song is still stuck in my gut. The most famous bucking horse song ever written. *The Strawberry Roan.*

I   Let us Now Praise The Bard of the Bucking Horse

My earliest memory is of cowmen and cattle.
I spent my best years as a cowboy of the old school.
I knew every water hole, I think, from the Sierra
Nevada to Utah. And I still look back to long days
and nights in the saddle, at $30 a month,
as the happiest of my existence.

— **Curley Fletcher**
Letter to John I. White

If you're talking cowboy songs and the foundation of Western Music then, at some point, you have to deal with several pioneer poets, among them Charles Badger Clark, Gail Gardner and Curley Fletcher. We'd also give a backwards nod to the lasting influence of Robert W. Service, *The Bard of the Yukon*, and the epic rhymes of Rudyard Kipling. I'm sure you could carry it back to Chaucer, the Old Testament, and Homer, and end up with whatever the old cave painters were trying to say, when they painted running lines of horses on cave walls seventeen thousand years ago.

The old ballad mongers and versifiers, like Service and Kipling, could spin a rhymed yarn and build the action. You were there with them in the trenches. Add Scots-Irish melodies and rank horses to the evolution of the rhyming ballad, and you arrive at Carmen William Fletcher, the bucking-stock bard from the Great American Desert. *Curley* for short.

The original poem *The Outlaw Broncho*, which later became *The Strawberry Roan*, can be attributed to Curley Fletcher (1892-1954). He wrote it. He'd lived it. He saw his poem swirl into western history. The swirling became a cyclone that knocked Curley backwards and taught him hard lessons about the *ins and outs* of the music business, song publishing, and the fleeting nature of fame and fortune.

The poem contains archetypal western ingredients: a great bronc fighter comes to town, brags a little, and takes on the horse *that could never be rode*. The cowboy ends up bucked off and transfigured by the ride of his life. The reader is with him in every twist and spin. In the belly of that original poem lay classic and colorful horse and bucking-stock descriptions that have never been bested.

Respected folklore authority Hal Cannon, after an informative phone chat with Curley's daughter, discovered that Curley wrote the poem one night in pencil on the back of an envelope. The envelope had held Curley's winnings in the bareback bronc riding at Cheyenne in 1914. Curley lost all the money in a poker game and was writing the poem to charm his wife, Minnie, into letting him back into their hotel room.

Curley didn't know, as Hal Cannon states, *that he was the first person to take the excitement and sheer kinetic power of a bronc ride and encapsulate it in verse.* He'd concocted a classic.

Curley Fletcher was born in San Francisco and raised in the high desert near Bishop, on the eastern side of the Sierra Nevada. Curley called it: *The Great American Desert.* He caught the last wild end of the deal. Fletcher learned about broncs, early on, rounding up wild horses with a band of Paiute Indians out in the desolate Owens Valley of California. The scenario reminds me of John Huston's *The Misfits*. *Mustanging.* Horse herds running hell bent across desert flats and dry salt lakes. Indian cowboys in their wake.

Fletcher's early bronc stomping days pulled him towards the rodeo arena. He rode bulls, broncs, and steer-wrestled, until a steer jerked its head back and took out one of Fletcher's eyes. Curley kept following the circuit, but turned more to poetry and poker. He was better at verse than cards. He took what he'd learned from his mustanging experience and folded it all into long colorful ballads. Curley conjured them up on envelopes and scraps of paper and gave them away to friends.

Curley published *The Outlaw Broncho* as a poem for the newspaper *The Arizona Globe* in 1915. He changed the title to *The Strawberry Roan* in 1917, in his first song and poetry collection, *Rhymes of the Roundup.* He sold these little songbooks when he travelled to rodeos across the west. Perfect size for the back pocket library of the working buckaroo.

Cowboys began *singing* Curley's ballad as a slow, deliberate waltz. The tune came from *an unknown balladeer.* Or maybe a dude ranch wrangler. Or was it twisted around and borrowed from an Irish fiddle tune. Who knows? Thus begins *the folk process,* and the long rag tag journey of Curley's bucking horse poem, through the glory days of western music.

If we take a strong gander at Curley's original poem, it bears raw resemblance to what evolved into the popular song, *The Strawberry Roan*, recorded throughout the 1930s, 40s and 50s, by folks like Gene Autry, Marty Robbins, and Wilf Carter. The song became legend in a matter of three decades: millions of 78s sold; two motion pictures produced under the *Strawberry Roan* title; dozens of parodies and follow-ups.

The core of the tale remained the same in all versions. The bronc ride and the athletic prowess of the roan horse. Curley's original draft of the poem was rough around the edges. He wanted the lingo to sound authentic. He called it *the vernacular of the early pioneer of the traditional west*. His poem was filled with words spelled like: *gits*, and *sez* and *wuz* and *hoss*, capturing the tone and the slang of the working cowboy. Spelling and grammar *be damned*:

> *I wuz hangin' 'round town just uh spendin' muh time,*
> *I wuz out of a job an' not makin' uh dime,*
> *When uh feller steps up an' he sez,*
> *"I suppose you're a bronc ridin' guy from the looks uh yure clothes."*

With that ragged, bumpy lingo, Curley was not implying cowboys were stupid. Far from it. In his songbook, *Songs of the Sage*, he declares that it is a mistake to consider the early cowboys as illiterate:

> *It would indeed surprise the misinformed individual, were he to hear discussed at the campfire, chuck wagon, or water hole, the myths of the Greeks and the Norsemen, The Rise and Fall of the Roman Empire, or the works of Shakespeare. He would be dumbfounded to find, upon the table in the bunkhouse,* **The Rubaiyat of Omar Khayyam**, *the works of Keats, Voltaire, Dumas, Shaw, Wilde and many others.*

Indeed. Curley's anecdote impressed me enough to make a list of a few authors I might have missed in school. Maybe these literary references reveal how in the hell a wild horse wrangler from the high desert could have writ' such a masterpiece on an empty rodeo winnings envelope.

I found this little gem from a translation of the *Rubaiyat*:

> *A book of verses underneath the Bough,*
> *A Jug of Wine, a Loaf of bread – and Thou,*
> *Beside me singing in the Wilderness,*
> *And oh, Wilderness is Paradise now.*
> *If chance supplied a loaf of white bread,*
> *Two casks of wine and a leg of mutton,*
> *In the corner of a garden with a tulip-cheeked girl,*
> *There'd be enjoyment no Sultan could outdo.*

I'm with Omar. Give me a cask of wine, a leg of lamb, and that tulip-cheeked gal. I'd be singing in the wilderness too. Khayyam, a Persian, wrote this in the eleventh century. He was a poet, philosopher, mathematician, and astronomer. He seemed to have pioneered the *quatrain* form. I imagine if there were a buckaroo in the bunkhouse with *The Rubaiyat of Omar Khayyam* on his bedside table, it must have been Curley Fletcher.

In fact Hall Cannon, in his fine introduction to the reissue of Curley's *Songs of the Sage,* states that Curley was an avid reader and carried *The Rubaiyat of Omar Khayyam* with him religiously. Though Curley only finished sixth grade, he could speak French and Spanish fluently. The plot thickens.

Let's cut loose of the biographical stuff, for a moment, and look at the heart of the poem. Eyeball those great *bronc lyrics.*

II The Art of the Bucking Stock Lyric

We drank the rivers, we rode the twisters
We stumbled down to the ground
But we'll rake and ride, we'll spend our glory
On our last go round

— **Rosalie Sorrels,** *The Last Go Round*

When dust rising off the backs
Of large animals
Makes a racket you can't think in....

— **Paul Zarzyski,** *All this Way for the Short Ride*

Curley kept that dog eared copy of *The Rubaiyat* in his back pocket, the cover beat to hell from saddle leather and the rock and roll of rank horses. From reading Khayyam, Curley surely knew and appreciated the *quatrain form.* He also had a great ear for the elements of rhyme. The art of rhyming words goes back to 10th century B.C. in China. Rhyming is also found in ancient Greek literature, and in the Bible. Irish literature introduced rhyme to medieval Europe. The Irish were masters of the ballad form, and the news of the day was composed into rhyming ballads and broadsheets by the wandering bards and minstrels, hundreds of years ago. Forerunners of the songwriter.

When I think of Curley Fletcher, and the great balladeers or history, I recall hearing about a colorful ballad-monger of note: the Irish bard *M.P. Moran* of Faddle Alley, Dublin. Moran was born in 1793. He was blind. From an early age Moran could memorize entire books of the bible after one or two hearings. He was later transfigured as the ballad singer *Zozimus*; renaming himself after an early Christian mystic from Palestine, who lived in the desert and spoke in tongues.

This character *Zozimus* prowled the streets of Dublin, in long black cape and a beaver-skinned top hat, hammering the cobblestones with a gnarly blackthorn walking stick, shouting his lyrics to the heavens, as they *reverberated out of the gutters of Dublin*. He would spend the early hours of the morning in a pub called *The Brazen Head*. (The pub is still there, Ireland's oldest, established in the year 1198. James Joyce mentions it in *Ulysses*.)

Zozimus prepared his daily ballads at the pub, after having the newspaper read to him. He'd versify the news, in his mind, and then stomp off to his regular spot near Carlisle Bridge, where he'd bellow and sing his ballads and topical songs. His voice had a *piercing raspy quality* on the top end, and a *cannon boom roar* at the bottom. He could roar all day and night.

The Irish folk singer Dominic Behan noted: *Dublin folks woke up in their sleep and could hear Zozimus, tap-tap-tapping down the cobblestones, his blind face thrust up at the stars, and his blackthorn stick tapping menacingly. If anyone dared interrupt him, he would heap tremendous abuse on them and shout them down. He brooked no interference. The greatest of ballad singers had been born.*

Zozimus wrote a few lines, now and again, about old milk horses making their way in the morning. Though blind, he retained a wondrous knack for the description of working steeds. Horses conjured up in quatrain and rhyme. A forbearer to our ballad maker, Curley Fletcher.

The core beauty of Curley Fletcher's original *Strawberry Roan* poem lies in the description of the horse, and the poetry of the wild ride. Curley had a stout hold on bronc vernacular.

Here's the key verse, in a cleaned up rendition by Marty Robbins:

Down in the horse corral standin' alone
Is an old Caballo, a Strawberry Roan
His legs are all spavined, he's got pigeon toes
Little pig eyes and a big Roman nose
Little pin ears that touch at the tip
A big 44 brand was on his left hip,

> *U-necked and old, with a long, lower jaw*
> *I could see with one eye, he's a regular outlaw.*

I guess Curley *did see* with only one eye. *A poet's eye.* If there's a better sketch of a rank, plumb-ugly bronc, I haven't heard or read it. I'm surprised there wasn't sawdust coming out of the nag. Some writers wonder what the hell Curley meant by *u-necked*. Actually the original was *yew-necked*. Did he mean *ewe-necked*, like a sheep? He never changed the spelling and we'll never know. His roan had spavined hocks and the ugliest head in hoss history. Later versions would throw the word *cayuse* into the mix, which might mean a northern mustang associated with the *Cayuse* tribe of Oregon, or any scrubby looking little horse.

Pin ears? Harry Webb, an old cowboy who used to work for Buffalo Bill's Wild West Show, described a *pin eared horse* in a chat with Walt Thayer in 1979. Harry was talking about the great bucking horses of the 1920s and 30s.

> *The greatest of them all, in my opinion, was a beautiful blood bay called* **Pin Ears**. *The tips of this horse's ears were frozen at the time he was born. He made 53 riders bite the dust before anyone rode to the finish. That was long before the sissy Hollywooders thought up the flank strap.*

Then we proceed to the wild ride itself. We can see why Curley, later in life, was hired as a dialogue and color-adviser for western films. From the original poem:

> And he goes toward the east an' he goes toward the west,
> An' tuh stay in the middle I'm doin' my best;
> Now he's sure walkin' frog an' he heaves uh big sigh
> And he only lacks wings fer tuh be on the fly.
> Then he turns his old belly right up tuh the sun
> An' he sure is a sun fishin' son uv uh gun...

Frog Walking might be described as crow hopping, or a horse that bucks and hops with an arched back and stiff knees. *Sun Fishin'* is described in Ramon Adams' book *Western Words* as:

> *A horse when he twists his body into a crescent, alternately to the right and to the left, in other words*

> *he seems to touch the ground with one shoulder
> and then the other, letting the sunlight hit his belly.*

Back to old *Pin Ears*. Harry Webb gives us a real example of the term *sun fishin'*, and an added lesson on the great old broncs, before the age of the flank strap:

> ***Pin Ears** was a 'sun fisher' and sometimes it looked like he'd come down flat on one side or the other, but he always hit the ground on his feet. With a tight buckled flank strap a horse can't get his head down to buck like the old timers. That's why every bucker of later years comes out just kicking his heels up and all but standing on his head. Hard to sit, sure, but I wouldn't walk across the street to watch a bucker nowadays.*

Amen Harry. There wasn't a flank strap on the Strawberry Roan. And what about that brand on the bronc's left hip? In the original, published in 1915, Curley wrote: *X. Y. Z. iron*. Later he changed it to *double square brand*. In the Marty Robbins' version it's changed to: *big 44 brand. Glen* Ohrlin, in his fine song book, *The Hellbound Train*, says that some cowboys even sang: *a map of Chihuahua branded on his left hip*. I like that one. It's proof that the folk process is damned interesting. Ohrlin goes on to illuminate facts about the brand:

> *Curley's double square brand refers to the old Double Square Ranch in Nevada which was actually known among cowboys as having a cantankerous bunch of horses. I've seen several broncs in West Coast rodeo strings bearing this brand.*

Once Curley hit his stride with the success of *The Strawberry Roan* he cranked out more bucking-stock ballads, like *The Ridge Running Roan*, and *That Bucking Bronc, Coyote*. *The Ridge Running Roan* ran to twenty-one verses, as Curley tried to outdo himself with the rankness of this new roan horse. It doesn't have the poetic balance, however, and the *impact* of the original roan poem.

Curley explored the physics of bucking in another ballad, *Bad Brahma Bull*, recorded by Tex Ritter. The bull is a *sun fisher* and a *fence rower (*scraping cowboys off on fences, I presume*)*, and has dust is *fogging 'right out of his skin.*

Back to the poem's journey.

III Where Good Men Die Like Dogs

If you steal my purse, you do me no wrong,
But God forbid you should steal my songs
For it's down in hell such likes belong
And not with decent people.

— **M.J. Moran,** *Zozimus*

In 1931 *The Strawberry Roan* was sung by Everett Cheatham in the Broadway play *Green Grow the Lilacs*. Tex Ritter sang four songs in this show, as the character *Cord Elam*. The play utilized traditional cowboy songs and told the story of a cowboy falling in love with a farm girl.

Cowboy themes were "in." In the early 1940s Rodgers and Hammerstein were much intrigued by the success of *Lilacs*. They collaborated on their first classic musical, *Oklahoma*, based on the plot of the *Green Grow the Lilacs*. In 1934 Cole Porter concocted the western hit, *Don't Fence Me In*, from a poem he'd purchased for $250 from a Montana poet named Bob Fletcher, no relation to Curley. Bob Fletcher had to sue Porter's publishers to get his name on the song, which was later recorded by Roy Rogers, Bing Crosby (*a million seller*), Ella Fitzgerald, and Willie Nelson.

In 1938, the renowned American classical composer, Aaron Copland, utilized traditional cowboy songs in his popular ballet *Billy the Kid*. Copland also used western and folk music in the ballet *Rodeo*, and portions of that score were used in commercials for the American Beef Industry.

By the mid-1930s, western music was popular and *The Strawberry Roan* was growing famous, while Curley Fletcher was mostly ignored. *Old Strawberry* entered that netherworld where lyrics were duded-up by Tin Pan Alley pros, and copyrights were applied for. The checks were *in the mail*, but not for Curley Fletcher. Around this time there was a singing duo who called themselves: *The Happy Chappies*, made up of Fred Howard and Nat Vincent. They published and sang several versions of the songs; some with a refrain added:

Oh that Strawberry Roan, Oh that Strawberry Roan
They say he's a cayuse that's never been rode
And the guy that gets on him is sure to get throw'd...

I remember hearing my Grandfather sing this chorus. *The Happy Chappies* version was a minor hit, later recorded by *The Sons of the Pioneers*, with Leonard Slye (*Roy Rogers*) on vocals.

Curley met *The Happy Chappies*, and he was eventually given credit on the back of their song folio for composing the original poem. Most of the money still went to the duo. Curley kept trying to set the record straight. If you didn't *lawyer-up*, back then, you were lost. I am reminded of a quote on the music business attributed to the late Dr. Hunter S. Thompson:

> *The music business is a cruel and shallow money trench, a long plastic hallway where thieves and pimps run free, and good men die like dogs. There's also a negative side.*

Cowboys didn't have the inclination to pick up a phone and hire a lawyer. *Naw*. Instead Curley published his original version of the song, once again, in his *Ballads of the Badlands*, a song folio sitting here on my desk. It states inside that the song was written to be sung in *cowboy style*. I can only imagine that *cowboy style* means a slow waltz on a plunky guitar, sung with a dust-blown slur or a mouth full of chaw. The illustrations in *Ballads of the Badlands* were drawn by Curley's father in law, Guy Welch, a painter and muralist I've written about in the essay: *The Michelangelo of the Western Saloon*. Welch painted cowboy murals up and down the west coast, trading drawings, paintings, and murals, for drinks and food.

The songbook *Ballad of the Badlands* includes a brief note from Curley:

> *The author has spent his life in that part of the West known as the Great American Desert...he has been a cowboy, muleskinner, prospector and what not, but refuses to admit ever having herded sheep.*

Then Curley discovered that the roan song had appeared in John Lomax's early cowboy and folksong collections, but Curley Fletcher's poem wasn't mentioned. The Lomax family were early pioneers of song collecting, but their sources and attributions towards authorship were sometimes questionable, or at the very least *imaginative*. They also understood copyright law. Back in those days it was open season on the so-called *traditional ballads*. Even musical *arrangements* can be copyrighted, so the publication of major song collections could be a lucrative endeavor.

John Lomax first attributed *The Strawberry Roan* to a dude ranch cowboy named *Whistle* in 1929. Go figure. Curley was fed up with the Lomax tribe, publishers, song stealers, and the bogus huckster-life outside the high desert and the real west. He fired off a letter to John Lomax indicating the authentic date when the song was first published under his name. He added:

> Anyone laying claim to having heard or read the **The Strawberry Roan** prior to those dates, above mentioned, is a damned liar, branded so in the eyes of God, myself, himself and the devil.

Lomax eventually set the record straight, but culled the song from future editions. Lomax probably didn't want to be involved in monetary or legal hassles. But the saga goes on, and song-mongers and ballad thieves clustered around the *Roan* like flies.

To quote folklorist Austin Fife:

> How could Curley Fletcher anticipate, as he sent his Strawberry Roan to the Arizona Record, where it was first printed in 1915, that it would sell a few million 78 rpm records, appear in scores of song folios and other books, and provide the making for a movie script? He even ended up paying royalties for a right to publish a tune and refrain for his own song!

Curley thought the authorship matter was finally settled. *Hold on, partners.* Enter, *stage left*, vaudeville cowboy singer, arch-Hawaiian crooner, and world class *windy story teller: Powder River Jack Lee*, who performed with his wife Kitty. Powder River Jack made bogus claims to having written the *Roan* song, and also asserted he'd written Gail Gardner's classic *Sierry Petes (Tying Knots in the Devil's Tail.)* Author John I. White says that Powder River Jack suffered from *an overactive imagination.*

Curley Fletcher and Gail Gardener, who'd become pals, went searching for Jack's head, and tracked him down in Phoenix. But Powder River was a slippery character.

Gail Gardner reminisces thirty years later:

> *That dude come swingin' into Phoenix thirty years ago packin' a steel guitar and a hula skirt fer his wife, Kitty. They found a rather sorry reception for that sorta music on the radio, so he bought hisself a fancy cowboy outfit, loaded him and Kitty down with belt buckles 'n boots and began singin' every cow song he could wrap his tonsils around. Curley and me got pretty damn sore about his liftin' our songs without so much as a by-your-leave, but when we got together to see what we could do about it, we found our only recourse was to sue him. Hell, he didn't own the clothes he stood in, and of course neither of us wanted Kitty.*

Next, Hollywood took interest in *The Roan*. In 1933 Ken Maynard appeared in a movie titled: *The Strawberry Roan*. In that scenario the roan is a renegade stallion, and ranch wranglers are trying to round him up. In 1948 Gene Autry starred in another version, this time a young kid is injured by being bucked off a wild roan, and his father wants to shoot the horse. Gene Autry steps in, *singing all the way*, and tames the horse, hoping to give it back to the kid and cheer him up. It was Gene's first color film.

Then came the parodies and take offs. In the early 1940s a *blue* version surfaced, titled: *The Castration of the Strawberry Roan*. One source claims Curley wrote it himself in New York City. Maybe Curley wanted to douse his frustrations, and kill off, or *neuter,* his beloved old roan. Lord knows they'd never put *this version* in a Broadway Musical. *Parental guidance suggested.*

A bootleg version of this bawdy song exists, and the vocals are alleged to be *The Sons of the Pioneers*, though they didn't put their name on it for obvious reasons. In my first meeting with Ian Tyson, back in 1986 in New York City, we began work on the song *Navajo Rug* and drank *mucho* red wine. Later in the evening Ian sang *The Castration of the Strawberry Roan* into my reel to reel tape recorder. Unfortunately, the tape has disappeared into history. Maybe it surfaced in The Bronx, and ended up as a rap song. *The folk process prevails.*

The version begins thusly:

I was layin' round town in a house of ill fame,
Laid up with a rough, tough hustlin' dame,
When a hop-headed pimp with his nose full of coke
Beat me outta that woman and left me stone broke.

That's the *tame* part. You'll have to hunt up the rest for your own edification. Omar Khayyam is turning pink.

IV Endings

> *But I bets all muh money thar's no man alive*
> *That kin stay with that bronc when he makes that high dive.*
>
> — **Curley Fletcher**

So it goes. We could look even deeper into the song, but the sum power and mystery of the balladeer's art is greater that the dissection of lines. The song has endured. The parodies and imitations abound. Curley went on to work as a magazine columnist, essayist, and prospector. His last years were spent seeking out mining properties in California. At one point he owned a mine with Tex Ritter. The money never lasted. Curley gambled or gave it away to cowboys down on their luck. The fame and fortune hustle always paled against those early days and nights in the saddle, at *$30 a month*.

Curley died in San Jose, California, in 1954. I'd like to think his grave marker says something raw, like: *I Never Herded Sheep*. I hope they buried him with his copy of *The Rubaiyat of Omar Khayyam,* and the empty rodeo-winnings envelope, upon which he'd scrawled, in pencil, the classic bronc poem of all time. *The Strawberry Roan*. Writ' by a great poet, *branded so in the eyes of God*.

Rhymes of a Recluse

In old California, I could have lived
And maybe I did, who knows?
With the center-fire saddle
And wild Spanish cattle
Those horseback times I'd a chose...

— **Dickie Gibford**
Joaquin Murrieta

Cowboys up and down California's Cuyama valley talk about the night Dickie Gibford re-enacted Paul Revere's midnight ride. It had a little to do with a long night of drinking at the Buckhorn Saloon, then Dickie mounting his horse at two in the morning, riding up and down the streets and across lawns, knocking over plaster dwarves and ceramic deer, shouting: *The British Are Coming*! *The British Are Coming*!

Those were the old days when Dickie Gibford would *go on a spree*, then sober up and disappear for months, following the songlines on his own vision quests. There were times when he'd pack two horses and ride from California to Nevada. Other times he just take off walking in a straight line across the mountains, from Cuyama to Santa Barbara, carrying little but a bag of carrots and dried fruit. We suppose he talked plenty with the *Great Spirit*, or conversed with the creatures of the night. Dickie isn't saying – and those old drinking and walkabout days are long past him. At least the *drinking* part. He stares back on all of it with a sober eye and sly grin. He saw *some things* out there. Things recognizable only to mystic seers and buckaroo metaphysicians.

Dickie Gibford is a rawhide philosopher, line rider, brush popper, and cowboy poet. He's a *seer* who meditates in an ancient Chumash Indian cave, as he communes with the native spirits. He returned from his wilderness tours with pages of epic rhyme that were drenched in Western and California history and always laced with a heap of Dickie's arcane and labyrinthine introspection. A typical Dick Gibford poem spirals through history, then suddenly takes a mystical turn and arrives at a personal and spiritual summing up. His thoughts sidewind into wonderful philosophical gullies, and every deviation makes perfect sense to Dickie Gibford.

The way Gibford writes about California landscape reminds me of Bruce Chatwin's fine book, *The Songlines* – a tome about Australian aboriginals who walk across their homeland, singing up the spirit of their ancestors in every dry creek bed, ant mound, and ancient rock formation. *Wanderabos* calling forth the songs that are buried in the territory. Gibford's self dialogue with history, nature, horses, Native American spirits, wildlife and the cowboy *querencia,* is deep cowboy poetry.

The old Buckhorn Motel and Bar in Cuyama is closed down now. There's a grocery store and a *Burger Barn* and a few dozen houses, peopled by folks who might work the oil rigs or just plain wish to live at a dust blown crossroads in the middle of nowhere. There's something about this valley, which runs between the San Joaquin and the Pacific Coast, which still echoes with that old *Californio* spirit. When the full moon shines down on the onion fields it's easy to forget that Los Angles is just a few hundred miles away. Dickie Gibford is seen in town every few months, buying supplies or washing his saddle blankets at the laundry, or grabbing breakfast at The Burger Barn. A *spectre.* Then he's gone. Back into the hills.

I mean no disrespect to Mr. Gibford for calling him "Dickie" instead of Dick. *Dickie* was what we knew him as when he worked for my brother and sister-in-law, Claudia, on the *Chimeneas* and *Check R* ranches twenty years back. That's where I first heard of his mystic wandering ways and his poetry. I want to head back into the hills now and catch up with him.

I   Gibford's World: The Setting

There's a race of me that don't fit in –
A race that can't sit still
So they break the hearts of kith and kin
And they roam the world at will...

— **Robert W. Service,** The Men That Don't Fit In

From Arabia – Spain
From Mexico – California they came
A horseback culture unequaled on this earth
Trigger-reined and trained for battle
And then for herding cattle...

— **Dick Gibford,** Joaquin Murrieta

The hills surrounding the Cuyama valley are deep in old vaquero country. Trails lead past five hundred year old oak trees, dark red Manzanita, and varieties of sage and *chimesa*. The is the night hunting ground of the black bear, mountain lion, wild pig, coyote, and bobcat. There are flocks of wild turkeys in the back country, and elk and antelope have been re-introduced across Highway 66, on the old Chimeneas.

Look up and you might see hawks, buzzards and occasional eagle, or even a California condor. Look down and you might trip over a Chumash mortar bowl in a dry creek bed, or unearth a Mexican spur that ole Joaquin Murrieta dropped when he was herding stolen horses away, *a la* one of Gibford's poem. We'll deal with Joaquin in a moment. This is a country which maintains a deep and enduring link with the Spanish past. There are still wild grasses here brought into the valley hundreds of years ago in the wool of Basque sheep.

Dickie Gibford, in fact, lives like a Basque sheepherder, in a small beat-up trailer crowded with woodstove, bedroll, soup cans, oil paints, sketchbooks and dozens of dog-eared paperbacks of history and verse. Outside there's a pole corral holding three colts that Gibford is patiently starting up, the old way: *Tie up a back leg. Sack em out. Saddle 'em. Take off up the trail for six hours. Check on the cows. Watch for bear and lion track. Chat with The Great Spirit. Make sure the territory is secure. Cow camp work.*

In the old days they called this job: *line rider* – a man who patrols a prescribed boundary to look after the interests of his employer. The venerable J. Frank Dobie describes the task of the line rider as such:

> *The fence rider looks primarily for breaks in the fence.*
> *The line rider looks for everything. Including the condition*
> *of the watering places and the grazing lands. He pushes strays*
> *of his brand back on the range and drives off those who*
> *do not belong...holes have to be chopped in frozen water*
> *places, and weak stock have to be tended...it's a lonely job.*

Loneliness, or *aloneness*, suits Dickie Gibford. Splendid isolation. A man needs time to think and conjure up a verse or two. In addition to the line riding, Dickie practices the ancient art of rawhide braiding. Today, when we venture upon Dickie's camp, he's in the middle of two rawhide works-in-progress. A *reata* is curled around a post, almost finished, and a braided rein is stretched between two corral poles.

Gibford hears us coming and shuffles around the corner of his little trailer with a black Labrador puppy trailing behind him. He says *hello*, then looks up to the mountain and considers how he might formulate a few more spoken words. He's a grizzled human sort, resembling one of Marshal Dillon's *Gunsmoke* sidekicks – the one they called *Festus*. Dickie is a *coot* in the making. A *wise* coot. His face is a mask of weather-beaten flesh. His grin is shadowed beneath a cowboy that looks like something a man might have watered a mule out of in the Mojave.

Gibford begins speaking again in a measured drawl, as if he's dusting off his language skills. You don't encounter many human beings out here, and if so, they might be a poacher or Mexican cartel gunsel growing illegal marijuana on top a mountain in the wilderness. Human contact takes some considering. We chat and make up for the lost years.

With a little encouraging, and another cup of coffee, Gibford begins to spin out his story. He starts *en media res*, employing the epic convention of jumping into the middle of things, and then working backwards and forwards through the current situation while throwing in odd biographical details. *En media res* is a literary device which can be traced back to *The Odyssey*. Dickie knows all the epic-poetic tricks of the trade. He's probably even memorized *The Odyssey*. I'll let him speak for himself.

II Thin Soup in Winter, Cow Hides and Cowboy Leanin's

The true religion is out here in the mountains. Same
As the Indians thought. They believed in the Great
Spirit. And I think most of us cowboys out in the wild
country kind of get along with that same line of thinking.

— **Dickie Gibford**

"I leave my winter camp in November," he says, "and come down here to this canyon where it's a lot lower. We have the cattle all in this canyon and they range for fifteen or twenty miles, all through these foothills. In May we'll take the cattle back up to the high country. Just take 'em up the trail. We don't have to do none of that haulin' in trucks and that makes it less stressful on the cattle.

"Around here in camp I'll just train a few young colts, break 'em to saddle and get 'em going with cattle. I'm ridin' trails, doing the trail work and always watching for sign of mountain lion and bear. I see bears up here quite a bit. It's just nice to know what's goin' on. It's nice to be back here, 'cause I'm kind of a hermit anyway. I might be inspired to write a few poems, do a lot of rawhide braiding in the wintertime. Working the hides and braiding hackamores and reins and quirts to sell. That buys my groceries, 'cause it's kind of thin soup in the winter time around here, as far as wages go.

"A choice hide for a rawhide *reata* would be an old cow that was skinny, and she was dying of old age. You see these little rough things sticking out? That means it's a good hide. That's the flesh. There was no fat on this animal, that's why it's so strong. Takes me about six or seven days to braid a *reata*. It's a lot of doggone work.

"The craft of braiding started with the Moors in Arabia. They were mathematicians and they were pretty sharp cookies. These buttons, like on this quirt here, they're just little tiny strands, so the people that did the braiding had to be pretty good mathematicians to invent those little braided buttons, cause they have to be mathematically correct.

"It's an old art. Lord knows how many thousand of years ago braiding started. Probably the first braiding was done by cave men who took a bunch of vines and twisted 'em together or something. Braiding's different than hitching horsehair, of course. Hitching is just a series of half-hitches done right on top of one another. It's very repetitious. I think it would be kind of boring after awhile. I don't like to strain my eyes that much, because horsehair would be kind of meticulous to work with.

"I just read the life of Tom Horn, and he wrote it while he was waiting to be hung, and he did some horsehair hitching in that jail."

We pause for a moment and then jaw back and forth about horsehair hitching being practiced for over one hundred years in western prisons. Montana State Prison has had a horsehair hitching program for almost a century. A man holed up in prison likes to keep in touch with the horse trade and the feel of horsehair. Dickie mentions my song "The Sky Above and the Mud Below," and I tell him it was inspired by a pair of horsehair bridle stocks I saw in a Cochrane, Alberta museum which were marked: *braided by Mexican horse thieves, Montana State Prison, 1910.*

We finish up with the rawhide and horsehair discussion and I ask Dickie how he commences his day. I'm curious about the routine, and the poetry in the details.

"Well in the morning," he says, "I get up about five o'clock and it's dark and I make my strong coffee and listen to the short wave radio awhile after I build my fire. I feed the pup then go out and feed the horses. I may walk up and visit the Chumash cave up there in the high rock, and cowboy-meditate for a while. Back for breakfast, and then I saddle up around six thirty and make a ride up through the country here. Work on trails or maybe push some cows.

"If too many cows are in one area, I'll push 'em out a different trail. I keep an eye on the water troughs and make sure everything's workin'. There's not many fences to check out here, it's pretty much open country that way. Sometimes I'll be back by noon, and sometimes, if I go all day, I'll pack a lunch and tie it on my saddle. A sandwich or something. In the summertime days are longer and a person can spend a lot of time riding around.

"I'll switch off and ride one colt one day and the other one the next day. I have two younger colts that I'm training, and two older horses that are plenty broke. It works good to have four horses. If I pack out, I take two horses and leave two. That way the other horses have each other while I'm gone. Horses are gregarious, by nature, and they go nuts if they're left by themselves. I'd be afraid they'd get cut up in the wire.

"How'd I get into this life? Well, my dad was a cowboy. He grew up on a small farm in Southern California. But a neighbor down the road was an honest-to-goodness cowboy. He still wore a six shooter and he was a *bronc stomper*, and he doubled for Tom Mix in the early movies. My dad bought a horse and saddle from a sheepherder for $25, and he rode down to this guy's stable and he mucked out stalls. This guy's name was Ed Wright, and by the time my dad was fourteen or fifteen years old, he was climbing onto the backs of broncos and riding young horses.

"Now this Ed was pretty wild and western. They didn't do a lot of gentling back then. They just got the saddle on and away they went. So there was a lot of action. You should have had your camera around when my dad was a kid. This world has gotten a lot tamer since then. I like to be a little on the wild side, myself.

"I started poetry in the sixth grade. The assignment in class was *The Gettysburg Address* by Abraham Lincoln. Teacher said: *If you kids can memorize some lines you can recite 'em to the class.* I took it home and memorized the whole *Gettysburg Address*. Recited it word for word the next day. She was pretty impressed. That's when I knew I had the knack for memorization, and I got into Robert Service and all, and then cowboy poetry, cause I had cowboy leanin's. I guess the cowboy poetry movement started in 1985. It was all in the cards. I helped organize that first Elko deal. So Abraham Lincoln got me started through his *Gettysburg Address*."

III At the Painted Gate

> *By the painted gate*
> *Where the ancient ones left art...*
> *He sits beside his hobbled horse*
> *And meditates*
> *In the silence that was first...*
>
> **— Dickie Gibford**

Five years ago Dickie sent me a rough version of his poem: "By the Painted Gate". There were penciled corrections and coffee stains washing through some of the lines. On the back of the last sheet Dickie wrote: *Tom, this is the poem that got started from a dream I had last winter. I woke up at 2 a.m. and lit the lantern and finished it. Some time where you're in Cuyama I'll show you the cave and the Indian paintings.*

Now Dickie asks us if we'd like to accompany him on his ritual walk to the painted cave. He says there's cave art there dating back to the early Chumash Indians. He states that Chumash holy men and women might have performed sacred ceremonies inside the cave. He's felt their *presence* up there. Its Dickie's *church*.

"Yeah, I would consider it an old, old church," he says. "Inside there I have what I call my cowboy meditation. I sit there quietly and connect to nature and the land and *The Great Spirit*. There's something beyond the ordinary going on inside that cave. Meditation in there is sorta like a preparation for death. According to the mystics, death is like taking off an old coat and stepping into the Spirit world. I like that idea."

We follow Dickie about a half mile up a canyon trail until we reach a curve in the path which arches off to the right. A big old hawk is twining around up on top of the rock rim, far above the cave entrance. Dickie squints up at the raptor and wonders if it's an old medicine man reincarnated as a hawk, then he tells us that one time he felt a shadow fly over him so gigantic he thought it might be an airplane. It was a rare California condor. Now he points up to a sandstone and rock cliff.

"It's up there," he states. "*The cave.* You got to sort of crawl up on your hands and knees, so I wouldn't blame you if you want to wait down here. Myself I climb up most mornings and commune with the spirits."

Dickie leads us up the steep slope of disintegrating rock and sand. In five minutes we level off and reach the small cave carved out of the rock. It's about five feet deep and four foot high. Just big enough for Gibford to squat inside like a medicine man. He stares down at us and rubs his chin. We catch our breaths and clap the rock dust off of our hands, trying not to slide down the mountain. I'm thinking it's a long time 'til happy hour.

Dickie points with his index finger to a faded red figure on the inside wall. If you squint your eye you might imagine it to be a horse and rider. Or maybe it's just an old stain of rain water or berry juice that seeped through the rock. Go with your gut and heart on this one. We'll side with Dickie and believe it's a rare Chumash pictograph. *A sign.*

"They found an Indian head dress in this cave in the 1920s," says Dickie. "With eagle feathers on it. I just sort of sit here and listen and sometimes the spirits tell me things in my subconscious mind. They started writing a poem for me. I woke up at two in the morning one morning with lines of a poem and I'm thinking – yeah these guys are working with me on this.

"I'll recite a couple of stanzas of "By the Painted Gate". The Painted Gate is a gateway to other higher worlds. I sit here and my ordinary thought patterns just vanish and I just tune into the land. It's a good place to live and a good place to die here – gone like the sand that erodes from this cave."

Dickie begins his recitation:

By the Painted gate
Where the Ancient Ones left art
By caverns in the rocks
Where the ocean tides slapped and shaped
The stone
A million years ago
Beyond time, beyond all sound
In the silence of the universe

The poem goes on through a prayer for rain, and then the poem's narrator mounts up and rides off on his line rider job: *turning back* to the duty, to the trail he takes, back to the Cowboy...the Equine Steed...The poem rolls on and carries the cowboy poet down to a water tank: *horse and dog drink from the trough, where windmill rod has pumped and coughed.* Cowboy, horse, and dog finally trot into the sunset where darkness will soon fall. The Ancient Ones have heard Dickie's prayer.

We let the poem drift off into the silence of the charred hills. The land has recently been scorched by wildfires and Dickie looks out and seems to envision the tops of pine trees that are no longer there.

"It's a shame," he says, "to see the big pines get burned. It swept through here and burned 70,000 acres in three or four days. Changed a lot, but it's not ugly to me because I still have the same feeling for the land. I love this land here, no matter how many fires come though. You can't erase the bond a man will get with the land or a place that he feels is his home. I may have been an Indian here in a past life, who knows? But I've always been connected real strong with this mountainous area right here, because it's wild, and I'm the kind of guy that likes wild country to cowboy in..."

We slide down and walk slowly back to camp as Dickie begins to tell us of the early days in the Cuyama Valley. He states this is the country the *bandito* Murrieta rode through. In fact Dickie's latest poem is about the Mexican outlaw. We arrive back at camp and Dickie offers to recite the poem for us, *horseback*, so we get the full effect. He wanders off to saddle a colt. The black puppy trots behind Gibford, and I hum a song I try to remember, about Joaquin Murrieta. *And his head.*

IV Bring me the Head of Joaquin Murrieta

Come saddle up boys cause the governor said,
He'll pay three thousand dollars for Murrieta's head...
He's the devil's bloody bastard, wicked and no good,
But all the Mexican's swear that he's Robin Hood

— **Dave Alvin,** *Murrieta's Head*

You might dig up two dozen different fragmented versions of Joaquin Murrieta's history. Throw in another dozen dime novel plots, film treatments, songs, ballads, and *corridos*, and you still wouldn't have your finger on the pulse of whom this legendary California bandito *was*, or where he came from, or why he went to the bad. I suppose that's why they call him a *legend*.

Take your pick: He was from Chile, or Mexico. He was a miner or a *monte* dealer during the gold rush days in California. He was a victim of racism. His wife was raped and murdered. His brother was lynched. *Anglos* stole his mining rights and shot his horse. After they took his horse, the *gringos* horse-whipped Joaquin for good measure. Hell, it's no wonder he had a *bad attitude*. *Whoever he was*. I'll stick with Dickie Gibford's version on this one. But Dickie's still trying to throw a loop on his horse.

I've heard an old story that Joaquin's head ended up in a specimen jar, and travelled the Wild West circuit, before disappearing, or exploding, in the great San Francisco fire. Lately I've been listening to *Murrieta's Head,* on the Dave Alvin record: *Eleven/Eleven*. Dave Stamey and other western writers have also written good songs about Murrieta, but what's with this head situation? I would suppose it's an old carnival tradition – the displaying of outlaw body parts: *Pancho Villas head, Three Finger Jack's missing finger, Elmer McCarty's arm*.

While Dickie's trying to catch that horse I'll tell you a colorful little California side story about Elmer McCarty's arm. When I grew up near Los Angles we used to visit the Long Beach Pike and ride the Cyclone Racers, the twin roller coaster that plunged towards the Pacific Ocean. One of the old sideshow buildings was being used in a movie in 1976. Inside a funhouse ride called *Laugh in the Dark* the film crew pulled down a cowboy dummy that was hanging on the wall. They thought it was wax. One of the dummy's arms fell off. It was a mummified *human arm*. The arm was identified as belonging to one Elmer McCarty, an Oklahoma train robber *who refused to be taken alive*.

In 1911 McCarty was mummified and carted around the old west in a travelling exhibit. Spectators were invited to: *put a nickel in the mouth of the dead gunfighter*. Elmer ended up on the wall at Long Beach Pike. *Until his arm fell off*. The even found a nickel in his mouth. I'm just sharing this with you because we're waiting for the Murrieta poem and Dickie Gibford.

But wait, Dickie is mounted on a sorrel colt. His hat is thrown back and his spurs are a jingling, and as he approaches he begins to recite his Joaquin Murrieta epic.

V The Murrieta Poem

Where Joaquin Murrieta swung his reata
And galloped stolen horses away
Where bones of the grizzly
Beneath giant oak trees
Have long since dissolved into clay...

Dickie tries out a verse or two, and then stumbles on a word. It's a long poem. *Take two*. In order to loosen him up, I ask what he knew about Murrieta. I'd like to get his take on the background material.

"I don't know," he says, "what kind of horsemanship Joaquin had, but he must have been pretty good. He stayed ahead of the Sherriff for a long time. You can't think of early Gold Rush days in California without thinking of him. His hay days were in the 1850s. A posse caught up with him and surrounded him at daylight, surprised his camp. Joaquin made a run but they shot him out of his saddle.

"He came from Sonora, Mexico. By some reports he turned outlaw because his young wife had been brutalized and murdered by miners. And so he went out on a rampage, became an outlaw and hated whites, and you know that seems like a pretty justifiable reason to turn outlaw.

"So this poem starts out about Joaquin, and then goes into California and the evolution of the California horseman from Arabia to Spain. And I talk about the spiritual side. When you're touched by that it's a gift, you know. To me the true religion is out here in the mountains. Same as the Indian thought. They believed in The Great Spirit. And I think most of us cowboys in the wild country kind of get along with that same line of thinkin'."

Dickie pulls on the reins and stares for a moment into the charred mountains. Summoning the proper focus, he begins again:

Here the mustang's sure tread, and the songs of the dead
told of a past that was free
It comes from the soul, where the oaken hills roll
from the Sierra on down to the sea.

Dickie is flying now, lost in the poetry. It's a century ago and he's chasing Spanish cattle and throwing his rawhide reata at that spiritual essence of what he refers to as *the gift* – the knack of seeing into the mystic core of *things western*.

Deep into the poem Murrieta gallops off as Dickie ponders *real knowledge* and *timeless lands* and *the genius which uncocks the mystery of our peers.* Finally Dickie is centered on the mind of man. Gibford reckons that man's mind suffices as compared to *computered devices.* He doesn't stop there. Now Dickie's wishing, in verse, that *one might go beyond ordinary time...to a higher state of mind...across space and time...where we are no longer a pawn in the game of life's abrasions.*

He's nearing the end. We're trying to hold on, and follow his thought line. He arrives at the conclusion and for a wild moment the poem and Dickie become one. He's Joaquin Murietta, and he's the mystic poet Dickie Gibford. It all makes sense and the poem trails away and melts back into the landscape which inspired it.

The mystic comes in nature
You can't hold it and it can't be caught
It can't be sold or bought
It's a gift to our being
It's a special way of seeing
And it remains elusive and free,
Like Joaquin Murrieta
Where he swung his reata
And galloped stolen horses away.

Silence. Someone say, *amen.* There's a whistle of wind through the sage and chimesa. The whine of a puppy. The *caw caw* of a raven. The pawing of a colt in the far corral. More silence. Dickie Gibford reckons he's said more than enough. He dismounts and walks off to his trailer. He comes back and hands me the poem, handwritten on three pieces of thick drawing paper. *Here,* he says, *I don't have another copy, so sometime when your secretary has time, maybe I can get a typed copy?*

We laugh at that, make our goodbyes, and walk down the path that leads to our truck and the road back to Cuyama. I'll never forget seeing him up there in that cave – St. Augustine in a beat-up cowboy hat, reciting the ending to his "Painted Gate", with the Chumash pictograph next to his right ear. Dickie Gibford will be a hawk or a condor in his next life, circling above our camps forever, illusive and free, with a lyrical *gift* and special way of seeing deep down into the mystic in western nature.

Then mounting in the fading light
Dog and horse and cowboy go
Trotting – trotting
In The Glow
Of winter afternoon
Daylight's spare
And not too long
Darkness will be back
And soon.

— **Dickie Gibford,** *"The Painted Gate"*

Ox Driver

In the Shadows of The Joshua Tree
Gram Parsons & the Lost Angels of Americana

*I spend a lot of time up at Joshua Tree,
in the desert, just looking at the San Andreas Fault
and I say to myself, 'I wish I were a bird
drifting above it.'*

— **Gram Parsons,** July 1973

The seed of our destruction will blossom in the desert, the alexin of our cure grows by a mountain rock, and our lives are haunted by a Georgia slattern...flies buzz home to death, and every moment is a window on all time.

— **Thomas Wolfe,** Look Homeward Angel

I   Joshua Tree National Monument

The land remains as wild and starkly beautiful as two hundred years back, when the Indians roamed through, digging roots and building fires against the huge boulders. These were the Mojave tribes, or specifically the *Serranos*, and the *Chemehuevi*, sometimes called the Southern Paiutes, and the *Cahuilla*.

The desert valley is surrounded by mountains with names like *Sheep Hole*, *Turtle*, and *Old Woman*. The desert here is *biblical* in tenor – a mystical landscape of tree, rock, yucca, and sand. An apocalyptic tone colors every sunrise and sunset, as the light sifts through the prickly Joshua Trees.

The Mormons gave the name *Joshua* to the spiny Yucca tree which abounds in the Monument. The trees reminded the Mormons of *Joshua*, the Old Testament patriarch, raising his arms towards the heavens. Joshua was the archetypal *voice crying out in the wilderness*, a prophet who spouted hair-raising admonitions, warning us against creating burnt offerings, and all that.

Los Angeles is 150 miles to the north of the Joshua Tree Monument. Up yonder where the freeways begin to snake and strangle the irrigated desert. On a sunny afternoon in September of 1973 a Georgia boy, age 26, with a cracked country voice that could break your heart, drove out of L.A. and down into his desert. To *dry out*. The hour of darkness he'd sung about was very near.

His lyrics were revelatory:

*It's a hard way to find out, that trouble is real
In a far away city, with a far away feel...*

The Joshua Tree desert is about as far and you can travel, *feel wise*, from Waycross, Georgia. His place of birth. There was to be no drying out. *Au contraire*. Destiny's flames roared up in his face, Hank Williams style, and blistered the boy upwards from earth in a fiery arc that splintered back down in ashes over the Monument.

Considering this Georgia boy's final days, we could rustle up a stew of his divinatory lyrics, throw in the prophetic words of the patriarch Joshua about *burnt offerings* and sacrifice, and ultimately arrive at Thomas Wolfe's lines dealing with *the seeds of destruction lying in the desert*, the *mountain rock*, and the haunting by a *Georgia slattern*. Roll over Tennessee Williams, there's a cat on a hot tin roof.

The kid was born Ingram Cecil Connor III. He was to be known professionally as Gram Parsons.

Young Gram was of an era when country music banged head-on into rock and roll in the late 1960s. This Southern kid was in front of the parade. How could you ignore him, with his long hair, satin bellbottoms, and embroidered Nudie suit? The suit with naked women, marijuana leaves, and pill capsules on the front. A flaming red crucifix was stitched upon the back. The old Porter Waggoner routine turned upside down and taken to the cosmic limit.

These days the suit is draped over a dummy in the Country Music Hall of Fame, next to Gram's big Gibson guitar. Around the corner is Hank Williams' suit and guitar. An appropriate collocation. Two Southern boys who changed the shape of country music and flamed out before the age of thirty.

Gram was an American singer-songwriter. He died September 1973 in Joshua Tree, California. His ashes blew through the monument and, for the next forty years, fans would trek out there and leave roses, candles, and old guitar strings on the sand – in the shadows of an isolated boulder fifty feet high.

The rock still bears charred marks from where the Georgia kid was cremated. Once upon a better time the kid and his pal Keith Richards, of the Rolling Stones, sat atop that rock, wrapped in Indian blankets, staring out at the wild landscape, fueling their song-visions with a little powder from the coca leaf. Keith is still with us. And a wonderful surprise that is.

II In Search of the Grievous Angel

I headed West to grow up with the country
Across those prairies with those waves of grain
And I saw my devil, and I saw my deep blue sea
And I thought about a calico bonnet
from Cheyenne to Tennessee

— **Gram Parsons,** "The Return of the Grievous Angel"

His songs roared out of a rental car cassette player when I first drove to Joshua Tree in 1974. I was a fledgling songwriter on a spirit quest, inspired by the dark country edge in his songs. I was picking up the crumbs and bones along the trail, searching for the witch's house where all the big songs were hidden. I had a pocket full of guitar picks.

Forty years later I'm still searching.

In the early 1970s I'd started playing this music they called *country rock* in the bars of the world. It was *Gram Parsons era* country. The soul of a George Jones song mixed with the hard beat and irreverent lyrics of The Rolling Stones. *Drinking music.* Four to six sets a night on Skid Row, Vancouver.

My old set lists, taped to the top of the Martin guitar, held George Jones songs, Hank Williams, Gram Parsons, The Rolling Stones, Merle Haggard, Buck Owens, John Prine, Bob Dylan, and whatever early original I could sneak in. I wrote some damn bad ones, trying to copy Gram. One was titled: "Strung Out Like the Tightest Wire on a Frozen Barbed Wire Fence." What a lousy metaphor.

The song made the jukebox in four or five Vancouver bars. We were called The Mule Train, *skid row's finest band.* Proud of it. I was the same age as Gram. But by the time I was crawling around the bottom rung of the *music biz*, Gram was nearing the end.

Burning the candle at both ends and in the middle.

In spring of '74 I cranked up the cassette tape volume with his music and sailed into Joshua Tree Monument. At the intersection of two desert roads stands an outcropping of monzonite boulders called *Cap Rocks*. The assemblage of boulders resembles a skull falling from the sky into the desert sand.

I stopped the car and parked it in the shade. I hiked around the base of the skull until I reached a cave-like indent in the rock where the surface was charred from smoke. The topsoil was covered with ash and charcoal. On the ash and sand there were a few candles and a long poem, framed under glass, from a Parsons' fan in Germany.

The ashes were the remains of Gram and his coffin. I reached down and picked up what I assumed was a bit of charred bone. I brushed it off lodged it inside my hatband. No disrespect intended. I said a prayer for Gram and that aching country boy voice that seemed to echo through the eerie Joshua Trees and twirl up and join the circling hawks. Then I walked away.

Gram died on September 19, 1973 in The Joshua Tree Inn, a motel a few miles outside the Monument. The newspapers claimed it was *heart failure due to natural causes*. Later it was determined Gram died from a lethal combination of drugs and alcohol.

The ambulance arrived and Gram's body was hauled back to Los Angeles, slated to be air-shipped to New Orleans for burial. The coffin never made the flight. By the next morning it was a mound of smoldering ashes in the Joshua Tree desert. Out of the ashes the legend of Gram Parsons began to form.

And why should we care now, forty years down the line? His voice and vision echoed through 1970s rock and roll. He brought country music to the rock crowd and rock and soul music to the country folk. Gram was a first hand influence on the music of The Byrds, The Rolling Stones, Emmy Lou Harris, The Eagles, and the dozens of Country Rock Bands that emerged from the West Coast in the early seventies.

When you consider that Parsons turned the above artists onto deep country music, then estimate the millions of people they reached with their more refined, commercial approach – you arrive at the importance of Gram Parsons. His influence on bringing country music to Rock n' Roll might be as important as Bob Dylan's combining Folk Music with Rock. And I'm a Bob Dylan fan.

III Cosmic American Music Melts into Americana (And What the Hell is All That?)

*The music he had in him was incredible...
he was a walking encyclopedia of songs...*

— Emmy Lou Harris

"When I first came to California," said Gram, "my ambition was to go to the honkytonks and win the talent contests and show them that a guy with long hair could be accepted. It took me two years to win The Palomino Club's contest. Every Thursday I would religiously drive out there and wait my turn, and for two years I was beaten by yodeling grandmothers and the same guy who sang *El Paso* every week."

"I wasn't to be stopped. When things got tough at the Palomino I started to go out to the tougher ones. I heard about The Aces Club in The City of Industry, where they keep it open all night long on Saturday and reopen the bar at six in the morning. I started going out there every weekend. The first couple of times I nearly got killed. I was wearing satin bellbottoms and people couldn't believe it.

"I got up on stage and when I got off a guy said to me, 'I want you to meet my five brothers. We were gonna kick your ass but you can sing real good so we'll buy you a drink instead.' Thank God I got up on that stage."

Gram aimed to defy the strict boundaries the music press had established. That myth that hippies and city folk wouldn't dig country and country rednecks and cowboys didn't dig rock. His personal goals were messianic in tone, like a child preacher from the Deep South healing cripples and drunks with God's own country music.

Gram was one of the godfathers of what some now call *Americana* music. In our obsession with naming genres (then killing them) the hybrid once called *Country Rock,* transitioned into *Progressive Country, New Country, No Depression Country, Alt-Country, Roots Rock, Outlaw Country,* and now *Americana* is the flavor of the day.

In truth, Virgil Thomson and Aaron Copland were creating *Americana* music, in the 30s and 40s, when they mixed folk and cowboy songs with ballet and symphonic works – like *Billy the Kid.* Moses *Clear Rock* Platt and *Lead Belly* were creating Americana music in the Texas and Louisiana prisons when they mixed cowboy music with blues and early rap – *call and response* songs. Chain gang Americana.

Americana music encompasses folk, blues, rock, soul, jazz, gospel,

Mexican and South American Music, Cajun music, Swiss yodel, German drinking songs...all of it. And more. Give a nod to the classical composers above and all the street singers of eighty years ago who sang Gospel, blues, country, folk, and a grand mix of poetry from our rattle bag heritage. Hank Williams was listening. And Gram Parsons.

Allow me a quick, necessary detour. If we're eyeballing folk and country-rock pioneers from the 1960s, a more neglected voice, deserves a moment of light. Another Georgia boy. Steve Young.

IV Crying up a Thunderstorm Chain: Steve Young

There are stars in the Southern sky
Southward as you go
There is moonlight and moss in the trees
Down the Seven Bridges Road...

— **Steve Young,** "Seven Bridges Road"

Thirty years ago I met Steve Young in Los Angeles. He was living in a studio apartment in Silver Lake above an oriental food store. He slept most of the day and wrote music at night. Called himself a *vampire*. There were sheets over the windows and a pallet on the floor. Overwhelming the main room was a mad-professor recording setup with keyboards, guitars, synthesizers, and microphones. Wires ran in all directions. Along the wall, on the floor, were dozens of *Our Lady of Guadalupe* votive candles from the local Mexican grocery store. Steve was not Catholic, that I know of, just wired into some other mystical universe for inspiration.

He told me then he was working on *weird new stuff* that was maybe *too far out* for the folk and country world. He was digging deep, pondering the roots of love and pain and writing about his divorce, about an old drinking problem, and death. He wouldn't play me the new songs yet, but he gave me a recording of his version of a Merle Haggard song that chilled me – "Sometimes I Dream."

There's no magic way for me to get over you
There's not much I can say, not a thing left to do
Seldom I laugh and seldom I ever cry
Sometimes I drink too much, and sometimes I lie
Sometimes I hate myself and wish I could scream
Sometimes I give up on love but sometimes I dream

A haunted lyric firmly based in self-truth. He sang it to the core. This was the terrain where Steve was heading with his songs. I went on my way thinking he was one of the pioneer songwriters who'd invented country rock in L.A., then outlaw music in Nashville. Now he was way out on a polar expedition, out yonder where you might end up on an isolated ice flow, disappearing forever.

Two years later I was walking down a back street in Oslo, Norway, five thousand miles from Los Angeles, and there was Steve Young walking toward me. As if we'd just chatted in Silver Lake. Nonchalant grin. Lost in thought. The vampire who'd emerged from the song caves. He was in Norway to record an album with a Norwegian backup band. He thrust a cassette into my hand and told me to check it out. *His new songs.* The fruit of the years in the room above the Oriental store.

"It might scare you," he said. "Maybe too far out. I don't know."

Steve looked down the street and out onto the *fjord* where the shrimp boats were coming in with the day's catch. He told me he'd tried to play the new songs in a folk clubs in Los Angeles, but club owners weren't interested in a folk or country singer playing solo, standing at a synthesizer. The songs and new sounds *scared* people. I thought of Bob Dylan walking onstage with an electric guitar at The Newport Folk Festival in '65. The old folk elite began weeping and gnashing their teeth. American music was never the same.

That night in my little room on the east side of Oslo I listened to the tape over and over. A new form of electric folk music. Honest revelations set to a synth drone. The finished songs, about love, lost love, divorce, drinking, and death, were potent. It was like eavesdropping in a confessional. A self-intervention. The songs were titled: "Look Homeward Angel," "War of Ancient Days," and "Long Time Rider."

Here's a bit of the divorce lyric:

> *I didn't come here to see who gets the best deal*
> *You can have the stuff I will survive*
> *But I came here to wage war on the poverty*
> *That I see in our eyes*
> *And I'm here to pay the tallest price*
> *For now I'm willing to change my ways*
> *And I'm here to lay the wreath of peace at your feet*
> *And end this war of ancient days.*

This was not Tammy Wynette *D-I-V-O-R-C-E* stuff. Nobody was blurting out songs this direct. And almost 20 years prior to this Steve had recorded his first record on A&M, *Rock, Salt, and Nails*, right down the hall from where Gram Parsons was recording in 1968.

Then Steve went to Nashville, and recorded two definitive records for RCA. His songs were covered by Hank Williams Jr. and Waylon Jennings, and the spirit of the songs almost single-handedly created the *outlaw movement*. Two Steve Young songs set the tone: "Montgomery in the Rain," and "Lonesome, Onr'y and Mean."

At that same time Willie Nelson moved to Austin and the outlaw movement became centered there.

If Gram Parsons was a soul cousin to George Jones, then Steve Young might be the lost godson of Faulkner or Thomas Wolfe. But Steve had, and still has, no flamboyance to his persona. Unless he was on stage, solo, with that huge voice and great guitar playing, he was shy and withdrawn. *An enigma* critics called him. A Zen warrior. No Nudie suit for Steve. He was meditating on how love devastates all of us. And how we might heal.

As I write this, in 2015, Steve Young is in a rehab facility in Nashville because of a bad fall. He should be given his due as a pioneer. The scribes are not usually attracted to the *legend* stories 'til the poet dies or flames out.

In truth, with the gift of forty years of hindsight – who truly created Folk Rock and Country Rock in the late 1960s and early 70s? Surely Bob Dylan, Gram Parsons, Steve Young, *Dillard and Clark*, Ian and Sylvia Tyson and their band *The Great Speckled Bird*, Doug Sahm's records on Atlantic (Bob Dylan attending), Billy Joe Shaver, Johnny Rodrigues, Jesse Winchester, Commander Cody, The Everly Brothers, The Band, Ramblin' Jack Elliott, John Stewart, Hoyt Axton, Katy Moffatt, Barbara Keith, Willie Nelson, Guy Clark, Linda Ronstadt, and on and on.

All of them and more.

And the bands who found commercial success in the formula: The Byrds, The Rolling Stones (some country tracks), Credence Clearwater...and finally The Eagles. And one of the Eagles biggest hits was Steve Young's "Seven Bridges Road." That's how he pays the rent.

Back to the Gram finale.

V The Messianic Country Soul Of Gram Parsons

Some called him a seer
flying blind and soaring free
like a bird above the fault line
in the land of the Joshua Tree

— **Tom Russell**, "Joshua Tree,"

There I was, three years after Gram's death, with that bone shard in my cowboy hat, trying to carve my own path through the snaky realms of show biz. Wandering around the Mojave Desert. There's ghosts a plenty out in that country – hillbilly ghosts with voices that reach across the years. In truth Gram was trailing a long line of Southerners and Texans who came to California in search of work, and brought their guitars and fiddles along.

I drove around the desert for days, and every crossroad led to another highway with a country music story behind it. Spade Cooley killed his wife out there somewhere. The old Roy Rogers museum in used to be in Apple Valley, with Bullet and Trigger stuffed, and if you took back roads north you'd eventually hit Bakersfield where Merle Haggard grew up in a boxcar and broke into and robbed a bar that he didn't know was still open for business. Next stop San Quentin.

I circled around and drove back into Joshua Tree, towards Gram's last motel stop. The Joshua Tree Inn was on the right as you entered town. An air conditioner rattled and spit in the small room where Gram died. The place smelled of ivory soap, bleach, and stale beer. Outside a semi-truck rolled by and flew past the *High-Ho Lounge* where Gram had sung and shot pool.

I'd last seen Gram alive in 1969, in the old Charlie Chaplin studios near Hollywood and Vine. The night the critics claimed Country Rock was born. The night of the Nudie suits.

A&M had invited the Rock press and DJs, as well as an odd mix of Hollywood cowboys, stuntmen, movie ranch folks, hippie chicks and groupies – a mix designed to confound the mind yet play host to Gram's cosmic dream. And sell records.

"There wasn't any music similar to ours," he'd said, "we were trying to come up with a new genre, a dream that I called in my early days, Cosmic American Music."

Nudie, *the rodeo tailor,* originally from Brooklyn, was in attendance to see how his suits looked on the boys. Nudie had parked his Cadillac near the back entrance – a big convertible with tooled leather seats and longhorn steer horns on the hood. There was a saddle lodged between the two front seats. Inside the gig there was free beer, cheap vin-rose wine, and a box lunch of chicken and beans. A square dance band opened the show. As per Gram's dream, hippies and rednecks drank and danced under one roof.

A wrangler I knew from the L.A. Horse and Mule auction recognized me and waltzed over:

"Who in hell is this hippie kid in the marijuana suit?"

"Gram Parsons," I said.

"Gotta' be Southern.

"Waycross," I said. "Georgia swamps."

"No shit? He's got that warble in his voice. The *hurt*. It's in the food down there. In the drink. You ever been to Waycross?"

"No," I said.

"The earth down there shakes. Like this kid's voice."

VI Waycross – The Land of the Trembling Earth

Oh My Land is Like a Wild Goose
Wonders all around everywhere
It trembles and it shakes 'til every tree's loose...

— **Gram Parsons,** "A Song For You"

Gram originally hailed from Waycross, Georgia, near the Okefeenoke Swamp, in the heart of the Old South. A peat-filled wetland straddling the Georgia-Florida border.

"Swamps," Gram said. "Okefeenokee, you know, means land of the trembling earth and everything down there is mush. I never fit in. I was a misfit from the start. There's an old saying about Waycross...as soon as you learn to walk, you start walking out of town."

The family history parallels anything in Tennessee Williams'. Old money, citrus groves, a mansion in Winterhaven, Florida, where *Gone with the Wind* was filmed, big business, packing plants, the family's founding of Cypress Gardens, and a father nicknamed *Coon Dog* Conner – part time country singer, full time drinker.

Money could not waylay the ravages of alcohol, insanity, and suicide, which ran up and down the family tree. *Coon* Dog blew his own head off on Christmas day 1959 with a small gauge shogun. The trembling earth and the family troubles filtered up into Gram's singing voice as he retreated into music. He taught himself piano and guitar and formed bands. His first group was a folk unit called the Shilohs.

Fast forward to Harvard Divinity school:

"I did a back dive into Harvard. I think I was there about four hours and fifteen minutes. I was out of the mold."

After Harvard, circa 1966, Gram began to formulate his dream of a *Cosmic American Music* – a combination of folk, country, blues, R & B, and rock, which would unite all audiences. The Harvard Divinity student felt his music could heal the world. He had formulated his divine mission and began to sermonize.

"If people want to get hold of something real, young people, they should listen to some good ole country music," Gram said. "Good country music teaches a lot of simple lessons. Rock and roll has probably contributed to the creation of more musical prejudices then it has broken down."

Gram and friends recorded *The International Submarine Band*, an album produced by Lee Hazelwood. The vision was there, but half formed, so Gram joined *The Byrds* and tried to convince them that their future wasn't in re-interpreting Bob Dylan songs. The result was *Sweetheart of the Rodeo*, one of the first country music albums by a known rock band.

Gram left the Byrds to hang out with the Rolling Stones in France. His influence showed up Stones' songs: "Wild Horses," "Dead Flowers," "Sweet Virginia," and "Faraway Eyes." Gram and Keith Richards bonded deeply – drugs, alcohol, and country music tightened the bond – but Gram didn't seem to have the constitution that Keith Richard still retains. They cut Gram loose.

Gram returned to L.A, entrenched in his *physical abuse program*, as Chris Hillman called it. Together Chris (of The Byrds) and Gram formed *The Flying Burrito Brothers*. Their first album, *The Gilded Palace of Sin*, finally captured what Gram had been visualizing – Cosmic American Country Rock, erasing all boundaries. This was the Nudie Suit record. The second album was unfocused and Gram lost interest. He took a room at the Chateau Marmont Hotel, on Sunset, dug into his inheritance money, and reverted back to the wild side of life. Plum wine for breakfast and the five martini lunch.

He came out of the fog long enough to land a solo deal with

Warner-Reprise, and was slated to be produced by his new idol, Merle Haggard. Merle eventually pulled out at the last minute, evidently involved in marital troubles.

Gram straightened up a notch, but he needed a harmony singer. Enter Emmy Lou Harris. Chris Hillman had spoken of this lady folksinger in Washington DC and Gram drove down from Baltimore one night and he and Emmy sang a few old George Jones duets. Instant magic. *The sound.*

"The power of his art," Emmy stated, "was his ability to incorporate vision, his gut feeling about what he was doing. That's where a new art form comes from. There's something in my voice that just wasn't there until I sang with Gram...a great deal of what I am as an artist is coming from him."

The second and final solo album was *The Return of the Grievous Angel.* Gram's masterwork. The record ended with Gram and Emmy Lou's "In My Hour of Darkness," a plea for the Lord to grant the singer speed and vision in his hour of death. The song was a fitting close to an album and a career.

Two days after the final session Gram Parsons was dead, age 26.

VII The Hour of Darkness & the Wilderness on Fire

We poured on the five gallons and threw in the match.
We were unencumbered by sobriety, so we got away.

— **Phil "Road-Mangler" Kaufman**

I was in the wilderness and the canyon was on fire...
I would walk all the way from Boulder to Birmingham
If I thought I could see, I could see your face.

— **Emmy Lou Harris,** "Boulder to Birmingham"

Gram Parsons was pronounced dead at a Yucca Valley Hospital on September 19, 1973. The coffin went to LAX, slated for flight to New Orleans and the family plot. Enter Gram's drinking buddy and road manager Phil Kaufman. From stage left.

"Gram and I had talked about this. Gram's thing was he wanted to die at Joshua Tree. He wanted to be cremated at Joshua Tree and have his ashes spread over Cap Rock."

The immediate family had other ideas. Gram's remains were to be flown home to the family plot – entombed forever alongside the Faulknerian tribe he'd fled from. The ghost of *Coon Dog* Conner was awaiting the return of the prodigal son.

Phil Kaufman and a friend came up with a plan to honor Gram's wishes. "It was something I'd promised him," said Phil. "I saw Keith Richards and he hugged me and said, 'Nice one, Phil, you took care of Gram.'"

Phil borrowed a hearse from a girlfriend and drove out to LAX – right up to the funeral home driver who was carting Gram's coffin to the plane. Phil told him the family had changed their minds. After some repartee the man shrugged and handed over the goods, and Phil drove off with Gram's body. They stopped at a liquor store for beer and Jack Daniels, then at a gas station for a gallon of gas. The wake began.

"We drove out to the desert, drinking with Gram. Went out to Cap Rock in Joshua Tree. I opened the casket to make sure it was Gram." The legend has it that Phil then put a can of beer in Gram's pocket for the long ride home.

"We poured on the five gallons and threw in the match. You aren't supposed to have open fires in National Parks, and this one created an unbelievable fireball seen by the forest rangers. They chased us, but we were unencumbered by sobriety, so we got away."

Most of Gram's friends agreed Kaufman had done the right thing. Kaufman was eventually busted, but got off lightly. He had to pay for the coffin. Gram's friend Kathy Miles provides the coda to the Gram Finale: "I can see Gram up there in hillbilly heaven, laughing his ass off."

I have a recurring daydream of Gram Parsons, at The Aces Club in The City of Industry, in a cape and satin bellbottoms, facing a beating for his attire, then winning the rednecks over in the talent contest. Saving his life with the country-truth of a George Jones song.

Since then I've returned to the desert many times. I buried the bone chard back in the sandy earth behind Cap Rock. I've written songs at The Twenty Nine Palms Inn, with Katy Moffatt, and I co-wrote "The Rose of the San Joaquin," with Ian Tyson, in The Pioneer Town Motel near Yucca Valley.

I've felt Gram's spirit out there – *like a bird drifting above the faultline,* singing up his cosmic visions, where every moment is a window on all time and the spiny Joshua Trees raise their arms toward the heavens.

He was just a country boy
His simple songs confessed
And the music he had in him
so very few possesed.

              — **Gram Parsons & Emmy Lou Harris,**
                        "In My Hour of Darkness"

Tom Russell

Singer songwriter, painter, essayist – Tom Russell has recorded thirty five highly acclaimed records, & published five books: *120 Songs of Tom Russell*; *Tough Company – Letters with Charles Bukowski*; *Blue Horse Red Desert: the Art of Tom Russell*; *Blodsport* a crime novel published by Aschehoug, Norway; and *And Then I Wrote: The Songwriter Speaks*, with Sylvia Tyson.

Tom Russell songs have been recorded by Johnny Cash, Doug Sahm, Nanci Griffith, K.D. Lang, Ramblin' Jack Elliott, Ian Tyson, Iris Dement, Joe Ely, and a hundred others.

Tom Russell graduated from The University of California with a Master's Degree in Criminology. He was recently awarded the 2015 *ASCAP Deems Taylor Award* for excellence in music journalism

In 2015 Russell released a 52 track "folk opera" on the West. *The Rose of Roscrae*, was deemed: *maybe the most important Americana record of all time* by **UK Folk**, **the top Folk album of 2105 by** *Mojo* **Magazine**, and hailed in top ten lists in two dozen publications including *The Los Angeles Times*. He has appeared on the David Letterman TV show five times.

His latest release (May 2016) is *The Tom Russell Anthology 2 (Gunpowder Sunsets)* – 19 Tracks.

www.TomRussell.com

Recent Quotes on Tom Russell

(May 2016) *These songs on The Tom Russell Anthology 2: Gunpowder Sunsets leaves me in anticipation of whatever might be coming next from the best songwriter of my generation.*

— **Mike Regenstreiff,** Montreal Gazette, Sing Out

Tom Russell is Johnny Cash, Jim Harrison and Charles Bukowski rolled into one. I feel a great affinity with Tom Russell's songs, for he is writing out of the wounded heart of America.

— **Lawrence Ferlinghetti,** Poet

Tom Russell is an original, a brilliant songwriter with a restless curiosity and an almost violent imagination. "Blood and Candle Smoke" is vintage Russell, and the Graham Greene connection is a 'beaut.

— **Annie Proulx,** The Shipping News, Brokeback Mountain

Tom Russell is the last great American voice.

— **Ken Bruen,** The Dramatist, The Cross

How great is Tom Russell? Isn't he the best? I'd like to quit my job and travel with him…if the money can be worked out…

— **David Letterman,** Late Night with David Letterman

The greatest living folk-country songwriter is a man named Tom Russell…

— **John Swenson,** Rolling Stone

Tom Russell is the best songwriter of the generation following Bob Dylan…

— *The Montreal Gazette*

The Rose of Roscrae

The #1 Album of the Year, *The Irish Post*, Joe Giltrap, Dec 19, 2015
The album of the year goes to Tom Russell's terrific The Rose of Roscrae...a great piece of work and a fine testament to a wonderfully talented singer songwriter.

Los Angeles Times Top Ten Albums, Dec, 2015, Randy Lewis
Masterful songwriter Russell enlists the help of friends and peers such as Maura O'Connell and others over a staggering 52 tracks in an extraordinary piece of Americana with an expansive narrative and scope.

***MOJO* Magazine, Dec 2015**
The Top Folk Album of 2015

***UNCUT* Magazine "Album of the Month", June 2015, Peter Watts**
It is an epic tale, a blend of Rodgers and Hammerstein, Berthold Brecht, Cormac McCarthy and Louis L'Amour, thick with references to U.S. history, music and myth...the scope is majestic, the ambition outrageous and the music magnificent. A unique accomplishment.

***The Guardian*, UK, 4/5 stars, April 10, 2015**
A bravely original epic.

Folk Radio, UK
A game changer – it could just be the single most important Americana release of all time.

Best Country Music Albums of 2015: *The Telegraph* UK
A bold two-disc country-folk-rock opera about a young 19th-century Irish immigrant drawn to a new life as a cowboy in the west after a failed love affair. It's a sprawling beast of an album and a remarkable piece of creativity. ★★★★

***Financial Times*, UK, 4/18**
It is novelistic in scope, full of detailed historiography and musical verve, a proud addition to the great American tradition of the immigrant epic.

Craig McDonald, Author, The Hector Lassiter Series
> *This time, Russell's previous western albums collide with Les Miserables and David Milch's "Deadwood." The result is a staggering feat of the imagination. No other living singer-songwriter even contemplates making albums like this one.*

Thom Jurek, *All Music Guide*, April 14, 2015
> *The journey is Homeric...Real and fictional characters are hard-stitched into his seamless narrative...soulful and moving for its reach...Russell's view of history may be romantic but it is also gritty as hell, and enduring. This is his masterpiece.*

Mike Regenstreif, *Folk Roots/Folk Branches*, *Sing Out*, *Montreal Gazette*
> *Yet another masterwork. It is a work of rare ambition and rare brilliance that is beautifully and artfully executed. There is an embarrassment of riches among the songs Tom composed for The Rose of Roscrae.*

Arthur Wood, *No Depression*, April 2015
> *Russell's Roscrae masterpiece, as well as his back catalogue, totally outstrips (so much of) the music by contemporaries that masquerades as Americana. Approached very much in the panoramic spirit of classical composer Aaron Copland...*

Maverick, UK, 5 Stars, 2015
> *Subtitled A Ballad Of The West, this is an expansive, cowboy culture wonderland from the man they call America's Greatest Living Songwriter.*

July 16, 2015, *R2* Magazine, UK, 5 Stars
> *A sprawling masterpiece...*

Printed in Great Britain
by Amazon